SPECIFICATION AND DESIGN OF CONCURRENT SYSTEMS

THE McGRAW-HILL INTERNATIONAL SERIES IN SOFTWARE ENGINEERING

Consulting Editor

Professor D. Ince
The Open University

Titles in this Series

Portable Modula-2 Programming	Woodman, Griffiths, Souter and Davies
SSADM: A Practical Approach	Ashworth and Goodland
Software Engineering: Analysis and Design	Easteal and Davies
Introduction to Compiling Techniques: A First Course Using ANSI C, LEX and YACC	Bennett
An Introduction to Program Design	Sargent
Object-Oriented Databases: Applications in Software Engineering	Brown
Object-Oriented Software Engineering with C++	Ince
Expert Database Systems: A Gentle Introduction	Beynon-Davies
Practical Formal Methods with VDM	Andrews and Ince
SSADM Version 4: A User's Guide	Eva
A Structured Approach to Systems Development	Heap, Stanway and Windsor
Rapid Information Systems Development	Bell and Wood-Harper
Software Engineering Environments: Automated Support for Software Engineering	Brown, Earl and McDermid
Systems Construction and Analysis: A Mathematical and Logical Framework	Fenton and Hill
SSADM V4 Project Manager's Handbook	Hammer
Knowledge Engineering for Information Systems	Beynon-Davies
Introduction to Software Project Management and Quality Assurance	Ince, Sharp and Woodman
Software System Development: A Gentle Introduction	Britton and Doake
Introduction to VDM	Woodman and Heal
An Introduction to SSADM Version 4	Ashworth and Slater
Discrete Event Simulation in C	Watkins
Objects and Databases	Kroha
Object-Oriented Specification and Design with C++	Henderson
Software Engineering Metrics Volume 1: Measures and Validations	Shepperd
Software Tools and Techniques for Electronic Engineers	Jobes
Reverse Engineering and Software Maintenance: A practical Approach	Lano and Haughton
Coding in Turbo Pascal	Sargent
A Primer on Formal Specification	Turner and McCluskey
Specification and Design of Concurrent Systems	Mett, Crowe and Strain-Clark
An Introduction to Software Engineering Using Z	Ratcliff

CONTENTS

Preface		ix
Trademark		xii
List of CSP symbols		xiii

PART I   CONCURRENT PROCESSES

1	**Introduction to concurrency and ODM**		**3**
	1.1	Concurrency	3
	1.2	Models of processing	5
	1.3	Multiprogramming	7
	1.4	The Open Development Method	9
	1.5	Summary	12
2	**Process analysis**		**13**
	2.1	The model of concurrency: processes and channels	13
	2.2	Examples of process analysis	17
	2.3	Inter-process communication	19
	2.4	Summary	23
3	**Process configurations**		**24**
	3.1	Evaluating functions	24
	3.2	Polynomial evaluation	28
	3.3	The funnel	30
	3.4	Star networks	34
	3.5	Summary	37
4	**Arrays of processes**		**38**
	4.1	Systolic arrays	38
	4.2	Image processing	42
	4.3	Non-communicating cell processes	44
	4.4	Operations involving cell communication	49
	4.5	Summary	53
5	**A simple telephone system**		**55**
	5.1	The two-telephone system	56
	5.2	A state transition model	57
	5.3	Process analysis of a telephone system	61
	5.4	Summary	66
	Summary of Part I		**68**
	Solutions to Part I Review Questions		**69**

PART II CSP SPECIFICATION

6 Building up processes — 75
- 6.1 Elements of process description — 75
- 6.2 The prefix construction — 80
- 6.3 *SKIP* and *STOP*: friend and foe! — 85
- 6.4 Summary — 88

7 Traces — 90

8 Choice — 93
- 8.1 Choice by input value—the | operator — 94
- 8.2 Choice by channel—the [] operator — 98
- 8.3 Non-deterministic choice—the ⊓ operator — 103
- 8.4 Summary — 104

9 Combinations of non-interacting processes — 105
- 9.1 Sequential composition of processes — 105
- 9.2 Interleaved processes — 109
- 9.3 Summary — 112

10 Composition of interacting processes — 114
- 10.1 Parallelism and traces — 114
- 10.2 Parallelism and choice — 117
- 10.3 Multiple parallel processes — 122
- 10.4 Summary — 124

11 Infinite processes and recursion — 125
- 11.1 Recursive processes — 125
- 11.2 Recursion with choice — 129
- 11.3 Sequential composition and recursion — 130
- 11.4 Parallel composition and recursion — 131
- 11.5 Summary — 133

Summary of Part II — 134

Solutions to Part II Review Questions — 136

PART III REFINEMENT AND OCCAM

12 Counting holes — 143
- 12.1 The hole-counting problem — 144
- 12.2 Requirements — 144
- 12.3 The hole-counting algorithm — 146
- 12.4 Summary — 149

13 Specification and design — 150
- 13.1 Process analysis — 150
- 13.2 The CSP specification — 151
- 13.3 Refinement — 151
- 13.4 The main channels — 153

	13.5	Exploding the CELLS process	153
	13.6	Internal communication within CELLS	155
	13.7	Process replication	158
	13.8	Summary	159
14	**More CSP**	**161**
	14.1	Input, output and variables	161
	14.2	Double buffers	164
	14.3	Specifying a funnel adder	169
	14.4	Summary	172
15	**Detailed design**	**173**
	15.1	The strategy	173
	15.2	The process *CONTROLLER*	174
	15.3	The process CELLS	177
	15.4	The process *FUNNEL*	183
	15.5	Summary	184
16	**Selection and repetition**	**185**
	16.1	Assignment, variables and arrays	185
	16.2	Selection	186
	16.3	The while construct	189
	16.4	Removing recursion	191
	16.5	Summary	195
17	**Transforming the design**	**197**
	17.1	The process *CONTROLLER*	197
	17.2	The process *CELLS*	198
	17.3	The process *FUNNEL*	201
	17.4	Summary	202
18	**An Occam version of *SYSTEM***	**203**
	18.1	Atomic processes	203
	18.2	The main control structures	204
	18.3	Defining a named process	205
	18.4	The process `Controller`	207
	18.5	The process `Cells`	211
	18.6	The process `Funnel`	215
	18.7	Summary	215
	Summary of Part III	**217**
	Solutions to Part III Review Questions	**218**
	PART IV CURRENCY CASE STUDIES	
19	**A model of a simple telephone network**	**225**
	19.1	The scope of the model	225
	19.2	Initial process analysis	227
	19.3	Refinement of the process *NETWORK*	228
	19.4	A state-based description	229

	19.5 The state DIAL	233
	19.6 The states CALLING, TALK and BUZZING	235
	19.7 The process *NETWORK*	237
	19.8 Summary	239
20	**Blockers and soft switching**	**240**
	20.1 The blocker	240
	20.2 Guarded communications	243
	20.3 Infinite starvation	245
	20.4 Summary	246
21	**Revised specification of the telephone network**	**248**
	21.1 The process *BL*	249
	21.2 Deadlock analysis	250
	21.3 The processes *DOWN* and *BUZZING*	251
	21.4 The processes *DIAL* and *TALK*	252
	21.5 Summary	254
22	**Coding the telephone network**	**255**
	22.1 The Occam folding editor	255
	22.2 The process `Phone`	256
	22.3 The process `Block`	257
	22.4 The process `Tel`	259
	22.5 Implementing the process *TALK*	263
	22.6 Summary	267
23	**The Towers of Hanoi**	**269**
	23.1 Specification	269
	23.2 Coding the Towers of Hanoi	278
	Summary of Part IV	**281**
	Solutions to Part IV Review Questions	**282**
	Appendix—Occam	**285**
	A.1 Data types	286
	A.2 Declarations	287
	A.3 Expressions	288
	A.4 Actions	289
	A.5 Processes	289
	A.6 Constructions	290
	A.7 Process definitions	293
	A.8 Occam programs	294
	Glossary of terms	**295**
	Index	**298**

PREFACE

The production of code for large-scale software systems with many components requires the use of carefully defined techniques. There are several different approaches, with varying degrees of formality, in vogue. Graphical techniques, in particular, tend to emphasize the individuality of the separate data structures and processes of the real-world system under consideration. Generally speaking, the component processes may operate concurrently, that is to say, various processes are active at the same time. In most methods of software development these various concurrent components must be reconciled to produce sequential code. This arises from the phenomenon that most computing has traditionally been carried out on essentially serial computers, which are programmed using sequential programming languages.

The pivotal role of the mainframe computer as the powerhouse of computing has steadily been eroded in recent years. In its place have come multiprocessor architectures, transputer-based mini-supercomputers, and microcomputer networks. These all point to a fundamentally different approach, one which forms the underlying philosophy of this book.

Instead of designing away the concurrent aspects inherent in real-world systems, to coerce the problem description into the strait-jacket imposed by sequential programming languages, we shall present the Open Development Method (ODM), which is able to maintain aspects of the concurrency inherent in a particular system. Indeed, our method allows explicitly for several processes to be active simultaneously and to communicate with each other.

Our method begins with an informal graphical specification. The next stage employs a mathematical formalism, CSP (Communicating Sequential Processes), which allows us to express formally the dynamic communication between processes, and so can be used to generate a formal description of a system composed of concurrent processes. These techniques allow us to analyse systems in a way that actively seeks out the concurrent features of a system. The top-level formal description is used as a basis for the design phase of program development. The design is then worked into code in the programming language Occam, which was created for the purpose of implementing concurrent processes.

ODM provides a well-defined progression from a specification in CSP, through refinement, to code in Occam which can be implemented on a transputer-based network. In fact, the CSP formalism was one of the motivating forces behind the development of the transputer and its associated programming language, Occam.

The plan of this book is as follows. Concurrent processes are introduced in Part I, as are process networks. Two simple case studies, image processing and a simple telephone system, are then described and analysed using process networks. These case studies are typical of problems whose natural description entails concurrency. Image processing is concerned with a picture or graphic composed of an array of digital components. It is natural to describe any processing of the whole image in terms of the array of processes each concerned with a single picture component. In a telephone network there are many individual telephones, each capable of the same sort of interactions with the others. All telephones in the network function at the same time.

In Part II we present the elements of CSP notation, which can be used for the formal design of concurrent systems. These provide the necessary degree of formality to:

(a) specify a process at various levels of abstraction; and

(b) investigate networks of concurrent processes for potential deadlock and (hopefully) to prove its absence.

The notation of CSP is introduced gradually, by considering a wide variety of examples. The first step is to discuss what is meant by a process; in this respect our approach is pragmatic. We shall consider how, starting with two very simple processes, we may generate new processes from old. We assume that you are familiar with the essential types of program design structures: selection, repetition and combination. However, concurrency allows a much richer range of situations than purely sequential descriptions. Thus selection constructs may exercise choice between values or channels, and may even be non-deterministic. The discussion of repetition is in terms of recursion, enabling us to describe infinite processes, which turn out to be of considerable importance. Combination of processes is not restricted to sequential composition; another way of forming processes will be to allow two or more processes to operate concurrently, treating the whole system as a single process.

Investigating these ideas will involve a degree of abstraction which is appropriate to solving problems in concurrent processing. You need not expect to master all the notation at a first reading; rather you should treat much of Part II as reference material to be consulted again whenever necessary. A brief summary of CSP notation can be found on page xiii.

CSP is a powerful and natural mathematical formalism for specifying processes and their intercommunications and for reasoning about their behaviour. Once we have a specification we are able to use the formalism to prove that it behaves in accordance with the customer's requirements and also that it does not exhibit undesirable behaviour, such as deadlock.

In Parts III and IV we use these techniques to apply the full development method to more realistic versions of the case studies. Firstly, we take an in-depth look at the statement of requirements and derive a CSP process description. We then show how to refine the process description into a detailed program design. Finally, we transform the design into executable Occam code, which can be used to program a transputer-based device. The version of Occam currently implemented is Occam 2, which includes a number of subtleties beyond the scope of this text. In order to avoid confusing the reader, we have adopted a simplified version of the language which contains the essential features. Once you have mastered the principles discussed in this book you will have no difficulty in progressing to an Occam 2 implementation.

How to use this book

As an introductory text on the application of formal methods to concurrent systems, this book adopts a pragmatic and didactic approach. Exercises are interspersed liberally within the main text—you, the reader, will learn by applying in practice what you have just read. In addition there are many review questions, many with brief two- and three-line answers, whose function is to reinforce your understanding of the text. Solutions to the review questions are collected at the end of each part of the book.

The main teaching chapters introduce new terminology which can be readily identified by the use of ***bold italics***.

The text makes free use of conventional notations for the description of sets, which you should be familiar with.

Acknowledgement

This book has been adapted from the Open University course *M355: Topics in Software Engineering* in which ODM is propounded. We would like to acknowledge the contribution made by our colleagues on the Course Team and the assistance of Steve Best in drawing the numerous diagrams.

Percy Mett
David Crowe
Peter Strain-Clark

TRADE MARKS

INMOS and Occam are trade marks of the INMOS Group of companies.
Figure 1.3 is adapted from a diagrammatic representation of the IMS T80 transputer by INMOS.

LIST OF CSP SYMBOLS

P, Q	processes
$T(1), T(2), T(3), \ldots$	several copies of a particular process
Q_{cmd}	a subprocess of Q which describes the state CMD
αP	the *alphabet* of the process P (i.e. the set of potential events for P)
$c.m$	the event consisting of the message m being transmitted synchronously on the channel c
$c!e$	the event which outputs e on the channel c
$c?x$	the event that receives a message on channel c and assigns it to the local variable x
SKIP	successful process
STOP	failed process
$a \rightarrow P$	event a followed by process P
;	process sequencing operator
$\parallel$	concurrency operator
$\interleave$	interleaving operator
$c.a \rightarrow P \mid c.b \rightarrow Q \mid \ldots$	choice by input value
$c.a \rightarrow P \,\square\, d.b \rightarrow Q \,\square\, \ldots$	choice by channel
$(c.a \rightarrow R) \boxplus (d.b \rightarrow S)$	prioritized choice by channel
$(b_1 \,\&\, c_1?x \rightarrow R) \,\square\, (b_2 \,\&\, c_2?y \rightarrow S)$	guarded choice by channel
$P \triangleleft b \triangleright Q$	if-then-else

$P \sqcap Q$	non-deterministic choice
$\mu X_A.\ F(X)$	recursion
$<>, <a>, <a,b>\checkmark, <c>_x$	traces

Precedence of operators

Wherever any ambiguity arises, the prefix operator is assumed to take precedence over all other operators.

The following general notation from set theory and logic is used:

$a \in S$
$S = \{x \mid P(x)\}$
$\wedge$ and
$\vee$ or
$A \backslash B$ The subset of A which excludes all elements of B

PART I

CONCURRENT PROCESSES

1 INTRODUCTION TO CONCURRENCY AND ODM

We begin with a general discussion of concurrency. We shall then show, in Chapters 2 and 3, how to analyse problems so as to emphasize concurrency, and introduce process networks as a means of producing informal specifications. We call this phase of the development *process analysis*. The remaining phases of the development method will be covered in Parts II and III. Our two case studies, image processing and telephone networks, are introduced in Chapters 4 and 5 respectively.

To set the scene, this chapter consists of a general discussion of our underlying theme, concurrency. We shall illustrate the relevance of concurrent processing to typical problems, and take a look at the way conventional computer hardware constrains such an approach.

1.1 Concurrency

A system which is capable of engaging in some activity or observable behaviour will be called a ***process***. A process may represent the whole of a system, or just some part of it whose behaviour we wish to describe. In general, we find that many real-world systems are composed of several identifiable processes that are active at the same time. We say that such processes are ***concurrent***. We shall be particularly concerned with the way in which concurrent processes interrelate in the description of a system.

Example
1.1 A chemical manufacturing complex typically contains numerous reaction vessels that can be operating simultaneously. Before one particular reaction can take place there may be a need to produce several different compounds in separate processes. These compounds are then fed into a reaction vessel so that a reaction can take place. In addition to these reaction vessels, which may be thought of as separate processes, a chemical plant needs to include devices for the measurement of temperature, pressure and volume. Even the individual personnel working in the plant might be thought of as processes. Each process in the plant is engaged in its own sequence of activities, and all the processes may be active simultaneously. Thus the whole complex is described as a collection of concurrent processes.

□

Review Question 1.1 Identify some concurrent processes which might arise in a description of:
(a) the system of road traffic in a town;
(b) a multi-user mainframe computer system.

This book aims to present a development method for producing software that is relevant to concurrent processes. It is only fair to ask: why should we be interested in modelling concurrent processes?

We may answer this question on two levels: an abstract one and a practical one. On the abstract level, we observe that real-time problems exhibit concurrency, so a model which incorporates this is far more realistic than one that can only treat activities in a purely sequential fashion. We have already mentioned a chemical plant; consider also a telephone network and the national grid of power stations. These are systems which inherently consist of many components operating concurrently.

This is not just an argument for elegance. The whole discipline of software engineering has been driven by the need to produce reliable, easy-to-maintain code. In particular a system specification should be understandable by the customer. This aim can be more easily met if the concurrency that exists in a system can be modelled in the specification.

On the practical level there is the issue of speed of execution. In a complex computation there is scope for more efficiency if we have several processors working concurrently on a problem, rather than just a single processor. With modern technology the high volume production of processor chips is not expensive. We therefore require methods which are relevant to the use of multiple processors.

Concurrency may be observed both in the most natural description of certain problems, and also in the particular method adopted for the solution of other problems which exhibit no inherent concurrency. We shall sketch briefly some examples of types of problems that exhibit concurrency in various guises.

The most common sources of concurrency examples are found in real-time systems. We have already mentioned the example of a chemical plant in which several physical processes are active simultaneously. Clearly, the most natural description of such a plant requires the use of notations for concurrency. Other real-time systems which contain concurrent component processes are an airline booking system, a telephone network and a point-of-sale system used at supermarket and chain store checkouts for credit-card purchases and electronic funds transfer. In each case the component processes communicate with each other by exchanging messages. We shall be investigating some of the issues which arise in modelling a telephone network in Chapter 5 and, in greater detail, in Part IV.

Another important area which exhibits concurrency is digital image processing. This is concerned with the transformation of images which are represented as an array of dots or *pixels*. The text you are now reading has been printed using high-resolution digital composition, rather than being composed from individual made-up characters. An important element in the development of digital composition is the ability to manipulate images consisting of millions of dots. One approach to such image processing is to isolate the sequence of transformations that takes place at each position in the array representing the image. The transformations undergone at each position may then be thought of as a separate process, and the transformation of the whole image is then modelled by an array of communicating processes.

Finally, some mathematical problems are amenable to methods which can be modelled as communicating processes. This is not only of theoretical interest but also has a practical application in that a concurrent solution can be implemented more efficiently on a network of processors.

Matrix manipulation, such as multiplication of matrices, has a fairly obvious concurrent application whereby identical computations on the elements of an array of data may be modelled by an array of processes. We shall also see, in Chapter 3, how polynomial evaluation may be performed by a *pipeline* of processes, using a suitable algorithm.

1.2 Models of processing

The 1980s have seen considerable development in terms of computer architectures which incorporate multiple processors operating concurrently. One particular development in this direction, the *transputer*, has been the source of motivation for a considerable part of the theoretical approach presented in this book. In this section we present a brief review of some important milestones in the evolution of computer architectures, leading up to the design of the transputer.

The Turing machine

The earliest theoretical basis for modern computing dates back to the 1930s and the work of the British mathematician Alan Turing. His computational model consisted of an abstract machine capable of being in any one of a finite number of states, a read–write head, a tape on which symbols could be stored, and a state transition function. Such a machine is known as a **Turing machine.** A mathematical function is called *computable* if it is capable of being computed by defining a suitable Turing machine which reads the arguments of the function from the tape and writes the result on to the tape. Figure 1.1 illustrates a notional Turing machine with four states.

Computations are performed on a Turing machine in a sequence of cycles. Each cycle

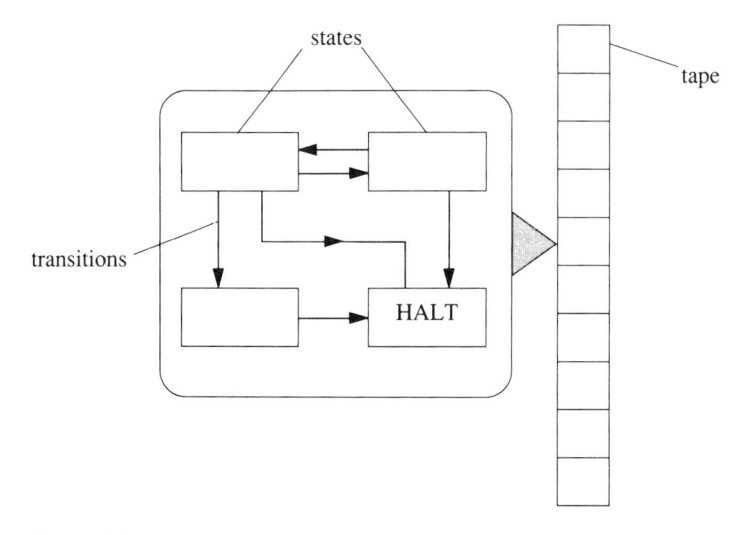

Figure 1.1

involves reading the character at the current tape position; depending on this character and the current state of the machine, certain actions take place. These actions may include a transition to a new state, writing a character to the tape and moving the tape. If and when the machine reaches a special state HALT, the result of the computation is read from the tape.

In principle, a different Turing machine would be required for each and every computation that is required. It took Turing's genius to see that a single universal Turing machine could be constructed that would be capable of exhibiting the functional behaviour of any other Turing machine. This is achieved by sequentially encoding a description of the machine to be simulated as part of the initial tape presented to the universal Turing machine.

von Neumann architecture

From the earliest practical electronic computers to this day, most computers have shared a common design, first described in 1945 by John von Neumann in a paper propounding the construction of a machine called EDVAC.

Although modelled only very loosely on the idea of a universal Turing machine, the von Neumann machine exhibits some features which correspond to its theoretical predecessor.

In a von Neumann machine, the universal Turing machine is replaced by a central processing unit (CPU) with a finite number of *registers*, whose contents determine the current state. In place of the (infinite) tape we now have an electronic memory with a (necessarily finite) sequence of addresses. However, one improvement of the von Neumann architecture is that the memory is capable of random access, which makes the machine considerably more efficient than one in which memory must be stepped through one cell at a time. As with the universal Turing machine, the initially stored data includes a sequential representation of how the computation should be performed, which we now refer to as the program. A symbolic representation of a machine with a von Neumann architecture is shown in Figure 1.2.

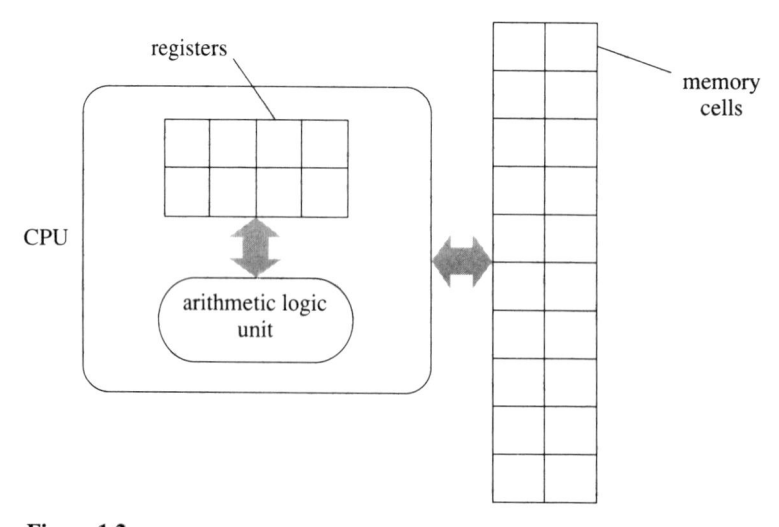

Figure 1.2

The CPU performs each instruction of the computation in strict sequence. Each instruction cycle consists of two phases: first the instruction is fetched, then it is executed. To perform a computation on a von Neumann machine, the computation must therefore be reduced to a sequence of individual instructions, which are fetched singly from memory into the CPU. The need for the instructions to be fetched sequentially into the CPU is referred to as the *von Neumann bottleneck*, and is a major constraint on the speed of such devices when applied to processes that are not inherently sequential.

Simple concurrency

It was soon realized that the full potential of a high-speed CPU was effectively thwarted by the need to interface it with slow devices for input and output. One method of addressing this problem is the use of a separate, dedicated processor which deals with the input/output process while the main processor handles the main instruction sequence. This concurrent use of two processors results in an increase in efficiency.

Another improvement of a similar nature is to break up the fetch–execute sequence for a single instruction into several steps which are performed by different hardware elements. This arrangement is called a *pipeline processor*. This enables the different steps of several instructions to be activated concurrently, while maintaining the basic sequence of instructions.

1.3 Multiprogramming

However much more power can be squeezed out of the computer, it always seems desirable to devise and solve problems for which contemporary computers are inadequate. An obvious solution to the problem of speeding up the processing time appears to be to reduce the time taken to fetch and execute a single basic instruction. This has been achieved over the years by dramatic technological improvements. However, there are limits to the reduction in time that can be achieved and, at the time of writing, it appears that the technology may be getting close to those limits. So the search for increased power must take a different direction.

Batch systems

The earliest computers were relatively slow and catered for a small group of users. As such, they were operated in single-user mode—by one user at a time. As improvements were made, hardware costs increased; additionally the pool of users grew, so it became desirable to investigate the possibility of sharing efficiently the use of the computer. The first method of sharing a fast processor was the introduction of batch systems, whereby a large number of user tasks were batched together (on decks of cards) for automatic input without human intervention, as this had become the slowest part of the whole operation. By the late 1960s primitive versions of *operating systems* began to appear. These are able to handle a queue of several executing programs or tasks which are all at some stage of their processing at the same time. This mode of operation is called *multiprogramming* and can handle several tasks, submitted by one or more users, simultaneously. Although the processing of all the tasks is carried out by the same processor, there is an illusion of concurrent execution. The allocation of short time slots of processor time to each task is called *time slicing*, and is carried out according to a scheduling algorithm implemented in the operating system.

Multi-user systems

Here more than one user is linked via a terminal to a computer with a time-sharing operating system. This is a more sophisticated time-slicing operation than a batch system, since online users must be given a reasonable real-time response. Although these systems still run on a single processor, we recognize that this situation has elements of a genuine concurrent processing system. Specifically, each terminal may be viewed as a separate process, and the whole system consists of the CPU, peripherals and terminals running concurrently in communication with each other.

Multiprocessing

With the continued fall in the price of hardware, opportunities have become more widely available for the concurrent use of several processors in the execution of a single program. The rationale behind this approach is that many hands make light work, so that throughput times for complex programs should be reduced by setting several processors to work on a task which had hitherto been executed on a single processor.

How can multiprocessing be used to good advantage? Clearly it is open to the programmer to describe the problem in a way which lends itself to the allocation of processes within the program to different processors. In order to achieve this aim, the programmer requires suitable tools. One of these tools is the use of a concurrent programming language. Extended versions of Pascal are available that allow concurrent programs to be written. In addition, newer languages such as Ada have been designed to incorporate concurrency fully. These languages allow the programmer to describe the activities involved in the various processes, but ultimately they are designed for execution on a computer system with a single CPU. In other words, they enable simulation of concurrent tasking on essentially sequential computers. Our target language in this book is Occam, which has been designed specifically to enable programs to be run on a multiprocessor system.

With this target in mind, we are able to specify the process model in as much detail as is appropriate to the problem in hand. This approach leaves open the possibility of implementation either on separate processors all working concurrently, each using its own memory, and interacting through distinct communication channels or on a single processor under a multiprogramming operating system.

The transputer

The transputer is a general-purpose processor which can be connected to other transputers to form a distributed processing system. A *transputer* is a computer on a chip; one particular feature is that a transputer has four autonomous *link interface controllers* for communication with other transputers. Transputers are designed to function in a local network. Unlike some novel computer architectures currently being investigated, the transputer philosophy still incorporates a CPU which functions according to the principles of the basic von Neumann architecture. Thus a network of transputers is a ***distributed processing system*** which functions as a set of communicating sequential processes.

Figure 1.3 illustrates the layout of the T800 transputer, manufactured by INMOS. It consists of a 32-bit CPU capable of 10 million instructions per second; a hardware floating-point unit which performs floating-point arithmetic operations concurrently with the CPU,

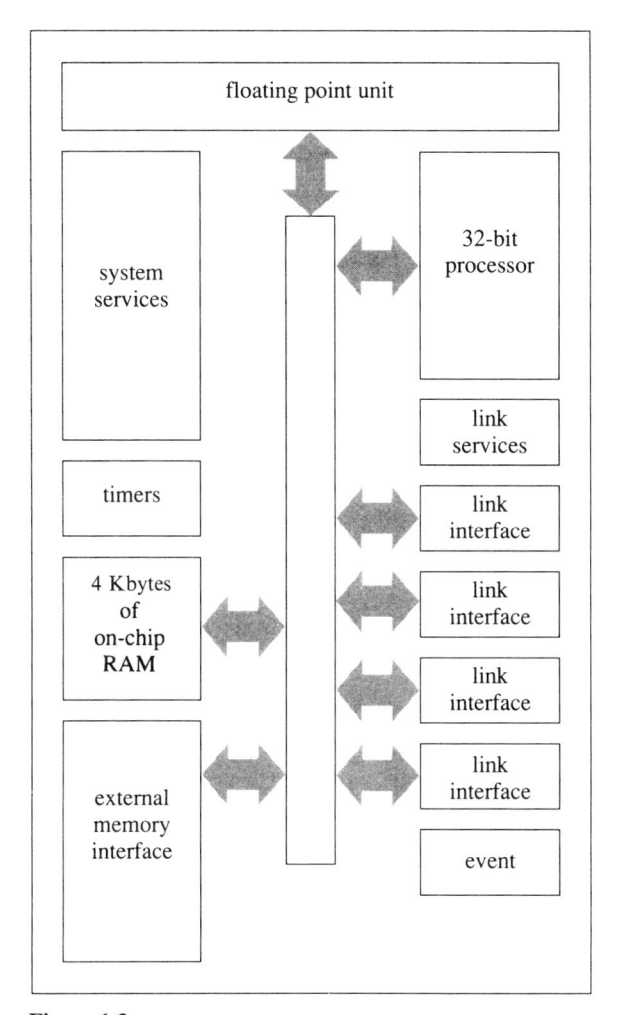

Figure 1.3

and a small amount (4 Kbytes) of very fast, on-chip RAM. Its highly novel feature is a set of four bi-directional links capable of inputting and outputting up to 20 Mbits (million bits) per second.

1.4 The Open Development Method

There are several software development methods which, to differing degrees, recognize concurrency inherent in a problem, but aim to produce sequential code. The essential activities involved in the development of software for a system are illustrated in Figure 1.4.

It is our aim to exploit concurrency fully. To this end we shall describe a development method, the Open Development Method, which emphasizes concurrent aspects of a problem at the requirements analysis stage and uses an appropriate notation for the design stages.

The starting point for our method is the primitive notion of a *process*. In a conventional statement of requirements there is no attempt to identify subsidiary processes that form part

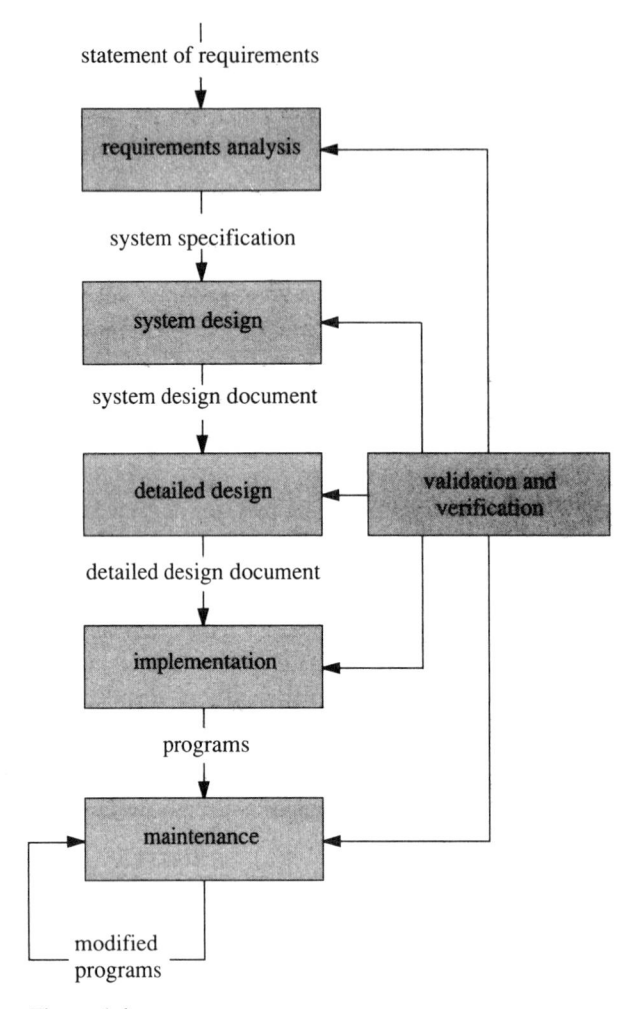

```
                    |
         statement of requirements
                    ↓
          ┌─────────────────────┐
          │ requirements analysis │◄──────────┐
          └─────────────────────┘           │
                    │                       │
         system specification               │
                    ↓                       │
          ┌─────────────────────┐           │
          │    system design    │◄────┐     │
          └─────────────────────┘     │     │
                    │                 │     │
         system design document       │     │
                    ↓                 │     │
          ┌─────────────────────┐  ┌──────────────┐
          │   detailed design   │◄─│ validation and│
          └─────────────────────┘  │  verification │
                    │              └──────────────┘
         detailed design document        │
                    ↓                    │
          ┌─────────────────────┐        │
          │   implementation    │◄───────┘
          └─────────────────────┘
                    │
                programs
                    ↓
      ┌───►┌─────────────────────┐◄──────────┘
      │    │     maintenance     │
      │    └─────────────────────┘
      │             │
      │    modified │
      └── programs ─┘
```

Figure 1.4

of the main problem description. However, our aim is to exploit as much concurrency as possible. To this end we incorporate into requirements analysis the specific task of identifying concurrent, component processes within a problem. We shall refer to this type of analysis as *process analysis*. The objective is to divide the problem repeatedly into communicating processes, each of which can then be developed individually.

The next step is to specify the individual processes in a formalism which captures the notion of communication between processes.

It is possible to identify three models of communication between concurrent processes. In the *shared variables* model, several processes may access a common memory. By updating the variables in the common memory, the processes communicate with each other.

Another model is the *mailbox* model of *message passing*. In this model a process communicates with another by sending a message to its mailbox. This message can be retrieved subsequently by the recipient process. If the recipient arrives at the mailbox too early, it must wait for the message. However, the sender process can continue whatever it is doing once it has sent its message—it does not have to wait for the message to be received. If an acknowledgement is required, this must be achieved by the recipient process initiating a reply message to the first process's mailbox.

Finally, there is the *synchronous message passing* model, in which the sender and recipient must synchronize for communication to take place. If either process is ready to communicate before the other, it must wait. Both processes participate in the communication synchronously. In this model of communication there is, in general, no need for acknowledgement. If the communication takes place at all, the recipient process must have received it.

Our preferred model in this course is the third one: synchronous message passing. In Chapter 2 we shall introduce *process networks* that incorporate the description of a system as a collection of processes with synchronized communication. This will be followed up in Part II by a formal notation, CSP, for the specification and description of such a system. Analysis using process networks and its formalization into CSP notation form major elements of the Open Development Method—ODM for short. The use of a formal notation allows the system to be developed in parts, by enabling us to verify that the behaviour of the whole system can be reconstructed from the behaviour of the parts.

The CSP formalism enables code to be developed in Occam. This language is particularly suited to implementation on a distributed processing system, especially in a network of transputers.

Review Question 1.2 How does ODM contrast with conventional software development methods?

We now ask: what advantages might there be in a development method that incorporates concurrency into problems that do not obviously exhibit it?

Concurrency is inherent in far more situations than those where we perceive it as obvious. Our blindness in this direction is due to a long history of programming computers that are unable to exploit this concurrency. Indeed, even when describing problems which obviously exhibit concurrency, much of the work involved in program development has been in effectively removing concurrency. An important aim has been to produce sequential code that can be executed on a single processor.

What about the disadvantages of a concurrent description? Real-time systems exhibit particular snags of their own; when events may occur in an unspecified order (because they occur within different processes) there are usually too many possible sequences of events, so that an exhaustive check is not feasible. It is always possible that some particular sequence will lock up the system and prevent further progress. You will meet examples of this in Chapter 2. Given a formal mathematical specification, though, it may be possible to prove that such sequences will not occur.

Fragmentation

We have mentioned the existence of a multiprocessing facility—a transputer network—as a powerful motivation for our development method. At some stage we are going to have to take into account the available transputers and their interconnections. It is most unlikely that the description of a problem in terms of communicating processes will map directly on to a given hardware configuration. The question therefore arises: at what stage in the development should the detailed construction of the transputer network be taken into account?

Should such considerations play a part at an early stage, such as during process analysis, or should they wait until after the production of Occam code?

This leads to two radically different approaches to a problem. In the first, referred to as *pre-fragmentation*, we break the problem up from the outset bearing in mind the arrangement of transputers on which the resulting code will be executed. In other words, an early part of process analysis consists of establishing the processes and communications links that map on to the hardware. These top-level processes are then analysed further into component processes in a hardware-independent way, to be implemented by concurrency simulation software.

The other approach is to treat the problem on its merits, introducing whatever processes and communications channels best fit the concurrency inherent in it. Only at the last stages of implementation do we make sure that the code is divided in such a way as to match the processor network. This final allocation of the code to processors is referred to as *post-fragmentation*.

We shall not concern ourselves further with the problems of fragmentation, but shall concentrate on bringing out aspects of concurrency in the analysis.

1.5 Summary

This chapter serves both as an introduction to Part I and as a window on the book as a whole, whose theme is software development for systems involving concurrency.

We began by discussing concurrency in general, and showed that concurrency is playing an increasingly important role in designing more efficient computer architectures as well as being inherent in many classes of important real-time and spatial processes.

We introduced the development method, ODM, and emphasized that the requirements analysis phase should identify concurrent processes within a system. ODM uses a model of inter-process communication via synchronous message passing. We shall enlarge on this topic in Chapter 2.

Each process within a concurrent system proceeds in its own time-scale until it needs to participate in a communication. A network of transputers forms a suitable hardware implementation for a set of concurrent processes that communicate by synchronous message passing.

2 PROCESS ANALYSIS

In this chapter we study process analysis; this is the first stage of our development method. Our model of concurrency is introduced in terms of processes that communicate along synchronous channels. The first step in process analysis will be to draw a suitable *process network*. This is illustrated by way of some introductory examples. There follows a section which investigates the issues that arise when studying communications between processes.

2.1 The model of concurrency: processes and channels

The use of ODM depends on two basic notions: processes and channels. A ***process*** will be regarded in a deliberately vague way as an activity, or some identifiable, self-contained collection of activities. A process may be thought of as a black box, the details of whose operation can, and subsequently will, be refined. The reason for vagueness at this stage is the enormous variety of situations which we may wish to model. A process may describe the behaviour of a machine, or an object which may exhibit more than one state. (A *state* is a mode of system behaviour which is externally observable.) However, a process is not necessarily mechanical, or inanimate—an organization can be modelled as a single process.

By analogy with functional decomposition, a process may be subdivided into component processes. The table below lists some examples of processes, with possible components. You might like to extend the table with examples of your own from real-life situations with which you are familiar.

Main process	Component processes
Central heating system	Boiler Hot-water tank Radiators
A chemical plant	An individual reaction vessel, with its input and output pipes and regulating valves

(*continued overleaf*)

Main process	Component processes
The Open University	A regional centre A professor A course tutor
Pelican crossing	Each traffic signal A pedestrian push-button A vehicle detector The control box
A lift system	The lift controller A lift cage The control panel in the lift cage The control panel at each floor Each display panel

Review Question 2.1 Consider the UK public telephone system. Can you suggest any component processes which model aspects of the system?

Let us consider the central heating system. This system is too complex to describe in its totality without considering its component parts. A radiator is quite a simple component, which can be in one of two states—hot or cold. (A thermostatically-controlled radiator could have many temperature states, but we shall ignore that sophistication.) In a simple central heating system, there are two *events* that affect the state of the radiator: turning on the valve allows the radiator to reach the hot state, and turning off the valve causes the radiator to return to the cold state.

Similarly, a traffic signal for a pelican crossing has four states: red, flashing amber, green and amber. The signal cycles between these states under the control of a control box, which responds to pedestrians pressing the push-button and vehicles passing the vehicle detector.

In addition to processes that cycle endlessly, we may consider a process which passes through a finite sequence of states. Students in the Open University are required to complete tutor-marked assignments (TMAs) as part of their course requirements. A TMA process is created when a student submits an assignment to his or her tutor. The TMA next participates in an event *grading*, as a result of which it acquires a mark. It then participates in an event whereby the mark is recorded in the Open University student database. The final event in the life cycle of the TMA is *return to student*, after which this TMA process terminates. Note that, although a TMA is a passive object, its life cycle may be described by a sequence of *events*; the sequence in which the events evolve forms the description of a process.

Communication

If a number of concurrent processes are to model a single system, there must be some means of communication between the processes. In our model of concurrency, processes can communicate with each other by means of **channels**. A channel is a directed communications link between two processes; these are its **source** and its **sink**. The source process may send messages along the channel to the sink process. If bi-directional communication is required between a pair of processes, two channels are necessary—one in each direction.

A process is represented by an ellipse labelled by a word in upper-case letters. A general or anonymous process is often labelled with the letter *P*, as shown in Figure 2.1.

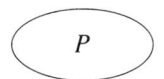

Figure 2.1

A channel connecting two processes is represented as a directed arrow from one process to the other. The channel is usually labelled for ease of reference, e.g. *link* in Figure 2.2.

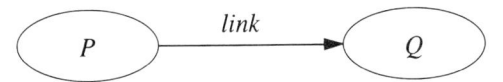

Figure 2.2

A *process network* shows all the processes under consideration and all the channels connecting them. The simplest non-trivial example of a process network is shown in Figure 2.2. Communication can only occur in the direction of the arrow: in this case from *P* to *Q*, but not vice versa. For *Q* to be able to send messages to *P* an additional channel would be necessary, as in Figure 2.3, which illustrates *two-way* communication.

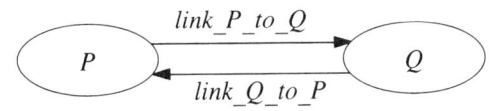

Figure 2.3

A system with any degree of complexity will contain many processes; there may also be many channels between any two given processes. A possible process network is shown in Figure 2.4. In principle, it is always sufficient to have two channels between a given pair of processes, *P* and *Q*: one in each direction. However, there may be several types of communication from *P* to *Q*, say. Rather than attach a tag to each communication to identify its type, we may find it convenient to use a different channel for each type of communication.

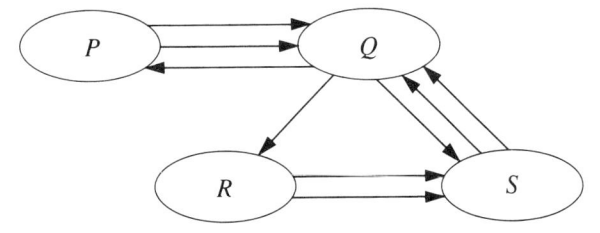

Figure 2.4

The environment

The process networks shown so far describe *closed systems*, that is, groups of processes capable of communicating with each other but not with any external process. Sometimes we may wish to indicate a channel for communication with some unspecified process—either because we are not interested in describing the behaviour of the other process, or because we wish to defer description of the other process to a later occasion. In this case, we say that the process is capable of communicating with its **environment** through **external** channels.

Example

2.1 As an example of a simple process, let us consider an individual traffic signal in a pelican crossing. At any time the signal produces one of the following outputs: red, flashing amber, green or amber. Each of these outputs may be thought of as a message on an external channel called *colour*. Thus the signal interacts with its environment through the channel *colour*.

The signal changes colour in response to a message from the control unit for the crossing. Thus we must also introduce an entry channel, which may be called *control*. An individual signal has a single **entry channel** and a single **exit channel**; this is illustrated in Figure 2.5.

```
control ──▶( SIGNAL )── colour ──▶
```

Figure 2.5

☐

Exercise

2.1 A pelican crossing includes the following components, each of which may be thought of as a separate process: two traffic signals, two push-buttons, and a control unit.

Use your knowledge of how pelican crossings work to identify appropriate channels for (a) the push-button process, (b) the control unit.

Solution 2.1 (a) The push-button process requires the following channels: an entry channel, *button,* to carry the message generated when someone pushes the button; and an exit channel, *stop*, to notify the control unit.
(b) The control unit must have an exit channel, *control*, which sends messages to the traffic signals; an exit channel, *wait*, to switch the WAIT displays on and off; and an entry channel, to carry the message generated when a vehicle passes over one of the detectors. It has another entry channel, identified in part (a), which carries the notification from the push-button process.

☐

Piecing together the component processes of the pelican crossing using the channels identified above, we may obtain the process network given in Figure 2.6. (We could have used two separate *wait* channels, one for each display, and two separate *vehicle_detector* channels, one for each detector. However, it is frequently better to opt for conceptual simplicity, as in Figure 2.6.)

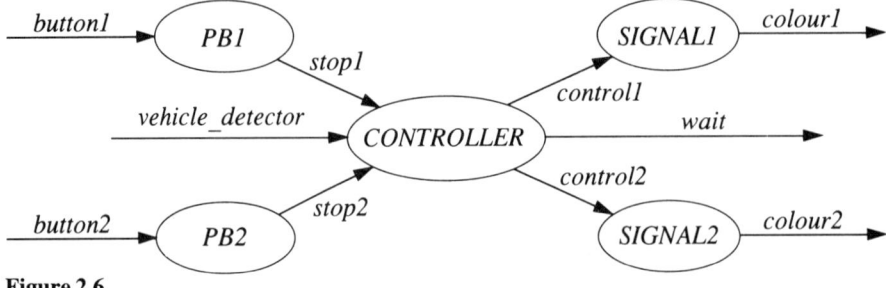

Figure 2.6

2.2 Examples of process analysis

We now present some examples from a variety of contexts. We shall consider a telephone linked to an exchange, a chemical plant and an executing computer program.

Example

2.2 Our first example in this section concerns a local telephone exchange. Figure 2.7 shows the channels associated with a single telephone receiver. A similar set of channels would be required for each receiver linked to the exchange. In addition to a pair of channels linking the receiver to the exchange, there are additional channels that allow the *PHONE* process to receive inputs from and send outputs to the *environment* in which *PHONE* is assumed to operate.

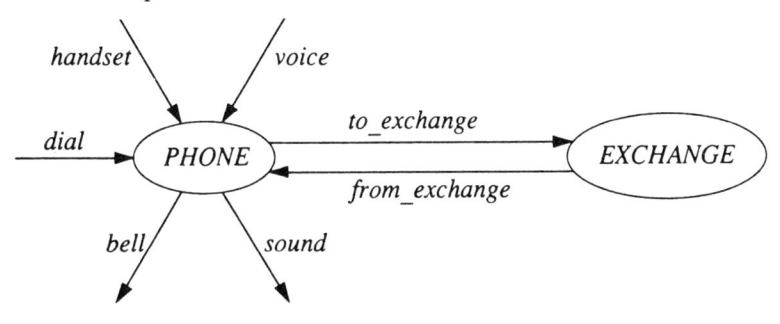

Figure 2.7

The *PHONE* process responds to several types of input from the external environment of *PHONE* and *EXCHANGE*: lifting or replacing the handset, dialling a number, and voice input to the mouthpiece. The channel labelled *handset* conveys a message indicating a change in status of the telephone handset. There are two possible messages: *handset up* and *handset down*. Similarly, the channel labelled *dial* carries the sequence of numbers dialled or, in a push-button phone, the sequence of buttons pressed. The other two external channels are *bell*, which carries the output signal that activates and switches off the telephone bell, and *sound*, which carries the output from the earpiece.

Example

2.3 Consider a chemical plant. We may have to take into account the following components:

- several reaction vessels, interconnected by pipes;
- a heater and a temperature gauge, in physical contact with one of the vessels;
- a computer which has control of the heater and other devices.

A first attempt at a process network might be as shown in Figure 2.8. The two reaction vessels are modelled as processes *R1* and *R2*. The control computer is modelled as the process *CC*, and the processing of the waste is modelled as the process *WP*. The figure indicates a view of the chemical plant as four separate processes in communication with each other.

The environment may influence the chemical plant by sending messages along the entry channels to the processes *R1* and *R2*. These messages could be the rate of flow of raw materials and the mix of chemicals. The chemical plant influences the environment by its

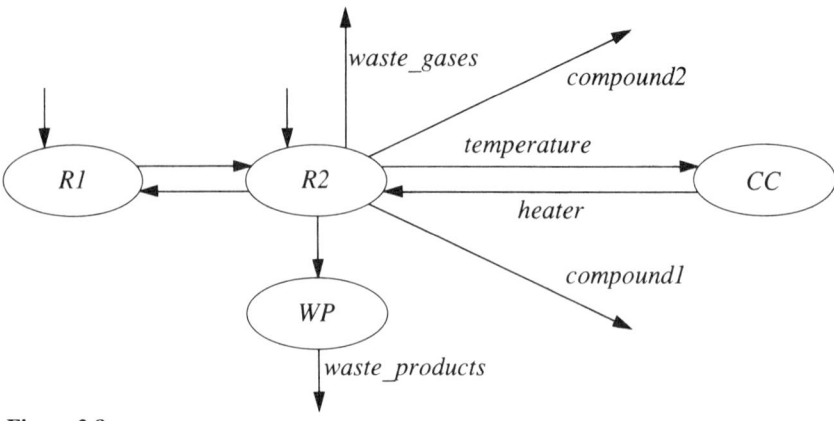

Figure 2.8

products; these are represented as the exit channels called *waste_gases*, *compound1*, *compound2* and *waste_products*. In addition we have identified channels that link the component processes, such as *temperature*, which carries the temperature reading from *R2* to *CC*, and *heater*, which carries the control signal that operates the heater in reaction vessel 2.

It may be argued further that this network is incomplete. There may be input to the control computer by an operator, and output from it to a monitor screen. The external sources (for incoming channels) and the external sinks (for outgoing channels) have not been shown. Here the external sources are the suppliers of raw materials, the external sinks are the users of the products, and there is a waste disposal facility. It would certainly be appropriate, if required, to include these processes explicitly. It is part of the process analysis phase to elucidate the customer's relevant requirements that have to be modelled.

No hard and fast rule can be laid down as to what should and should not be included. As much or as little must be included as is relevant to the customer's needs.

□

Example

2.4 Our next example covers a rather more familiar problem: execution of a computer program. When we use a computer to solve a problem, we may run a specific program which makes use of certain peripheral devices. In a first attempt at a process analysis of this problem, we would certainly expect to identify the executing program as a process, as well as the obvious input and output devices, such as a keyboard and a screen. Disk memory and individual files accessed by the program are also candidates for processes. (Other input devices, such as a mouse, would also qualify, if present.) This is represented pictorially as shown in Figure 2.9.

□

Exercise

2.2 Draw a process network for the execution of a computer program, as indicated above, showing clearly the channels.

Solution 2.2 The individual processes have essentially been identified in Example 2.4. We therefore label them with suitable names. A channel must be provided from each input device to the program, and from the program to each output device. In addition, a pair of channels is needed between the *PROGRAM* process and each of the *DISK* and *FILE* processes, to cater for two-way communication. A process network is shown in Figure 2.10.

□

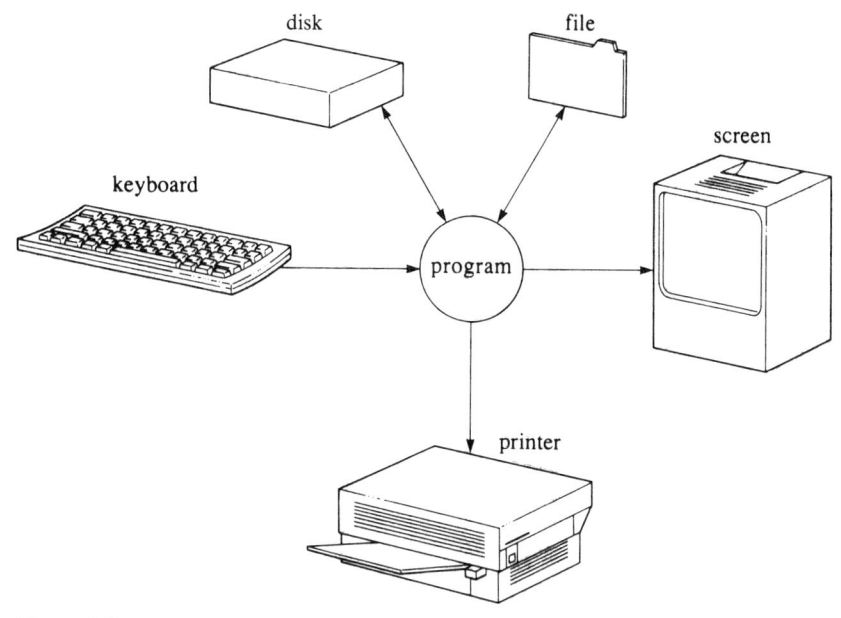

Figure 2.9

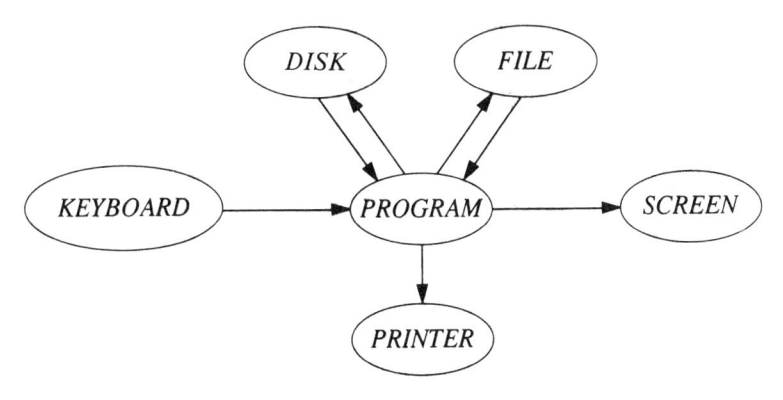

Figure 2.10

2.3 Inter-process communication

At a suitable level of detail, each process can be thought of as *sequential*. A process *evolves* by engaging in a sequence of events. In other words, the life history of a process is a sequence of events. An *event* is simply any observable activity which is of interest. As such, it may be specified and refined using well-known techniques. Our main consideration will be in analysing how a collection of these sequential processes behave when there is inter-process communication. We shall need to make some assumptions about the timing of activities within a process and, in particular, the timing of the communication between processes.

Synchronous communication

The first assumption in our model is crucial to much of what follows. We assume that processes are *asynchronous*, in the sense that each process evolves in its own time-scale. There is no notion of global time, and processes that are not communicating are free to engage in events at their own rate, quite independently of any other process. Only when two processes communicate is there any link between them, because in our model communication is *synchronous*. That is, if two processes reach a state where they wish to communicate (one to send, the other to receive) then the communication event takes place. On the other hand, if only one of the processes is ready and the other is not, then the communication is delayed until both parties are ready. In the meantime, the process that is ready remains in suspense until the communication can take place. The communication event is indivisible—it effectively synchronizes the sending and receiving processes. After a communication event, both processes are free to evolve asynchronously until such time as they need to communicate again.

Example

2.5 Consider two workers, *W1* and *W2* say, performing mainly unrelated activities, except that worker *W1* needs to pass an object to *W2* at some stage (Figure 2.11).

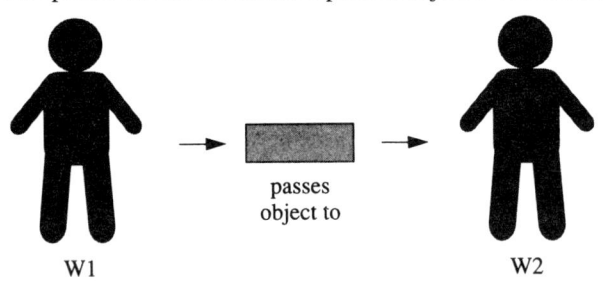

Figure 2.11

The workers *W1* and *W2* work simultaneously and independently so we may think of them as two concurrent processes, as shown in Figure 2.12. We model the possibility of *W1* passing the object to *W2* by providing a channel.

Figure 2.12

Each worker continues with his own work, oblivious of the other, until either *W1* needs to pass the object or *W2* needs the object. If *W1* needs to pass the object, but *W2* does not yet need it, then *W1* cannot continue. The process *W1* is suspended or **blocked** and cannot get on with anything else until the object has been passed. As soon as *W2* is ready to receive, the object is passed and then both are free to continue work. Alternatively, if *W2* must have the object to make further progress but *W1* is not ready to pass it, then *W2* is blocked until *W1* is ready to oblige. Once again, the object is then passed and both are free to work asynchronously. More formally, the process *W1* is capable of engaging in the event *pass object*, and *W2* is capable of engaging in the event *receive object*. However, these two events must take place simultaneously.

□

Review Question 2.2 Given our model of concurrency, is it possible for communicating processes to run in sequence? In other words, given the simple process network of Figure 2.2, is it possible for all the events of *P* to occur *before* any of the events of *Q*, or vice versa?

□

Deadlock and livelock

In order to help you to master the concept of synchronous communication between asynchronous processes we shall use the analogy of conversation between people. In the course of the discussion, you will be introduced to two problems that can arise with communicating processes—*deadlock* and *livelock*.

Our discussion centres round two people, whom we call Peter and Chris, living in separate houses.

Suppose first that the two houses have no communication between them. Peter and Chris get on with their own lives oblivious of each other. Their clocks may tell different times—perhaps Peter's clock is forever ten minutes fast, or maybe it gains a minute a day—but no one will be any the wiser. In this situation Peter and Chris act as *asynchronous processes*, with independent time-scales. There is no notion of global time.

A second situation to consider allows some communication between the houses. This is a fundamental change from the previous lack of communication. Suppose there is a single directed link from Peter's house to Chris's house. Communication is achieved using a microphone in Peter's house linked to a loudspeaker in Chris's house. The microphone and loudspeaker may each be switched on and off by its user. A lamp in each house indicates whether the other end of the link is live. For example, when Peter switches on the microphone, Chris's indicator lamp is lit. With this arrangement a message can be transferred (from Peter to Chris) only when both lamps are lit (indicating that both the microphone and the loudspeaker are live). This ensures that no message will get lost; Peter will not transmit when his lamp (controlled by Chris) is off, and Chris will switch the lamp on only when she is prepared to listen. This differs from normal conversation, where the speaker may talk at any time, irrespective of whether the person being spoken to is listening.

In all likelihood, one party will become ready to send (or receive) a message before the other. If Peter is ready to send, but Chris is not ready to receive, Peter's lamp remains unlit. Peter will therefore wait before sending a message—possibly indefinitely. This could arise in two ways, as illustrated in Figure 2.13. Firstly, maybe Chris does not choose to listen. Peter is therefore totally frustrated in his wish to send a message. The situation is deadlocked: Peter is unable to continue, since he resolutely wishes to transmit to Chris, who has no intention of listening. A second possibility is that Chris is willing to listen, but has a heavy schedule and continually postpones switching on the loudspeaker. Peter is not deadlocked, since Chris may eventually get round to listening, in which case he can continue with his planned activities. But Peter does not get to transmit, because Chris does not actually switch on. In this case Peter is in *livelock*. This is a singularly unpalatable situation, since future activity is not ruled out—it merely fails to happen. It is clearly desirable to set up communicating processes in such a way as to eliminate deadlock and livelock. Indeed, this is a prime aim in the design of concurrent systems.

Consider now that Chris may be ready to listen, indicating this by switching on the loudspeaker and illuminating Peter's lamp. To achieve progress, Peter must be prepared to

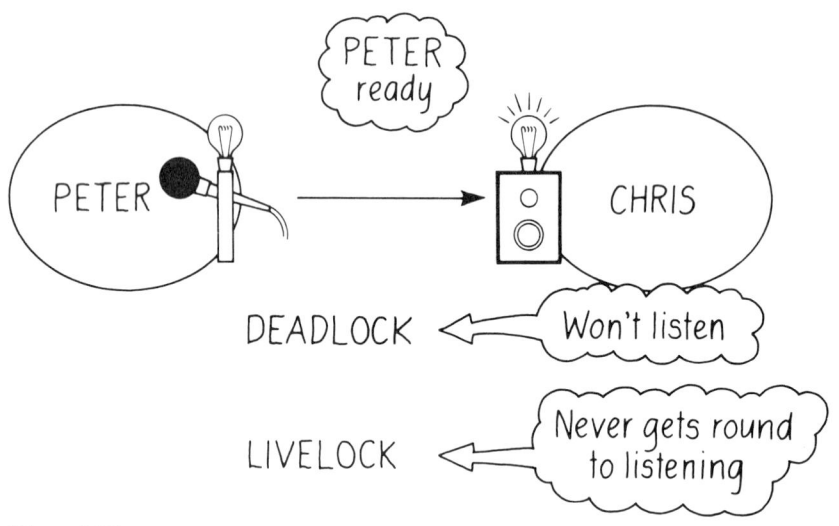

Figure 2.13

transmit. If Peter is never willing to transmit, Chris has reached deadlock; and if Peter might transmit, but never gets round to it, Chris is in livelock. However, in the case of a waiting receiver, our model will allow a further alternative. Rather than being committed to listening for a message, Chris is allowed to engage in one of a set of alternative activities. Listening out for a message from Peter is just one of these alternatives. If a message arrives, then Chris is available to receive it. If Peter is not ready to transmit when Chris is listening, Chris continues with something else; she can check periodically to discover whether Peter is waiting to send a message. This arrangement avoids deadlock and livelock: Peter switches on the microphone when he wishes to transmit, and sooner or later Chris will make a periodic check by switching on the loudspeaker. At this instant both lamps are illuminated simultaneously and communication takes place.

Two-way communication

Let us extend our analogy to cover the case of two-way conversation. In order to avoid deadlock, such a conversation must be carefully planned. For example, each party might have the intention of talking first and then listening; this would result in immediate deadlock. We must set things up so that each person listens while the other is talking, according to some suitable convention. A convention to regulate communication between two parties is called a *protocol*. One protocol which we shall find useful is for each party to send and receive simultaneously. Whenever a message is sent, it is done in parallel with listening for incoming messages. In our analogy this could be achieved by each party possessing a message recorder attached to the loudspeaker. Anyone who wishes to send a message first switches on the recorder to intercept incoming messages. Thus, when Peter wishes to speak to Chris, he switches on his recorder. No communication can yet take place, as Chris is not yet ready to listen. When Chris is ready to participate, she switches on her recorder. The two can then speak in parallel, each message being received by the other's recorder.

More complicated situations arise when more than two parties are involved. We do not consider these in detail, but merely note that careful consideration must be given to the available sequences of events. In particular, we must prevent the situation arising where an attempt is made to send a message to a party who is unwilling to listen—causing deadlock—or who never gets round to listening—causing livelock.

2.4 Summary

We began this section by introducing process analysis; this involves modelling a system as a set of processes that communicate by passing messages (from a fixed set) along channels between them. The model is represented as a process network. Each process runs in its own time-scale, subject to synchronization when a communication event takes place. A process may interact with its environment along an external channel.

For our model of communication, it is essential that two processes that wish to communicate are running concurrently. It is possible, though, for the situation to arise where one or more processes are forever prevented from further progress, because they cannot agree on a communication. This situation, which must be avoided, is called ***deadlock***. It could arise, for example, because each process wishes to send a message, and neither is ready to receive. In this case, deadlock can be overcome by specifying that the communications take place in parallel. Another situation which is to be avoided is where the second party to a communication is able to make the link but may never get around to doing so; for example, the second party may always engage in some other activity in preference to receiving the communication; this is called ***livelock***.

In a system of more than two processes, it is useful to be able to choose to act on the communication that first becomes available for input. Such a choice between alternative inputs will turn out to be a powerful element in our discussion of concurrent processes. In our model no element of choice is available on output; the intention to transmit a message commits the sender to the transmission.

3 PROCESS CONFIGURATIONS

We now turn our attention to some configurations of processes and channels which may arise in various contexts. In principle, there is no limit to the number of different process networks which can be drawn. However, there are some configurations, such as *pipelines* and *funnels*, which arise in many situations. We shall introduce these in appropriate contexts. We shall also introduce an additional feature into our process networks—a semi-formal annotation which describes the activities performed by a process. To illustrate this feature, we consider the use of process analysis in evaluating mathematical functions. This will lead us naturally into some of the process configurations we wish to discuss.

In this chapter the problems we address are fully specified. We are using process analysis as a design tool.

3.1 Evaluating functions

A function of one variable can be modelled as a process with one entry channel and one exit channel. A process for a simple function can be described as engaging in the following three events, in sequence:

- receive a value on the entry channel;
- evaluate the result;
- send the result on the exit channel.

This process might be implemented as a button on a calculator—it transforms a single input value to a single result.

For example, the function $f(x) = x + 3$ is described semi-formally by the **process annotation** in Figure 3.1.

Note that we have annotated the process ellipse with a semi-formal description of the process. The process, which we have called *ADD_3*, engages in a sequence of three events. This is made clear by prefixing the list of events that comprise the *ADD_3* process with the qualifying phrase, IN SEQUENCE, and indenting the list. (Later we shall consider processes that can engage in a list of events in parallel, and processes that select a single event from a list of possibilities.) Synchronization of communication means that when

PROCESS CONFIGURATIONS 25

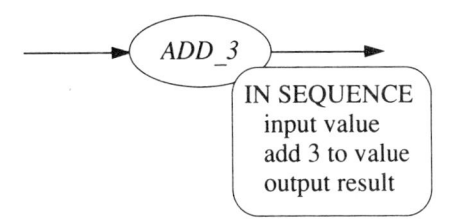

```
     ┌─────────┐
────▶│  ADD_3  │────▶
     └─────────┘
     ╭─────────────╮
     │ IN SEQUENCE │
     │  input value│
     │  add 3 to value│
     │  output result│
     ╰─────────────╯
```

Figure 3.1

ADD_3 is activated, it is quiescent until a value arrives on the entry channel. This value is then increased by 3 and the result is available for transmission on the exit channel—when the process at the other end of the channel is ready to receive it. *ADD_3* has then completed its task and engages in no further activity. More realistically, it would be desirable for *ADD_3* to be available to process a stream of input values. To achieve this, *ADD_3* needs to accept another value on its entry channel as soon as it has completed its output event. We indicate this by prefacing the group of events to be repeated by the qualifier REPEATEDLY, as shown in Figure 3.2. The process *ADD_3R* so defined engages in a never-ending sequence of events. As soon as it has output one result, it continues by receiving the next value on the entry channel.

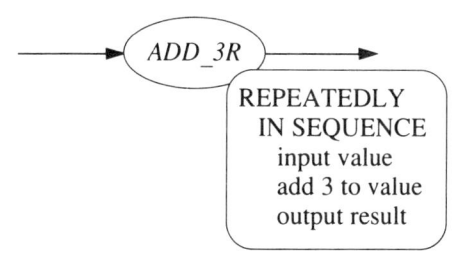

```
     ┌─────────┐
────▶│ ADD_3R  │────▶
     └─────────┘
     ╭─────────────╮
     │ REPEATEDLY  │
     │ IN SEQUENCE │
     │  input value│
     │  add 3 to value│
     │  output result│
     ╰─────────────╯
```

Figure 3.2

Note the scheme of indentation used in our process annotations to delineate the scope of each qualifier. Thus, in Figure 3.2, there is a sequence of three events. This sequence forms a single compound activity which is qualified by REPEATEDLY.

Exercise

3.1 Draw a process network for the process that computes the value $3x - 7$ for each x in the input stream. Annotate your network with a semi-formal description.

Solution 3.1 The process network for the process to compute $3x - 7$ is given in Figure 3.3.

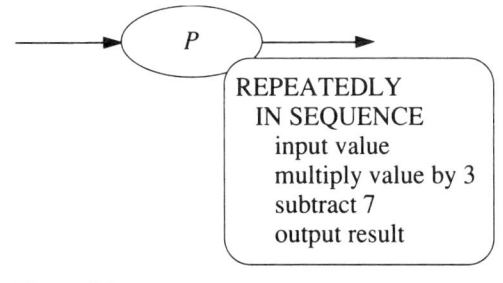

```
     ┌─────────┐
────▶│    P    │────▶
     └─────────┘
     ╭─────────────────╮
     │ REPEATEDLY      │
     │ IN SEQUENCE     │
     │  input value    │
     │  multiply value by 3│
     │  subtract 7     │
     │  output result  │
     ╰─────────────────╯
```

Figure 3.3

An alternative solution to Exercise 3.1 is to separate out the events *multiply value by 3* and *subtract 7* as distinct processes, as shown in Figure 3.4. The process TIMES_3 has one entry channel and one exit channel; each input value is multiplied by 3, and the result is output.

⟶(TIMES_3)⟶(MINUS_7)⟶

Figure 3.4

Exercise

3.2 Give a process annotation for TIMES_3 in the manner of Figure 3.3.

Solution 3.2 The process annotation for TIMES_3 is given in Fig. 3.5.

(TIMES_3)
REPEATEDLY
IN SEQUENCE
  input value
  multiply by 3
  output result

Figure 3.5

Review Question 3.1 Describe the process MINUS_7 in words, and provide a suitable process annotation.

Splitting the function $3x-7$ into two concurrent processes provides an interesting exercise, but does it serve any useful purpose? The answer is yes. Suppose we have a stream of input values for which we require the corresponding outputs $3x - 7$. The process P of Figure 3.3, which includes both a multiplication and a subtraction, will clearly take longer to perform than either of the processes TIMES_3 and MINUS_7. Now, as soon as TIMES_3 outputs its result, it is ready to accept the next number from the input stream. Meanwhile MINUS_7 has input the value that TIMES_3 output, since these two events are synchronized. So MINUS_7 can continue to subtract 7 and output the answer while TIMES_3 is working on its next input. The two processes can continue concurrently, MINUS_7 always processing one value while TIMES_3 is working on the next one. The two processes are synchronized each time a value is communicated from TIMES_3 to MINUS_7. The time saving may be insignificant for a single input value, but could be considerable for a stream consisting of thousands or even millions of input values. In practice, calculating this function as a pair of concurrent processes (on two physical processors) may not yield a saving in time, owing to the communication overhead. However, a complex calculation may be broken down in this way so that each part is performed in a separate processor, yielding an appreciable saving in time.

Buffers and pipelines

A process which has a single entry channel and a single exit channel is called a *pipe*. Thus the processes *ADD_3* and *TIMES_3* are examples of pipes. Two or more pipes may be joined together so that the exit channel of one process is the entry channel of the next. A set of concurrent processes linked in this manner is a *pipeline*. Figure 3.4 is an example of a pipeline of two processes. The environment of a pipeline 'sees' one entry channel and one exit channel. The internal channels are not visible to the environment. A pipeline in which a separate processor is allocated to each component process is often a good way of speeding up a computation.

The simplest example of a repeating process inputs values and outputs them unchanged; this is a *one-place buffer*, with a process network as in Figure 3.6.

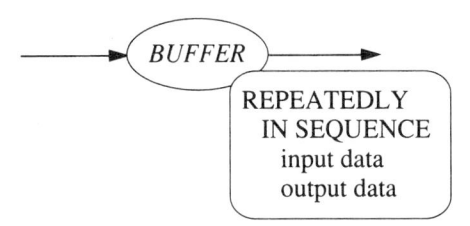

```
    ──▶( BUFFER )──▶
         ┌─────────────┐
         │ REPEATEDLY  │
         │ IN SEQUENCE │
         │  input data │
         │ output data │
         └─────────────┘
```

Figure 3.6

The *BUFFER* process in Figure 3.6 takes a data item transmitted on its entry channel. The process, *BUFFER*, is then dormant until it is able to send this data item on its exit channel. Having done so, it is ready to accept the next item on its entry channel, and so on.

Thus a one-place buffer serves as a single memory cell. It is capable of storing a single data item until it detects a demand on its exit channel. Suppose now that we connect several buffers together in a pipeline. Figure 3.7 illustrates three *BUFFER* processes linked as a pipeline. The external channels are called *data_in* and *data_out*; the internal channels are called *link1* and *link2*.

```
 data_in           link1            link2           data_out
────▶( BUFFER )────▶( BUFFER )────▶( BUFFER )────▶
```

Figure 3.7

The individual one-place buffers operate concurrently, transferring data by communication along the pipeline. Since each buffer can store only one data item at a time, our pipeline serves as a queue which can have up to three such items passing through it at any one time.

Exercise

3.3 Describe, in a few sentences, the mode of operation of the pipeline in Figure 3.7.

Solution 3.3 The first event for each *BUFFER* is the input of data (on its entry channel). Before any data arrives on the external channel *data_in*, the three *BUFFER* processes are dormant. When the first data item arrives along *data_in*, the first *BUFFER* is woken up. The data item is output along *link1* to the second *BUFFER*, which is awaiting communication. The second *BUFFER* then proceeds to output the item on *link2* to

28   SPECIFICATION AND DESIGN OF CONCURRENT SYSTEMS

the third *BUFFER*. When the receiving end of *data_out* is ready for a communication, the data item will be transmitted along that channel.

In the meantime, as soon as the first data item has been sent on *link1*, the first *BUFFER* is ready for the 'input data' event, so another data item can be input on *data_in*. Whenever insufficient data requests appear for *data_out*, up to three data items can be held by the three *BUFFER* processes, each being blocked while waiting to perform its output activity.

3.2 Polynomial evaluation

We can use a pipeline of processes to describe the evaluation of polynomials.

One way to evaluate the polynomial $2x^2 - 3x + 4$ is by rewriting it in the form $x(2x - 3) + 4$. This can be broken down into the following sequence of elementary calculations, using names for the intermediate values:

(a) input a value x;
(b) multiply x by 2 to obtain the intermediate result c_1;
(c) subtract 3 from c_1 to obtain a new intermediate value c_2;
(d) multiply c_2 by the original value x;
(e) add 4 to obtain the answer.

Exercise
3.4 Show how the calculation of this expression for a stream of input data can be modelled by a pipeline of annotated processes.

Solution 3.4   The annotated process network is given in Figure 3.8.

Each process *P1*, *P2*, *P3* and *P4* is a sequential process. Linked in a pipeline, and executing concurrently, they implement the required polynomial evaluation. For each value x arriving on the channel *input*, the corresponding value of the polynomial appears on the channel *output*.

Review Question 3.2   Suggest a descriptive name for the process *P4*.

Review Question 3.3   Describe in words the behaviour of the pipe *P3*.

You should notice that since no data is shared between processes, the variables called c and x are distinct for each process in Fig. 3.8. In other words, c and x are local variables whose scope is restricted to a single process. However, the value of x does not change as it is passed along the pipeline. In addition to the value of x, the intermediate output of each process *P1* and *P2* is passed along as additional input to the next process in the pipeline. The interesting thing about this arrangement is that, as a sequence of values is transmitted along the entry channel, the processes act concurrently on different values from the input stream. Thus, when the first value in the input stream has reached *P4*, the second value can be processed in *P3*, the third in *P2*, and so on. As soon as each process has output the result of its computation, it is ready to accept a new value of x. The results of the computations appear in a stream on the exit channel.

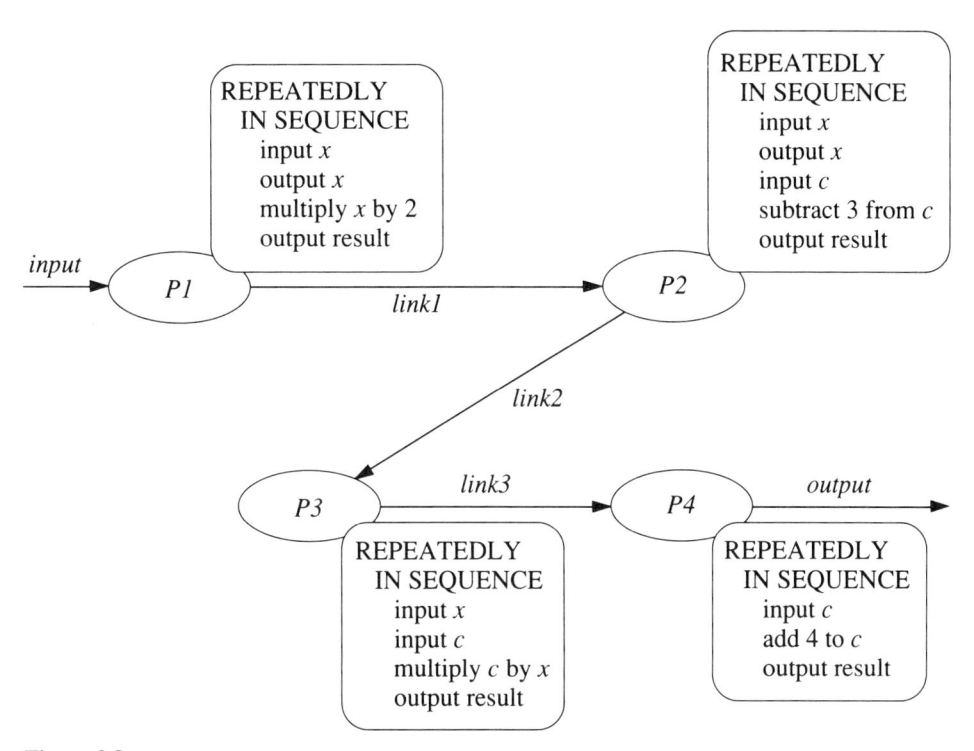

Figure 3.8

```
                REPEATEDLY              REPEATEDLY
                IN SEQUENCE             IN SEQUENCE
                  input x                 input x
                  output x                output x
                  multiply x by 2         input c
                  output result           subtract 3 from c
                                          output result
  input
  ─────▶ ( P1 ) ──────────────▶ ( P2 )
                    link1

                              link2
                                    ╲
                                     ▼
                         link3                  output
              ( P3 ) ─────────▶ ( P4 ) ──────▶

                REPEATEDLY              REPEATEDLY
                IN SEQUENCE             IN SEQUENCE
                  input x                 input c
                  input c                 add 4 to c
                  multiply c by x         output result
                  output result
```

Further consideration of Figure 3.8 reveals an inefficiency in the process *P2*. The problem is that *P2* has to pass along the value of *x* even though the part of the calculation that it handles does not involve the value of *x* at all. In addition to subtracting 3 from the input value *c*, it must also input and output the value *x*. If there are many values on the input stream to be processed, a significant delay can accumulate. The apparent way round this is to use a bypass, as shown in Figure 3.9.

We have introduced the additional channel *bypass,* which carries the value *x* directly. This enables the process *P2* to be replaced by the simpler process *P2'*. The processes *P1* and *P3* must also be modified to take into account the new channel.

Unfortunately, though, this process is less efficient than the one it replaces. Each data item is processed more rapidly, since some of the steps in *P2* have been eliminated. But the overall throughput for a stream of input is not improved! When *P3'*, the new *P3*, receives a value *x* on *bypass*, it must wait to receive the result from *P2'*. After *P1'*, the new *P1*, has accepted an input it cannot output that value until *P3'* is ready to receive it—*P1'* is blocked. So *P2'* will be idle after sending its result to *P3'* until *P1'* is ready with the next result.

Review Question 3.4 Why would it be wrong to describe the process network of Figure 3.9 as a pipeline?

Exercise

3.5 How could a buffer be used to make the process network of Figure 3.9 more efficient?

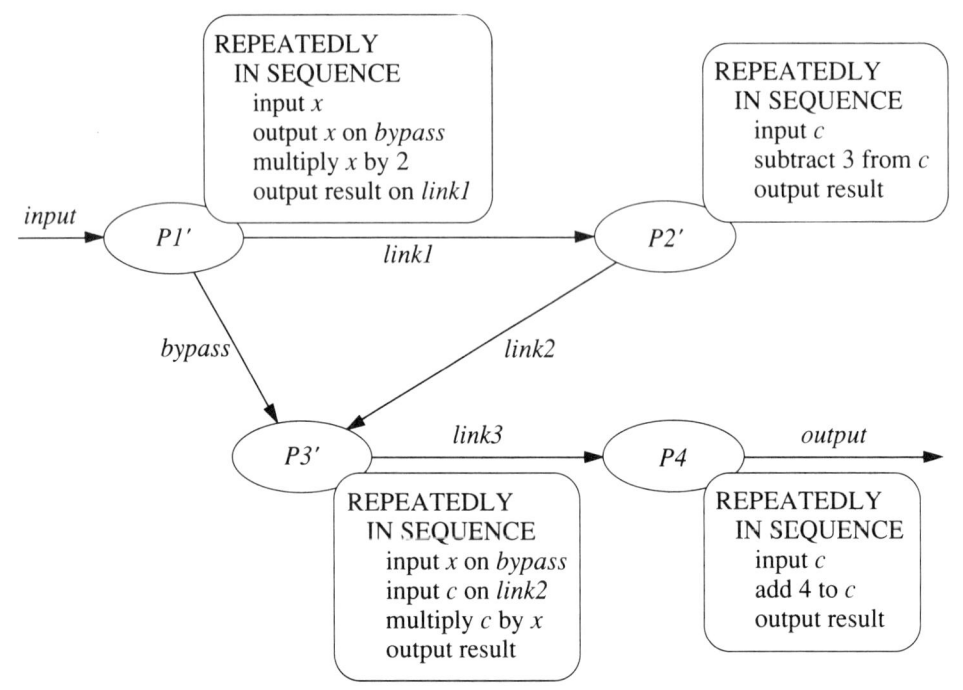

30 SPECIFICATION AND DESIGN OF CONCURRENT SYSTEMS

```
                    REPEATEDLY
                    IN SEQUENCE
                       input x                         REPEATEDLY
                       output x on bypass              IN SEQUENCE
                       multiply x by 2                    input c
                       output result on link1             subtract 3 from c
                                                          output result
  input
   ───▶  P1' ──────────── link1 ──────────▶ P2'

         bypass ╲                  ╱ link2
                 ╲                ╱
                  ▼              ▼
                     P3' ── link3 ──▶ P4 ──▶ output

                    REPEATEDLY                   REPEATEDLY
                    IN SEQUENCE                  IN SEQUENCE
                       input x on bypass            input c
                       input c on link2             add 4 to c
                       multiply c by x              output result
                       output result
```

Figure 3.9

Solution 3.5 If a buffer process is introduced between processes *P1'* and *P3'*, *P1'* will not be kept waiting for *P3'*. Thus, at any one time, four calculations are in progress. While *P4* is completing the computation of the first result, *P3'* is engaged in evaluating the second, *P2'* is engaged in the third with the corresponding value from the input stream waiting in the buffer *B*, and *P1'* is beginning the fourth computation. This is illustrated in Figure 3.10.

Thus new values of *x* can be input continually. Values are then passed steadily along from process *P1'* to *P2'* and from *P2'* to *P3'* to meet the correct value of *x* that has passed through the buffer.

3.3 The funnel

The problem of polynomial evaluation has indicated that even when the pipeline provides a proper description of a problem, efficiency of computation may require an alternative topology of processes and channels. We shall now take a look at another problem that could be modelled by a pipeline, but which has an alternative process network leading to a more efficient computation.

Consider the process *ADD*, which sums the values on its two entry channels and places the result on its exit channel (Figure 3.11).

Exercise

3.6 Draw a process network for the computation that adds eight numbers; for example, $1+3+5+3+2+0+7+1$.

PROCESS CONFIGURATIONS 31

Figure 3.10

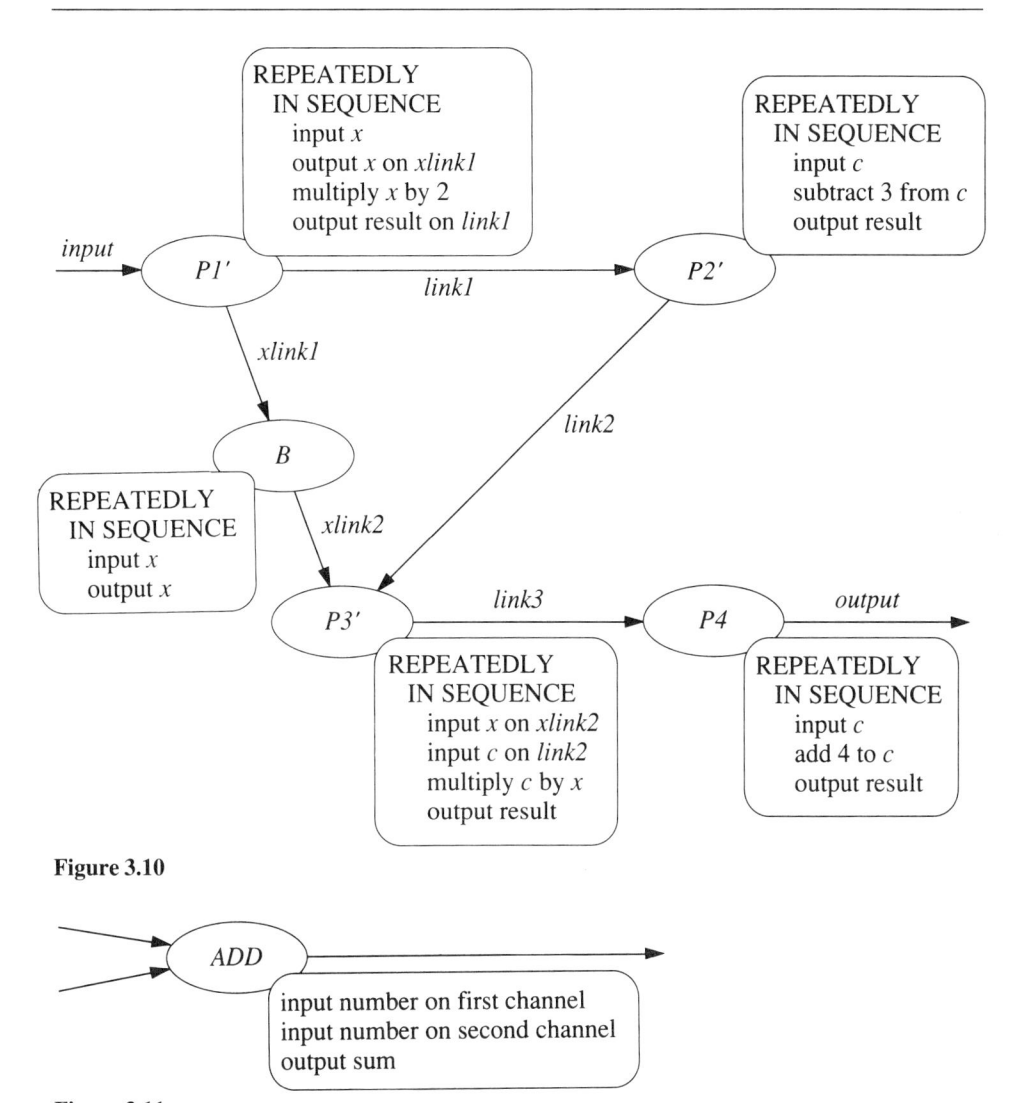

Figure 3.11

Solution 3.6 When eight numbers are added there are seven additions, so seven *ADD* processes are needed. We have labelled the incoming channels from the environment with the names *input1*, *input2*, ..., *input8*.

Alongside each channel in Figure 3.12, we have shown the value that is transmitted for the sample computation.

□

The process network in Figure 3.12 generates the *sequential* computation of the sum. Is there any way that the concurrent capabilities of the *ADD* process might be exploited to achieve the same computation more efficiently? It turns out that we can use the associative property of addition to speed up the computation. As shown in Figure 3.13, if there are eight numbers to be summed, it is possible to perform four separate additions concurrently. We are still using seven identical *ADD* processes, but they are linked in a new configuration.

Figure 3.12

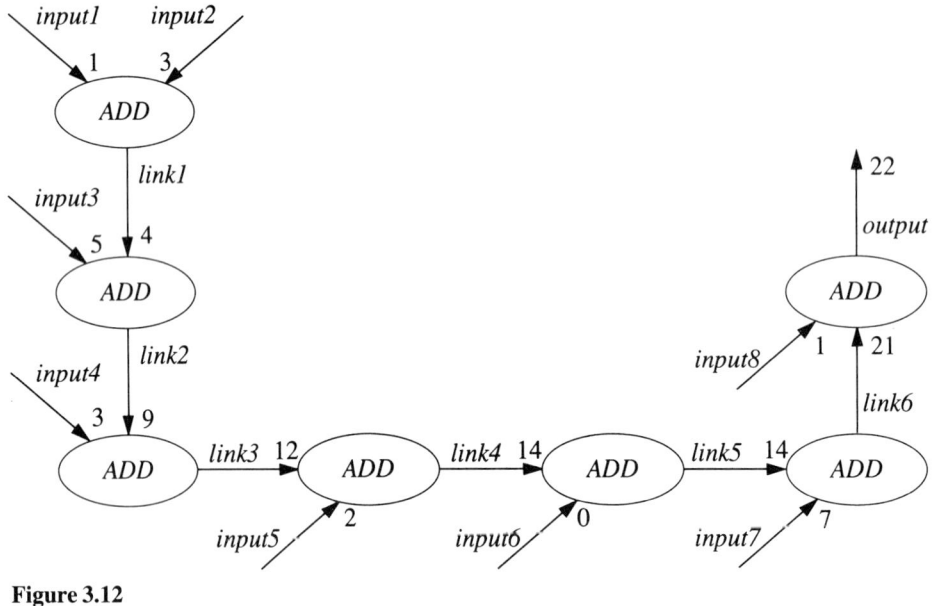

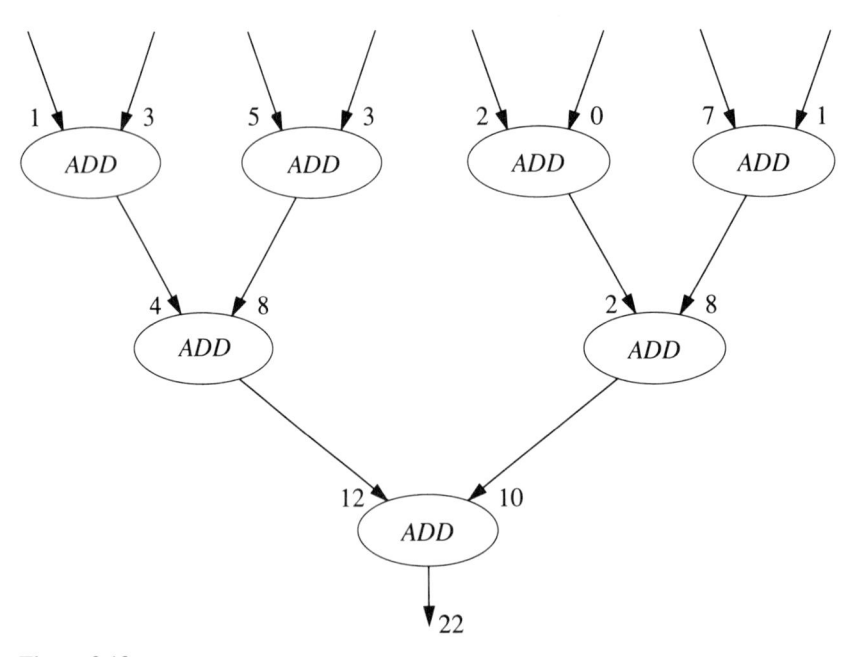

Figure 3.13

The arrangement of processes in Figure 3.13 is called a *funnel*. All four processes in the top row act simultaneously. After one time period, the two processes in row two receive their inputs; they too can execute simultaneously. The total time lapse in adding eight numbers is just three activations of the *ADD* process.

A funnel may be used wherever an associative operation is required.

Merge sort

Another, quite different, context in which a funnel processor may also be used is the sorting of a collection of items. The basic process *MERGE* has two entry channels and one exit channel, as illustrated in Figure 3.14. Each input string carries an ordered (sorted) string; the *MERGE* process merges them into a single sorted string which is transmitted on the exit channel.

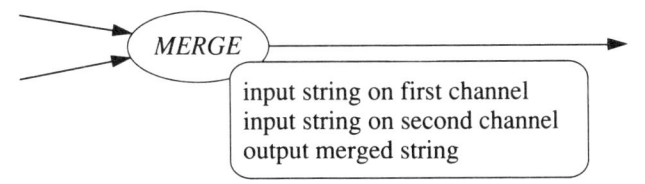

Figure 3.14

A string of arbitrary length may be sorted into alphabetic order by using sufficient *MERGE* processes, as follows. Since a string consisting of one character only is certainly sorted, we begin by splitting our given string into its individual characters. These may now be merged, using copies of the *MERGE* process until a single output string is obtained. This output string will consist of the same letters as the original string, rearranged into alphabetical order. In fact, it does not matter precisely how the *MERGE* processes are linked in order to achieve this result, but the most efficient arrangement is a funnel. Figure 3.15 illustrates a funnel arrangement to sort an eight-letter string; there are eight entry channels from the environment and one exit channel. We have not labelled the internal channels. The figure also shows the progress of the letters of the word 'elephant' as they are sorted using the *MERGE* funnel. Notice how the two entry channels to each *MERGE* carry sorted

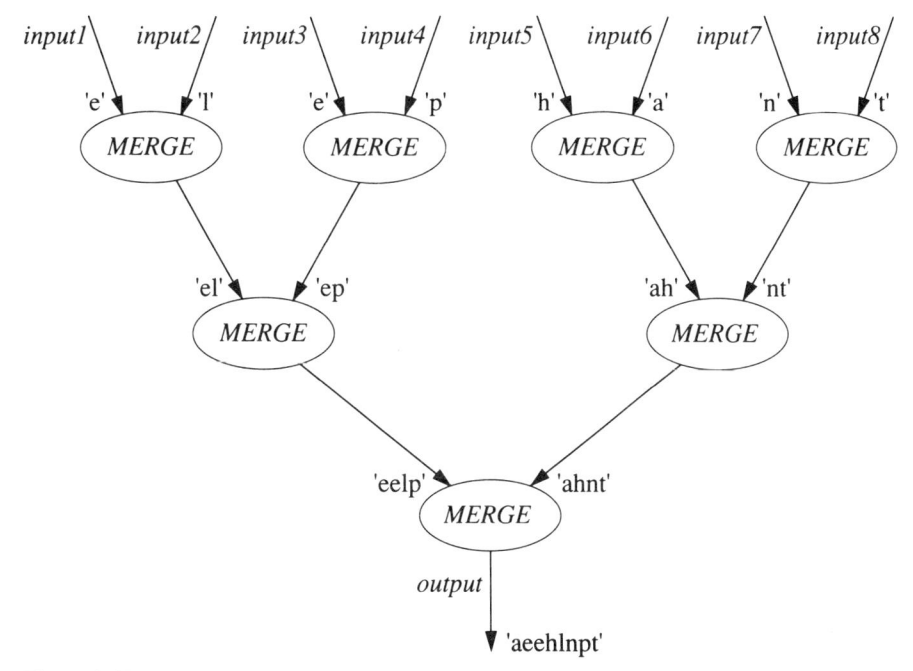

Figure 3.15

strings, and the corresponding exit channel carries the merged string. As a result of the concurrent execution of these processes, the time lapse from the instant when the string is presented to the funnel until the result is delivered on the exit channel is equivalent to three executions of the *MERGE* process.

3.4 Star networks

A process network in which one process is connected to each of the other processes (and there are no direct channels between the other processes) is called a ***star network***. In this section we shall discuss briefly two types of situations that may be modelled as star networks.

Controller and slaves

Often, one process is in a privileged position. For example, referring back to the chemical plant (Figure 2.8), there is a control computer which has responsibility for all the other processes. Similarly, in an interactive computer environment it is the user who initiates various tasks and interacts with them. A more general example, relevant to multiprocessing, arises where a supervisor process allocates tasks to different processors for autonomous execution as and when the processors are available.

The common thread is a central *controlling* process which issues signals or instructions to each of a number of *slave* processes, receives their responses, and performs some subsequent processing. Since the slave processes evolve concurrently, it is appropriate for communication between the *CONTROLLER* process and each slave process (which may be called *SLAVE1*, *SLAVE2* and so on) to take place in parallel. We describe such a situation in a process annotation using the qualifying phrase, IN PARALLEL. As usual, the events within the scope of this qualifier are indented. A typical process network for such a situation with three slave processes is shown in Figure 3.16. We have labelled the outgoing channels *control1* and so on, and the incoming channels *response1* and so on.

```
REPEATEDLY
  IN SEQUENCE
    prepare to control
    IN PARALLEL
      send control signal to each slave
    IN PARALLEL
      receive slave responses
    process responses
```

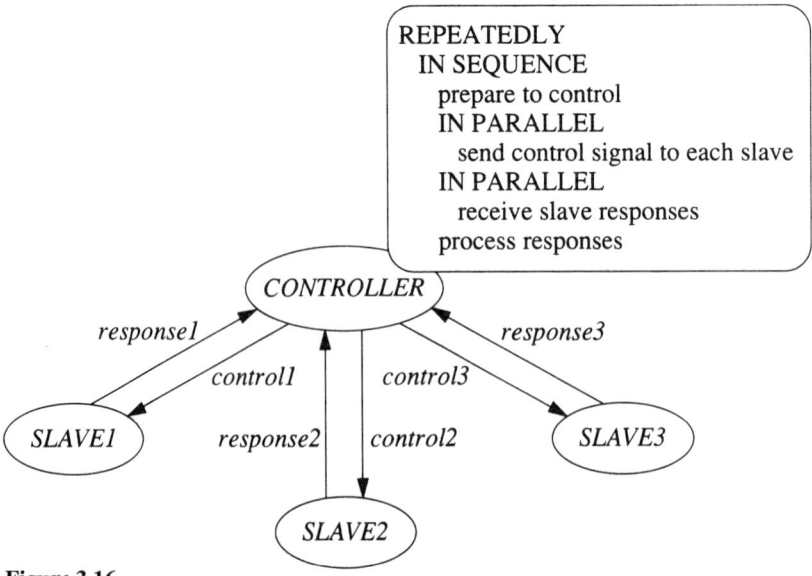

CONTROLLER connected to SLAVE1 (response1, control1), SLAVE2 (response2, control2), SLAVE3 (response3, control3)

Figure 3.16

In the version of the *CONTROLLER* process given above, no response can be received from any one slave until the control signals have been sent to all the slaves. This is the effect of the qualifier IN SEQUENCE, which means that *CONTROLLER* is blocked until all the control signals have been transmitted. Consequently no slave process can respond until the *CONTROLLER* is ready. Suppose, however, that we require an alternative interpretation, namely that each slave should be able to respond to its control signal without delay. For this purpose the pair of communications between the *CONTROLLER* and each slave must be treated as a composite activity; the slaves can then be controlled in parallel, as shown in Figure 3.17. For greater clarity, the qualifier IN PARALLEL is followed by the phrase 'over all slaves'.

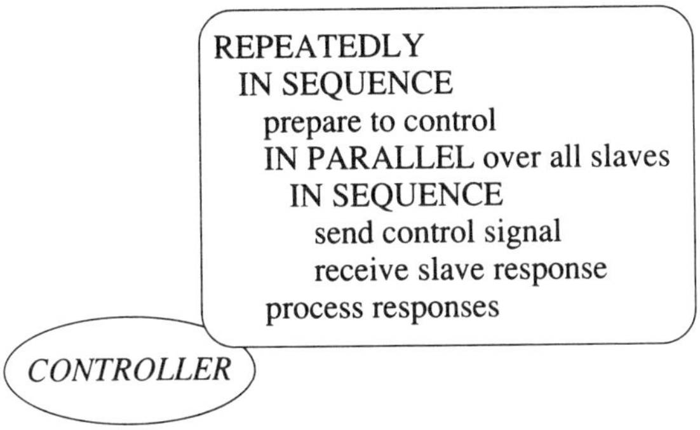

```
REPEATEDLY
  IN SEQUENCE
    prepare to control
    IN PARALLEL over all slaves
      IN SEQUENCE
        send control signal
        receive slave response
    process responses
```

(CONTROLLER)

Figure 3.17

Note that the sequence qualified by IN SEQUENCE consists of three activities. The first activity in the sequence is 'prepare to control', as in the previous description. The second activity is a compound activity performed concurrently for each of the slaves. Each component of this concurrent activity consists of the 'sequence' send control signal followed by 'receive slave' response. The third and final activity is 'process responses'.

With this version of the *CONTROLLER*, the response from each slave can be received as soon as it is available, without necessarily having to wait for every slave to receive the control communication.

Note carefully that both versions of *CONTROLLER* described here need responses to come from all the slaves before the activity 'process responses' can begin. This is appropriate to a situation in which the controller requires information from all slaves to determine the nature of the subsequent processing activity.

Review Question 3.5 Write down a suitable process annotation for the behaviour of one of the slave processes.

Clients and resource

The situation we have just discussed consists of several slave processes subordinate to one controller process. We now consider the reverse situation, in which one process serves as a resource subordinate to several client processes. For example, in a large factory complex several workshops may need to draw stores from a common warehouse; in a public house several bar staff may need to use a single handpump; or in an electronic office several operators may need access to a single laser printer.

36 SPECIFICATION AND DESIGN OF CONCURRENT SYSTEMS

```
REPEATEDLY
  IN SEQUENCE
    prepare
    send demand signal
    receive supply
    use supply
```

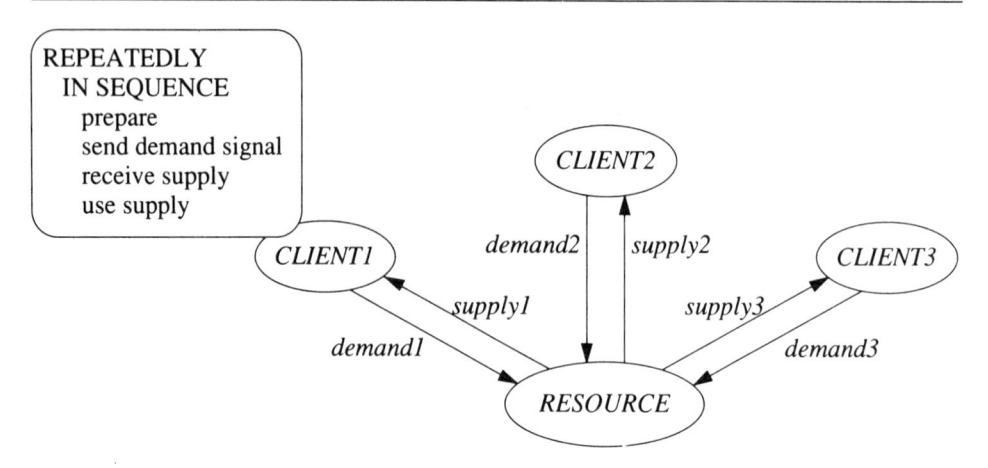

Figure 3.18

The typical process network for this situation is shown in Figure 3.18. The process *CLIENT1* communicates with the *RESOURCE* process using channels *demand1* and *supply1*, and similarly for the processes *CLIENT2* and *CLIENT3*.

Let us now analyse the *RESOURCE* process. This process has to service a request made by a client on a *demand* channel, by furnishing it with a supply, modelled here as a message on the corresponding *supply* channel. So we expect the *RESOURCE* process to include the following in its description:

```
REPEATEDLY
  ...
  IN SEQUENCE
    receive demand
    process demand
    deliver supply
```

Here the compound event controlled by IN SEQUENCE services the demand made by a single client. The line of dots has to be replaced by a suitable annotation which represents the strategy for servicing the clients.

> **Review Question 3.6** Why is the qualifier IN PARALLEL unsuitable for the missing line of the *RESOURCE* process?

A simple method of servicing the clients is to serve them in strict order. This means that *RESOURCE* waits for a demand from *CLIENT1*, services it, then waits for a demand from *CLIENT2*, services it, and so on. When all the client processes have been serviced, *RESOURCE* starts again from *CLIENT1*.

> **Review Question 3.7** Complete the process annotation for *RESOURCE* using the above strategy.

While this strict order ensures a fair allocation of supplies, it is perhaps too fair. If the client whose turn is next should fail to make a demand, *RESOURCE* will become blocked, so that no other client can be serviced either.

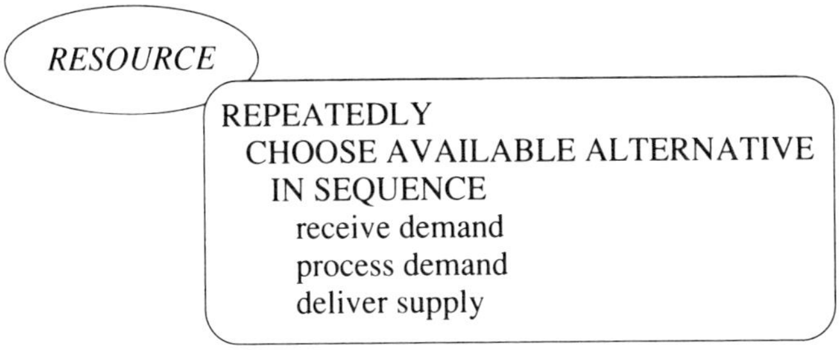

```
RESOURCE
    REPEATEDLY
       CHOOSE AVAILABLE ALTERNATIVE
       IN SEQUENCE
          receive demand
          process demand
          deliver supply
```

Figure 3.19

Another way of handling clients, which overcomes this problem, is for *RESOURCE* to choose a client which is ready with a demand, service that request, and then look again. This means that the *RESOURCE* process must be capable of detecting whether any clients are waiting to communicate and if so to accept the communication, making a choice between clients if more than one is ready. We deal with this situation by introducing the qualifier CHOOSE AVAILABLE ALTERNATIVE. We shall see, in Chapter 5 and subsequently, that this form of choice between available channels has a significant role to play in the study of concurrent processes. We illustrate the use of this construction in Figure 3.19.

Notice that it may be the case that none of the clients is ready to make a demand. If so, the *RESOURCE* process must wait until one does. If two or more clients are ready to communicate a request, the *RESOURCE* process chooses one at random. A consequence of this fact is that a very persistent client *may* just end up with all the resource. Put another way, there is no notion of fairness built in to the choice operation.

3.5 Summary

We have extended the process analysis phase of the Open Development Method (ODM) to include a semi-formal annotation of processes in process networks. Each component process may be further specified, taking care to distinguish sequential and parallel activities. A non-terminating process may be described using an infinite loop. We introduced the terms REPEATEDLY, IN SEQUENCE and IN PARALLEL to qualify a list of events; the events so qualified are indented relative to the qualifier. We also introduced the phrase CHOOSE AVAILABLE ALTERNATIVE that indicates a selection between a set of communications which may be available.

In the course of this chapter we encountered a number of examples of process networks. These include buffers and pipelines (for polynomial evaluation) and funnels (for performing arithmetic and sorting). We also saw how a star network could be used as a controller with slaves, as well as for clients of a shared resource.

4 ARRAYS OF PROCESSES

This chapter introduces some simple examples of process arrays. The two topics we shall investigate are systolic arrays and image processing. Much modern computing is concerned with processing arrays of data: mathematical models often involve systems of differential equations in many variables, linear programming deals with systems of linear equations, and so on. Whenever an array of data is to be processed, there is a good chance that parallel methods may help by processing all the array elements concurrently. We illustrate this firstly with the example of matrix multiplication. Image processing deals with arrays of pictorial data, and interest in this is growing rapidly. The remainder of the chapter presents some simple operations on images, which can be described as arrays of identical image processes each operating on a single element of the image.

4.1 Systolic arrays

The pipeline processes introduced in Chapter 3 have the property that signals are sent from process to process, in a definite sequence of processes. The *PHONE–EXCHANGE* process network (Figure 2.7), on the other hand, contains a bi-directional link so that signals can be sent from either process to the other. Arrays of processes in which the flow of signals is entirely one-way (with no return routes) are called ***systolic arrays***. This name derives from the flow of blood through the chambers of the heart.

The following example exhibits specific mathematical techniques. However, for our present purpose the mathematics is secondary—it is the use of a systolic array of concurrent processes that interests us.

Matrix multiplication

Suppose we have a fixed 2×2 matrix of real numbers

$$\begin{pmatrix} a & b \\ c & d \end{pmatrix}.$$

The operation of this matrix on a vector

$$\begin{pmatrix} v \\ w \end{pmatrix}$$

produces another vector defined by the equation

$$\begin{pmatrix} a & b \\ c & d \end{pmatrix} \begin{pmatrix} v \\ w \end{pmatrix} = \begin{pmatrix} av + bw \\ cv + dw \end{pmatrix}.$$

A quick glance at the result shows that four multiplications and two additions must be performed. Just as we saw in Chapter 3 in connection with function evaluation, if we wish to compute only one matrix product using a 2×2 matrix, it is not really worth introducing concurrent methods. We might, however, need to work with a 100×100 matrix, in which case concurrent computation of the result vector could certainly speed things up.

Even with a 2×2 matrix, there are situations where concurrency is useful. As an example of how this need may arise, consider a polygonal shape defined by its vertices $V_1, \ldots, V_n$ as in Figure 4.1. The position of each vertex is represented by a vector of two coordinates. In order to determine the image after the polygon has been rotated through some fixed angle, it is necessary to apply the appropriate rotation matrix to the vector of each of the vertices. In this way the new positions are calculated and the figure can then be drawn in its new orientation. Since there are many vertices to compute, it may take a considerable amount of time to perform the computations.

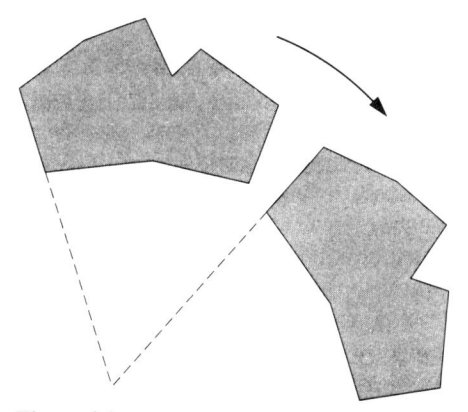

Figure 4.1

The speed of the computation now assumes some importance. If the figure is part of a visual display, on a screen, say, it is desirable to minimize the delay. Even if the figure is to be printed, so that a short delay does not matter, the cumulative effect of many such computations may impose a heavy time penalty. Since a portion of the data is static—the rotation matrix is fixed—we are encouraged to seek a pipeline-type analysis to exploit the use of concurrency.

We shall develop the approach of pipeline evaluation. Let us first concentrate on the calculation of the first coordinate of the image, $av + bw$. The values for v and w arrive in two streams. Process A computes av while process B computes bw and adds it to the result received from process *A*. This is illustrated in Figure 4.2, which also shows a similar pipeline for the calculation of *cv + dw*.

(a)

(b)

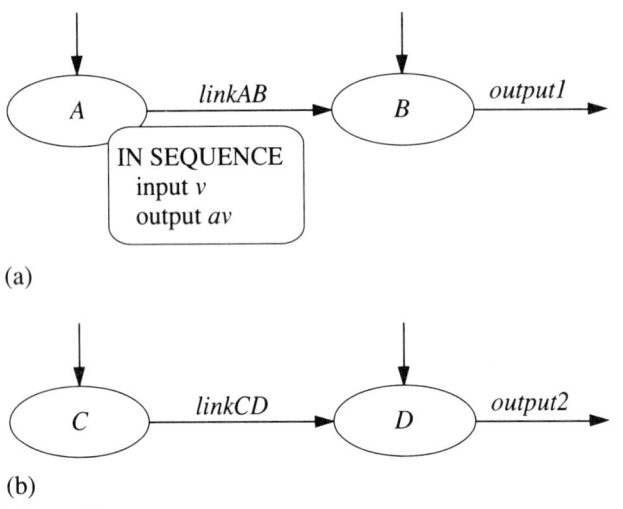

Figure 4.2

We may now link these two process diagrams to yield an array of processes, as shown in Figure 4.3. For convenience in following the discussion, the value that is transmitted along each channel is shown.

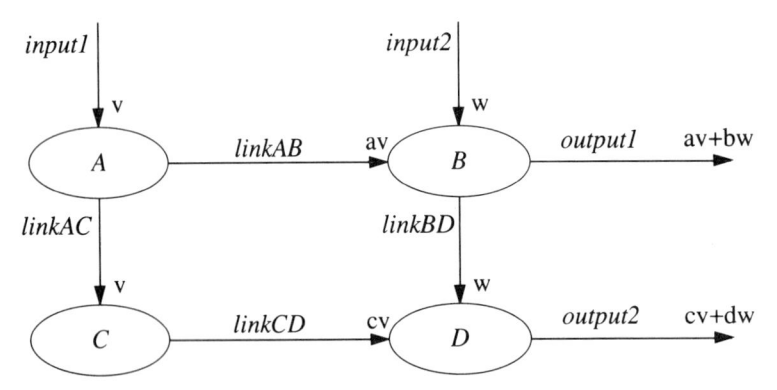

Figure 4.3

Let us follow a typical vector:

$$\begin{pmatrix} v \\ w \end{pmatrix}$$

through the overall process. The values *v* and *w* arrive along channels *input1* and *input2* respectively. The process *A* must perform the multiplication *av* and pass the resulting value to process *B*. It also has the responsibility of passing the value *v* to process *C*. In the meantime, *B* computes *bw*, and when it receives the value *av* it can add the two values, passing the answer along channel *output1*. It also passes the value *w* on channel *linkBD*. This deals with the first component of the required vector.

A single cycle for process A might therefore be specified as follows:

>IN SEQUENCE
>>input *v* from *input1*
>>IN PARALLEL
>>>output *av* on *linkAB*
>>>output *v* on *linkAC*

We could have omitted the name of the entry channel here, but the two exit channels must be clearly distinguished. Notice that once the input value is supplied, it is immaterial in which order the subsequent output events occur. It is therefore preferable not to specify a sequence, but to allow them to occur in parallel. Note, too, that the event 'output *av*' could have been analysed further into 'multiply *v* by *a*' followed by 'output result'.

Review Question 4.1   Write a similar specification for process *C*.

□

The situation for process *B* is slightly more complicated because it has two inputs and two outputs. The important restriction on *B* is that it performs its computation after it has received both the input *w* and the intermediate result *av*. Process *B* must engage in the following four communications:

1   input a value on *linkAB* (*t*, say);
2   input *w* on *input2*;
3   output *t* + *bw* on *output1*;
4   output *w* on *linkBD*.

These events are constrained as follows: 1 must precede 3; 2 must precede 3; 2 must precede 4. Otherwise they can occur in any order. Unfortunately our process annotations cannot capture this generality. Both of the following descriptions are valid:

IN SEQUENCE	IN SEQUENCE
IN PARALLEL	IN PARALLEL
input *t* on *linkAB*	input *t* on *linkAB*
input *w* on *input2*	IN SEQUENCE
IN PARALLEL	input *w* on *input2*
output *t* + *bw* on *output1*	output *w* on *linkBD*
output *w* on *linkBD*	output *t* + *bw* on *output1*

Review Question 4.2   Write a similar description of process *D*.

□

Note that we have described processes to handle a single input vector:

$$\begin{pmatrix} v \\ w \end{pmatrix}.$$

In practice, each process would be active repeatedly to cater for a stream of input vectors (*n* vectors for our problem). That would be achieved by prefixing each of the processes with REPEATEDLY. We should also specify a mechanism for terminating the processes when the last vector has been input. These are details which we shall not develop here.

Notice how the use of an array of processes serves to increase the speed with which the output vector is computed for a given input vector. The longest route through the network is taken by v, passing from A to C, then to D and finally out on *output2*. The time lag on this trip is one multiplication (in C) and one addition (in D). By contrast, the sequential computation of the output vector entails a time lag of four multiplications and two additions. Although there is an additional overhead due to the various communications between the processes, these are outweighed by the significant computational advantage.

When the gain in speed is applied to a stream of input vectors, this advantage becomes decisive. You can think of this as a sort of two-dimensional extension of pipelining. Of course, the idea can be extended to larger arrays, and even to higher dimensions.

4.2 Image processing

Perhaps the most significant application of the use of arrays of processes arises in the field of *image processing*. Satellite images have great economic and political importance. Examples of such use include the location of resource-bearing geological features, the detection of the movement of equipment or people, and weather prediction. Satellite images are generated by electromagnetic radiation with a spectrum of wavelengths. This radiation can be focused either on to sensitized film, or on to an electronic array (as in television). In addition to visible light, infrared waves are particularly useful because they can pass through certain obstacles, such as clouds. Image processing is also helpful in astronomy where radio waves and X-rays, as well as visible light and infrared waves, are used.

Modern digital imaging techniques build up a picture as an array of picture elements, or *pixels*. A typical satellite image may consist of eight or more *frames*, each of which may be 6000 pixels square. Bearing in mind the sheer quantity of data involved—10^8 pixels per image—the use of concurrent processes provides a significant advantage over sequential methods.

The analysis and processing of these images consists typically of a standard transformation which is applied uniformly to each pixel in the image. A process diagram consisting of identical processes, whose evolution is synchronized, is said to exhibit **geometric parallelism**. One might therefore expect that the best results would be obtained using an array of identical processors all executing in step with each other.[1] This is far removed from our model of asynchronous processes. Nevertheless, there is widespread use of transputers for image processing—the subject of one of the case studies in this book.

The amount of data necessary to describe a particular pixel varies with the sophistication of the system. We shall study digitized pictures in which each pixel carries a unique value; the range of possible values may be large as, for example, in a multicolour, multitone image. Since we are interested in illustrating the principles, rather than developing a full-blown, real-life system, we shall keep our examples as simple as possible; in most of our examples only two possible values will be allowed: black and white.

The matrix convention

Before considering specific images and transformations, we need to agree on how they are arranged. Though each pixel in an array could be hexagonal, or triangular, as illustrated in Figures 4.4 and 4.5, we shall restrict our attention to rectangular arrays.

---

[1] This approach, known technically as *single instruction, multiple data*, may be implemented using a synchronized array of identical processing elements.

Figure 4.4

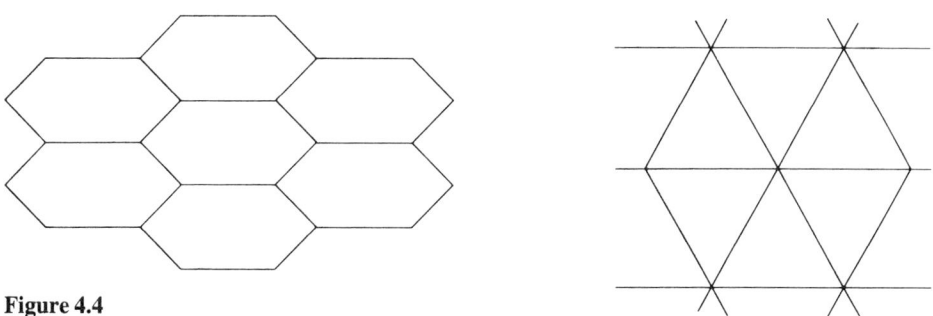

Figure 4.5

We use a matrix representation for a rectangular array of pixels. We adopt the usual mathematical convention for matrices and refer to the position of a cell using its *row* number and *column* number, in that order. As shown in Figure 4.6, the row number increases as we move downwards, and the column number increases as we move from left to right. A cell position is represented collectively as a bracketed pair: (*row*, *column*). Notice that we have begun at cell (0, 0), rather than the more usual (1, 1). This will prove to be a convenience when we need to use modular arithmetic to handle the edges of an array.

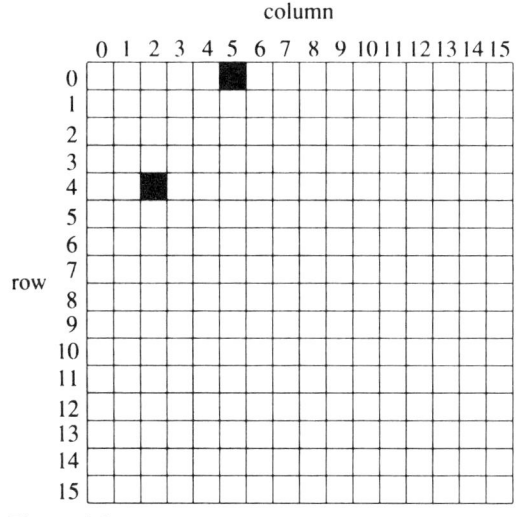

Figure 4.6

Review Question 4.3 This question refers to Figure 4.6.

(a) Name the cells shown in black.
(b) Shade in the cells (6, 6) and (4, 0) on the diagram.

We shall use the name *rows* to signify the number of rows in the array under discussion. Thus the rows of the array will be labelled 0, 1, ..., *rows* − 1. In a similar way, we shall use the name *cols* to signify the number of columns in an array, and the columns of the array will be labelled 0, 1, ..., *cols* − 1. We shall also use the name *cells* for the number of cells in the array. Note that

$$cells = rows \times cols.$$

Array wraparound

In our study of image processing we shall frequently be concerned with the immediate neighbours of a cell in an array. For example, we may wish each cell to communicate with its right-hand neighbour. This is clearly impossible for cells in the right-hand column. It will assist us to avoid unnecessary, exceptional cases if we adopt the *wraparound* convention for arrays; that is, at each edge of the array we consider the array to continue with the opposite edge. Thus each cell in column 0 of an array (the leftmost column) is a right-hand neighbour of a cell in column *cols* −1 (the rightmost column).

As an example, consider again the array in Figure 4.6. The cell on the left of cell (2, 0) is cell (2, 15), and the cell *down* from cell (15, 2) is cell (0, 2).

> **Review Question 4.4** Which are the cells above cell (0, 3) and to the right of (1, 15) in Figure 4.6?
>
> ☐

In a general array, what are the cells above and to the left of cell (i, j)? The cell above (i, j) is $(i-1, j)$ except when i is 0. The cell above $(0, j)$ is $(rows-1, j)$. Similarly, the cell to the right of (i, j) is $(i, j+1)$ unless j is $cols-1$; in the latter case, the cell to the right of $(i, cols-1)$ is $(i, 0)$. These results can be written using the notation of modular arithmetic as:

$(i \ominus 1, j)$ and $(i, j \oplus 1)$

where the subtraction is modulo *rows* and the addition is modulo *cols*.

4.3 Non-communicating cell processes

The objects of specific interest in image processing are the pixels. We may consider the problem of processing an image as an array of cell processes, each storing a pixel value and capable of communicating with all of its immediate neighbours. Each cell process describes the possible transformations of a single pixel.

We begin with some simple problems, in which each pixel is transformed without reference to the colours of its neighbours. Such transformations do not entail any communication between the individual cell processes, but they will help you to get a feel for the nature of image processing.

Reversing an image

One of the simplest transformations of a black and white image is to *reverse* it. That is, the black cells become white and the white cells become black. The outcome of this transformation depends only on the state of each pixel, and not on the states of any of its neighbours.

Exercise
4.1 Apply the *reverse* operation to the array of cells in Figure 4.7.

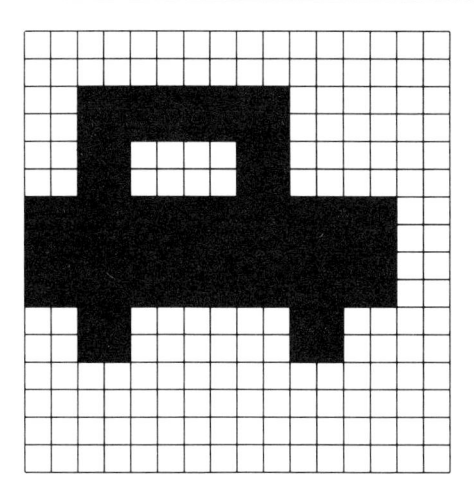

Figure 4.7

Solution 4.1

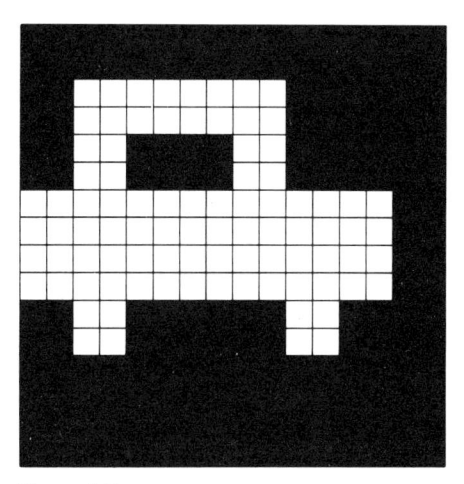

Figure 4.8

We shall model the operation *reverse* by the process *REVERSE_IMAGE*. Note that the action taken by this process depends on the current state of each pixel. We therefore extend our process annotations to include a ***selection*** mechanism:

    IF
      condition1
        THEN *action1*
      condition2
        THEN *action2*
          .
          .
          .
    ENDIF

46 SPECIFICATION AND DESIGN OF CONCURRENT SYSTEMS

It is essential that *condition1*, *condition2*, ..., do not overlap; that is, they are mutually exclusive.

With this notation, the operation *reverse* as applied to a single pixel may be described as *REVERSE_CELL* as shown in Figure 4.9.

```
REVERSE_CELL
    IF
        cell is black
            THEN make cell white
        cell is white
            THEN make cell black
    ENDIF
```

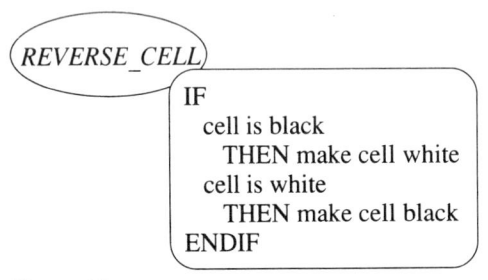

Figure 4.9

The stylized use of IF and ENDIF, and indentation of the alternatives, help to make the meaning clear. The choices here are understood to be alternatives; they are not sequential. The ENDIF may be omitted if the lines are clearly indented to indicate the scope of the IF construct.

Exercise

4.2 Describe the *REVERSE_IMAGE* process.

Solution 4.2

    IN PARALLEL for each cell
        IF
            cell is black
                THEN make cell white
            cell is white
                THEN make cell black
        ENDIF

This could be expressed more simply as follows:

    IN PARALLEL for each cell
        REVERSE_CELL

Notice that this process does not require the cells to communicate with each other.

Thresholding

Suppose now that we have an image composed of pixels each of which can take one of four tone values: *white*, *light grey*, *dark grey*, or *black*. In some circumstances, this may produce an image which is insufficiently defined. This lack of contrast may be cured by ***thresholding***. This means sharpening up one or both of the greys.

Suppose we wish to sharpen the tone of an image into just black and white, by making all the light grey cells white and all the dark grey cells black. At the cell level, this operation might be described as follows:

```
IF
    cell is light grey
        THEN make cell white
    cell is dark grey
        THEN make cell black
    otherwise
        do nothing
ENDIF
```

The *otherwise* event is a catch-all; since it is *do nothing* it could just as well be omitted.
Other similar thresholding operations might amend just one of the colours.

Exercise

4.3 Suppose an image is transmitted, on a white background, and is rather faint on reception. It is desired to set up a process *INTENSIFY_IMAGE*, with the following process description:

```
IN PARALLEL for all cells
    INTENSIFY_CELL
```

Suggest a suitable description for the cell process *INTENSIFY_CELL*, using the four-tone model where each grey cell is sharpened up one tone.

Solution 4.3 The following answer should be self explanatory:

```
IF
    cell is light grey
        THEN make cell dark grey
    cell is dark grey
        THEN make cell black
ENDIF
```

Detecting motion

Our final example of a non-communicating array of processes arises in considering two related images. This could arise when capturing two images of the same scene at different times, to detect changes in the scene. Such problems arise in the study of stellar motion.

Consider two related images of a black object on a white background, as shown in Figure 4.10. The pair of images can be modelled as a *single* combined image, with two data items per cell: *colour1* and *colour2*. *colour1* is the pixel value in the first image and *colour2* the value of the same pixel in the second image. Thus, for example, for cell (0, 0) *colour1* = *white* and *colour2* = *white*. The interesting cells are, of course, the ones where *colour1* and *colour2* are different. For an individual cell, the data items *colour1* and *colour2* can each take the value *black* or *white*. This is illustrated in Figure 4.11.

Exercise

4.4 Describe a process which picks out the cells of Figure 4.11 that represent change in colour between the first and second images, by colouring dark grey all the cells that changed from white to black and by colouring light grey all the cells that have changed from black to white. All unchanged cells are coloured white.

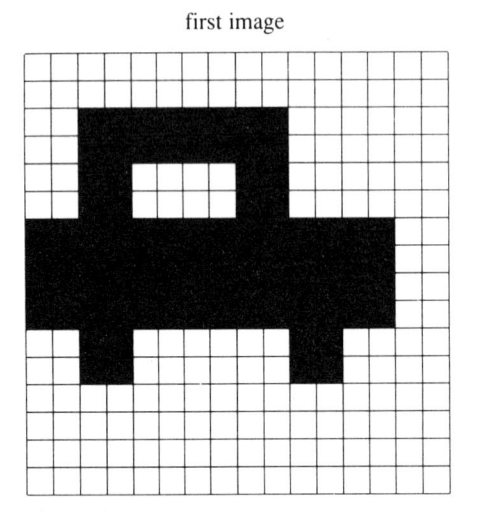

first image   second image

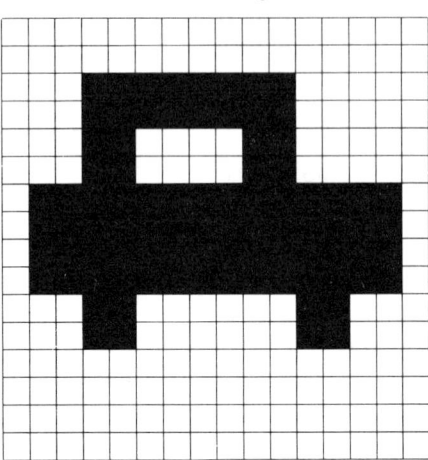

Figure 4.10

colour 1
colour 2

(a) Each cell   (b) Combined image

Figure 4.11

Solution 4.4 This is not unlike the thresholding examples. We might have:

    IN PARALLEL for all cells
        CELL_CHANGE

where the *CELL_CHANGE* process is described by:

    IF
        colour1 = colour2
            THEN make cell white
        colour1 = white and colour2 = black
            THEN make cell dark grey
        colour1 = black and colour2 = white
            THEN make cell light grey
    ENDIF

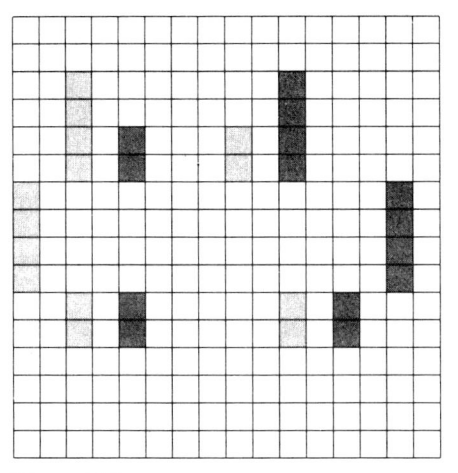

When the *CELL_CHANGE* operation is applied in parallel to all the cells we obtain Fig. 4.12.

Figure 4.12

A human observer could see that the car in Figure 4.10 had moved from left to right. One of the problems in image processing is to develop an automatic process which could detect from this final image that the two images in Figure 4.10 differ by a sideways shift. It would be possible for a machine to detect that Figure 4.12 represents a sideways shift.

From the performance point of view, the benefits of the concurrent approach to these operations is clear. If there are N processors available, then the array can be split into N blocks of cells and the processing of each block is done in parallel. Since there is no communication involved, the processing will be done N times faster than on a single processor. In fact, even if communication between cells is necessary there can still be a large gain, as we shall see in the next section.

4.4 Operations involving cell communication

It is now time to examine some more complicated (and interesting) operations, where each cell process must communicate with (some of) its neighbours. Specifically, we consider that each cell has eight immediate neighbours. The *state value* that identifies the tone or colour of each cell is denoted by one of the letters a–i, as shown in Figure 4.13; e denotes the state value of the cell under consideration. In the given example, we have the following values:

a = black b = black c = white
d = white e = grey f = white
g = white h = grey i = white

(a)   (b)

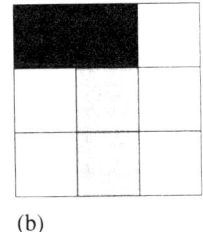

Figure 4.13

We shall describe three operations which require knowledge of neighbouring pixel values—dot removal, thickening and edge detection.

Dot removal

Any mechanical or electronic system is prone to error. When capturing a large image, it is fairly common for an individual cell to receive a spurious signal. In transmission, the remote sensing device may receive the wrong signal. Even if the correct signal reaches the remote sensing device, the electronics associated with a particular cell may be malfunctioning—either randomly or systematically. The result is that the final image may include some spurious isolated dots—single black or white cells in the middle of a region that should uniformly be the opposite colour. These dots are easy to pick out, as they are in contrast to all their neighbouring cells.

Exercise

4.5 Describe, for a single cell, a process *REMOVE* which adjusts a spurious dot to the colour of all its neighbours. (A cell is a spurious dot if all its neighbours have the same state value, which is different from the state value of the given cell.)

Solution 4.5 The given cell has eight neighbours, and their states must be examined. If all of them have the same state value, then this value should also be the value of the given cell. Bear in mind that the *REMOVE* process for each neighbouring cell needs to know the state value, e, of the given cell, since all the *REMOVE* processes function concurrently. Here is a suitable annotation for *REMOVE*:

IN SEQUENCE
  IN PARALLEL
    output value e to all neighbours
    receive state values a, b, c, d, f, g, h, i of eight neighbours
  IF
    all neighbours have same colour
      THEN change e to this colour

Notice that the eight outputs and the eight inputs are performed in parallel. It might be possible to determine a fixed sequential order for all the communications between the cells, but this would be very tedious. Worse still, it would remove almost all the benefits of concurrent processing. And the slightest inaccuracy in specifying an order of communication would result in deadlock!

Thickening

Owing to bad illumination, say, a single large object may leave a fragmentary image, resulting in it being misinterpreted as a collection of small objects. For example, the object in Figure 4.14 may be received, after transmission, as Figure 4.15(a).

Thickening can be used to reveal the single object. In its simplest form, we consider a black image on a white background. Thickening changes a white cell to black if it originally had a black cell as one of its neighbours. Thus a black image is thickened by extending it at its boundary. This should remove fragmentation of a single image, as shown in Figure 4.15(b).

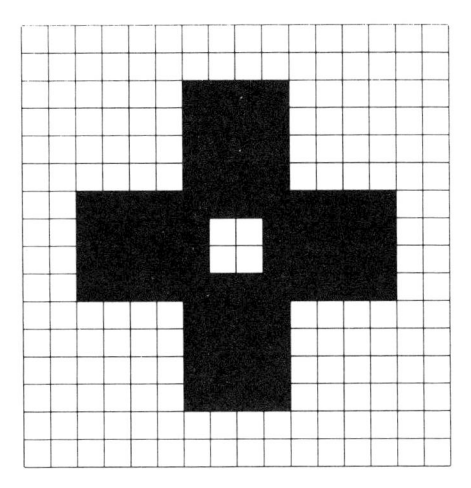

Figure 4.14

(a)   (b)

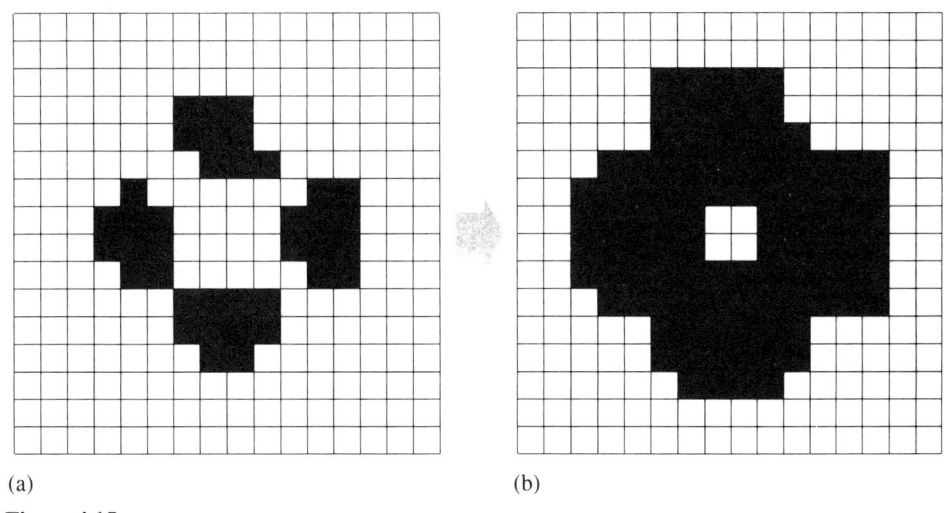

Figure 4.15

The thickened image may not be a true likeness of the original, but it is a considerable improvement on the received image.

Of course, isolated dots may have to be removed first, or spurious images may achieve solidity, as illustrated in Figure 4.16, where the original image (a) is received as (b), and thickens to the totally different image (c).

Review Question 4.5   Describe, for a single cell, the process *THICKEN*.

Edge detection

It is often useful to be able to detect the edges of an image. One of the many algorithms which can help in this is the *Sobel edge detector*. The underlying process is very similar to

(a)

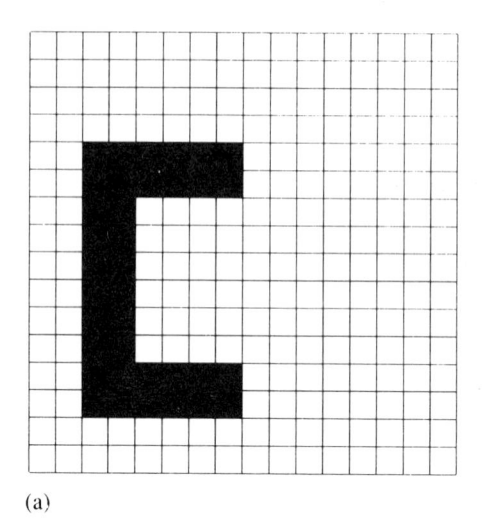

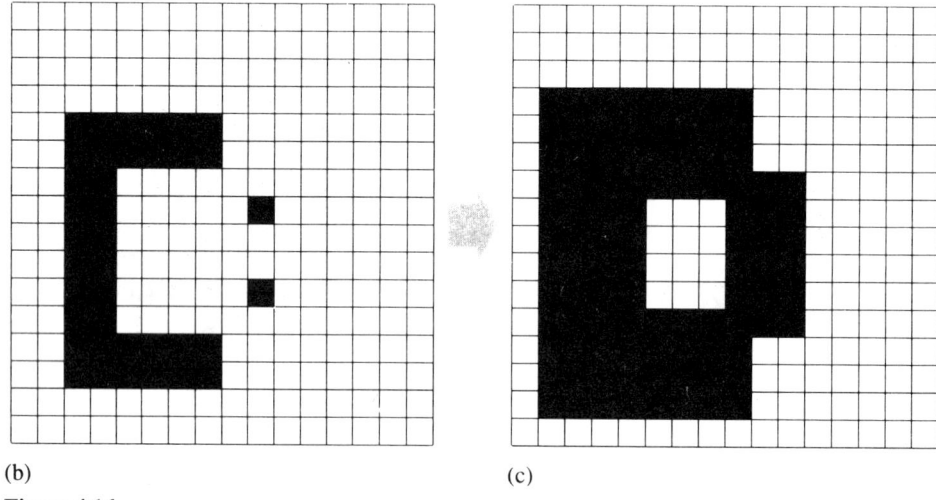

(b)   (c)

Figure 4.16

thickening, but involves a rather more detailed calculation step. The essence of the method is to compute the new value of e by combining checks for vertical edges and horizontal edges. We quote the formulas here without proof or justification. For a monochrome image we assign the value 1 to black (foreground colour) and 0 to white (background colour). The Sobel edge detector calculates values x_edge and y_edge according to the following formulae, where $a,\ldots,i$ are the state values of the neighbouring cells as defined in Figure 4.13(a):

$$x\_edge := |a + 2d + g - c - 2f - i|$$

$$y\_edge := |a + 2b + c - g - 2h - i|$$

If the sum $x\_edge + y\_edge$ reaches a threshold value (which turns out to be 4 for a monochrome image), we identify the current cell as an edge cell.

Exercise

4.6 Calculate *x_edge* and *y_edge* for the following cells of Figure 4.17:

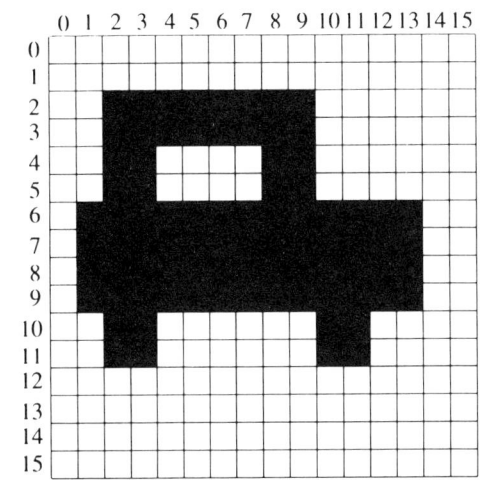

(2, 2), (1, 12), (5, 9)

Figure 4.17

Solution 4.6 (2, 2) is the black cell at the top left of the car. We have:

$x\_edge = |0 + 0 + 0 - 0 - 2 - 1| = 3$
$y\_edge = |0 + 0 + 0 - 0 - 2 - 1| = 3$

Thus $x\_edge + y\_edge = 6$ which is greater than 4; so (2, 2) is identified correctly as an edge cell.

For (1, 12) we have:

$x\_edge = |0 + 0 + 0 - 0 - 0 - 0| = 0$
$y\_edge = |0 + 0 + 0 - 0 - 0 - 0| = 0$

So $x\_edge + y\_edge = 0$ and (1, 12) is not an edge cell.

For (5, 9) we have:

$x\_edge = |1 + 2 + 1 - 0 - 0 - 1| = 3$
$y\_edge = |1 + 2 + 0 - 1 - 2 - 1| = 1$

Thus $x\_edge + y\_edge = 4$ and (5, 9) is identified as an edge cell.

4.5 Summary

In this chapter we studied arrays of processes. We saw how systolic arrays arise in matrix computations. The important area of image processing was introduced; we represented an image using a rectangular array of pixels. Particular operations were described on an image. These operations may be described by associating with each pixel a process which knows the current pixel values; we shall develop this approach further in Part III.

We met operations that reverse images, perform thresholding or compare two images; these cell processes do not involve communication. We also introduced operations involving parallel communication with neighbours, which remove dots, thicken images and detect edges. The convention we adopt for labelling cells in an array is the matrix convention and, by using modular arithmetic, we were able to discuss wraparound.

We extended our conventions for process annotation by introducing a selection construct which allows one of a set of alternative actions to be selected by a set of conditions.

5 A SIMPLE TELEPHONE SYSTEM

In this final chapter of Part I we continue our study of *communication*. Rather than person-to-person conversation, we now consider an artificial communication system which is an essential feature of modern life and provides a good example of a large-scale parallel system. We are particularly interested in the telephone network, which has the advantage of being familiar to us all. The system is parallel in the sense that at any instant many people may be using it. In point of fact, a telephone network of any size is very complicated indeed. In each local area, telephones are connected to an area exchange through which they can communicate. These local exchanges are, in turn, linked to trunk exchanges, through which telephones on different exchanges can be connected.

We shall not attempt to deal with the full generality of a telephone network. Instead, we shall concentrate on some very simple (and idealized) systems. It turns out that even an elementary model of a small network is surprisingly complicated, so in order to reduce the problem to manageable proportions we must make some simplifying assumptions. Bearing this in mind, we aim to develop a network of four telephones as a case study in Part IV.

To this end we set the scene here with a process analysis of the simplest possible system, consisting of just two users, either of whom may wish to talk to the other. We shall construct a simulation, or model, of this simple system, limiting our consideration to the control aspects of the system. (That is, we shall not be concerned with the actual transmission of voice data, but merely with the sequencing of events so as to obtain a connection or break it.) This is a good example of a real-time problem where potential deadlocks abound, and so steps *must* be taken to avoid them.

In the course of analysing our telephone system, we shall introduce two new elements of our development method. The first has to do with modelling a complex process which has various states associated with it. As the process evolves, it passes indefinitely through a finite set of states in a non-repeating fashion. We shall find it convenient to modularize the process specification in terms of these states. This approach has something in common with the use of procedures to modularize a sequential program. The second element we introduce in this chapter arises from the real-time nature of our process. We shall find that, at each juncture, the future behaviour of a process may depend on which channel carries the next input. Because we are now in a real-time situation, the next channel to respond is determined by factors outside the process. Thus the evolution of the process is controlled by its environment. Of course, when two entry channels both carry an input, the process selects one of the inputs, often in an unspecified fashion.

5.1 The two-telephone system

We begin by discussing the scope of the model. This is, if you like, in place of the customer's statement of requirements document. As usual, ambiguities and omissions owing to the vague nature of an English-language description emerge as the specification proceeds.

The model is to be a discrete simulation of a network consisting of two telephones. Our chief aim in this modelling exercise is to ensure that the control flows between the two telephone processes are correct. In particular, we ignore all details pertaining to the passage of voice data through the network: we shall concentrate wholly on aspects of control.

In this context, either user must be able to engage in two activities. The first is to pick up the handset. The other activity is to alert the other user of the wish to communicate; this corresponds to dialling a number on a conventional telephone. For this purpose, each telephone has a push-button which, provided the handset is lifted, causes a buzzer to be sounded at the other telephone. The caller can abort a call by replacing the handset. If, on hearing the buzzer, the other party lifts the receiver, the two may converse until the connection is terminated. In our model, we assume that either party can terminate the connection by replacing the handset.

> **Review Question 5.1** Explain why the push-button is required. Could not lifting the handset serve to activate the other party's buzzer?
>
> ▫

The top-level process analysis identifies two processes, *PHONE1* and *PHONE2*. Channels are required both for communication between these two processes and for communication between the environment and each process.

Exercise

5.1 Draw a process diagram for the two-telephone system.

Solution 5.1 A suitable process diagram is shown in Figure 5.1.

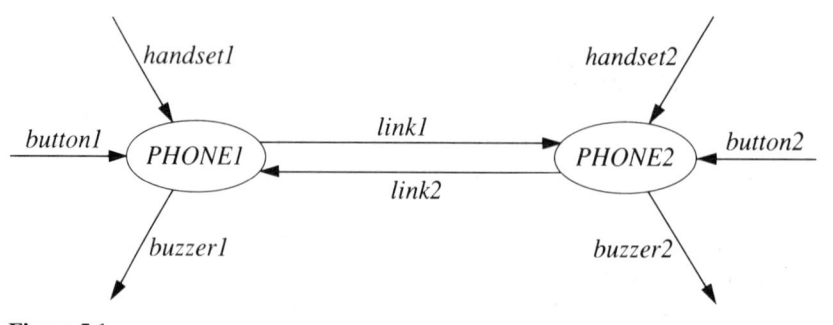

Figure 5.1

Note that each telephone process has a single *handset* channel which can carry two distinct signals—*up* and *down*. When a user lifts the handset, the *up* signal is sent on the corresponding *handset* channel. Likewise, when the handset is replaced, the *down* signal is sent. We shall also see that several different signals may need to be sent down the *link* channels. □

It is evident from Figure 5.1 that the two processes *PHONE1* and *PHONE2* have similar communications channels. In fact, further consideration should reveal that these two processes should exhibit the same behaviour; after all, it would be rather strange if different telephones responded differently to the same inputs. This situation, with a pair of identical processes evolving concurrently, is superficially like the geometric parallelism that we encountered in Chapter 4. There is, however, one important difference. Whereas the array of processes that perform image processing all evolve in step with each other, the *PHONE* processes respond to inputs that are not in step—at any time the two phones are likely to be in different states. Thus the *PHONE* processes evolve according to a common set of rules, but without being constrained to keep in step. A network of identical processes with this behaviour is said to exhibit **temporal parallelism**.

5.2 A state transition model

The real work comes when we try to analyse the processes *PHONE1* and *PHONE2*. We shall find it convenient to identify the various states that a phone can be in, and to consider the events that trigger transitions between these states:

DOWN	dormant phone
DIAL	ready to dial (push-button)
BUZZING	ringing phone
CALLING	a call has been placed
TALK	ready to transmit and receive voice communication

On a conventional telephone system, a receiver in the state DIAL emits a dialling tone. In the CALLING state, a ringing tone is heard while waiting for the other party to answer the call.

> **Review Question 5.2** When phone 1 is in the state BUZZING, what can be deduced about the state of phone 2? □

Initially (when the system is commissioned) both phones are in the state DOWN. We shall assume that only two events can happen when a phone is dormant, as follows:

1. Someone picks up the handset; this is modelled by a signal *up* on the *handset* channel. The phone now proceeds to the state DIAL.

2. The phone is buzzed by the other phone; this is modelled by a signal *buzz* on the incoming *link* channel. The phone now proceeds to the state BUZZING.

This may be summarized in a ***state transition diagram***, as in Figure 5.2. Each state is represented by a rectangle. The arrows in this diagram represent the transitions between states as a result of the occurrence of an event—a signal on an entry channel—in the *PHONE* process. Each transition arrow is labelled by the event that triggers the transition.[1] *Note how we prefix each signal name with the channel name and a dot.*

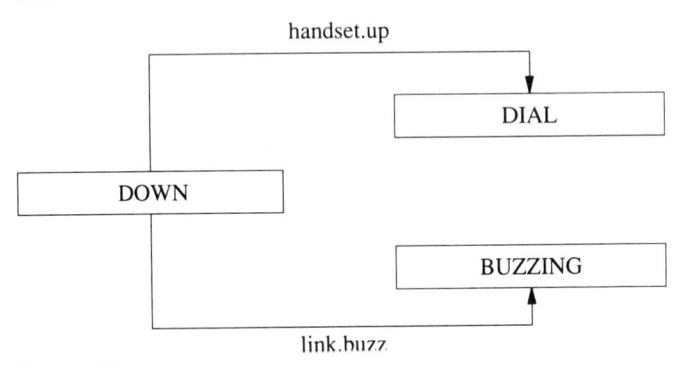

```
                    handset.up
         ┌─────────────────────────┐
         │                         ▼
         │                      ┌──────┐
         │                      │ DIAL │
         │                      └──────┘
      ┌──────┐
      │ DOWN │
      └──────┘
         ▲                      ┌─────────┐
         │                      │ BUZZING │
         │                      └─────────┘
         │                         ▲
         └─────────────────────────┘
                    link.buzz
```

Figure 5.2

When in state DIAL, the phone can also respond to just one of two events:

1 The caller replaces the handset (deciding to abandon the call after all). The phone then reverts to the state DOWN.

2 The caller presses the button to call the destination. The phone now proceeds to the state CALLING.

These transitions are illustrated in Figure 5.3.

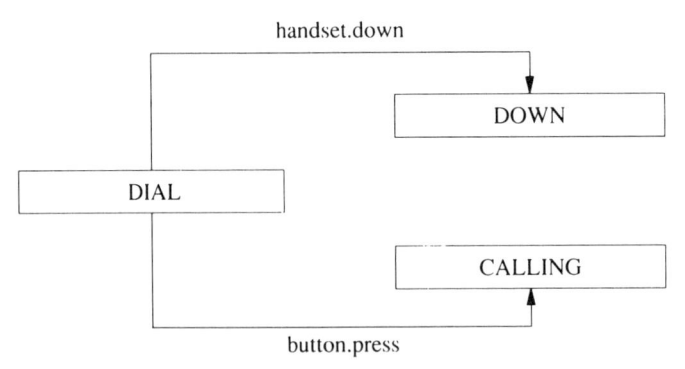

```
                    handset.down
         ┌─────────────────────────┐
         │                         ▼
         │                      ┌──────┐
         │                      │ DOWN │
         │                      └──────┘
      ┌──────┐
      │ DIAL │
      └──────┘
         │                      ┌─────────┐
         │                      │ CALLING │
         │                      └─────────┘
         │                         ▲
         └─────────────────────────┘
                    button.press
```

Figure 5.3

Exercises

5.2 Draw a single state transition diagram incorporating both Figures 5.2 and 5.3.

---

[1] Note that a state transition diagram does not detail the actions that take place.

Solution 5.2

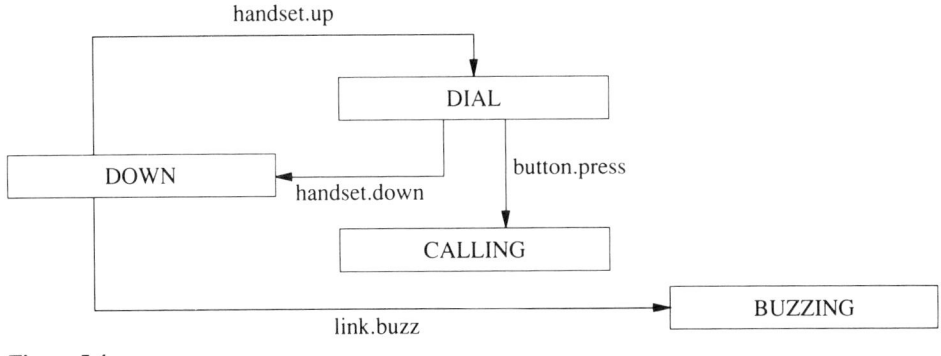

```
                    handset.up
         ┌─────────────┬──────┐
         │          ┌──▼───┐  │
         │          │ DIAL │  │
         │          └──┬───┘  │
    ┌────┴───┐         │ button.press
    │  DOWN  │◄────────┤
    └────┬───┘ handset.down
         │         ┌───▼─────┐
         │         │ CALLING │
         │         └─────────┘
         │                       ┌──────────┐
         └──────────────────────►│ BUZZING  │
                  link.buzz      └──────────┘
```
Figure 5.4

5.3 When the phone is in the state CALLING, the following two events can happen:
1. The caller abandons the call, replacing the handset. The phone returns to the state DOWN.
2. The called party lifts the receiver of the destination phone. This is modelled by a signal *answer* on the incoming *link* channel. In this case, the calling phone proceeds to the state TALK.

Draw a state transition diagram for the transitions from the state CALLING.

Solution 5.3

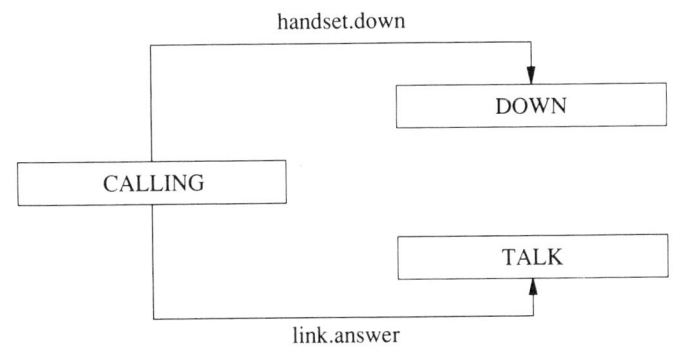

```
                  handset.down
              ┌───────┬──────┐
              │    ┌──▼───┐  │
              │    │ DOWN │  │
              │    └──────┘  │
       ┌──────┴──┐           │
       │ CALLING │           │
       └──────┬──┘           │
              │    ┌──────┐  │
              │    │ TALK │  │
              │    └──▲───┘  │
              └───────┴──────┘
                  link.answer
```
Figure 5.5

Review Question 5.3 What communication between the two telephones must accompany:
(a) the transition from state CALLING to state TALK?
(b) the transition from state CALLING to state DOWN?

We have considered so far the states of the calling phone. What about the destination phone? As shown in Figure 5.4, the destination phone enters the state BUZZING on being called. Let us see what happens next.

Exercise

5.4 Describe the transitions from BUZZING.

Solution 5.4 In the state BUZZING, the possible events are as follows:

1. The handset is lifted to answer the call, indicated by the signal *up* on the *handset* channel. This generates a suitable signal to the calling party (on the outgoing *link* channel) and a transition to the state TALK.

2. A signal on the incoming *link* channel (the calling party has rung off). The consequence is a transition to the state DOWN.

This analysis is illustrated in Figure 5.6.

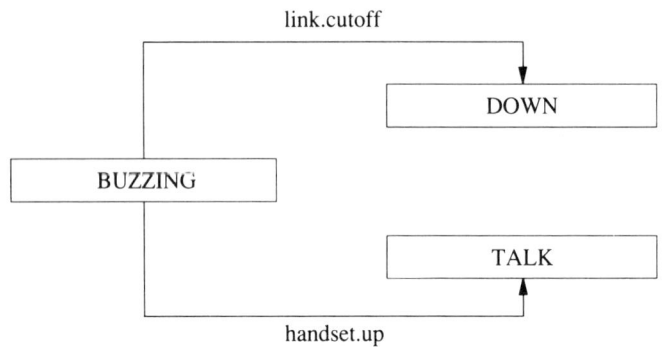

Figure 5.6

Let us pause for a moment to consider the sequence of events which take place in placing a call from phone 1 to phone 2, and the corresponding states of the two phones:

After event	Phone 1	Phone 2
(Initially)	DOWN	DOWN
Phone 1 handset lifted	DIAL	DOWN
Phone 1 button pressed	CALLING	BUZZING
Phone 2 handset lifted	TALK	TALK

> **Review Question 5.4** List all possible pairs of corresponding states of the two telephones.

There is one more question to resolve before we complete the transitions between states. What are the possible events that can occur when a phone is in the state TALK? According to our discussion of requirements in Section 5.1, either party can terminate a connection (indicated by both phones being in the state TALK) by hanging up the handset. From the point of view of a particular phone, either of the following two events may occur:

1. The signal *down* arrives on the *handset* channel, thus returning the phone to state DOWN. (Before changing state, a *cutoff* signal is sent to the remote phone to confirm that the connection is broken.)

2   The remote phone signals that the connection is cut off (because the other party has hung up). In this case, the telephone (whose handset is still raised but with no connection to the other party) changes state to DIAL. (This was not made explicit in the outline assumptions, but is sensible on the grounds of logical design.)

Exercise
5.5 Draw a state transition diagram which summarizes all the transitions we have analysed so far.

Solution 5.5

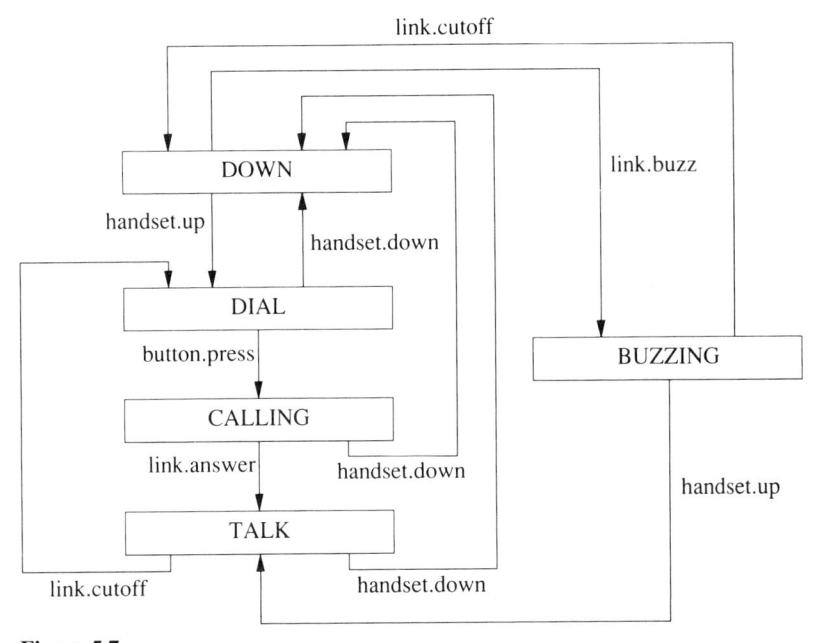

Figure 5.7

5.3 Process analysis of a telephone system

The final transition diagram for the two-telephone system can be used to provide a good basis for specifying the telephone processes. Each *PHONE* process is an infinite process which passes through the various states in accordance with the next signal received. This pattern of behaviour is too complex to be specified in a sequential manner. Instead, we shall describe a separate process for the behaviour of a telephone in each state. Thus, the behaviour of a telephone in the DOWN state is described by the *DOWN* process; when it is in the CALLING state its behaviour is given by the *CALLING* process, and so on. The essence of the description is that in each state certain communications are allowed, followed by a transition to another state. We model the transition by invoking the relevant process.

For example, here is how we might specify the *DOWN* process. The possible communications are signals on the *handset* and *link* channels, as shown in Figure 5.7. If the *handset.up* signal is received, the telephone moves into the DIAL state; the future evolution of the

DOWN process is thus governed by the *DIAL* process. If, on the other hand, the *link.buzz* signal is received, the buzzer must be activated and the *BUZZING* process invoked. The *DOWN* process can be summarized as follows:

>   CHOOSE AVAILABLE ALTERNATIVE
>   handset.up:
>   DIAL
>   link.buzz:
>   IN SEQUENCE
>   sound buzzer
>   BUZZING

We have extended the notation here to cater for the alternative communications that may arrive. Following the phrase CHOOSE AVAILABLE ALTERNATIVE we list the two choices of events. Each choice is given a header which consists of the name of the entry channel (and the name of the signal) followed by a colon. Note carefully that the *DOWN* process cannot control which communication will arrive. It must be prepared to receive whichever signal is available first and react accordingly. If both signals are available simultaneously the *DOWN* process will select one of them.

Similarly, we may annotate the *DIAL* process as follows:

>   CHOOSE AVAILABLE ALTERNATIVE
>   handset.down:
>   DOWN
>   button.press:
>   IN SEQUENCE
>   alert destination
>   CALLING

The interpretation of this annotation is that the *DIAL* process can either receive the *handset.down* signal and behave like the *DOWN* process, or it can receive the *button.press* signal, in which case it issues a signal to alert the destination phone and then it behaves like the *CALLING* process.

We could continue the analysis in this fashion to specify the *CALLING*, *BUZZING* and *TALK* processes, which describe the behaviour of the *PHONE* process in the corresponding states. Note that each of these processes completely represents the behaviour of the *PHONE* process from one state until it enters the next state. Effectively, this description is a modularization of the *PHONE* process.

Unfortunately, this type of specification is liable to break down. There are fundamental problems involved in applying purely sequential thinking to concurrent real-time problems, and this example demonstrates them very well.

Exercise

5.6 Discover the flaw in our (partial) system specification, by considering what happens if both telephone users try to call each other at the same time.

Solution 5.6 We disregard the possibility that the two users press their buttons at exactly the same instant. Indeed, the concept of simultaneity has serious philosophical problems when applied to different processes. However, in our present example it is certainly reasonable that an observer might agree that the two events occurred within a very short interval of time—so short that the devices that implement our simulation are unable to tell which occurred first. Since activating a switch takes a minute amount of time, it is possible for one user to press the button while the other phone is adjusting to the situation of having its button pressed. If both telephones enter the state DIAL and both callers press their buttons, then both phones will be trying to send an alert to the other, and *neither* will be willing to listen until this has been done!

The situation begins to resemble one of our ill-fated, two-person conversations. This is a classic deadlock—the phones will never work again, and the poor users cannot even hang up effectively.

□

There is, in fact, a very elegant way out of this dilemma—at the expense of amending our specifications. We adopt a communications protocol which is admirably suited to the task. In fact the convention we are about to describe is well worth mastering, because it guarantees that deadlock due to incompatible communications cannot occur. The essence of the protocol is that whenever a phone sends a signal on its outgoing *link* channel, it simultaneously listens on the corresponding incoming *link* channel.

Communications protocol

1	Whenever a process needs to output a control signal to another process that is in two-way communication with it, it does so in parallel with receiving a response.
2	Whenever a process receives an unsolicited signal from another process, it must eventually acknowledge receipt.

Note that the second part of the protocol is required as a direct consequence of the first—if the receiving process does not acknowledge receipt of a signal, the calling process will be blocked awaiting a response.

In fact, it is desirable that the acknowledgement required by 2 in the above protocol should be sent at the earliest opportunity. The receiving process may have to perform certain internal housekeeping tasks before it can send an acknowledgement, but it is bad practice to keep the sender waiting unnecessarily.

We must now revise our specifications of the *DOWN* and *DIAL* processes to conform with the protocol. Here is the amended version of *DOWN*:

    CHOOSE AVAILABLE ALTERNATIVE
      handset.up:
        DIAL
      link.buzz:
        IN SEQUENCE
          acknowledge
          sound buzzer
          BUZZING

Here the convention has forced us to acknowledge the incoming signal on the *link* channel. The *DIAL* process must be amended in accordance with part 2 of the protocol, as follows:

CHOOSE AVAILABLE ALTERNATIVE
   handset.down:
     DOWN
   button.press:
     IN SEQUENCE
       IN PARALLEL
         alert destination
         receive response
       act on response

Note how invoking the *CALLING* process has been replaced by the non-specific phrase 'act on response'. The purpose of this is to cater for the situation we are worried about.

Exercise

5.7 What are the possible responses to be catered for?

Solution 5.7 There are two possible responses. The expected response is an acknowledgement to say that the receiving phone will sound its buzzer, so the calling process now moves in to the state CALLING.

The unusual response is precisely the situation which would previously have caused deadlock! In other words, the other possible response to our alert is the receipt of an alert from the other telephone. ▫

Exercise

5.8 If the response from the destination phone is *acknowledge*, the calling phone enters the state CALLING. Suggest what transition should take place if the response is an *alert* signal.

Solution 5.8 Since both the users are trying to contact each other, it seems sensible to proceed straight to state TALK. (This is not the behaviour of the public telephone network.) However, our statement of requirements does not cover the case of two users trying to contact each other simultaneously. We therefore ought to obtain further instructions from our client on this matter. ▫

Let us assume that the client is in agreement with our eminently sensible suggestion that the connection between the users should be established in this case. The annotation of *DIAL* now becomes:

CHOOSE AVAILABLE ALTERNATIVE
   handset.down:
     DOWN
   button.press:
     IN SEQUENCE
       IN PARALLEL
         alert destination
         receive response
       IF
         response is acknowledge
           THEN CALLING
         response is alert
           THEN TALK
       ENDIF

Exercise

5.9 Write an annotation for the process *CALLING*.

Solution 5.9

    CHOOSE AVAILABLE ALTERNATIVE
      link.answer:
        IN SEQUENCE
          acknowledge
          TALK
      handset.down:
        IN SEQUENCE
          IN PARALLEL
            send cutoff on outgoing link
            receive response on incoming link
          DOWN

It is perhaps worth noting that, in this case, the actual response received to the cutoff signal is immaterial. But it is vital that there is a response, in accordance with the communications protocol.

Review Question 5.5 Why must the *CALLING* process send an acknowledgement before entering the process *TALK*?

Review Question 5.6 Which process (or processes) can receive the *cutoff* signal issued by the *CALLING* process?

Let us now deal with the *BUZZING* process.

Exercise

5.10 Devise a process annotation for *BUZZING*.

Solution 5.10

    CHOOSE AVAILABLE ALTERNATIVE
      link.cutoff:
        IN SEQUENCE
          acknowledge
          DOWN
      handset.up:
        IN SEQUENCE
          IN PARALLEL
            send answer signal on outgoing link
            receive response on incoming link
          IF
            response is acknowledge
              THEN TALK
            response is cutoff
              THEN DIAL
          ENDIF

The last choice option in the *BUZZING* process, 'response is cutoff', represents a familiar problem—answering a ringing phone just as the caller hangs up. This usually happens after a sprint across the garden! Notice that, in this event (handset up, no connection), we have identified the next state as DIAL. Once again this did not appear in the original requirements, but seems acceptable, since you have lifted the handset and have no one to talk to.

It is useful to summarize here the possible signals on each of the channels:

Channel	Signals
button	press
buzz	sound buzzer
link	alert, acknowledge, answer, buzz, cutoff
handset	handset up, handset down

This completes our first simple telephone model. There are a couple of points worthy of note. Many of the process states are specified *recursively*. In several instances, we have pairs of states leading to each other, as the following state transition diagram, abstracted from Figure 5.7, shows:

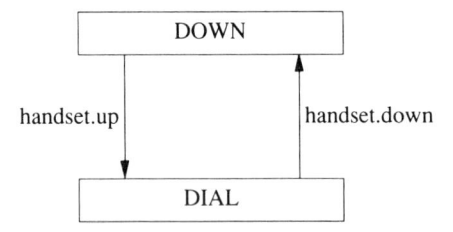

Figure 5.8

This is a form of recursion, which can be handled by our methodology: we shall see how to deal with it in Part IV.

More importantly, notice how complicated the process analysis turns out to be, even for such a trivial system. Much of the complication arises from the need to avoid deadlock. When we come to use CSP specifications we shall find that we can be slightly more cavalier about process analysis, leaving much of the hard work to be handled more easily in the formal mathematical setting of CSP.

5.4 Summary

This chapter has been devoted to a discussion of a relatively simple example of a system of processes which exhibits temporal parallelism. Our chosen example dealt with the control aspects of a two-telephone system. Despite its apparent simplicity, the discussion turned out to have a fair degree of complexity.

Our approach was to identify states of the system being modelled. The system consisted of two identical phones that could each be in one of a number of defined states. In each state there are certain allowable events, each leading to some other state. We then modelled each state as a separate process, which must in turn invoke one of the processes corresponding to the successor states. Since a phone may be in a given state, and eventually return to that state, the corresponding description in terms of processes must lead to a *recursive* specification in which a process ultimately calls itself.

We discovered that certain combinations of events in which the two phones participate may lead to deadlock. Our solution to this problem was to enforce a communications protocol whereby each signal on one *link* channel is required to be accompanied by some signal on the reverse *link* channel.

SUMMARY OF PART I

We have introduced the notion of concurrent processes, both to model real-world concurrency and to exploit the use of multiple processors in the solution of problems; consequently it is desirable to incorporate notions of concurrency in the course of program development. The particular model of concurrency which we use is synchronous message passing.

As the first step in the Open Development Method, we introduced the topic of process analysis. This seeks to analyse systems with a view to identifying concurrent asynchronous processes communicating along channels. We gave a specific communication model in which a communication synchronizes its source and its sink. When the only options open to a process are to communicate (either as sender or as receiver) with processes that are not yet ready to communicate, the process is *blocked*. A problem peculiar to concurrent systems is deadlock, which can be difficult to detect and diagnose. By introducing a formal development method we hope to eliminate the causes of deadlock from our designs. By way of example, we gave a communications protocol for the avoidance of deadlock in a particular process.

We illustrated the method of process analysis with a number of examples, including the description of buffers and pipelines for the evaluation of simple functions on a stream of input data. In addition we performed a process analysis of two systems which will play a significant role later in this book: an image processor and a two-telephone hook-up. These systems will be developed as significant case studies later, in Parts III and IV.

SOLUTIONS TO PART I REVIEW QUESTIONS

1.1

(a) Examples of concurrent processes are individual vehicles and road users, as well as traffic-lights and zebra crossings.

(b) In a multi-user system, different users, their terminals, the mainframe itself and peripheral devices can be thought of as concurrent processes. The mainframe may have more than one processing unit operating concurrently; but even if it has only a single processor and a time-slicing operating system we can think of different tasks as concurrent processes.

1.2 The conventional development methods are used for producing sequential code, but they have no facilities for identifying autonomous processes and communication between them.

By contrast, our development method, ODM, is aimed at a distributed processing system, and hence concentrates on a process-and-communications based approach to problem solving.

2.1 The entire system could be modelled as a single process. An exchange (or even a single telephone) could be modelled as a component process.

2.2 This is only possible as long as the channel *link* is never used! For if *Q* follows *P* sequentially, and *P* wishes to output to *Q* on channel *link*, it will be unable to do so. The reason is that *Q*, being sequentially after *P*, cannot input from *link* until after *P* has performed the output. But *P* cannot perform the output until *Q* is ready to input.

It is, however, possible that the final event of *P* is to output on *link*, and the first event of *Q* is to input from *link*. The two processes could then synchronize on the communication event. However, in this case, *P* and *Q* would not be sequential: *Q* would have to begin while *P* performs its last event, not after *P* has terminated.

3.1 The process *MINUS_7* has one entry channel and one exit channel; 7 is subtracted from each input value, and the result is output:

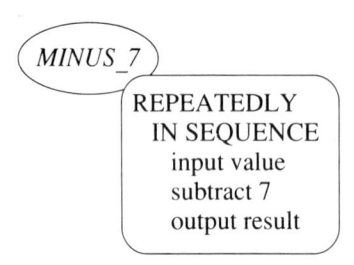

```
    MINUS_7
         REPEATEDLY
           IN SEQUENCE
             input value
             subtract 7
             output result
```

3.2 *P4* is a pipe which adds 4 to each number on the input stream and outputs the result. We might therefore rename it *ADD_4*.

3.3 *P3* accepts two values in succession on its entry channel and outputs their product.

3.4 A pipeline must be composed of pipes, each having one entry and one exit channel. *P1'* is not a pipe because it has two exit channels; similarly *P3'* has two entry channels.

3.5
```
    REPEATEDLY
      IN SEQUENCE
        prepare for control
        receive control signal
        act on signal
        send response
```

3.6 The whole point of the *RESOURCE* process is to manage the resource, exercising control over it. This may be because the resource is essentially indivisible, e.g. a printer, so that each client must have exclusive access for a period of time, or because the resource might become exhausted by two clients simultaneously trying to grab the last unit of resource. IN PARALLEL allows simultaneous access to the resource, whereas we require exclusive access by clients in a controlled fashion.

3.7
```
    REPEATEDLY
      IN SEQUENCE over all clients
        IN SEQUENCE
          receive demand
          process demand
          deliver supply
```

4.1
```
    IN SEQUENCE
      input v on linkAC
      output cv on linkCD
```

This specification is quite straightforward. In fact, we could have omitted the channel names, as *C* has only one entry channel and one exit channel.

4.2
    IN SEQUENCE
        IN PARALLEL
            input *w* on *linkBD*
            input *t* on *linkCD*
        output *t + dw* on *output2*

4.3

(a) The cells in black are (4, 2) and (0, 5).

(b) The shaded cells are shown in the following figure:

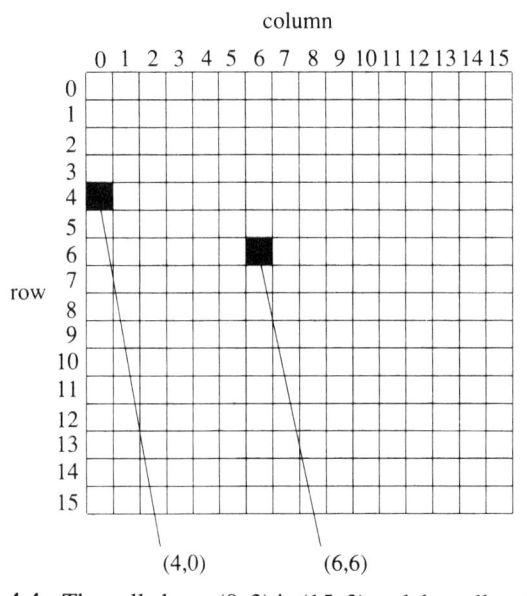

4.4 The cell above (0, 3) is (15, 3) and the cell to the right of (1, 15) is (1, 0).

4.5   IN SEQUENCE
       IN PARALLEL
          output value *e* to all neighbours
          receive state values of eight neighbours
       IF
          e = white and any neighbour is black
            THEN set *e* to black
          otherwise
            do nothing
       END IF

5.1 When the phone rings, the local user will lift the handset to answer the call. If lifting the handset activates the other party's buzzer then, when someone answers a call by lifting the handset, the caller's phone would ring!

5.2 Phone 2 must be in the state CALLING.

5.3

(a) The calling phone must receive a signal from the destination phone.

(b) The phone originating the call must alert the destination phone that the call has been aborted and the connection has been broken.

5.4 You should have been able to enumerate the following.

Phone 1	Phone 2
DOWN	DOWN
DIAL	DOWN
CALLING	BUZZING
TALK	TALK
DOWN	DIAL
BUZZING	CALLING

You may also have included

DIAL	DIAL

which can arise if both users lift their handsets before either has dialled.

5.5 So that it conforms with part 2 of the communications protocol.

5.6 When a telephone is in the CALLING state, the other telephone must be in the BUZZING state. Thus the *cutoff* signal issued by the *CALLING* process can only be received by the *BUZZING* process.

PART II

CSP SPECIFICATION

6 BUILDING UP PROCESSES

In Part I we introduced the idea of analysing a problem or a system into communicating processes that operate concurrently. The processes are connected by named channels, and each process may be described individually using a semi-formal annotation. This description expresses the evolution of the process in terms of certain elementary activities and the way they are combined.

Once a problem has been broken down, using process analysis, into a family of (concurrent) processes it is possible to get a feel for how the solution should be developed. Each process may be annotated by an informal description, but this is far from adequate. What is needed now is something more formal which will enable us to make progress towards the implementation stage in a manner which conforms with the user requirements. It is absolutely vital that we provide a rigorous description of the communications between the processes, especially if the project is a large one with many development teams at work. Without this degree of rigour there could be no confidence in the concurrent execution of the separately constructed solutions. Indeed, even if only one person is working on the project it is very likely that a totally informal approach will produce a solution which is prone to deadlock. In view of the difficulty in debugging concurrent programs, the extra effort involved in adhering to a well-defined development method is very worthwhile.

As yet we have been less than precise about what legitimately constitutes a process. In this chapter we begin by introducing the CSP notations that allow us to describe sequential processes in terms of events. In particular, we shall introduce *prefixing* and the two elementary processes, *SKIP* and *STOP*.

6.1 Elements of process description

The very word 'process' suggests activity—something is happening. In order to describe a process, we assume that some collection of activities has been identified as being of interest. We shall therefore redefine process analysis to include the identification of relevant activities in which the process might participate. For example, in a chemical plant the activities of interest might include measuring temperature and pressure, operating pumps, and sounding alarms. In the case of a function evaluation, the activities of interest will include input and output, the evaluation of expressions and the assignment of values to variables.

Events

We shall refer to the occurrence of each activity of interest in the description of a process as an *event*. Precisely which events are included in the description of a process will depend on the level of refinement.

Example

6.1 Consider the execution of a computer program. Let us call the process that describes the program execution *PROGRAM*. We might identify the following events for *PROGRAM*:

load_code, run_program, print_result

At this level of description we are not interested in the activities inherent in loading code, running a program or printing out results. We are just concerned with the fact that each of these occurs.

□

Example

6.2 A customer owning a chemical plant provided the following overview of one of its components:

```
Reactor Vessel (Version X)

Chemical C1 enters via pipe A, alongside chemical C2
from pipe B. Subsequently the required product issues
from pipe C and the waste products from pipe D.
```

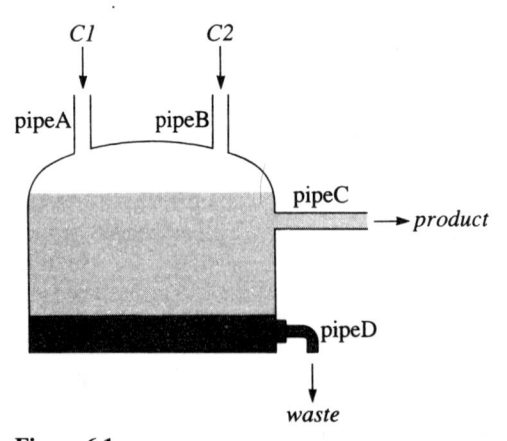

Figure 6.1

Process analysis leads to a description with two entry channels, which we call *pipeA* and *pipeB*, and two exit channels, *pipeC* and *pipeD*. This is illustrated by the process network in Figure 6.2, in which the process has been named *REACTOR_VESSEL_X*. The events may then be treated as communications along these channels. Using the notation introduced in Section 5.2 for a named signal transmitted on a channel, an appropriate set of events is:

{*pipeA.C1, pipeB.C2, pipeC.product, pipeD.waste*}

pipeA   *pipeB*

REACTOR_VESSEL_X

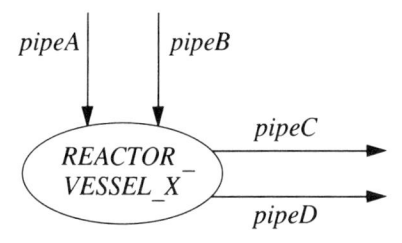

pipeC

pipeD

Figure 6.2

The set of events derived in Example 6.2 is not the only one possible, but it is appropriate to the given statement of requirements. However, discussions with the customer might produce the following, more detailed, statement of requirements:

```
Reactor Vessel (Version Y)

Chemical C1 enters via pipe A, alongside chemical C2
from pipe B. The chemicals are mixed, and then they are
heated. The pressure is increased, after which the
reaction takes place. Very rarely, impurities in C1
and C2 can cause the reaction to go wrong. This would
be characterized by an immediate rise in temperature.
If this happens, the safety valve must open and the fire
brigade must be alerted. Otherwise the product issues
from pipe C and the waste from pipe D.
```

In order to model this revised statement of requirements we shall use the process *REACTOR_VESSEL_Y*.

Exercise

6.1 Introduce a suitable channel (in addition to those attached to *REACTOR_VESSEL_X*) for the process *REACTOR_VESSEL_Y*, and suggest a relevant set of events.

Solution 6.1   One answer is depicted in Figure 6.3.

pipeA   *pipeB*

REACTOR_VESSEL_Y

pipeC

pipeD

fire_brigade

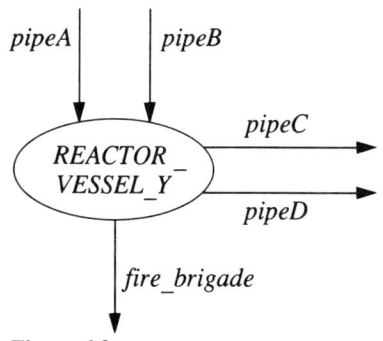

Figure 6.3

In addition to the channels of *REACTOR_VESSEL_X* we have added the outgoing channel *fire_brigade* that can carry an *alert* signal to the fire brigade. An appropriate set of events is:

{*pipeA.C1, pipeB.C2, mix_and_heat_chemicals, increase_pressure, detect_high_temperature, open_safety_valve, fire_brigade.alert, pipeC.product, pipeD.waste*}

We have identified a single event *mix_and_heat_chemicals*; this event occurs when the chemicals have been mixed and heated. However, you might have decided to model two distinct events, *mix_chemicals* and *heat_mixture*. There are certain design decisions in the process analysis phase that depend on the interpretation of the analyst. Likewise you may have chosen different names for some of the events.

⊡

The important point to note is that the set of relevant events depends on the points of interest in the process description. A more detailed description is provided by a larger set of events. An even fuller description of the reactor vessel would involve knowing how to increase the pressure, how temperature is measured, and so on.

Review Question 6.1 Give a set of events for the *BUFFER* process of Section 3.1.

⊡

Communication events and internal events

A close look at the preceding discussion reveals that an event can be thought of as being either an **internal event**, such as *increase_pressure* and *run_program*, or a **communication event**, such as *pipeC.product* and *input_data*.

Exactly which type an event is may depend on the level of specification. An event which appears as an internal event of a given process may, on refinement of the design, be modelled as a communication between two lower-level processes.

Exercise
6.2 Identify the internal and communication events for the process *REACTOR_VESSEL_Y*.

Solution 6.2 The communication events are precisely those that involve the transmission of a signal along a channel. All other events are internal events (at the current level of description).

Thus the set of communication events is:

{*pipeA.C1, pipeB.C2, pipeC.product, pipeD.waste, fire_brigade.alert*}

⊡

Every communication event can be specified by identifying the channel used for the communication and giving a name to the signal transmitted. We use the notation *c.v* to identify the event that describes the transmission of the signal or *value v* on the channel *c*. This is the only use of a dot in naming an event. In particular, an internal event never contains a dot as part of its name.

Processes and alphabets

We now embark on the topic that underpins our development method—the formal specification of communicating processes. Unsurprisingly, there is more than one formal method currently in use for the specification of concurrent systems. The particular formalism that we are about to introduce is called CSP—an abbreviation for Communicating Sequential Processes.

In CSP notation identifiers are used to name two types of elements: *processes* and *events*. The convention adopted is that process identifiers use upper-case letters and event identifiers use (mainly) lower-case letters. Channel names are used to identify events, and so are in lower case. We may also use digits and the underscore symbol within names to aid clarity.

We shall suppose that we have a notion of the level of abstraction required to describe a given process and its channels, and have drawn up a corresponding list of events. This is the phase of the development covered by process analysis.

The set of events for a process is called the **alphabet** of the process. Specifically, we write αP for the alphabet of process P. For example, for the first reactor vessel process described above, we have:

$\alpha REACTOR\_VESSEL\_X$
$= \{ pipeA.C1, pipeB.C2, pipeC.product, pipeD.waste \}$

Review Question 6.2 What is $\alpha REACTOR\_VESSEL\_Y$?

Processes and states

So far we have considered the relationship between a process and its alphabet. The process covers the totality of activity from the time the process starts until it finishes, if ever. Let us consider the evolution of a purely sequential process. When the process starts, it is able to engage in one specific event in its alphabet. After the occurrence of the event, the object or problem described by the process is in a new *state*. It is then able to engage in another event in the alphabet. As the process evolves, it passes through a sequence of states; in each state it may engage in some specific event in its alphabet.

What does this tell us about intermediate states? That is, what happens if we start observing the process at a later time? We shall investigate this with an example.

Consider the process that describes the execution of a computer program. We may obtain Figure 6.4 as a result of process analysis.

The alphabet is:

$\alpha PROGRAM = \{ load.code, run\_program, print.results \}$

```
           load              print
        ──────▶ ( PROGRAM ) ──────▶
                ┌─────────────┐
                │ IN SEQUENCE │
                │ load.code   │
                │ run_program │
                │ print.results│
                └─────────────┘
```

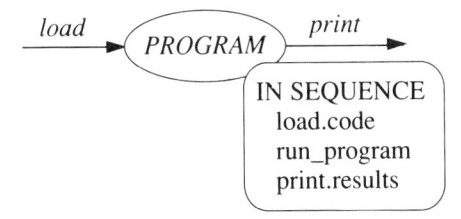

Figure 6.4

The process annotation describes *PROGRAM* as follows. First the code is input as a message on the channel *load*. Then the event *run_program* takes place; this may signify that the program has run to completion, leaving the results available for output. Finally the results are transmitted as a message on the channel *print*. Now, we might wish to consider the program as entering a new state, RUN, after the code has been loaded. The RUN state is the starting point for another process *RUN* which takes care of everything from the time the program starts running until its successful conclusion. Then the processes *PROGRAM* and *RUN* can be described as shown in Figure 6.5. Although, strictly speaking, *RUN* does not use the channel *load*, it seems desirable to retain it to emphasize that the context of *RUN* is in fact the context of *PROGRAM*. In other words, *RUN* is not being studied in its own right as a separate process, but is defined as a *subprocess* of *PROGRAM*. For this reason we assert that both processes have the same alphabet:

$$\alpha RUN = \alpha PROGRAM$$
$$= \{load.code, run\_program, print.results\}$$

Whenever we extract a subprocess from the description of a process, we define the alphabet

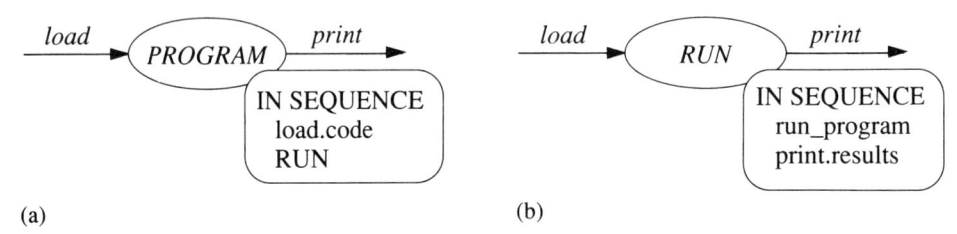

Figure 6.5

of the subprocess to be the alphabet of the original process.

Note that the process *PROGRAM* has this alphabet, even though some of the activities are not explicit but hidden in the body of the process *RUN*. Expressing *PROGRAM* in terms of *RUN* does not change the set of events which *PROGRAM* is capable of engaging in. The process *RUN* also has this alphabet, even though it does not engage in the event *load.code*, because it entered our analysis as a subprocess of *PROGRAM*. The alphabet of a process consists of the set of events which the process might engage in.

The process *PROGRAM* describes the execution of a program from its initial state; following the event *load.code* the program enters the state RUN that determines the subprocess *RUN*; after the event *run_program* the program is in the state PRINT and its subsequent behaviour is described by a suitable subprocess.

This notion, treating a process as the occurrence of an event followed by some subprocess, turns out to be the fundamental building block in the CSP formalism for the specification of processes. In fact, we found this approach invaluable in Chapter 5 when we developed a description of the two-telephone network.

6.2 The prefix construction

Suppose we have a process *P*, and let *a* be any event of αP. Then:

$a \to P$ (read as '*a* then *P*')

denotes a new process, with the same alphabet as *P*, which first engages in the event *a* and then behaves like the process *P*.

The → operation is called *prefixing*, and the new process is sometimes called:

'*P* prefixed by *a*'.

When a process *Q* has been defined by prefixing, as above, we write it as:

$Q = a \rightarrow P$

and we also know that $\alpha Q = \alpha P$.

Note carefully that the syntax for → requires its left-hand operand to be an event and its right-hand operand to be a process. Thus the following constructions are *not permissible* in CSP.

$a \rightarrow b$ where *a* and *b* are both events

$P \rightarrow Q$ where *P* and *Q* are both processes

For example, the content of Figure 6.5(a) is captured by the equation:

$PROGRAM = load.code \rightarrow RUN$

In studying the behaviour of processes, we may consider prefixing from two viewpoints. We frequently specify and design a process *P* in top-down fashion. In this case, if we identify the first event of *P* as *a* we may write:

$P = a \rightarrow S$

where the subprocess *S*, whose alphabet must be αP, has yet to be defined. Alternatively, we may develop a process description in bottom-up fashion. In this case we may have reached the stage where we have designed a process *S*. The alphabet of *S* will include all the events of the ultimate process, whether or not they occur in the description of *S*. We may now build the process *T* defined by:

$T = e \rightarrow S$

where $e \in \alpha S$.

Review Question 6.3 What can you say about the process *T*?

Let *PRINT* be the subprocess that describes the evolution of the process *PROGRAM* from the PRINT state just before the event *print.results*, as illustrated in Figure 6.6.

Note that we have:

$\alpha PRINT = \alpha RUN = \{load.code, run\_program, print.results\}$

even though the process *PRINT* engages in only the last activity.

Figure 6.6

Review Question 6.4 Specify *RUN* in terms of *PRINT* using prefixing.

Repeated prefixing

Many simple processes are built by repeated prefixing. As an example, consider the process *PROGRAM*. We have:

$PROGRAM = load.code \rightarrow RUN$

and

$RUN = run\_program \rightarrow PRINT$

so that:

$PROGRAM = load.code \rightarrow (run\_program \rightarrow PRINT)$

We have included the parentheses here to indicate the order in which the prefixing took place. However, the parentheses are not essential. Since the $\rightarrow$ operator is defined only for an event on the left and a process on the right, there is no possible ambiguity if we write:

$PROGRAM = load.code \rightarrow run\_program \rightarrow PRINT$

We say that the binary operator $\rightarrow$ *associates to the right*. (The only other possible interpretation would be:

$PROGRAM = (load.code \rightarrow run\_program) \rightarrow PRINT$

but this is not defined—the combination of two events using prefixing is not meaningful.)

Vending machines

As a case study for presenting the CSP formalism, we shall consider vending machines, which will be a source of useful examples of processes.

A vending machine has one or more slots for the insertion of coins. It may have buttons to select a product; and it will, in response to a suitable sequence of activities, dispense the desired product. Of course, vending machines may run out of products to dispense, and it is not unheard of for a vending machine to get jammed and fail to perform to its specification. We shall treat the behaviour of a vending machine as a process; by considering the properties of various designs of machine, we hope to illustrate some of the important features of CSP. We shall first build up a CSP description of vending machines in an unspecified environment; this does not yet entail any concurrency. In Chapter 10 we model the interaction of a vending machine with a user; in so doing we see how concurrency is represented in the CSP formalism.

Our first vending machine, illustrated in Figure 6.7, dispenses a cup of tea in return for a 10p coin. Various models of this machine are available; the basic model is designed to perform this combination of activities exactly once.

The behaviour of the basic machine is described by a process with two channels: an entry channel which we call *coinslot* and an exit channel *hatch*. There are two events in the life of this machine, *coinslot.10p* and *hatch.tea*, after which it has successfully completed the purpose for which it was designed. A process network for this basic machine is shown in Figure 6.8.

Figure 6.7

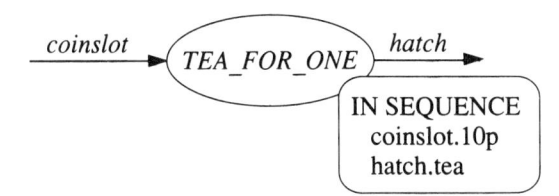

Figure 6.8

A suitable alphabet is therefore:

$\alpha TEA\_FOR\_ONE = \{coinslot.10p, hatch.tea\}$

The machine does nothing until a 10p coin is supplied, whereupon it serves a cup of tea and terminates successfully. We may usefully identify two states of our machine: the initial state, in which it can accept a coin, and the final state, in which it has done what it was designed to do and can engage in no further events. Since we have sought to associate each state of a process with an appropriate subprocess, we shall introduce the subprocess *NO_MORE_TEA* that describes the behaviour of a vending machine which has not yet been filled with supplies. The correct behaviour of this machine is to accept no coins and dispense no tea; it engages in neither of the events in its alphabet. We may now give the formal specification:

$TEA\_FOR\_ONE = coinslot.10p \rightarrow hatch.tea \rightarrow NO\_MORE\_TEA$

Note that the IN SEQUENCE of the informal annotation translates directly into prefixing in the formal specification.

The box notation

We shall now introduce a convenient notation for collecting together the formal specification of a process in terms of its alphabet. The constituents of this specification are collected together in a box, as shown below. The process name appears in the top line; the alphabet of the process appears in the top part of the box; and the body of the CSP specification appears in the bottom part.

If the alphabet is obvious it can be omitted, but strictly speaking it should appear, especially when it involves activities that the process does not engage in explicitly:

TEA_FOR_ONE

{ coinslot.10p, hatch.tea }

---
coinslot.10p $\to$ hatch.tea $\to$ NO_MORE_TEA

Let us now consider a few more realistic variants of the vending machine. An obvious possibility is that the machine will serve more than one customer. In fact a modern machine may be able to serve hundreds of customers successfully. To specify such a machine using prefixing is easy but very cumbersome, so we seek notational devices to ease the task. In this case it is helpful to consider the state of the machine each time it is ready to engage in the event *coinslot.10p*. The state represents the number of cups of tea still available to be dispensed. Corresponding to each state we have a subprocess. This gives us a family of subprocesses, which can best be written using a suffix notation. For example, when there are thirty cups of tea left in the machine the process that describes its future behaviour is called TEA_{30}, and when there are six cups of tea left the future behaviour of the machine is described by the process TEA_6. This enables a straightforward specification of a machine which will dispense, say, 50 cups of tea before terminating successfully:

$TEA\_FOR\_FIFTY = TEA_{50}$

Review Question 6.5 Express the specification of the basic model TEA_FOR_ONE in terms of the suffix notation. □

Let us now see how to give a complete specification of TEA_FOR_FIFTY. We note first that, for example:

$TEA_{50} = coinslot.10p \to hatch.tea \to TEA_{49}$

and that:

$TEA_{22} = coinslot.10p \to hatch.tea \to TEA_{21}$

More generally:

$TEA_n = coinslot.10p \to hatch.tea \to TEA_{n-1}$ (if $n > 0$).

For each value of n, TEA_n describes the future behaviour of the machine in the state where n cups remain. This can be shown in box notation:

TEA_FOR_FIFTY

{ coinslot.10p, hatch.tea }

TEA_{50}
where
$\quad TEA_n = coinslot.10p \to hatch.tea \to TEA_{n-1}$ (if $n > 0$)
$\quad TEA_0 = NO\_MORE\_TEA$

In this box specification the word 'where' is used to qualify the process TEA_{50} that precedes it. The following lines complete the specification. It is assumed here that the process *NO_MORE_TEA* has been defined to specify a machine designed to do nothing.

The specification in terms of the family of processes TEA_n ($0 \leq n \leq 50$) is much more compact than fifty lines of:

> *coinslot.10p* → *hatch.tea* →
> *coinslot.10p* → *hatch.tea* → ...

and loses nothing of the exactness required of the specification. The equivalence of the two specifications could be established by expanding the shorthand version in terms of sub-processes.

We shall now increase the realism by allowing a different ending. You will almost certainly have experienced a vending machine whose ultimate behaviour differs from *NO_MORE_TEA*. Consider a vending machine which jams after accepting its first coin. Such a machine dispenses no tea, and will never do anything useful again. It will certainly not terminate in the manner it was designed to do. (We discount the possibility that the machine was designed to gobble up the coin of the first unwary passer-by.) Let us call the process that describes the behaviour of a jammed machine *JAMMED*. Then our faulty machine is specified by the process *JAM*:

```
┌──── JAM ────────────────────────┐
│                                 │
│  { coinslot.10p, hatch.tea }    │
│                                 │
│  coinslot.10p → JAMMED          │
│                                 │
└─────────────────────────────────┘
```

Notice that the event *hatch.tea* is retained in αJAM, although it does not take place. The alphabet of a process includes all potential events—that is, all events in which the vending machine is designed to engage.

In the case of *TEA_FOR_ONE* the process terminates successfully via *NO_MORE_TEA*; though when this process has terminated the customer is free to walk away and engage in other processes. By contrast the process *JAM* leads to *JAMMED*. Not only is the machine in a sorry state, the customer is also profoundly unhappy. He has paid for the tea that will never arrive, nor does the machine give any indication that it has ceased performing. This state cannot be a prelude to further processes.

Review Question 6.6 Give a CSP specification for the process that describes the behaviour of a machine which successfully serves one customer with a cup of tea in return for 10p. However, as soon as another 10p coin is inserted the machine breaks—no more tea will be dispensed, and no further coin will be accepted. ▫

6.3 *SKIP* and *STOP*: friend and foe!

At this stage it is worth summarizing our progress so far. First we establish a set of events of interest—the alphabet, that we may call *A*. Then, using prefix notation, we have the rule that, if *P* is a process with alphabet *A* and *a* is an event in *A*:

86   SPECIFICATION AND DESIGN OF CONCURRENT SYSTEMS

$$a \to P$$

is also a process with alphabet A. We can therefore build up a sequential process as a sequence of events that prefix some terminating process.

There are two processes that describe the eventual behaviour of a vending machine—*NO_MORE_TEA* and *JAMMED*. Both of these processes have the same alphabet, {*coinslot.10p, hatch.tea*}, though neither actually engages in these events. Strictly speaking, we should define an event which represents successful termination in the alphabet of *NO_MORE_TEA*. However, we shall see presently that a process which does nothing other than terminate successfully arises whenever we consider a terminating sequential process, and we therefore adopt a more general approach.

Of course, it is possible that the process may not terminate successfully; for example an apparently correct program may crash or a chemical reactor may explode. Indeed, for any terminating process we must consider two possible subprocesses—one to describe *successful termination* and another to describe *irretrievable breakdown*. These processes are *atomic*—they engage in no events of the alphabet and cannot be analysed further.

We shall now study the two basic processes, corresponding to successful termination and irretrievable breakdown, which may appear in a CSP specification.

SKIP: *successful termination*

Suppose a process has been described by process analysis. It may turn out that the process is finite—after some finite sequence of events the description reaches a successful conclusion. The important point here is that for any successful finite process there must be termination.

Specifically, we assert that for any process *P* there is a subprocess *SKIP* which does nothing but terminate successfully.

Exercise

6.3 Consider the process *PROGRAM*, which was specified in Section 6.2 in terms of the subprocess *PRINT*. By identifying a suitable subprocess for successful termination, complete the specification of *PROGRAM*.

Solution 6.3 Let *END* be the process whose sole effect in the context of program execution is to terminate successfully. Then Figure 6.6 indicates that:

PRINT = print.results → *END*

Since we have already seen that

PROGRAM = load.code → *run_program* → *PRINT*

we may describe *PROGRAM* fully by

PROGRAM = load.code → *run_program* → *print.results* → *END*

However, we have stated that there is a *SKIP* process associated with any process—the process *END* is thus the *SKIP* associated with *PROGRAM*. You could therefore have written the specification of *PROGRAM* with *SKIP* in place of *END*.

□

Review Question 6.7 Consider the following alphabet for a process which describes a single shopping expedition by car:

{*enter_car, drive_to_shop, leave_car, enter_shop, buy_goods, leave_shop, drive_home*}

Use the box notation to give a CSP specification of such a process. You may make any reasonable assumption about the sequence of events.

⊡

Let *P* be a process; then there is an associated subprocess *SKIP*. As stated previously, the alphabet of *SKIP* is αP —the alphabet of its parent process. Thus, for example, the process *NO_MORE_TEA* is identical to the process *SKIP* with alphabet {*coinslot.10p, hatch.tea*}, and the process *END*—which appeared in the solution to Exercise 6.3—is identical to the process *SKIP* with alphabet {*load.code, run_program, print.results*}. In each case the alphabet is determined by the context. So, although both *SKIP* processes have the same effect—they both describe successful conclusions—they do so in different contexts, and are therefore not identical processes. Strictly speaking, they should not both have the same name. When we need to distinguish two *SKIP* processes by their alphabet, we add a subscript. We give names to the two alphabets as follows. Let:

A = {*coinslot.10p, hatch.tea*}

and

B = {*load.code, run_program, print.results*}

then

$NO\_MORE\_TEA = SKIP_A$

whereas

$PRINT = print.results \rightarrow SKIP_B$

We shall find, though, that in most cases we can safely omit the alphabet subscript and infer it from the context.

Any process which successfully performs only a finite number of events can be expressed in terms of a sequence of events ultimately leading to *SKIP*, because this primitive process is our *only* recognition of a successful conclusion. At this stage you should suppress the desire to challenge the philosophical validity of encapsulating success in a single, named process, just think of *SKIP* as *immediate success*.

Review Question 6.8 Use the box notation to specify the process *RUN*.

⊡

STOP: *irretrievable failure*

At the opposite end of the spectrum there is another atomic process: irretrievable failure. Processes sometimes do not achieve what their designers hoped for. A machine may break, a chemical plant may explode while the fire brigade is on holiday, or a concurrent program executing on several processors may reach the stage where no further progress is possible—the system deadlocks. The important point here is that having reached such a state there is no way out within the framework of the problem. For example, the total reconstruction of a chemical plant following a massive explosion is unlikely to have been one of the factors borne in mind at the design stage. By definition a program which crashes cannot have anticipated the fact that it was about to crash and then taken counter measures. To avoid such calamitous situations it is vital to countenance the disaster happening in the first place, and this certainly is an important factor in the design stage.

We cater for the possibility of a disaster situation by introducing the process *STOP*. Thus the process *JAMMED* that describes a broken vending machine is an instance of the *STOP* process. For any process we describe the situation in which no further progress is possible, but the process has not terminated successfully, by a *STOP* process. As in the case of *SKIP*, there is a dependence on context. To return to the example of the vending machine, the process *JAMMED* is an instance of *STOP*, with alphabet A defined previously. Once again, we may include the alphabet explicitly by subscripting, so that:

$$JAMMED = STOP_A$$

For the time being, you can think of *STOP* as a process which starts, but that is all it ever does. It will never do anything useful again, and in particular will never terminate. We shall see in due course that a pair of concurrent processes that have reached a deadlock can be described collectively by *STOP* with a suitably chosen alphabet.

Exercise
6.4 Given an alphabet $\{a, b\}$, describe some finite processes that we can specify at this stage of our theoretical development.

Solution 6.4 Given our development so far, every process must be formed by prefixing a subprocess. Since the only atomic processes are *SKIP* and *STOP*, the only finite processes we can specify are those that engage in a finite sequence of n (≥ 0) events followed by *SKIP* or *STOP*. These may be expressed as follows:

SKIP	*STOP*
$a \rightarrow SKIP$	$a \rightarrow STOP$
$b \rightarrow SKIP$	$b \rightarrow STOP$
$a \rightarrow b \rightarrow SKIP$	$a \rightarrow b \rightarrow STOP$
$b \rightarrow a \rightarrow SKIP$	$b \rightarrow a \rightarrow STOP$

and so on.

6.4 Summary

In this chapter we have introduced the CSP formalism. After discussing the nature of processes we described how internal and communication events could be incorporated into an alphabet for a process. Our approach to processes is constructive, using the prefix construction to specify a sequential process. We also discussed two fundamental atomic processes, *SKIP* (which terminates immediately and successfully) and *STOP* (which does nothing and in particular does not terminate). From these, the prefix construction can be used to build other processes. Given a process Q and an event a in its alphabet αQ, the process:

$$a \rightarrow Q$$

engages in the event a and then behaves like Q. By convention, a process and its sub-processes share the same alphabet.

We introduced the box notation as a compact way of specifying a process and its alphabet.

7 TRACES

A useful way of describing processes is to record what they do. To this end, consider a hypothetical observer, with pencil and notebook, who chronicles how the process evolves. Each time the process engages in an event, the observer notes the fact by recording the symbol for that event in the notebook. At any moment, the observer's notebook will contain a string of event symbols drawn from the alphabet of the process. For any process, we call the string of events so far a ***trace*** of the process.

Before a process has had a chance to accomplish anything, this string will be empty; we shall write < > to denote an empty trace. As time passes and the process engages in events from its alphabet, the observer records the appropriate string of symbols.

Example

7.1 The process *TEA_FOR_ONE*, introduced in Section 6.2, has the following possible traces:

    < >

    <coinslot.10p>

    <coinslot.10p, hatch.tea>

Before the insertion of the coin the observer's notebook is blank. The next trace reveals the recording of the coin event. Subsequently the delivery of the tea is recorded. This set of traces tells us nothing about what might happen next. □

The CSP model endows the observer with the gift of being able to tell whether the process being observed has terminated with the behaviour of *SKIP,* or has become deadlocked with the behaviour of *STOP*. Since these processes have no corresponding event symbols in the alphabet, two special symbols are used to describe these situations. When a process terminates successfully (by evolving into *SKIP*), the trace is annotated with a tick. When a process cannot engage in any further event but has not terminated it has become *STOP*; its trace is then annotated with a cross.

The process *TEA_FOR_ONE* therefore has the following additional trace:

    <coinslot.10p, hatch.tea> ✓

reflecting successful termination after the event *hatch.tea*. The possible traces of *STOP* are:

    $<>$

    $<>_x$

Note that no further event symbol can occur after either $\checkmark$ or $_x$.

Suppose now that the customer of our vending machine modelled by *TEA_FOR_ONE* has no 10p piece, only a 20p piece, and naively assumes that the insertion of 20p will buy a cup of tea.

Exercise

7.1 Give a CSP specification of the process *CUST20* that models the customer described informally above.

Solution 7.1

    $CUST20 = coinslot.20p \rightarrow hatch.tea \rightarrow Q$

Here Q stands for a process which remains unspecified, given the description above.

Figure 7.1 shows a process network for the complete process.

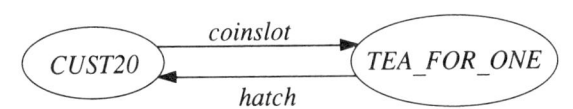

Figure 7.1

Now let us consider what happens to *TEA_FOR_ONE*. The first event that can take place is *coinslot.10p*. This is a communication event, and will take place only if the other party to it is willing to do so. However, as can be seen from Solution 7.1, *CUST20* will not cooperate, preferring to attempt the communication *coinslot.20p*. Thus the process is deadlocked, yielding the following trace:

    $<>_x$

Whenever a process is due to engage in a communication event, we must determine whether the environment of the process will allow the event to take place; if not, the process will deadlock.

Review Question 7.1 Write down all the traces of *SKIP*.

Review Question 7.2 Consider the process TEA_2 defined in Section 6.2. Write down:

(a) the trace of TEA_2 containing three events;
(b) the trace of TEA_2 that includes successful termination.

Each trace of a process gives a record of a possible sequence of events as seen by a hypothetical external observer. For a finite sequential process, such as we have discussed so far, the traces can be more or less read off from the specification. In the next chapter we shall investigate new ways of defining processes. The behaviour of these processes is not always transparent from the specification, and the traces can be a great help in discussing them.

8 CHOICE

Two asynchronous processes, P and Q, may be brought into temporary synchronization by a communication event along a channel c which links P and Q, as shown in Figure 8.1. If P is ready to participate in the event, but Q is not ready, process P suspends; it is **blocked**. P cannot transmit a value on channel c unless Q is simultaneously ready to receive it. On the other hand, if Q is ready to participate in a communication event, that is, to receive a value on channel c, but P is not ready, Q is not necessarily blocked. Q could choose to engage in an alternative event if no value is ready to be delivered on channel c. We met this kind of situation in Chapter 2 when we considered conversations between three people. We also saw examples of choice constructs in our discussions of image processing and the telephone system.

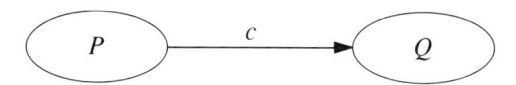

Figure 8.1

It is essential that we introduce an element of choice in order to describe complex processes because a process must be able to choose between different courses of action according to prevailing circumstances, and it is to this topic that we now turn. We shall find it convenient to distinguish the following forms of choice to abstract our experience of real-world processes:

- choice by input value;
- choice by channel;
- non-deterministic choice.

These different forms of choice may be illustrated by considering the control system for a lift. This is shown in Figure 8.2.

The *LIFT* process needs an entry channel *inlift* which carries signals from the control panel in the lift. A passenger inside the lift cage may select a destination by pressing the appropriate

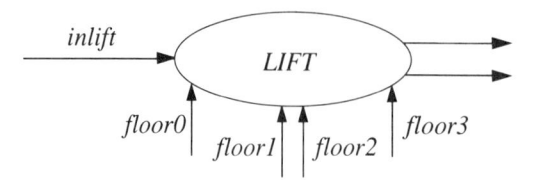

94   SPECIFICATION AND DESIGN OF CONCURRENT SYSTEMS

Figure 8.2

button. Each button sends a different signal on the channel *inlift*. The lift must now proceed according to the value of this signal—this is an example of *choice by input value*.

There are additional entry channels (one per floor) that carry signals from potential passengers. The *LIFT* process must respond appropriately to any calls received. This is modelled as *choice by channel*.

Finally, the lift may be at the second floor, say, with outstanding calls from potential passengers waiting on the first and third floors. In this case the behaviour of the lift would be modelled realistically by a *non-deterministic choice*. You could not predict whether it would go to the first or third floor.

We shall devote a section to each of these forms of choice.

8.1 Choice by input value—the | operator

In specifying the behaviour of a chemical plant, it is necessary to describe not only the normal sequence of events, but also the remedial action that is required in special circumstances. The concentration of a compound can be monitored by a transducer. As long as the concentration of a particular compound remains below a certain critical value, a *safe* signal is sent and the reaction is allowed to proceed normally. However, if an excess concentration is detected, the transducer sends an *excess* signal, so that remedial action can be taken. We may model this situation by a control process which can accept input on a *monitor* channel, as illustrated by Figure 8.3.

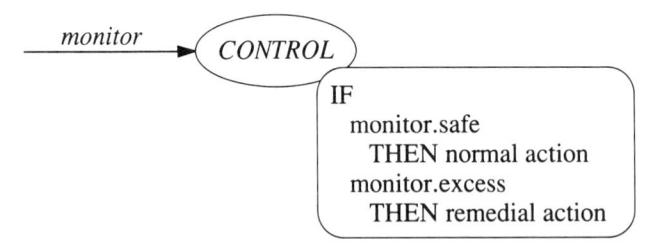

Figure 8.3

The process thus contains in its alphabet two communication events corresponding to the receipt of a signal on the *monitor* channel. Suppose these events are called *monitor.safe* and *monitor.excess*. The future behaviour of the control process now depends on which of these two events takes place. We may say that the process can enter two possible states, and there is then a branching of behaviour according to the current state.

Other examples in which a communication event may determine the future behaviour include a vending machine offering a choice of tea or coffee, and an automatic railway signalling system which applies the brakes to a train if it attempts to pass a signal at red.

These examples provide a motivation for including a mechanism in CSP to describe a process which selects a course of action according to the value of a communication input from the environment or from another process. The symbol | (called 'thinbar') is used to specify a process whose future behaviour depends on the value of an input event. Thus:

$$CONTROL = monitor.safe \rightarrow NORMAL \mid monitor.excess \rightarrow REMEDIAL$$

The | operator

The formal syntax of | is as follows. Let P and Q be two processes with the same alphabet, $\alpha P = \alpha Q$, and let x and y be two distinct events belonging to this alphabet. Then the process:

$$(x \rightarrow P \mid y \rightarrow Q)$$

first engages in either event x or event y, as determined by the environment. If the first event is x then the process continues by behaving like P; if the first event is y then the process continues by behaving like Q. Where no ambiguity can arise we shall omit the parentheses. Note that the prefix arrow takes precedence over thinbar. We never write $R \mid S$—the prefixing must be explicit. It is crucial that the events x and y are distinct. The choice is exercised not by the process but by the environment. Thus we are not permitted to define a process by, for example:

$$(x \rightarrow P \mid x \rightarrow Q)$$

as, in this case, the process would have to make the choice between continuing with P or continuing with Q and such a choice would be non-deterministic. Thinbar applies only to deterministic choice. We shall deal with non-deterministic choice later.

We remark that, by its interpretation, thinbar is commutative:

$$(x \rightarrow P \mid y \rightarrow Q) = (y \rightarrow Q \mid x \rightarrow P)$$

Exercise

8.1 A basic vending machine, Figure 8.4, dispenses one drink, but allows the customer a choice: it will deliver tea if a 10p coin is inserted, and coffee if it receives a 20p coin. Process analysis yields Figure 8.5. Give a boxed CSP specification of this process.

Figure 8.4

96 SPECIFICATION AND DESIGN OF CONCURRENT SYSTEMS

coinslot → TEA_OR_COFFEE → *hatch*

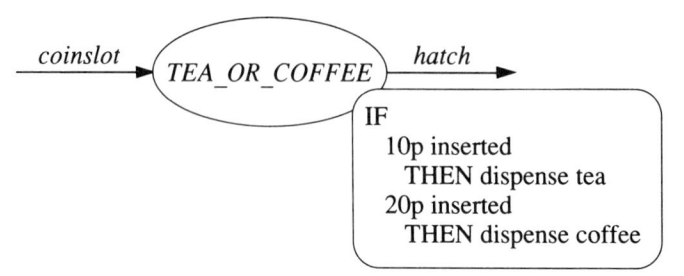

IF
 10p inserted
  THEN dispense tea
 20p inserted
  THEN dispense coffee

Figure 8.5

Solution 8.1 Depending on the initial input event, which is determined by the customer, the behaviour of the process is (in CSP notation) either:

coinslot.10p → *hatch.tea* → SKIP

or

coinslot.20p → *hatch.coffee* → SKIP

This gives the following specification. Note where we place the choice symbol | for a choice which spans more than one line:

TEA_OR_COFFEE

{*coinslot.10p, coinslot.20p, hatch.tea, hatch.coffee*}

(*coinslot.10p* → *hatch.tea* → SKIP
|
coinslot.20p → *hatch.coffee* → SKIP)

8.2 A family of processes is specified by

$P = a \rightarrow A \mid b \rightarrow B$
$A = a \rightarrow SKIP \mid b \rightarrow STOP \mid c \rightarrow C$
$B = a \rightarrow SKIP \mid b \rightarrow STOP$
$C = c \rightarrow SKIP$

Write down all the traces for each of the following processes:

(a) B

(b) P

Solution 8.2

(a) $<>, <a>, <a>\checkmark, <b>, <b>_\times$

(b) $<>, <a>, <a, a>, <a, a>\checkmark, <a, b>, <a, b>_\times, <a, c>, <a, c, c>, <a, c, c>\checkmark,$
$<b>, <b, a>, <b, a>\checkmark, <b, b>, <b, b>_\times$

The thinbar notation enables us to specify a process whose behaviour is a choice between a pair of prefixed processes. Each process is prefixed by a *guard* event; the environment participates in one of the guard events, thereby exercising the choice provided.

In the cases considered so far there are two possible guard events, and the subsequent behaviour of the process is completely determined by the one that occurs. There is no particular reason to limit the number of possible guard events to two. A process with three possible inputs may be defined using the extended notation

$$T = (x \rightarrow P \mid y \rightarrow Q \mid z \rightarrow R)$$

The process T may initially engage in any of the three distinct guard events x, y or z. The subsequent behaviour of T is like P, Q, or R, as the case may be. The notation may be extended in this way to accommodate any number of choices.

The choice does not even need to be restricted to a small number of guards that are enumerated individually. Indeed, we may allow a choice to be performed over any convenient subset of the alphabet of the process. We shall develop this idea further when we discuss input communications in Chapter 14.

Review Question 8.1 The vending machine of Figure 8.4 is replaced by a more up-to-date model (Figure 8.6), which can dispense a single cup of hot chocolate, at 5p, as an alternative to tea and coffee. Specify a process *HOT_DRINK* which describes this machine.

Figure 8.6

Review Question 8.2 List the possible traces of *HOT_DRINK*. (Remember that it dispenses only one drink.)

A process prefixed by an explicit guard event, or a choice between such guarded processes, is called a ***guarded expression***. We shall encounter guarded expressions in various situations.

Review Question 8.3 Which of the following are guarded expressions?

(a) $x \rightarrow P$
(b) *coinslot.10p* $\rightarrow$ *STOP*
(c) *SKIP*

(d) $(x \to P \mid y \to Q \mid z \to R)$

(e) X

(f) $t.press \to hatch.tea$

$\Box$

8.2 Choice by channel—the $\Box$ operator

A basic feature of our treatment of concurrency is that several processes may actively influence each other's behaviour. They do this using communication events along channels. We have seen that a process may choose different courses of action according to which input it receives from another process. For example, the *HOT_DRINK* process has its future behaviour determined by the value of the coin inserted in the slot.

There is another, equally valid, possibility: a vending machine may require the customer to exercise choice by pressing one of a number of buttons, each of which could be regarded as an entry channel.[1] This is a good example of a new form of choice: how the future behaviour of a process may depend on which of several channels is prepared to provide it with an input.

Consider a process P with two entry channels, c and d, on which it can receive input values, a and b respectively, as shown in Figure 8.7. The subsequent behaviour of P is either the process Q or the process R, depending on which of the alternative communications has occurred.

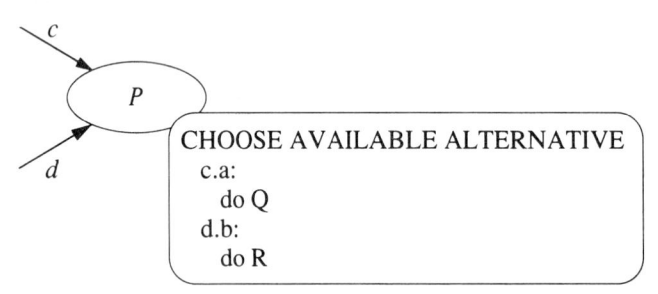

```
        c
         ↘
          ( P )
         ↗  ┌──────────────────────────────┐
        d   │ CHOOSE AVAILABLE ALTERNATIVE │
            │   c.a:                       │
            │     do Q                     │
            │   d.b:                       │
            │     do R                     │
            └──────────────────────────────┘
```

Figure 8.7

The CSP symbol $\Box$ (called 'fetbar') is used to specify a process whose future behaviour depends on a choice of communication events on different channels.[2] Thus the process P of Figure 8.7 is specified by:

$P = (c.a \to Q \,\Box\, d.b \to R)$

This process first engages in event $c.a$ or $d.b$, as determined by the environment. If neither channel is ready, P waits until a signal arrives on one of the channels, and then continues as stated. The syntax rule for $\Box$ is similar to the syntax rule for $\mid$, that is, each operand of $\Box$ must be a guarded expression.

---

[1] It would be possible, alternatively, to treat the choice of drinks as values on a single channel; this will be explored later in this section.

[2] The name *fetbar* arose as the result of a minor historical accident. The original notes for CSP were photocopied and circulated in a series of courses held by the Programming Research Group at Oxford. The two choice operators were called *thinbar* and *fatbar*. However, the name of the latter was mistyped, and the misprint stuck!

The crucial difference between | and ▯ is that while the allowable first events of | are required to be mutually exclusive, the environment may quite legitimately be willing to engage in *any* guard event of a ▯ choice. Put another way, both channels might be ready to transmit. When this situation occurs the process *P* makes a non-deterministic choice—it chooses at random whether to accept the input from channel *c* and then behave like *Q* or to accept the input from channel *d* and then behave like *R*.

Example

8.1 Consider a vending machine which supplies a single drink, which may be either tea or coffee, at the same price of 10p. After inserting a 10p coin, the customer indicates her choice of drink by pressing either the button marked tea or the one marked coffee. The machine responds accordingly (Figure 8.8).

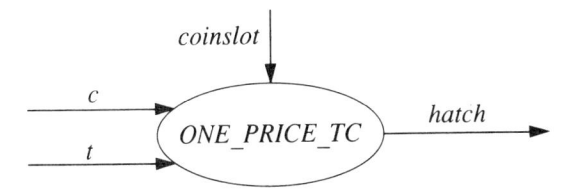

Figure 8.8

A suitable specification for this process is as follows:

ONE_PRICE_TC

{*coinslot.10p*, *t.press*, *c.press*, *hatch.tea*, *hatch.coffee*}

coinslot.10p →
  (*t.press* → *hatch.tea* → SKIP
  ▯
  c.press → *hatch.coffee* → SKIP)

Review Question 8.4 What happens if the customer presses the tea button or coffee button before inserting 10p?

Review Question 8.5 Why is it not possible to bracket the process *ONE_PRICE_TC* further by writing it as follows?

(*t.press* → *hatch.tea*
▯
c.press → *hatch.coffee*)→ SKIP

In Example 8.1 we modelled *ONE_PRICE_TC* using choice by channel. At first sight it might seem that we could have obtained a simpler, but equivalent specification using a single channel to model the choice of button pressed, with two values that can be discriminated using thinbar (choice by input value). However, this is not so. The difference between using

100 SPECIFICATION AND DESIGN OF CONCURRENT SYSTEMS

one channel and two channels is that on one channel the values must be transmitted in sequence, whereas the use of separate channels allows the model to take into account the possibility that both buttons are pressed simultaneously. The definition of fetbar states that if a communication event is available on just one channel, that event determines the choice. If, however, communication events are available on both channels, either alternative could proceed, and the choice is exercised non-deterministically. In our example this would be an acceptable mode of behaviour—if both buttons are pressed simultaneously the customer is presumably willing to accept tea or coffee, whichever the machine chooses to deliver.

Exercise

8.3 Specify a process *TCH* which describes a machine which provides a single cup of either tea, coffee or hot chocolate, all at a price of 10p. The customer exercises choice by pressing the appropriate button.

Solution 8.3   Process analysis gives a process network as in Figure 8.9.

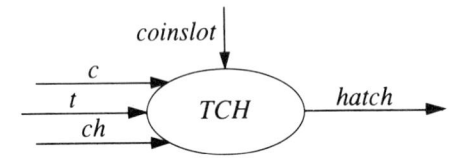

Figure 8.9

This leads to the following specification:

TCH

$\{coinslot.10p, t.press, c.press, ch.press, hatch.tea, hatch.coffee, hatch.choc\}$

$coinslot.10p \rightarrow$
  $(t.press \rightarrow hatch.tea \rightarrow SKIP$
  $\square$
  $c.press \rightarrow hatch.coffee \rightarrow SKIP$
  $\square$
  $ch.press \rightarrow hatch.choc \rightarrow SKIP\ )$

Exercise

8.4 Specify a machine which offers a choice of tea or coffee by button and will deliver a single cup of tea, at 10p, or coffee, at 20p. The machine accepts either 10p or 20p coins, up to a maximum of 20p. A customer inserting 20p for a cup of tea should receive 10p change.

Solution 8.4   This is a rather more complicated machine, and in fact we must be quite careful to avoid a design flaw! Firstly the alphabet must include a new output event which corresponds to giving change—we call the corresponding channel *change*. A process network for the coffee, tea, and change process is shown in Figure 8.10.

So the alphabet needs to be:

$\{coinslot.10p, coinslot.20p, t.press, c.press, hatch.tea, hatch.coffee,$
$change.10p\}$

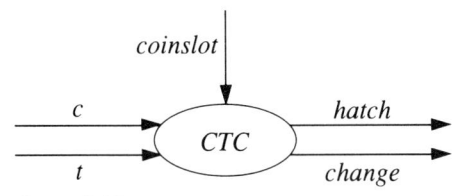

Figure 8.10

The behaviour of the machine depends on an initial choice by input—the value of the first coin inserted. Thus:

$$CTC = (coinslot.10p \rightarrow CTC_{10} \mid coinslot.20p \rightarrow CTC_{20})$$

where CTC_{10} and CTC_{20} have yet to be specified. Let us consider the two cases separately. In the first case, where 10p has been inserted, there are two courses legitimately open to a customer. Either he may press the button marked *t* and expect a cup of tea, or he may insert a further coin before making a selection. Thus:

$$CTC_{10} = (t.press \rightarrow hatch.tea \rightarrow SKIP) \;\Box\; (coinslot.10p \rightarrow CTC_{20})$$

The second case, where 20p has been inserted, is specified by CTC_{20}, which offers a choice of drink:

$$CTC_{20} = (t.press \rightarrow hatch.tea \rightarrow change.10p \rightarrow SKIP$$
$$\Box$$
$$c.press \rightarrow hatch.coffee \rightarrow SKIP)$$

Notice that in the solution we have made the arbitrary design decision that a drink is dispensed before change is given. The problem did not specify which order these events should occur in, so we could equally well have reversed the order. We shall see later that it is not necessary to incorporate a design decision at this stage—the indeterminacy can be left in the CSP specification to be resolved at a later stage.

We may summarize the result as follows:

CTC

{*coinslot.10p, coinslot.20p, t.press, c.press, hatch.tea, hatch.coffee, change.10p*}

($coinslot.10p \rightarrow CTC_{10}$
|
$coinslot.20p \rightarrow CTC_{20}$)
where
　　$CTC_{10} = (t.press \rightarrow hatch.tea \rightarrow SKIP$
　　　　　$\Box$
　　　　　$coinslot.10p \rightarrow CTC_{20})$
　　$CTC_{20} = (t.press \rightarrow hatch.tea \rightarrow change.10p \rightarrow SKIP$
　　　　　$\Box$
　　　　　$c.press \rightarrow hatch.coffee \rightarrow SKIP)$

Review Question 8.6 What is the behaviour of *CTC* if three 10p pieces are inserted in succession?

Prioritized choice

The choice-by-channel operator exercises a symmetric choice between its channels. If only one communication event is possible, that event takes place. If two (or more) communication events are possible, an arbitrary choice between them is made. In some circumstances this is not the appropriate response. For example, a lift may be provided with an emergency button for use in case of malfunction or other emergency. It would not do for the lift process to treat this event on a par with unfulfilled requests for stopping at various floors. Worse still, there may be people who are calling the lift from one of the floors who are unaware that an emergency has occurred; simple choice by channel would give equal priority to these events as to the emergency button. The need for prioritized choice may be expressed in CSP using the *modified fetbar*, ⇨.

Rather than attempt a formal description of the lift process, which is by no means trivial, we present a simple application here. We shall meet a more substantial application of ⇨ in the case study of Part IV.

Example

8.2 The process P can accept an input either on channel x, in which case it continues as process X, or on channel y, in which case it continues as process Y. However, it must not accept input from y when an input event is available on channel x. Suppose the input events are $x.a$ and $y.b$ respectively. We may specify P as follows:

$$P = x.a \to X \mathrel{⇨} y.b \to Y$$

The guarded expression to the left of ⇨ takes precedence over the guarded expression on the right.

Exercise

8.5 The process network in Figure 8.11 represents a simple buffer which can hold a single value for onward transmission. The buffer can be deactivated by a signal on the *halt* channel. Specify the process *BUFF*, assuming that

$$\alpha BUFF = \{in.x, out.x, halt.t\}$$

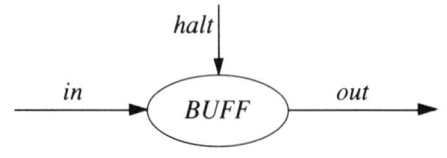

Figure 8.11

Solution 8.5

$$BUFF = (halt.t \to SKIP \mathrel{⇨} in.x \to out.x \to SKIP)$$

This buffer only works once and then terminates. A more realistic buffer would carry on indefinitely until halted, as follows:

$$BUFF = (halt.t \rightarrow SKIP$$
$$\Box\!\!\!\!>$$
$$in.x \rightarrow out.x \rightarrow BUFF)$$

8.3 Non-deterministic choice—the $\sqcap$ operator

We have seen, in our discussion of choice by channel, that a process may have to exercise choice between two courses of action in what may seem from the outside an arbitrary fashion. Non-determinism is a tricky area, and we shall steer a careful path round it. On occasion, however, it is convenient to have a notation to represent a process which behaves either like a process P or like a process Q—where the choice is made according to factors *that are beyond our current level of refinement*.

Consider a vending machine. It seems unlikely that whether it delivers tea or coffee is decided non-deterministically. However, if the vending machine is capable of offering change, so long as we get our 10p change we are not really bothered whether it is as a 10p piece or two 5p pieces. We hardly expect to choose the form in which change is given by a hot drinks machine. As far as we are concerned the subprocess of giving change is non-deterministic.

CSP has a special symbol $\sqcap$ (called 'piebar') for this form of choice. The process:

$P \sqcap Q$ where $\alpha(P \sqcap Q) = \alpha P = \alpha Q$

behaves either like P or like Q, but the factors controlling the choice are unknown to the environment at the current level of abstraction. P and Q do not need to be guarded expressions. Non-deterministic choice satisfies the following rules:

$P \sqcap Q = Q \sqcap P$
$P \sqcap (Q \sqcap R) = (P \sqcap Q) \sqcap R$
$x \rightarrow (P \sqcap Q) = (x \rightarrow P) \sqcap (x \rightarrow Q)$

Rules such as these are needed when deciding whether two process specifications are equivalent. The meanings of the first two rules should be fairly straightforward. The third rule states that the process that begins with the event x followed by a non-deterministic choice between process P and Q is equivalent to a non-deterministic choice between the processes $(x \rightarrow P)$ and $(x \rightarrow Q)$.

Example

8.3 Consider a vending machine which supplies a single cup of tea for 10p; it will accept in payment either a 10p or 20p coin, giving change as necessary. Here is a suitable specification:

```
┌─────── TEA_WITH_CHANGE ───────────────
│
│  {coinslot.10p, coinslot.20p, hatch.tea, change.5p, change.10p}
│
│  (coinslot.10p → hatch.tea → SKIP
│   |
│   coinslot.20p → hatch.tea → CHANGE)
│  where
│     CHANGE = (change.5p → change.5p → SKIP
│              ⊓
│              change.10p → SKIP )
```

In the example above we have assumed that the tea is dispensed before change is given. In Chapter 9 we shall see how to handle the case in which the tea may be dispensed either before or after giving change.

As with previous operators, there is no restriction on the number of processes between which a non-deterministic choice is made. We shall not often make use of this operator in the specification of processes, but we shall see later that it has its uses in the analysis of deadlock.

8.4 Summary

In this chapter we have shown how processes can be specified when their behaviour depends on choice. We dealt with the following different forms of choice:

- choice by input value, | thinbar;
- choice by channel,   ☐   fetbar;
- prioritized choice by channel, ⇸   modified fetbar;
- non-deterministic choice,   ⊓   piebar.

Choice by input occurs when two or more different values input on a given channel lead to different behaviour in the receiving process. The notation here is:

$$P = (x \rightarrow Q \mid y \rightarrow R \ldots)$$

where x and y are distinct events on the same entry channel.

Choice by channel occurs when the behaviour of a process is decided by which of a number of entry channels is first ready to transmit. The notation is

$$P = (x \rightarrow Q \,\square\, y \rightarrow R \ldots)$$

where x and y are events on distinct entry channels. The choice notations can be extended for choice among more than two inputs.

Non-determinism is something which refinement strives to remove, though we shall see its usefulness later in deadlock analysis.

9 COMBINATIONS OF NON-INTERACTING PROCESSES

We have so far seen how a process may be analysed, using prefixing, in terms of the first event in which it may engage. In particular, we have seen that the first event might not be determined uniquely, in which case there is an element of choice in how the process continues to evolve. In the next two chapters we shall discuss ways in which two or more subprocesses may be combined to form a composite process. If we consider a set of terminating subprocesses, amongst which there is no communication, one way of combining them is to perform them one after another, and treat the resulting sequence of events as a single process. Alternatively, a process may consist of several subprocesses combined in parallel, each evolving at its own pace.

We leave until Chapter 10 the most interesting case of several subprocesses evolving concurrently and communicating with each other.

9.1 Sequential composition of processes

We may be interested in a process that can be analysed as a sequence of subprocesses. For example, a compiler for a programming language will include a lexical analyser, a syntax analyser and a code generator. In a simple compiler these three subprocesses might take place in strict sequence. Thus the syntax analyser is invoked on successful termination of the lexical analyser, and, following successful termination of the syntax analyser, the code generator is invoked.

Given two processes P and Q with the same alphabet, we write:

$P\,;Q$

for their *sequential composition*. This combined process behaves like P until P successfully terminates with a *SKIP*, and then behaves like Q. If P fails to terminate successfully, so does the process $P\,;Q$ without ever reaching any of the events in Q.

Suppose, for example, that P and Q are two processes with the alphabet $\{a, b\}$. If:

$P = a \rightarrow SKIP$

and

$Q = b \rightarrow SKIP$

then

$P\,;Q = a \rightarrow b \rightarrow SKIP$

The intermediate *SKIP* does not appear in the sequential composition of *P* and *Q*. (It signifies the successful termination of *P*.)

Example

9.1 Consider the process:

TEA_FOR_TWO =
   (*coinslot.10p* → *hatch.tea* → *coinslot.10p* → *hatch.tea* → *SKIP*)

with alphabet:

   {*coinslot.10p, hatch.tea* }

This can be considered as a repetition of the process:

TEA_FOR_ONE = (*coinslot.10p* → *hatch.tea* → *SKIP*)

as follows. *TEA_FOR_TWO* is identical to the composite process:

TEA_FOR_ONE ; *TEA_FOR_ONE*
   = (*coinslot.10p* → *hatch.tea* → *SKIP*) ; (*coinslot.10p* → *hatch.tea* → *SKIP*)
   = *coinslot.10p* → *hatch.tea* → *coinslot.10p* → *hatch.tea* → *SKIP*

□

Review Question 9.1 Specify the process *TEA_FOR_THREE* in terms of *TEA_FOR_ONE* and *TEA_FOR_TWO*.

Review Question 9.2 In Section 8.3 we discussed a change-giving vending machine. Suppose:

   DISPENSE = *hatch.tea* → *SKIP*

and *CHANGE* is defined as in Example 8.3. Use sequential composition to specify a machine which dispenses tea and gives change, in that order.

Review Question 9.3 Consider the process *PROGRAM* of Chapter 6. By defining a suitable subprocess *LOAD_AND_RUN*, decompose *PROGRAM* into a sequential combination of processes, using CSP box notation.

Rules for sequential composition

We may use sequential composition as a tool in the top-down analysis of a process, if we can identify a suitable sequence of subprocesses. In doing so, we must be sure that the resulting sequence of subprocesses meets the same specification as the original top-level process. In proving that two process designs meet the same specification, it is helpful to have some formal rules.

We list here a few elementary rules for sequential composition.

For any process P, we have:

$SKIP ; P = P$ **SKIP rule**

$STOP ; P = STOP$ **STOP rule**

The meaning of these should be clear—after *SKIP* you can carry on immediately, while *STOP* stops you in your tracks permanently.

For prefixing we have the following rule (provided $a \in \alpha P$):

$(a \rightarrow SKIP) ; P = a \rightarrow P$ **prefix rule**

Note that the prefix arrow on the left-hand side of this equation takes precedence over the sequencing operator (;), so that the parentheses could safely be omitted.

It is also necessary to consider the possible need for parentheses when combining several processes—is sequential composition associative? Thus, does:

$P ; Q ; R$

mean

$(P ; Q) ; R$

or does it mean

$P ; (Q ; R)$?

The short answer is that it does not matter, because:

$(P ; Q) ; R = P ; (Q ; R)$ **associative rule**

To see this, consider the composite processes defined by each side of the equation. Observe that the order in which events occur in each process is the same, and so each side consists of the sequence of events in P leading to successful termination, followed by the sequence of events in Q leading to successful termination, followed by the sequence of events in R leading to successful termination. Sequential combinations of processes are dependent only on the order of the processes in the final combination, and not on the order in which this combination is built up. In particular, note that if:

$P = a \rightarrow SKIP, Q = b \rightarrow SKIP$ and $R = c \rightarrow SKIP$

then

$P ; Q ; R = a \rightarrow b \rightarrow c \rightarrow SKIP$

Review Question 9.4 Specify *TEA_FOR_THREE* in terms of *TEA_FOR_ONE*.

□

Exercises

9.1 Prove that, for any two processes P and Q and any event a such that $a \in \alpha P$ $(= \alpha Q)$:

$(a \rightarrow P) ; Q = a \rightarrow (P ; Q)$

Solution 9.1 By the prefix rule:

$$a \to P = a \to SKIP\,;\,P$$

Therefore:

$$\begin{aligned}(a \to P)\,;\,Q &= (a \to SKIP\,;\,P)\,;\,Q \\ &= a \to SKIP\,;\,(P\,;\,Q) \quad \text{by the associative rule} \\ &= a \to (P\,;\,Q) \quad \text{by the prefix rule}\end{aligned}$$

The meaning of this rule is that the process $a \to P$ followed by Q has the same effect as the composite process $P\,;\,Q$ prefixed by a. Thus the brackets are unnecessary—events can only happen in the obvious order.

9.2 Consider the process:

$$PROGRAM = load.code \to run\_program \to print.results \to SKIP$$

Use the rules to show that:

$$PROGRAM\,;\,SKIP = PROGRAM$$

Solution 9.2 Using the result of Exercise 9.1:

$$(a \to P)\,;\,SKIP = a \to (P\,;\,SKIP) \qquad (*)$$

Since:
$$\begin{aligned}&PROGRAM\,;\,SKIP \\ &= load.code \to (run\_program \to print.results \to SKIP)\,;\,SKIP \\ &= load.code \to (run\_program \to print.results \to SKIP\,;\,SKIP) \quad \text{by }(*) \\ &= load.code \to (run\_program \to (print.results \to SKIP)\,;\,SKIP) \\ &= load.code \to (run\_program \to (print.results \to SKIP\,;\,SKIP)) \\ &= load.code \to (run\_program \to (print.results \to SKIP)) \quad \text{by the prefix rule} \\ &= PROGRAM\end{aligned}$$

The method of Solution 9.2 can be adapted to prove the general rule

$$P\,;\,SKIP = P$$

We shall take this as the other half of the *SKIP* rule. Its meaning is that sequential composition with another process, which does nothing but terminates successfully, achieves nothing new.

On the other hand, we can say little in general about $P\,;\,STOP$. We are unlikely to wish to specify such a process except possibly as a diagnostic to step through the execution of some bigger process (on successful completion of P this would force a 'crash').

Sequential combination and alphabets

We shall now examine how sequential composition may be used in a bottom-up development of a process description. We shall see that it is necessary to exercise care, as the two processes to be composed may well have different alphabets.

Example

9.2 Turning aside from the rather impersonal world of vending machines, let us consider the everyday process of having dinner. The activities involved might form the alphabet:

$$A = \{lay\_table, eat\_food, clear\_table\}$$

and the process itself be written:

$$DINNER = lay\_table \rightarrow eat\_food \rightarrow clear\_table \rightarrow SKIP_A$$

Note that we have identified the alphabet of *SKIP* explicitly.

A sad consequence of eating is having to do the washing-up. This process is defined by:

$$WASH\_UP = wash\_dishes \rightarrow dry\_dishes \rightarrow put\_away \rightarrow SKIP_B$$

with alphabet:

$$B = \{wash\_dishes, dry\_dishes, put\_away\}$$

We might now want to define the composite process:

$$DINNER\_AND\_WASH = DINNER \,;\, WASH\_UP$$

But there is a problem with the alphabet. What alphabet does the process *DINNER_AND_WASH* possess? It should be clear that *DINNER_AND_WASH* engages in each of the events in the combined alphabet:

$$A \cup B = \{lay\_table, eat\_food, clear\_table, \\ wash\_dishes, dry\_dishes, put\_away\}$$

Thus, in order to be able to define *DINNER_AND_WASH* by sequential composition, we redefine the alphabets of the processes *DINNER* and *WASH_UP* so that they are both $A \cup B$.

□

In general, a new process defined by sequential composition has the union of the alphabets of its subprocesses as its alphabet. In order to define the process $P \,;\, Q$ we require:

$$\alpha P = \alpha Q = \alpha(P \,;\, Q)$$

9.2 Interleaved processes

As well as considering sequential composition, which we have defined in the previous section, we may sometimes wish to consider two or more processes, which are proceeding simultaneously, to be a single process. In this case the individual processes are running *concurrently*, or *in parallel*. We shall consider here the less interesting case of parallel composition where the processes proceed independently, without influencing each other's behaviour. Parallel composition of communicating processes, which is the underlying theme of this book, will be discussed in Chapter 10.

For the purposes of this discussion, we return to vending machines. Consider the case where two tea machines are standing side by side (Figure 9.1).

The machines are outwardly indistinguishable. We shall label them as L(eft) and R(ight), and assume that each has the individual behaviour of *TEA_FOR_ONE*. To avoid ambiguity we define the channels as $coinslot_L$ and $hatch_L$ for the left-hand machine and $coinslot_R$ and $hatch_R$ for the right-hand machine. Thus we have:

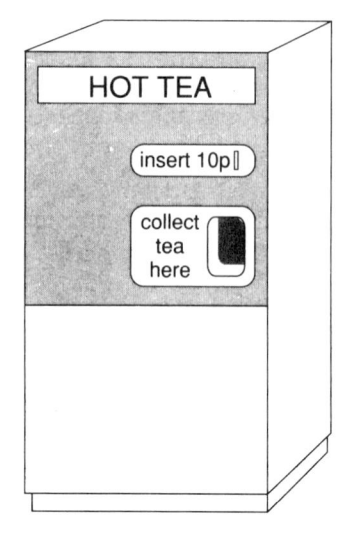

$$TEA_L = (coinslot_L.10p \rightarrow hatch_L.tea \rightarrow SKIP)$$

$$TEA_R = (coinslot_R.10p \rightarrow hatch_R.tea \rightarrow SKIP)$$

If we wish to consider tea-vending in this context as a single process then we may do so by using the **interleaving operator** |||, whose formal syntax is as follows. The process:

$P \;|||\; Q$ (read as 'P interleave Q')

engages in each of the events of each of the processes P and Q, and in no other event. The events of each of P and Q take place in their correct sequence, but, subject to this condition, the events of Q may be interleaved with the events of P in any fashion. Since the combined process can engage in all the events of its individual components, we impose the requirement:

$$\alpha(P \;|||\; Q) = \alpha P \cup \alpha Q$$

The interleaving operator is used to specify concurrency without communication. For our pair of vending machines, we may write:

$$DOUBLE\_TEA = TEA_L \;|||\; TEA_R$$

The combined process DOUBLE_TEA terminates when both TEA_L and TEA_R have terminated.

Review Question 9.5 Give the alphabet of DOUBLE_TEA.

Exercise
9.3 Suppose two processes are defined as follows:

$P = p \rightarrow SKIP$
$Q = q \rightarrow SKIP$

where p and q are internal events. What successful traces of $P \;|||\; Q$ are possible?

Solution 9.3 The behaviour of $P \;|||\; Q$ is given by either:

$$p \to q \to SKIP$$

or

$$q \to p \to SKIP$$

The traces $<p, q>\checkmark$ and $<q, p>\checkmark$ are both possible successful traces.

☐

Let us now consider the behaviour of *DOUBLE_TEA*, which is an interleaving of two processes that can each communicate with the environment. *DOUBLE_TEA* is the process that consists of TEA_L and TEA_R running asynchronously, with no communication between them. We may describe the behaviour of *DOUBLE_TEA* by attempting to list its traces. As usual, the initial trace is $<>$. The next event is when a customer arrives and inserts a coin in one of the machines. How this selection is made is beyond the control of the process *DOUBLE_TEA*. Thus both the following are allowable traces:

$$<coinslot_L.10p>, <coinslot_R.10p>$$

Following either of these traces there is again a choice of possible events. Suppose the customer chose TEA_R, so that the current trace is $<coinslot_R.10p>$. The next event is either the delivery of tea from $hatch_R$, or the insertion of a coin by a customer in TEA_L.[1] (TEA_R will never accept another coin.) Thus there are two possible extensions of our trace:

$$<coinslot_R.10p, coinslot_L.10p>$$

or

$$<coinslot_R.10p, hatch_R.tea> \qquad (*)$$

In the former case a further choice is possible. Unknown to us (and in any case not in our alphabet, and therefore beyond our present analysis), TEA_R might be slower at preparing the tea for dispatch. In this case, the next trace will be:

$$<coinslot_R.10p, coinslot_L.10p, hatch_L.tea>$$

If on the other hand TEA_R delivers first, the next trace is:

$$<coinslot_R.10p, coinslot_L.10p, hatch_R.tea>$$

For each of these traces there is a unique extension to the trace, namely that the second cup of tea is delivered.

Let us now consider the case (*) above, in which TEA_R has delivered its tea. Since TEA_R has no further event to engage in, the next event of *DOUBLE_TEA* must be $coinslot_L.10p$, and its subsequent behaviour is just that of TEA_L. Note carefully that the event $hatch_R.tea$ does not lead immediately to the successful conclusion of the process *DOUBLE_TEA*. Although TEA_R has completed its sequence of events and can now proceed to a successful conclusion, we are considering the composite process *DOUBLE_TEA* that does not terminate successfully until it has completed the sequences of events of *both* TEA_L and TEA_R.

---

[1] We discount the possibility of both events occurring simultaneously, since we have no notion of global time.

Thus the subsequent traces of (*) will eventually lead to:

$\langle coinslot_R.10p, hatch_R.tea, coinslot_L.10p, hatch_L.tea \rangle \checkmark$

This trace does represent a successful outcome of the parallel process. This illustrates an important point which you should always bear in mind:

> A parallel composition of processes does not terminate until all its component processes have terminated; a composite process terminates *successfully* only if each component process does so.

In summary, the following three successful traces of DOUBLE_TEA can arise beginning with the event $coinslot_R.10p$:

$\langle coinslot_R.10p, coinslot_L.10p, hatch_L.tea, hatch_R.tea \rangle \checkmark$
$\langle coinslot_R.10p, coinslot_L.10p, hatch_R.tea, hatch_L.tea \rangle \checkmark$
$\langle coinslot_R.10p, hatch_L.tea, coinslot_L.10p, hatch_L.tea \rangle \checkmark$

There is a similar set of traces that begin with the event $coinslot_L.10p$.

Thus the behaviour of DOUBLE_TEA incorporates both the processes TEA_L and TEA_R. The order in which events occur is arbitrary, subject only to the constraints imposed by the internal behaviour of each constituent process.

Exercise

9.4 Suppose that, owing to a wiring fault, the two tea machines have been interlinked so that neither can deliver tea until coins have been inserted in both of them. Use the interleaving operator to give a CSP specification of the process HATCHES that describes the behaviour of the machines after both coins have been inserted.

Solution 9.4

$HATCHES = (hatch_L.tea \rightarrow SKIP) \;|||\; (hatch_R.tea \rightarrow SKIP)$

$\square$

The behaviour of the linked tea machine of Exercise 9.4 can now be given in terms of choice by channel, as follows:

$LINKED\_TEA = coinslot_L.10p \rightarrow (coinslot_R.10p \rightarrow HATCHES)$
$\square$
$coinslot_R.10p \rightarrow (coinslot_L.10p \rightarrow HATCHES)$

The interleaving operator obeys the following two rules, whose meaning should be fairly obvious:

$P \;|||\; Q = Q \;|||\; P$
$P \;|||\; SKIP = P$

9.3 Summary

In this chapter we have introduced two operator symbols for processes that do not communicate—sequencing (;) and interleaving (|||). These operators may be used either to refine a process design in top-down fashion, or to build a process bottom-up from given component processes.

If P and Q are processes with the same alphabet then $P\ ;\ Q$ is a process, with the same alphabet, which behaves first like P and then (assuming P terminates successfully) like Q.

If P and Q have disjoint alphabets, then $P \,|||\, Q$ is a process with alphabet $\alpha P \cup \alpha Q$ and it represents the interleaved operation of P and Q.

10 COMPOSITION OF INTERACTING PROCESSES

We are now going to introduce the *concurrency operator* ||, which combines two (or more) processes that run concurrently and can communicate. This is probably the most important operator that we shall study, and you should make sure that you understand this chapter thoroughly.

In order to illustrate the ideas, we shall consider a number of instances of vending machines that communicate with a variety of customer processes.

10.1 Parallelism and traces

Given two communicating processes P and Q, the communication events must be in both alphabets, αP and αQ. As before we shall write $c.v$ to denote a communication of the value v on channel c, and we do not distinguish symbolically between input events and output events. Much of the groundwork has already been done. We have our model of communication in which processes temporarily synchronize their behaviour to permit a communication event in which both participate. For internal events the processes are free to proceed asynchronously.

Let us take as a specific example the interaction of a customer with a vending machine. We shall specify the behaviour of the customer and the machine as a pair of communicating processes, and we shall describe the whole system as the concurrent composition of these two processes. In order to make clear what is happening, we shall allow both customer and machine to engage in internal events in addition to their mutual communications.

Let *NOISY* represent the behaviour of a new model of tea machine, with alphabet:

$\alpha NOISY = \{coinslot.10p, hatch.tea, clink\}$

and specification:

$NOISY = coinslot.10p \rightarrow clink \rightarrow hatch.tea \rightarrow SKIP$

Now consider a happy customer who whistles after inserting a coin, whilst awaiting delivery of tea. The alphabet is:

$\alpha\,HAPPY = \{coinslot.10p, whistle, hatch.tea\}$

and the specification is given by:

$HAPPY = coinslot.10p \rightarrow whistle \rightarrow hatch.tea \rightarrow SKIP$

The process network for the combined parallel process is illustrated in Figure 10.1. We write:

$HAPPY \parallel NOISY$

for the combined process.

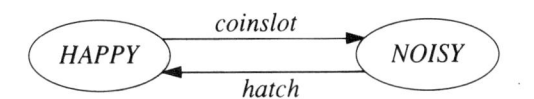

Figure 10.1

The alphabet of the combined process $HAPPY \parallel NOISY$ must include all the events that either might engage in. We therefore write:

$\alpha\,(HAPPY \parallel NOISY) = \alpha\,HAPPY \cup \alpha\,NOISY$

The behaviour of $HAPPY \parallel NOISY$ is as follows. The first event in each process is the communication event *coinslot.10p*, and this is synchronized: neither process can start without the other. After this event has taken place, the processes run asynchronously and an observer might record either *whistle* or *clink*. These events may actually appear to be simultaneous, but the observer who is recording the trace will still have to choose which one to record first. Suppose *whistle* is chosen. Then the trace of $HAPPY \parallel NOISY$ up to this point is:

<*coinslot.10p, whistle*>

The customer's next event is *hatch.tea*, but this is a communication which requires the synchronous participation of *NOISY*. The process *NOISY* is not able to engage in this event until it has performed *clink*, so the next trace must be:

<*coinslot.10p, whistle, clink*>

After this, both processes are able to participate in *hatch.tea*, so the terminal trace will be:

<*coinslot.10p, whistle, clink, hatch.tea*>✓

Review Question 10.1 What is the other possible terminal trace of $HAPPY \parallel NOISY$?

So the behaviour of a process $P \parallel Q$ is defined to incorporate the sequences of events of the two processes P and Q, subject to the following two caveats. Whenever a communication is due to take place, both P and Q must be ready to participate in the event. As far as internal events are concerned, these are interleaved as described in Section 9.2.

Correspondingly, in a trace of the composite process, a communication event shows up as a single event.

Returning to our example, if we define processes *CLINK* and *WHISTLE* by:

$$CLINK = clink \rightarrow SKIP$$

and

$$WHISTLE = whistle \rightarrow SKIP$$

then we can write:

$HAPPY \| NOISY =$
  $coinslot.10p \rightarrow (CLINK \,\|\|\, WHISTLE\,); (hatch.tea \rightarrow SKIP)$

Review Question 10.2 In the expansion of *HAPPY* ‖ *NOISY* above, why is the sequencing operator ; used before *hatch.tea* and not the prefix operator?

Exercise

10.1 Consider a chocolate-bar dispenser *CHOC* with alphabet:

$\alpha CHOC = \{coinslot.10p, clink, tray.choc, clunk\}$

and description:

$CHOC = coinslot.10p \rightarrow clink \rightarrow clunk \rightarrow tray.choc \rightarrow SKIP$

A hungry customer is specified by the process *HUNGRY* with alphabet:

$\alpha HUNGRY = \{coinslot.10p, slurp, mutter, tray.choc\}$

and description:

$HUNGRY = slurp \rightarrow coinslot.10p \rightarrow mutter \rightarrow tray.choc \rightarrow SKIP$

By defining suitable subprocesses, expand the specification of $HUNGRY \| CHOC$.

Solution 10.1 The alphabet of the composite process is:

$\alpha(HUNGRY \| CHOC\,)$
  $= \alpha HUNGRY \cup \alpha CHOC$
  $= \{coinslot.10p, slurp, mutter, tray.choc, clink, clunk\}$

The first event to be recorded will be *slurp*. Although *CHOC* is prepared to engage in *coinslot.10p* immediately, *HUNGRY* must perform *slurp* first. After this, the synchronized event *coinslot.10p* will occur. We cannot predict exactly what happens next. Each of the following sequences of events is possible:

  $mutter \rightarrow clink \rightarrow clunk$

  $clink \rightarrow mutter \rightarrow clunk$

  $clink \rightarrow clunk \rightarrow mutter$

Whichever sequence takes place, the following event will be *tray.choc*. By introducing the processes:

$CLONK = clink \rightarrow clunk \rightarrow SKIP$

and

$$MUTTER = mutter \to SKIP$$

we can write:

$$HUNGRY \parallel CHOC =$$
$$slurp \to coinslot.10p \to (CLONK \mid\mid\mid MUTTER) ; (tray.choc \to SKIP)$$

☐

Review Question 10.3 What are the possible terminal traces of *HUNGRY* ∥ *CHOC*?

☐

10.2 Parallelism and choice

We shall now extend our discussion of parallel composition to include processes that involve the use of choice operators. Here again, the key to successful interpretation is to adhere strictly to the synchronization of communications.

Example

10.1 Consider a chocolate/toffee machine which is unable to offer its normal choice of products because it has run out of chocolate. The machine will indicate to a customer who requires chocolate that none is available by emitting an audible beep; we shall name the channel for the sound output *noise*. A process network is shown in Figure 10.2.

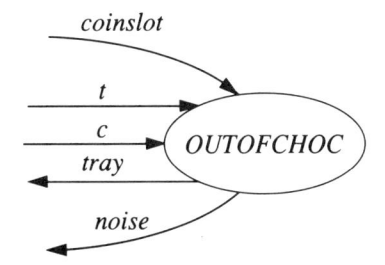

Figure 10.2

Here is a specification for the process:

```
┌─────── OUTOFCHOC ───────
│ {coinslot.10p, c.press, noise.beep, t.press, tray.choc, tray.toffee}
│
│ coinslot.10p →
│     (t.press → tray.toffee → SKIP
│     []
│     c.press → noise.beep → t.press → tray.toffee → SKIP)
```

Next let us consider a fussy customer who prefers chocolate, but is prepared as a last resort to accept toffee. The customer is aware that machines of this type will give an audible signal if they have no chocolate. A process network for the customer is shown in Figure 10.3.

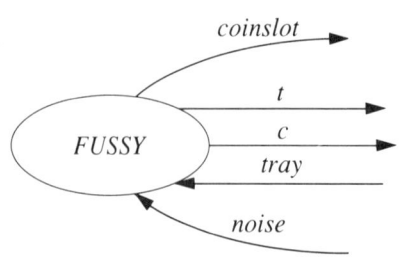

118　SPECIFICATION AND DESIGN OF CONCURRENT SYSTEMS

Figure 10.3

The alphabet of the customer includes the internal events *grin* and *curse* to cover the customer's reaction to the ability of the machine in meeting his preference. Here is a suitable specification for the customer process:

FUSSY

{*coinslot.10p, t.press, c.press, tray.choc, tray.toffee, noise.beep, grin, curse* }

coinslot.10p → *c.press* →
　(*tray.choc* → *grin* → *SKIP*
　▯
　noise.beep → *curse* → *t.press* → *tray.toffee* → *SKIP*)

We now wish to consider the composite process whose behaviour describes the interaction between the machine with no chocolate and the fussy customer. The two process networks are merged using the communication channels, as shown in Figure 10.4. Note that each channel is an exit channel from one of the processes and an entry channel to the other.

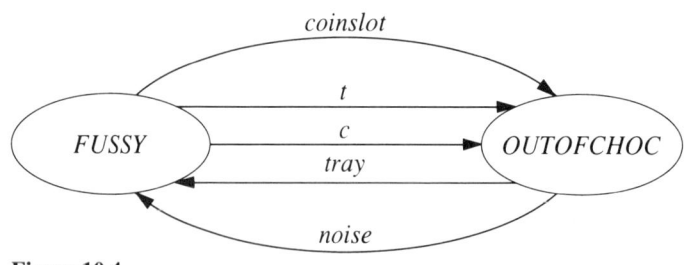

Figure 10.4

The behaviour of this combined process is specified by the parallel combination:

　OUTOFCHOC ∥ *FUSSY*

The first event in this process must be *coinslot.10p*, which is the first event in each of the component processes. The next event in *OUTOFCHOC* depends on a choice, which is exercised by *FUSSY* as the event *c.press*. In a concurrent process, choice by channel in one constituent (the receiving process) may be exercised by a specific communication event in the other (the sending process). The next choice by channel, in *FUSSY*, is exercised by the process *OUTOFCHOC*, which is committed to the event *noise.beep*. Now the choices in both processes have been exercised, so the remaining behaviour is fully determined. We see therefore that the only possible outcome is as follows, in which all communication events are acceptable to both *OUTOFCHOC* and *FUSSY*:

coinslot.10p →
    c.press → *noise.beep* → *curse* → *t.press* → *tray.toffee* → *SKIP*

In more general circumstances, parallel composition of processes involving choice will not necessarily result in uniquely determined behaviour; there may still be some element of interleaving. The method used here to reduce the specification of the process *OUTOFCHOC* ∥ *FUSSY* may be formalized in the following rules, which apply in general to combinations of concurrent processes. ☐

Rules for the concurrency operator ∥

In the following rules, P and Q are processes linked by the channels c and d, which carry messages from P to Q, and i is an internal event of the process P, that is, $i \in \alpha P$ but $i \notin \alpha Q$.

If the first event of each of two components in a concurrent combination is the same (communication) event, then both processes will engage in that event before engaging in any other:

$(c.v → P) \parallel (c.v → Q) = c.v → (P \parallel Q)$ *communication rule*

If the first event of one component of a concurrent combination is an internal event, that event will take place before there is any communication between the component processes.

$(i → P) \parallel (c.v → Q) = i → (P \parallel (c.v → Q))$ if $i \in \alpha P \setminus \alpha Q$
                                                                          internal event rule

If the first event of one component of a concurrent process combination is an output communication event and the first event of the component process that receives the communication is a choice by channel, the sending process will determine the choice:

$(c.v → P) \parallel (c.v → Q \,\square\, d.w → R) = c.v → (P \parallel Q)$ *choice-by-channel rule*

We remark that it does not matter in which order component processes are written when they are combined with the concurrency operator:

$P \parallel Q = Q \parallel P$ *commutativity rule*

The concurrency operator extends naturally to three or more concurrent processes, in which case the order of writing is immaterial. Thus:

$P \parallel Q \parallel R = P \parallel R \parallel Q = R \parallel Q \parallel P$

and so on; each of these expressions stands for the combination of processes P, Q, and R that are taking place concurrently.

Exercise

10.2 Formalize the reduction of the process description for *OUTOFCHOC* ∥ *FUSSY* using the rules, until the first three events are determined.

Solution 10.2 Let:

$P = tray.toffee → SKIP$

and

$$Q = noise.beep \to t.press \to tray.toffee \to SKIP$$

so that

$$OUTOFCHOC = coinslot.10p \to (t.press \to P \,[]\, c.press \to Q)$$

Similarly, let:

$$R = grin \to SKIP$$

and

$$S = curse \to t.press \to tray.toffee \to SKIP$$

so that

$$FUSSY = coinslot.10p \to c.press \to (tray.choc \to R \,[]\, noise.beep \to S).$$

Applying the communication rule, we obtain the following:

$$OUTOFCHOC \parallel FUSSY$$
$$= coinslot.10p \to$$
$$((t.press \to P \,[]\, c.press \to Q) \parallel$$
$$c.press \to (tray.choc \to R \,[]\, noise.beep \to S))$$

We continue by applying the commutativity rule and the choice by channel rule to the process following the event *coinslot.10p*. This gives us:

$$OUTOFCHOC \parallel FUSSY$$
$$= coinslot.10p \to$$
$$(c.press \to (Q \parallel (tray.choc \to R \,[]\, noise.beep \to S)))$$

Writing out Q in full, this becomes:

$$OUTOFCHOC \parallel FUSSY$$
$$= coinslot.10p \to c.press \to$$
$$((noise.beep \to t.press \to tray.toffee \to SKIP) \parallel$$
$$(tray.choc \to R \,[]\, noise.beep \to S))$$
$$= coinslot.10p \to c.press \to noise.beep \to$$
$$((t.press \to tray.toffee \to SKIP) \parallel S)$$

where the second equality is obtained by the choice-by-channel rule.

□

The reduction begun in Solution 10.2 could be continued until the evolution of the whole process is determined. As you can see, formal application of the rules is quite tedious. We shall mostly use informal arguments in our discussion of concurrent processes, relying on our ability to formalize our argument using the rules as necessary.

Review Question 10.4 Consider an extremely selective customer and a noisy chocolate/toffee machine which is bereft of chocolate; their behaviour is specified by the following processes:

VERYFUSSY
$$= coinslot.10p \to c.press \to$$
$$(tray.choc \to grin \to SKIP$$
$$\square$$
$$noise.beep \to curse \to groan \to t.press \to tray.toffee \to SKIP)$$

NOISY
$$= coinslot.10p \to$$
$$(t.press \to tray.toffee \to SKIP$$
$$\square$$
$$c.press \to noise.beep \to whirr \to t.press \to tray.toffee \to SKIP)$$

What are the possible successful traces of *VERYFUSSY* ‖ *NOISY*?

(Note that the inclusion of the additional internal events *groan,* and *whirr* does not alter the process networks.)

Exercise

10.3 Consider a tea machine that requires prior payment, and a suspicious customer who requires tea before payment. The process description is as follows:

$\alpha\,TEAONLY = \alpha\,SUSPICIOUS = \{t.press, coinslot.10p, hatch.tea\}$

$TEAONLY = t.press \to coinslot.10p \to hatch.tea \to SKIP$

$SUSPICIOUS = t.press \to hatch.tea \to coinslot.10p \to SKIP$

Describe the behaviour of the parallel combination given below:

TEAONLY ‖ *SUSPICIOUS*

Solution 10.3 In this case the two alphabets coincide; however, all that the parallel processes can agree on is the first communication *t.press*. Then one wants to receive the money, by the event *coinslot.10p*, while the other wants the tea, by the event *hatch.tea*. These are events in both alphabets, so they refer to communication and can only occur when both processes agree to participate. Since they cannot agree which to do next we have reached a state of deadlock. Hence we write:

TEAONLY ‖ *SUSPICIOUS* $= t.press \to STOP$

The final *STOP* tells us that the combined process can proceed no further.

The result of this exercise can be formalized as follows. If c and d are channels linking the processes P and Q, so that the events $c.v$ and $d.w$ belong to both αP and αQ, then:

$(c.v \to P) \,\|\, (d.w \to Q) = STOP$ **deadlock rule**

SKIP and STOP rules for concurrency

To complete the discussion, we shall take a brief look at the behaviour of concurrent processes when one of the components is *SKIP* or *STOP*.

For example, consider $SKIP_A \,\|\, SKIP_B$, where A and B are any two alphabets. Since there are no communications, this process cannot deadlock; and since the constituent processes terminate successfully, so does the composite process. In fact, this is all that happens, so the overall process is *SKIP* with a suitable alphabet. By the defining rule for the concurrency operator || the alphabet of the combined process is $A \cup B$, so:

$$SKIP_A \| SKIP_B = SKIP_{A \cup B}$$

for any alphabets A and B.

What can we say about the process:

$$(a \rightarrow SKIP_A) \| SKIP_B$$

There are two possibilities here. If a is an internal event of A, that is, not a communication included in $A \cap B$, then a is free to occur and is the only event that can occur, after which the process reaches a successful conclusion. So

$$(a \rightarrow SKIP_A) \| SKIP_B = a \rightarrow SKIP_{A \cup B}$$

when $a \in A$ and $a \notin B$. This is just an application of the internal event rule.

However, if a does occur as a communication event in the alphabets of A and B, then the left-hand process $a \rightarrow SKIP_A$ will never proceed, as the process $SKIP_B$ terminates successfully, and $SKIP_B$ will never engage in the communication that $a \rightarrow SKIP_A$ needs. Thus in this case we have:

$$(a \rightarrow SKIP_A) \| SKIP_B = STOP_{A \cup B}$$

when $a \in \alpha A \cap \alpha B$.

This means just what it says: since the processes cannot agree to terminate successfully together, neither is free to continue and the parallel composite process is in deadlock.

One more rule that may seem fairly intuitive is that if two processes are both deadlocked, then so is their parallel composite:

$$STOP_A \| STOP_B = STOP_{A \cup B}$$

More generally, a parallel combination is deadlocked if any component is deadlocked:

$$P \| STOP = STOP$$

10.3 Multiple parallel processes

As in the case of the choice operators, where we allow choice among several events, there is no need to restrict a parallel composition to just two processes. In fact a typical specification will be a parallel composition of many processes, some of which may themselves be parallel composites.

This is potentially more complicated, since now the communication channels between the processes may form a complex network. Nevertheless, the same principles as in the two-process case apply to interpreting the behaviour of the overall system. Processes are free to engage in internal events but must synchronize to communicate. In the case of more than two processes, however, the order of events appearing in traces can be indeterminate for communication events as well as for internal events. Since a communication event only engages two processes, there may be some interleaving of communication events between a given pair of components and the events of other component processes.

Example

10.2 Consider three processes *P1*, *P2* and *P3*, which each output their process number (1, 2 or 3) to each of their neighbours. To do this, they use a collection of channels $c[i, j]$ ($1 \le i \le 3$, $1 \le j \le 3$, $i \ne j$) as shown in Figure 10.5. We call such a systematic collection of channels a ***channel array***.

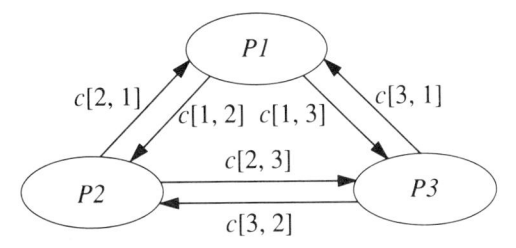

Figure 10.5

This is similar to the three-way conversation discussed in Chapter 2. Unless carefully handled, this is a potential source of deadlock—about which we shall have much to say later. In order to avoid deadlock, we can specify each process to be a parallel composition of component processes, as follows. Consider *P1*, and the events it is required to engage in. These are (in no particular order):

- output 1 to *P2* on $c[1, 2]$
- output 1 to *P3* on $c[1, 3]$
- input 2 from *P2* on $c[2, 1]$
- input 3 from *P3* on $c[3, 1]$

We define corresponding processes, thus:

- $P11 = (c[1, 2].1 \to SKIP)$
- $P12 = (c[1, 3].1 \to SKIP)$
- $P13 = (c[2, 1].2 \to SKIP)$
- $P14 = (c[3, 1].3 \to SKIP)$

We can now define *P1* by:

$$P1 = P11 \,|||\, P12 \,|||\, P13 \,|||\, P14$$

In isolation, *P1* will never get started because there would be no other process to communicate with. However if we define *P2* and *P3* in a similar fashion, the whole process can be specified as:

$$P = P1 \,\|\, P2 \,\|\, P3$$

There are many possible traces of this overall process. One possible initial pattern of behaviour is that *P1* and *P3* might first be observed to pass the value 3 on $c[3, 1]$. Whilst this is happening, neither can communicate with *P2*, which is temporarily suspended.

Eventually, it turns out, all the communication events will occur, and the overall process *P* will terminate successfully. Remember that a parallel composite process *does not terminate until all its component processes have terminated*. The usefulness of the interleaving operator ||| here is precisely to avoid imposing an ordering on the communication events, and it is this that actually guarantees the absence of deadlock. Our example is quite symmetric (apart from the actual values passed), and an order imposed at the specification stage would be wholly artificial.

You might like to contrast this example with the similar one in Chapter 5, where a bad attempt at ordering the communications can lead to deadlock!

□

Example 10.2 is a nice example of the freedom given by using a parallel specification, rather than imposing a fixed order on a situation where none is naturally apparent. Our formalism allows a system involving communication to be specified without building in any design decisions about the sequence in which communications take place. In fact, the requirement for a deadlock-free process drives the design and may eliminate many of the options. The formalism can then be used to generate the feasible options, if any.

Review Question 10.5 Specify the process *P3* in detail.

□

Note that when writing the parallel composite of several component processes, we do not bracket the components. When we write:

P1 || *P2* || *P3*

for example, we are referring to a process network of three communicating processes and considering them as a single unit. When we want to expand or simplify such composites we must consider the entire collection of communicating processes.

10.4 Summary

In this chapter we have seen how to combine processes using the concurrency operator (||).

If P and Q communicate, $P \| Q$ is a process with alphabet $\alpha P \cup \alpha Q$, and represents the concurrent operation of P and Q in which communication events are synchronized.

In attempting to unravel the behaviour of the parallel combination of two or more processes, we consider the first action in which each is able to engage. If this is an internal event, it can take place (at a time independent of events in all other processes). If it is a communication event, it will take place provided the partner to the communication is willing to do so. We may identify essentially three cases, as follows:

- If the next communication between two given processes is the same event, it can take place.
- If the receiver of the communication includes the event in a choice by channel, the sending process effectively exercises the choice by its need to participate in the communication.
- If two processes wish to communicate with each other, but cannot agree on the communication event, they become deadlocked.

11 INFINITE PROCESSES AND RECURSION

Up to now nearly all our examples have been of somewhat trivial, finite processes that lead through a set of events to either a successful conclusion, *SKIP* or, if the worst happens, *STOP*. This restriction is unsatisfactory because we may legitimately wish to describe a never-ending process.

As an example, consider again our drinks vending machine. We have resorted to various tactics to describe a machine which will deliver one, or two, or fifty, or, in fact, any fixed number of drinks. Now, in practice, it is true that a vending machine will deliver only as many drinks as it contains. But do we need to be concerned with this in a general sense? We can quite reasonably ignore the business of regularly restocking the machine. As far as the user is concerned, the machine should always be available for the supply of drinks. If indeed it does run out, it is effectively broken. So the customer is really interested in a machine which provides an uninterrupted supply; the mechanism of maintaining this supply is someone else's problem. There are many similar situations where we wish to specify an ever-repeating process and we address this topic in this chapter.

11.1 Recursive processes

In order to be able to discuss recursive processes, we shall introduce a suitable notation. Before giving a CSP formulation for an inexhaustible vending machine, we shall introduce the notation in the context of a clock, which alternately emits the sounds 'tick' and 'tock' forever. (We ignore such tedious matters as rewinding or new batteries at this level of abstraction.) The process network for the clock process is shown in Figure 11.1.

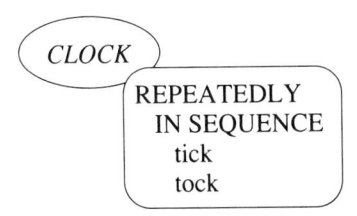

```
CLOCK
    REPEATEDLY
    IN SEQUENCE
        tick
        tock
```

Figure 11.1

Let the process that describes the behaviour of the clock be called *CLOCK*. We shall investigate the specification of the process *CLOCK*. To start with, we take:

$\alpha CLOCK = \{tick, tock\}$

(We could be more precise by treating the events as outputs on a sound channel to the environment, but for the present we shall keep the example as simple as possible.)

The real problem comes when we try to specify the process *CLOCK*. The process annotation suggests that we write:

$CLOCK = (tick \rightarrow tock \rightarrow tick \rightarrow tock \rightarrow tick \rightarrow tock \rightarrow \ldots)$

However, the meaning of the dots for indefinite repetition is not adequate if we are to use our specification in a rigorous analysis. The problem is that the qualifier REPEATEDLY that we use informally does not translate into any of the formal CSP operators introduced so far. The way forward is to spot that after the first two events the above process is back where it was to start with. That is, we can write:

$CLOCK = tick \rightarrow tock \rightarrow CLOCK$

This finite equation, together with the alphabet, characterizes the process *CLOCK*. There is one problem though—since *CLOCK* is defined implicitly (in terms of itself), can we be sure that there is only one process which has this property? In other words, if *PC* is another process with alphabet $\{tick, tock\}$, and specified by:

$PC = tick \rightarrow tock \rightarrow PC$

are we confident that *CLOCK* and *PC* are indeed the same process? Let us investigate the behaviour of *PC*. Clearly the first two events of *PC* are given by the trace:

<tick, tock>

What is the next event of *PC*? Well, the process *PC* on the right-hand side of the specification is the same as that on the left-hand side. In other words:

$PC = tick \rightarrow tock \rightarrow (tick \rightarrow tock \rightarrow PC)$

So the first four events of *PC* are given by the trace:

<tick, tock, tick, tock>

In fact, it rather looks as though the set of traces of *PC* is identical with the set of traces of *CLOCK*. Now, a process is characterized, in part at least, by its set of traces; so it looks as though *PC* and *CLOCK* are one and the same process.

This is only an informal proof that the two processes are the same. It is possible, though, to adopt an approach which enables one to prove formally that the two processes *CLOCK* and *PC*, defined as above, must be identical processes. We shall assume without further proof that recursive definitions of the above nature define processes uniquely.

The process *CLOCK* (or, equivalently, the process *PC*) may be said to *satisfy* the recursive definition:

$X = tick \rightarrow tock \rightarrow X$

Here *X* stands for an unnamed process; the definition is called recursive because *X* appears within the definition on the right-hand side. As stated above, we take it as axiomatic that the recursive definition of *X* is the complete definition of a process.

We shall find it convenient sometimes to have a self-contained notation for recursively specifying a process which does not yet have a name, in much the same way as we can specify a choice between processes or a parallel process without giving it a name. In CSP this is achieved using the μ *notation*. Thus, the process that satisfies the equation:

$X = tick \to tock \to X$

may be written:

$\mu X. tick \to tock \to X$

This is read as 'the process that begins with the event *tick* followed by the event *tock* and then starts again'. Note that we place a dot after the dummy symbol (X here) that serves as a local name for the process.

Using this notation, we can specify CLOCK as follows:

```
┌──── CLOCK ─────────────────────────┐
│  {tick, tock}                      │
├────────────────────────────────────┤
│  μX. tick → tock → X               │
└────────────────────────────────────┘
```

The process *PC* given above would have exactly the same definition. More generally, for any expression $F(X)$ which contains the symbol X, we write $\mu X_A. F(X)$ to specify the process with alphabet A and which satisfies the condition:

$X = F(X)$

As usual, the name of the alphabet may be omitted when it is clear from the context. Initially, $F(X)$ will be a simple expression involving one or more events prefixing X, but later we shall consider recursively defined processes that include choice by input value or channel and processes defined by sequential or parallel composition.

Review Question 11.1 A tea machine which never runs out of supplies is described by the process *TEA_FOR_EVER* with alphabet {*coinslot.10p, hatch.tea*}. Give a suitable process specification.

Exercise

11.1 The process *PPP* with alphabet $A = \{p\}$ is defined by

$PPP = \mu X_A. p \to X$

Determine the possible traces of P.

Solution 11.1 The traces of P are as follows.

$< >, <p>, <p, p>, <p, p, p>, <p, p, p, p>,$
$<p, p, p, p, p>, <p, p, p, p, p, p>, \ldots$

In other words, each trace consists of a finite number of occurrences of the event p.

Of course, the μ notation is only useful when it defines a unique process. There is no point in having a notation for a specification which is ambiguous and could apply to more than one process. Consider, for example, the process definition $\mu X_A . X$; this purports to specify a process with alphabet A which satisfies the equation:

$X = X$

Well, any process with the given alphabet satisfies this equation, so the formula does not actually specify a unique process.

It turns out that for a given class of expressions, the *guarded expressions*, the specification $\mu X_A . F(X)$ is well defined—provided $F(X)$ is a guarded expression, this specification does indeed yield a unique process. Guarded expressions were introduced in Section 8.1, and include expressions involving a choice of prefixed processes; where the number of choices is one, the expression is just a prefixed process, as in the specification of *CLOCK*. All the recursive definitions we permit will involve guarded expressions; we adopt as *axiomatic* that if two processes can be shown to satisfy the same guarded recursive definition then they are equivalent.

We make use of this property in the next example, which introduces *mutual recursion*, that is, a pair of processes defined in terms of each other.

Example

11.1 Consider the two processes *TICK* and *TOCK*, each of which has alphabet $\{tick, tock\}$. These processes satisfy the equations:

$TICK = tick \to TOCK$
$TOCK = tock \to TICK$

Using the condition satisfied by *TOCK*, the first equation can be rewritten:

$TICK = tick \to (tock \to TICK)$

Since parentheses may be removed from an expression with multiple prefixes, we see that both *TICK* and *CLOCK* satisfy the equation:

$X = tick \to tock \to X$

Thus the processes *TICK* and *CLOCK* are equivalent, both being given by the specification:

$\mu X . (tick \to tock \to X)$

We may therefore write:

$TICK = CLOCK$

□

Exercise

11.2 Show that the processes $(tock \to CLOCK)$ and *TOCK* are equivalent.

Solution 11.2 Since:

$CLOCK = tick \to tock \to CLOCK$

we have:

$tock \to CLOCK = tock \to (tick \to tock \to CLOCK)$

or, inserting suitable parentheses:

$(tock \rightarrow CLOCK) = tock \rightarrow tick \rightarrow (tock \rightarrow CLOCK)$

On the other hand:

$TOCK = tock \rightarrow TICK$
$= tock \rightarrow tick \rightarrow TOCK$

Hence both $TOCK$ and $(tock \rightarrow CLOCK)$ may be written as $\mu X.(tock \rightarrow tick \rightarrow X)$. Since $tock \rightarrow tick \rightarrow X$ is a guarded expression, we may deduce:

$TOCK = tock \rightarrow CLOCK$

that is, the processes $TOCK$ and $(tock \rightarrow CLOCK)$ are equivalent.

11.2 Recursion with choice

Recursive definitions become more complicated when the guarded expression takes the form of a choice rather than a simple sequence of prefixes. We shall examine choice by input value and by channel in turn.

Choice by input value

A vending machine which provides an uninterrupted supply of tea and coffee is described by the process *TCFE* (Tea or Coffee For Ever). Suppose we have:

$\alpha TCFE = \{coinslot.10p, coinslot.20p, hatch.tea, hatch.coffee\}$

and

$TCFE = (coinslot.10p \rightarrow hatch.tea \rightarrow TCFE$
$\qquad \mid$
$\qquad coinslot.20p \rightarrow hatch.coffee \rightarrow TCFE)$

We may express this in the μ notation as:

$TCFE = \mu X. (coinslot.10p \rightarrow hatch.tea \rightarrow X$
$\qquad \mid$
$\qquad coinslot.20p \rightarrow hatch.coffee \rightarrow X)$

Review Question 11.2 Identify the traces of *TCFE*.

So far we have given recursive definitions of processes that continue indefinitely. However, the notation can be used to specify a process which is also capable of successful termination. Termination will be achieved using a choice construct; one or more guards may lead to a terminating process. As an example, consider the process *AAAB*, with alphabet $\{a, b\}$, defined by:

$AAAB = \mu X.(b \rightarrow SKIP \mid a \rightarrow X)$

The effect of this recursively-defined process is to make an initial choice by input (|) between a and b. If b is chosen the process terminates successfully. If a is chosen the process repeats itself. To see what this process does, we shall examine its traces.

Review Question 11.3 Write out the first few traces of *AAAB*.

The complete set of traces of *AAAB* includes:

(a) the empty trace < >

(b) any arbitrarily long string of *a*s < *a, a, a, ..., a* >

(c) any arbitrarily long string of *a*s followed by one *b*, which successfully terminates the process: < *a, a, a, ..., a, b* >√

Notice that although the process is capable of terminating successfully, it might never terminate.

Choice by channel

We can apply a recursive specification in the case of choice by channel. We shall consider a computer game; after each game the user is offered the choice of another game or quitting. We suppose that the user exercises this choice by pressing the appropriate button.

Suppose the process *GAME* has alphabet:

$\alpha GAME = \{play, replay.press, quit.press\}$

and is specified by:

$GAME = play \rightarrow (replay.press \rightarrow GAME \,[]\, quit.press \rightarrow SKIP)$

You have to play at least once, and then have the choice of a replay or quitting.

Exercise

11.3 Specify *GAME* using the μ notation.

Solution 11.3

$GAME = \mu X. \, play \rightarrow (replay.press \rightarrow X \,[]\, quit.press \rightarrow SKIP)$

Review Question 11.4 A smoke alarm works by emitting a long-sounding buzz when smoke is detected. After such an occasion the alarm ends its useful life. The alarm has a battery tester: if the test button is depressed, the alarm emits a short buzz and then returns to its operational state.

Give a specification of the process *SMOKEALARM*, using channels *button* and *sensor* for the activating signals.

11.3 Sequential composition and recursion

Sequential composition of two processes gives us a process which behaves like the first process until its successful termination, and then behaves like the second process. If the first process fails to terminate successfully, the sequential composition behaves like the first process only. In particular, if *P* is a non-terminating process, then for any process *Q*

$P ; Q = P$

This means that the sequence of events in which $P \,;\, Q$ engages is identical to the sequence of events of P—the process Q is only invoked on successful termination of P, which never happens. Thus, for example, we may even write

$$CLOCK \,;\, STOP = CLOCK$$

Review question 11.5 Show that, for any process Q,

$$CLOCK \,;\, Q = CLOCK$$

(**Hint**: use the result of Exercise 9.1.) □

We shall now consider a rather complicated process specification which entails both sequential composition and choice.

The process *PPPQRRR* has alphabet $\{p, q, r\}$ and is specified by

$$\mu X.(q \rightarrow SKIP \mid p \rightarrow (X \,;\, r \rightarrow SKIP))$$

The effect of this is successively to choose n ps, then a single q, and then n rs (where n might possibly be zero). In other words, the successful traces of *PPPQRRR* will turn out to be

$$<q>\checkmark, <p, q, r>\checkmark, <p, p, q, r, r>\checkmark, <p, p, p, q, r, r, r>\checkmark, \ldots$$

By way of example, let us see how the last but one of the successful traces mentioned above is formed. We unfold the specification, making particular choices of the initial event. An initial choice of event p leads to the process:

$$p \rightarrow X \,;\, r \rightarrow SKIP$$

Since

$$X = (q \rightarrow SKIP \mid p \rightarrow (X \,;\, r \rightarrow SKIP))$$

the process becomes:

$$p \rightarrow (q \rightarrow SKIP \mid p \rightarrow (X \,;\, r \rightarrow SKIP)) \,;\, r \rightarrow SKIP$$

Exercising a second choice of p leads to:

$$p \rightarrow (p \rightarrow (X \,;\, r \rightarrow SKIP)) \,;\, r \rightarrow SKIP$$

Once again we can rewrite X; on this occasion, say, the event q is chosen so that X is replaced by $q \rightarrow SKIP$ and the whole expression becomes:

$$p \rightarrow (p \rightarrow (q \rightarrow SKIP \,;\, r \rightarrow SKIP)) \,;\, r \rightarrow SKIP$$
$$= p \rightarrow (p \rightarrow (q \rightarrow r \rightarrow SKIP) \,;\, r \rightarrow SKIP$$
$$= p \rightarrow p \rightarrow q \rightarrow r \rightarrow r \rightarrow SKIP$$

Hence our choices lead to an instance of the process with trace $<p, p, q, r, r>\checkmark$, as required.

11.4 Parallel composition and recursion

We now go on to consider concurrent non-terminating processes. If any process in a parallel composition is infinite, then so is the composite process (unless it is deadlocked). A simple example, which is also extremely useful, is a permanent buffer process, which repeatedly accepts a value on an entry channel and passes it to an exit channel.

Example

11.2 A one-place buffer has the following process network.

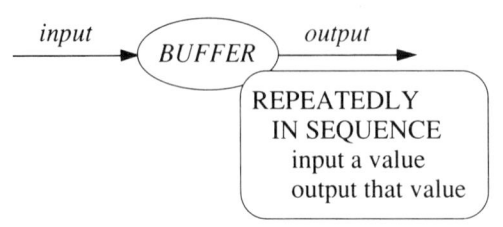

input → BUFFER → *output*

REPEATEDLY
IN SEQUENCE
input a value
output that value

Figure 11.2

Using the simple alphabet:

$$\{input.p, output.p, input.q, output.q, input.r, output.r\}$$

this process has the specification:

$$BUFFER = (input.p \rightarrow output.p \rightarrow BUFFER$$
$$|$$
$$input.q \rightarrow output.q \rightarrow BUFFER$$
$$|$$
$$input.r \rightarrow output.r \rightarrow BUFFER)$$

More formally, we may write:

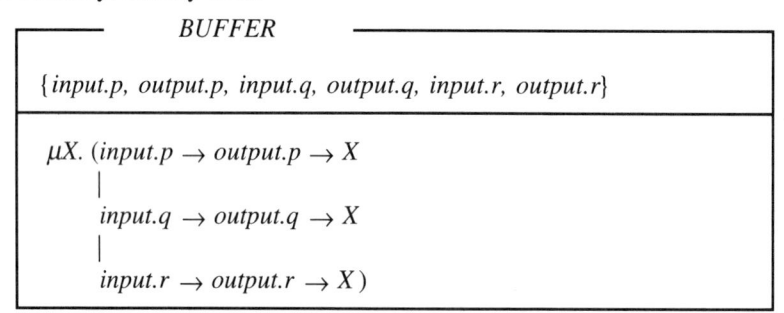

BUFFER

$\{input.p, output.p, input.q, output.q, input.r, output.r\}$

$\mu X. (input.p \rightarrow output.p \rightarrow X$
$\quad |$
$\quad input.q \rightarrow output.q \rightarrow X$
$\quad |$
$\quad input.r \rightarrow output.r \rightarrow X)$

This is a one-place buffer; by combining in parallel several of these, connected as a pipeline, we can obtain more complex buffers. □

Example

11.3 Consider a pipeline of two one-place buffers forming a process *BUFFER_TWO*.

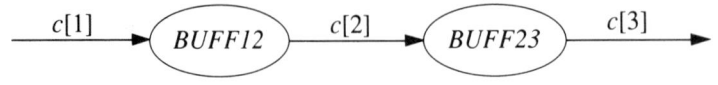

c[1] → BUFF12 → *c[2]* → BUFF23 → *c[3]*

Figure 11.3

The value that is output from one buffer acts as input for the other. Since a pipeline is unidirectional we need only to know the name of the channel to know whether it provides input or output for a given process. Hence for this pipeline of buffers we can take as our alphabet:

BUFFER_TWO

$\{c[1].p, c[1].q, c[1].r, c[2].p, c[2].q, c[2].r, c[3].p, c[3].q, c[3].r\}$

BUFF12 || BUFF23
where
$\quad BUFF12 = \mu X.(c[1].p \to c[2].p \to X$
$\quad\quad\quad\quad\quad\quad |$
$\quad\quad\quad\quad\quad\quad c[1].q \to c[2].q \to X$
$\quad\quad\quad\quad\quad\quad |$
$\quad\quad\quad\quad\quad\quad c[1].r \to c[2].r \to X)$
$\quad BUFF23 = \mu X.(c[2].p \to c[3].p \to X$
$\quad\quad\quad\quad\quad\quad |$
$\quad\quad\quad\quad\quad\quad c[2].q \to c[3].q \to X$
$\quad\quad\quad\quad\quad\quad |$
$\quad\quad\quad\quad\quad\quad c[2].r \to c[3].r \to X)$

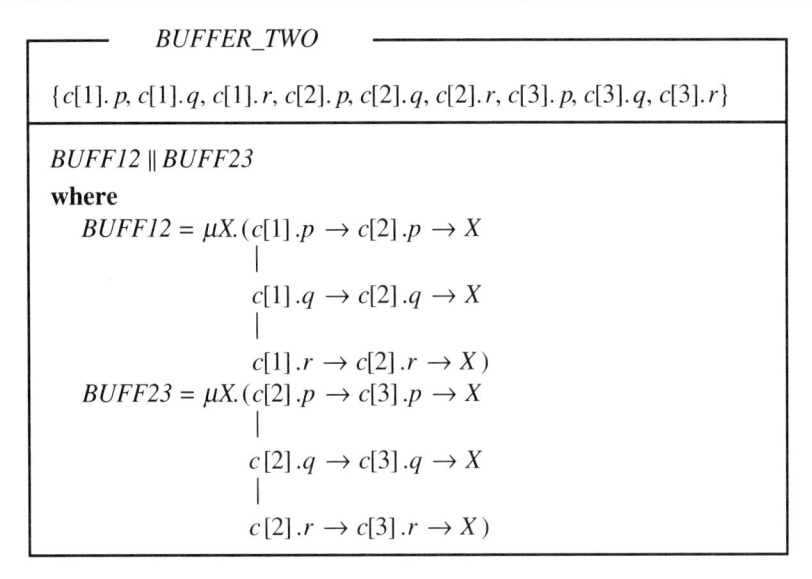

We now wish to investigate the composite process *BUFFER_TWO*.

The first event is an input on channel $c[1]$, and the next must be the transfer of this value on $c[2]$. At this stage, one of two activities can occur. Either *BUFF12* can input a new value on $c[1]$, or *BUFF23* can output on $c[3]$.

We cannot say in which order these events will occur—this is dependent on the external channels $c[1]$ and $c[3]$. What is clear is that both events must occur before there can be a further communication on $c[2]$.

□

11.5 Summary

We have used recursion as an additional tool in our CSP tool kit. Recursion can be used to define non-terminating processes, such as *CLOCK* and *BUFFER* as well as processes that might terminate, such as *GAME*. Termination of a recursively defined process can arise from a choice construct; thus the environment determines whether and when the process should terminate.

We illustrated the use of concurrency and recursion by defining a two-place buffer in terms of a pair of communicating one-place buffers.

SUMMARY OF PART II

We now stand back and take an overview of all the operations and symbols that have been introduced. We have developed a formal notation in which we can express the behaviour of processes. By using formal representations for choice, process composition and recursive processes, we can reason about how processes behave. The use of traces gives us a window on to the possible sequences of events in which a process might participate as it evolves.

We have met the following ways of specifying processes.

Atomic processes

For any alphabet A:

$SKIP_A$ and $STOP_A$

are processes.

Prefixing

If $\alpha P = \alpha Q = A$, then for any $a \in A$,:

$Q = a \rightarrow P$

is a process.

Choice by input value

For any distinct events $a, b, \ldots$ of A:

$a \rightarrow P \mid b \rightarrow Q \mid \ldots$

is a process.

Choice by channel

For distinct channels $c, d, \ldots$ the expression:

$c.v \rightarrow P \;[]\; d.w \rightarrow Q \;[]\; \ldots$

defines a process whose alphabet contains the events $c.v, d.w, \ldots$. When the first event has priority the operator $\boxplus\!\!\rightarrow$ is used.

Non-deterministic choice

The expression:

$P \sqcap Q \sqcap \ldots$

is a process which behaves like any one of $P, Q, \ldots$; the environment cannot control which is chosen.

Each of the notations for choice can be used for a choice between two or more processes.

In addition to these methods of constructing processes using events and guards, processes may be composed sequentially or in parallel. A parallel composition is either an interleaving or a concurrent combination.

Sequential composition

Two or more processes $P, Q, \ldots$ may be composed sequentially:

$P\,;Q\,;\ldots$

If P terminates successfully, the composite process continues with the evolution of Q, and so on. Otherwise $P\,;Q;\ldots = P$. We require the alphabets $\alpha P, \alpha Q, \ldots$ to be identical.

Interleaving

Two or more processes P and Q with disjoint alphabets may be interleaved. The process:

$P \,|||\, Q \,|||\, \ldots$

has the alphabet $\alpha P \cup \alpha Q \cup \ldots$ and engages in all the events of $P, Q, \ldots$. However, the order of these events is determined only by their ordering within the individual processes $P, Q, \ldots$.

Concurrency

Two or more processes $P, Q, \ldots$ with overlapping alphabets may be composed concurrently, $P \,\|\, Q \,\|\, \ldots$. A communication event in $\alpha P \cap \alpha Q$ can take place only if both P and Q are ready.

In order to simplify a concurrent composition we may use the rules given in Section 10.2. These rules allow the reduction of concurrent processes and the detection of deadlocked communications.

Recursion

The expression:

$\mu X_A .\, F(X)$

defines a process with alphabet A provided that $F(X)$ is a guarded expression.

In the remainder of this book, we shall apply these notations to our case studies.

SOLUTIONS TO PART II REVIEW QUESTIONS

6.1 $\{input\_data, output\_data\}$

6.2 $\alpha REACTOR\_VESSEL\_Y =$
$\{pipeA.C1, pipeB.C2, mix\_and\_heat\_chemicals,$
$increase\_pressure, open\_safety\_valve, fire\_brigade.alert,$
$pipeC.product, pipeD.waste\}$

6.3 T first engages in the event e and then behaves like the process S.

6.4 We have:

$RUN = run\_program \rightarrow PRINT$

6.5 $TEA\_FOR\_ONE = TEA_1 = coinslot.10p \rightarrow hatch.tea \rightarrow TEA_0$

6.6
┌── *TEA_THEN_JAM* ──────────────────────────┐
│ $\{coinslot.10p, hatch.tea\}$ │
│ │
│ $coinslot.10p \rightarrow hatch.tea \rightarrow JAM$ │
└──┘

6.7 Since our process has to describe a single shopping expedition, it should come to a definite conclusion. It may therefore be specified as a sequence of events terminated by *SKIP*:

┌── *SHOPPING* ──────────────────────────────┐
│ $\{enter\_car, drive\_to\_shop, leave\_car, enter\_shop, buy\_goods,$ │
│ $leave\_shop, drive\_home\}$ │
│ │
│ $enter\_car \rightarrow drive\_to\_shop \rightarrow leave\_car \rightarrow$ │
│ $enter\_shop \rightarrow buy\_goods \rightarrow leave\_shop \rightarrow$ │
│ $enter\_car \rightarrow drive\_home \rightarrow leave\_car \rightarrow SKIP$ │
└──┘

6.8

```
┌─── RUN ────────────────────────────────┐
│ {load.code, run_program, print.results} │
├─────────────────────────────────────────┤
│ run_program → print.results → SKIP      │
└─────────────────────────────────────────┘
```

7.1 The traces of *SKIP* are < > and < >✓

7.2

(a) <*coinslot.10p, hatch.tea, coinslot.10p*>

(b) <*coinslot.10p, hatch.tea, coinslot.10p, hatch.tea*>✓

8.1

```
┌─── HOT_DRINK ───────────────────────────────────────────┐
│ {coinslot.5p, coinslot.10p, coinslot.20p, hatch.choc,   │
│  hatch.tea, hatch.coffee}                               │
├─────────────────────────────────────────────────────────┤
│ (coinslot.5p  → hatch.choc   → SKIP                     │
│  |                                                      │
│  coinslot.10p → hatch.tea    → SKIP                     │
│  |                                                      │
│  coinslot.20p → hatch.coffee → SKIP )                   │
└─────────────────────────────────────────────────────────┘
```

8.2 As always, < > is a possible trace. To make progress a coin must be inserted, and therefore <*coinslot.5p*>, <*coinslot.10p*>, <*coinslot.20p*> are possible traces. A further set of traces will record the successful delivery of the drink. Here is the complete list of possible traces:

< >,
<*coinslot.5p*>, <*coinslot.5p, hatch.choc*>, <*coinslot.5p, hatch.choc*>✓,
<*coinslot.10p*>, <*coinslot.10p, hatch.tea*>, <*coinslot.10p, hatch.tea*>✓,
<*coinslot.20p*>, <*coinslot.20p, hatch.coffee*>, <*coinslot.20p, hatch.coffee*>✓

8.3 (a), (b), and (d) are guarded expressions; (c), (e), and (f) are not.

8.4 Nothing. The sequence of events in *ONE_PRICE_TC* guarantees that the process will not attempt to engage in *t.press* or *c.press* before it has engaged in the coinslot event.

8.5 The proposed notation breaks the syntax rules of CSP for two reasons:

(a) The fetbar operator [] must be placed between guarded expressions, but neither *t.press* → *hatch.tea* nor *c.press* → *hatch.coffee* qualifies as a guarded expression since *hatch.tea* and *hatch.coffee* are not processes.

(b) A prefix operator must be preceded by an event, but the expression in parentheses is not an event.

8.6 After the first two 10p pieces are inserted the process behaviour is governed by

138   SPECIFICATION AND DESIGN OF CONCURRENT SYSTEMS

CTC_{20}, which does not accept another coin. Strictly speaking, the coin slot should close, so that no more coins can be inserted. Alternatively, the machine might swallow the coin without changing its internal state. Such matters depend on a more detailed statement of requirements and suitable amendment of CTC_{20}.

9.1 Either:

   TEA_FOR_THREE = TEA_FOR_ONE ; TEA_FOR_TWO

or

   TEA_FOR_THREE = TEA_FOR_TWO ; TEA_FOR_ONE

In both cases, the combined process is:

coinslot.10p → hatch.tea →
    coinslot.10p → hatch.tea → coinslot.10p → hatch.tea → SKIP

9.2 The process:

DISPENSE ; CHANGE

has the required behaviour.

9.3

PROGRAM

{*load.code, run _ program, print.results*}

LOAD_AND_RUN; *PRINT*
where
  LOAD_AND_RUN = load.code → run _ program → SKIP
  PRINT = print.results → SKIP

9.4   *TEA_FOR_THREE =*
            TEA_FOR_ONE ; TEA_FOR_ONE ; TEA_FOR_ONE

9.5 We must include all events of the component processes:

$\alpha DOUBLE\_TEA$
   $= \alpha TEA_L \cup \alpha TEA_R$
   $= \{coinslot_L.10p, coinslot_R.10p, hatch_L.tea, hatch_R.tea\}$

10.1 The only other possibility is that the observer records *clink* before *whistle*, giving <*coinslot.10p, clink, whistle, hatch.tea*>✓.

10.2 *CLINK ||| WHISTLE* is a process, but the prefix operator can only follow an event, not a process.

10.3
   <*slurp, coinslot.10p, clink, clunk, mutter,tray.choc*>✓
   <*slurp, coinslot.10p, clink, mutter, clunk,tray.choc*>✓
   <*slurp, coinslot.10p, mutter, clink, clunk,tray.choc*>✓

10.4
    <coinslot.10p, c.press, noise.beep, curse, groan, whirr, t.press, tray.toffee>✓
    <coinslot.10p, c.press, noise.beep, curse, whirr, groan, t.press, tray.toffee>✓
    <coinslot.10p, c.press, noise.beep, whirr, curse, groan, t.press, tray.toffee>✓

10.5   We have the interleaved combination:

    $P3 = P31 \;|||\; P32 \;|||\; P33 \;|||\; P34$

where

    $P31 = (c[3, 1].3 \rightarrow SKIP)$
    $P32 = (c[3, 2].3 \rightarrow SKIP)$
    $P33 = (c[1, 3].1 \rightarrow SKIP)$
    $P34 = (c[2, 3].2 \rightarrow SKIP)$

(Of course, you may have numbered your component processes differently.)

11.1   Either:

    $TEA\_FOR\_EVER = coinslot.10p \rightarrow hatch.tea \rightarrow TEA\_FOR\_EVER$

or

    $TEA\_FOR\_EVER = \mu X.\; coinslot.10p \rightarrow hatch.tea \rightarrow X$

11.2   The initial choice of events allows either *coinslot.10p* or *coinslot.20p*, followed immediately by *hatch.tea* or *hatch.coffee*, respectively. Hence the traces are built up from arbitrary concatenations of the strings

    <coinslot.10p, hatch.tea>
    <coinslot.20p, hatch.coffee>

or any initial segment of such a string. Thus we may have

    < >, <coinslot.10p>, <coinslot.20p>,
    <coinslot.10p, hatch.tea>
    <coinslot.20p, hatch.coffee>
    <coinslot.10p, hatch.tea, coinslot.10p>
    <coinslot.20p, hatch.coffee, coinslot.10p>
    .
    .
    .
    <coinslot.10p, hatch.tea, coinslot.10p, hatch.tea,
            coinslot.20p, hatch.coffee, coinslot.20p>
    .
    .
    .

11.3

$<>, <b>, <b>\checkmark,$

$<a>, <a,b>, <a,b>\checkmark,$

$<a, a>, <a, a, b>, <a, a, b>\checkmark,$

$<a, a, a>, <a, a, a, b>, <a, a, a, b>\checkmark.$

11.4

$SMOKEALARM =$
$\quad (button.press \rightarrow shortbuzz \rightarrow SMOKEALARM$
$\quad \square$
$\quad sensor.smoke \rightarrow longbuzz \rightarrow SKIP)$

Alternatively:

$SMOKEALARM = \mu X.(button.press \rightarrow shortbuzz \rightarrow X$
$\quad \square$
$\quad sensor.smoke \rightarrow longbuzz \rightarrow SKIP)$

11.5 Since:

$CLOCK = tick \rightarrow tock \rightarrow CLOCK$

the left-hand side becomes:

$CLOCK \,;\, Q = (tick \rightarrow tock \rightarrow CLOCK)\,;\, Q$

By two applications of the result of Exercise 9.1, this can be rewritten as:

$CLOCK \,;\, Q = tick \rightarrow tock \rightarrow (CLOCK \,;\, Q)$

However, this equation is equivalent to the process definition:

$CLOCK \,;\, Q = \mu X.\, tick \rightarrow tock \rightarrow X$

which specifies a unique process since the expression is guarded. But this is exactly the specification for *CLOCK*. Therefore, we obtain the process equivalence:

$CLOCK = CLOCK \,;\, Q$

PART III

REFINEMENT AND OCCAM

12 COUNTING HOLES

Our software development method, ODM, which is suitable for dealing with problems involving concurrency, entails the following stages:

- The problem is formulated as a *statement of requirements*.
- Process analysis: a top-level *process network* is produced and annotated.
- Specification: the process network is formalized as a *CSP system specification*.
- Process design: the top-level processes are refined into component processes, with concomitant refinement of the specification into a refined *CSP system design document*.
- Detailed design: the design is reduced to executable actions; this leads to a detailed *CSP design with variables*.
- Code: the detailed CSP design is implemented as an *Occam program*.

We have already introduced, in Part I, the *process analysis* stage, in which the problem is represented by an annotated *process network*. In Part II we tackled the problem of formal specification in CSP notation, which forms the basis of our design methodology. The new areas on which we focus particularly in the case studies are process design, which uses the *explosion* technique, the introduction of variables into CSP, and the rudiments of coding programs in Occam (the language of the transputer).

Our first case study—which forms the subject matter for Part III—is centred on the theme of image processing. We introduce the case study in Section 12.1, and give an algorithm which will form the basis of our limited system in Section 12.2.

We are interested in illustrating all the stages of our development method, starting from a statement of requirements, through a verified design, leading eventually to reliable code; in order to do so, we shall restrict attention to a very simple system. Starting with a CSP specification for this system, we refine it into a detailed design document which can easily be implemented in Occam code. However, the same method could be used with a more detailed system to produce a sophisticated image-processing package.

We begin our development of the image-processing system in Chapter 13 with the CSP system specification and the process design. This entails subdividing the top-level processes into concurrent components and identifying the channels of communication between them.

In order to complete the formal specification, we need some tools, which are developed in Chapter 14; in particular we introduce a more convenient notation for handling communications and choice by input value in CSP. Various design issues are then considered in Chapter 15 which culminates in a complete CSP system design document.

This has now to be implemented as code. Before we are able to do this, we introduce appropriate notations for selection and repetition in the CSP context. This forms the subject matter of Chapter 16. These notations are used in Chapter 17 to formally transform our CSP design into a form from which it can be implemented directly in Occam code. The Occam code is then derived in Chapter 18.

12.1 The hole-counting problem

Machines in general are very poor at recognizing patterns. A five-year-old child can look at a crude sketch of a tree and recognize it immediately for what it represents. The most powerful of today's computers cannot begin to compete with this capability. Nevertheless some first steps have been taken to develop algorithms with which machines may analyse patterns. One area where this is of great potential importance is in the field of industrial automation—robotics. To take a very simple example, it might be very useful for a robot, presented with images of a nut and a bolt (established by an optical sensor), to detect the difference between them.

Figure 12.1

Consider the images in Figure 12.1. There are many differences between these images, relating largely to size and shape. Computations to spot these differences are likely to be very time-consuming, especially since the orientation of the objects may well be random. One crucial difference, however, which is relatively straightforward to spot is that a nut has a hole in it, whilst a bolt does not. It so happens that there is a highly parallel algorithm which can be applied to detect holes in images, and we shall make use of it in developing our case study.

We shall begin by setting the scene for our case-study, with a statement of requirements. The rest of this chapter will explore some aspects of the algorithm for counting the holes in an image.

12.2 Requirements

We shall be considering a fairly simple case study in image processing—counting the number of holes in an image. Our customer is able to supply a collection of images that have to be analysed for holes. Suppose that, after a lengthy discussion between the customer and the systems analyst, the following statement of requirements is agreed:

> The system should provide a facility for processing digitized two-dimensional images, which are held in a filestore. The following commands should be available.
>
> The LOAD IMAGE command: this loads a new image from the filestore and displays it on a screen. After completion of this command the system is available to receive another command.
>
> The COUNT HOLES command: this counts the number of holes in the current image, and displays this number. After completion of this command the system is available to receive another command.
>
> The TERMINATE command: this causes the program to terminate in an orderly fashion.

Exercise

12.1 Are there any areas of ambiguity you would like to eliminate?

Solution 12.1

(a) There are three legal commands, but there is no indication of how the system might respond to an illegal command.

(b) It would appear from the statement of requirements that all three options are always to be available. In particular, on starting up the program, it appears that you should be able to use the COUNT HOLES command before the LOAD IMAGE command. But in order to perform COUNT HOLES you clearly need some image—what should it be?

(c) It is not entirely clear what happens after the COUNT HOLES command has been invoked. The display should now include the hole count if it was not initially present, and the system is available to receive any of the commands. Is this meant to imply that the number displayed (for the hole count) is now part of a modified image? Probably not, but this point must be made clear in the specification.

(d) There is no statement of the manner in which the user might exercise choice over the images that are to be loaded.

▫

The simplest method of dealing with (a) is to ignore all illegal commands.

To resolve (b), one possibility is that there should be some default image which appears initially. We shall assume that the blank image—all pixels white—is displayed. An alternative way of resolving this problem is for the COUNT HOLES operation to be unavailable in the initial state.

As far as ambiguity (c) is concerned, we assume that the current image has an existence (in memory) which is independent of the screen display. In other words, a modification to the screen display—such as the appearance of the number of holes—does not affect the current image.

Concerning (d), in this case study we are actually more interested in designing the hole-counting algorithm than in developing a sophisticated image-handling system. We shall therefore make the simplifying assumption that the filestore is loaded externally (by hardware, or an external software system), and that the images are loaded from the filestore in a predetermined sequence. Of course, this now creates a new problem to be resolved—how does the system handle a request to load a new image after the last image in the filestore has been loaded. This could be dealt with, say, by issuing a warning message.

These assumptions could be incorporated in a more secure specification of our simple image-processing system.

Exercise

12.2 What implementation considerations do we need to take into account at this stage?

Solution 12.2 Details of input and output are still missing, but they do not affect the functionality of the system. At this stage we should be concerned purely with the functional description of the system. Implementation details should be left until a later stage.

There is, however, one implementation problem which may need to be considered in conjunction with the specification of the system: what transputer network is available for the implementation of the system? In principle, it should be open to us to refine the system specification either in the most elegant manner possible, or according to some absolute criteria. The question of mapping the processes to processors should, in theory, be left until after the system is fully specified. This approach, called *post-fragmentation*, leads to practical difficulties that cannot be easily resolved given the current state of the art. For this reason, given a large system and a limited choice of transputer networks it is often advisable in practice to employ *pre-fragmentation*—that is, specifying the transputer network first, and dividing the system according to how its component processes will be eventually placed on the given network before detailed analysis, specification and refinement.

We shall not be dealing with this problem in detail, but we shall attempt to develop a purely theoretical specification.

12.3 The hole-counting algorithm

We now examine the hole-counting algorithm that we intend to implement in our image-processing system. Although the objects that concern the customer are three dimensional, our statement of requirements confines the problem to the analysis of two-dimensional images. (Presumably, these are two-dimensional views of the original objects.)

Review Question 12.1 Will an algorithm to count holes be foolproof in distinguishing nuts from bolts?

Before we can describe the algorithm for counting holes we need to know how the image has been digitized. This would normally be specified as a constraint. As stated in Section 4.2, we restrict our attention to images that appear as rectangular arrays of pixels.

We shall also make the further assumption that the image is monochrome, represented by black cells on a white background.

The objects shown in Figure 12.1 are therefore represented by the images in Figure 12.2.

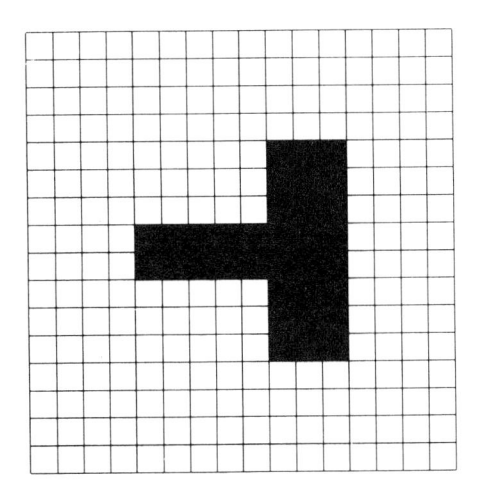

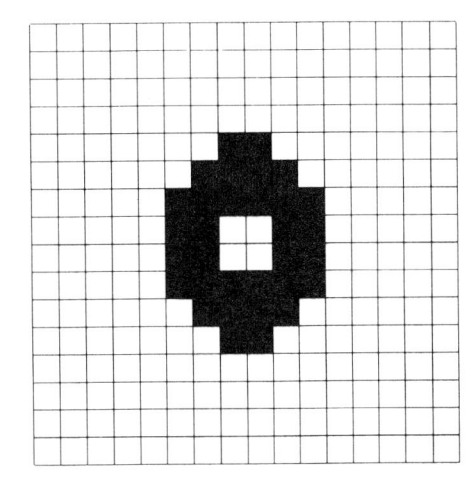

Figure 12.2

The algorithm that we shall use to count holes analyses the grid containing the image in square two-by-two blocks of four pixels each. For a monochrome image, there are $2^4 = 16$ possible patterns. Two of these sixteen patterns figure in the counting algorithm, as shown in Figure 12.3.

Type A   Type B

Figure 12.3

The following algorithm may be used to determine the number of holes in a black image on a white background (where all the pixels on the edges of the grid are white):

> Consider each two-by-two square within the image;
> to each square block of Type A assign the number -1;
> to each square block of Type B assign the number 1;
> to each square block of any other type, assign the number 0.

Now add together all these numbers, and add 1 to their sum. The final answer is the number of (white) holes in the black image.

A formal proof of this result is too complicated to be included here, and would divert attention from the main aim of this section, but we may reason informally as follows. A rectangular white hole would generate one Type B block and no Type A blocks. A rectangular black image generates one Type A block and no Type B blocks. Thus a rectangular black object containing n rectangular white holes generates one Type A block and n Type B blocks; the algorithm gives the number of holes correctly as $-1 + n + 1$. Irregular shapes actually introduce an equal number of Type A and Type B blocks, but we shall not pursue the proof any further.

148 SPECIFICATION AND DESIGN OF CONCURRENT SYSTEMS

Example

12.1 Let us test the algorithm on the images of a nut and a bolt.

(a)   (b)

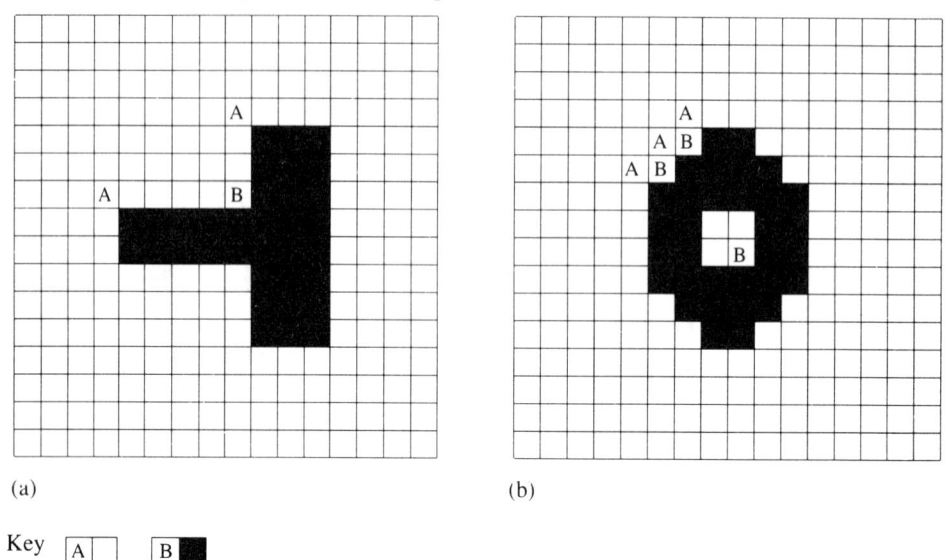

Key

Figure 12.4

In Figure 12.4 we have identified each two-by-two block as Type A or Type B by inserting the appropriate letter in the top, left cell of the block. For convenience, this is shown in the key. In the bolt there are two Type A blocks and one Type B giving a count of $(-2 + 1 + 1) = 0$ holes. The nut—Figure 12.4(b)—has three Type A blocks and three Type Bs; this gives a count of $(-3 + 3 + 1) = 1$ hole. □

Example

12.2 Here is a another example. The image in Figure 12.5 apparently has one hole. Let us see whether the algorithm agrees.

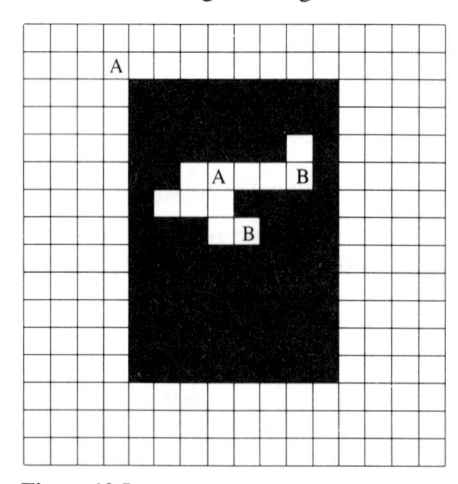

Figure 12.5

Applying the algorithm, this image has two blocks of Type A and two of Type B, so the overall score is $(-2 + 2 + 1) = 1$ hole.

Review Question 12.2 Apply the algorithm to compute the number of holes in the following two images (Figure 12.6).

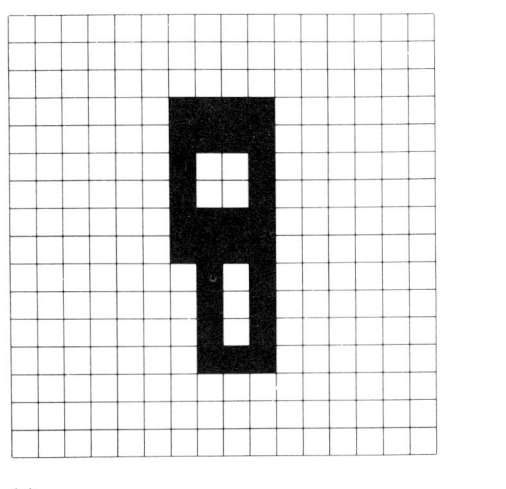

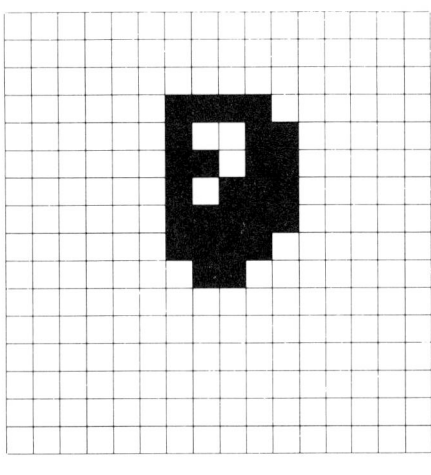

(a)   (b)

Figure 12.6

Exercise

12.3 There is a fundamental difference between this image-processing operation and operations like thickening and reversing that we looked at in Chapter 4. Can you spot it?

Solution 12.3 This one involves counting! As well as obtaining a local block count, which can be done in parallel over all blocks, the design of our system will have to make provision for globally summing the individual results.

12.4 Summary

We have now laid the groundwork for our image-processing case study. We first considered the user requirements, and established that we would be concerned with developing a system capable of counting holes in a collection of two-dimensional images. We then presented an algorithm for determining the number of holes in a monochrome image represented by the black cells on a white background within a rectangular array of pixels. This algorithm works by examining all the two-by-two blocks of the pixel array and looking for specific patterns.

13 SPECIFICATION AND DESIGN

In Chapter 12 you saw the statement of requirements for the image-processing system. We shall now proceed to specify this system using CSP. Our development will then continue by refining our top-level description into more detailed elements. In doing this we enter the design phase; at various stages our refinement will introduce intermediate steps that enable our process description to meet its specification.

The method by which we generate a CSP system design document is to *explode* the processes in the top-level process network; each explosion is represented in CSP by a set of concurrent component processes. In this chapter we shall develop the second level of our specification, giving a CSP description of each of the components in the exploded process network.

13.1 Process analysis

Once we have established the user requirements, the next stage in developing our simple system is to produce an annotated top-level process network. Our system has two entry channels—one for the command input and one for loading the images from the filestore—and one exit channel, for sending images and hole counts to the screen. We show this in Figure 13.1. Note that the actual input device and the nature of the input codes do not affect the specification of our system; all that matters is that the *command* channel is capable of carrying three messages—*load, count* and *terminate*. Whether the commands are input by depressing the keys 'l', 'c' and 't' on a conventional keyboard, by pointing a mouse at suitable icons, or by selection from a menu listing, the selections can in every case be treated as events on the *command* channel.

We call the channel from the filestore to *SYSTEM*, *filein*; but we do not require an exit channel from *SYSTEM* to the filestore as the images are presented in a predetermined sequence. Thus *SYSTEM* never sends any message to the filestore. The messages to the screen handler are communicated along the channel *screen*. We shall not consider the screen handler at all; we assume it can produce the appropriate displays using the messages communicated.

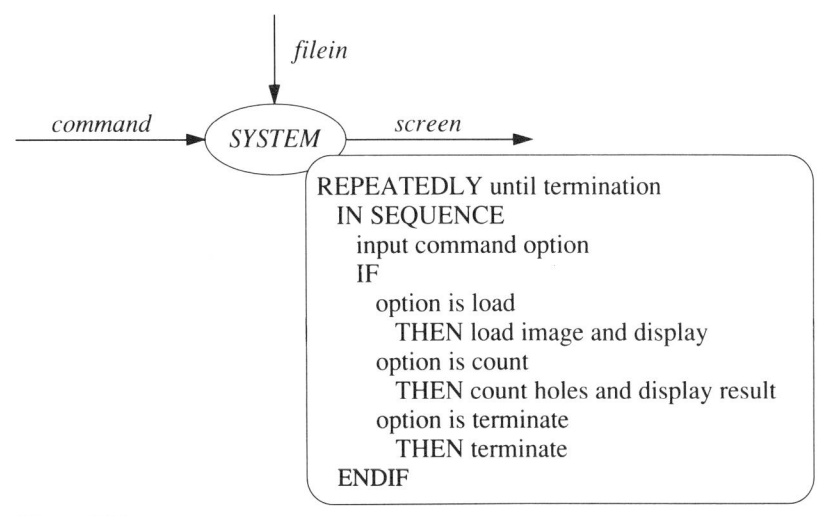

```
              filein
                ↓
  command   ┌────────┐   screen
 ─────────▶ │ SYSTEM │ ───────────▶
            └────────┘
         ╭────────────────────────────────────────╮
         │ REPEATEDLY until termination           │
         │   IN SEQUENCE                          │
         │     input command option               │
         │     IF                                 │
         │       option is load                   │
         │          THEN load image and display   │
         │       option is count                  │
         │          THEN count holes and display result │
         │       option is terminate              │
         │          THEN terminate                │
         │     ENDIF                              │
         ╰────────────────────────────────────────╯
```

Figure 13.1

13.2 The CSP specification

The next step in the development method is to formalize the process network into a top-level CSP system specification.

The annotation contains a REPEATEDLY, which calls for recursion, and a triple choice by input value. The process can thus be specified as follows.

SYSTEM
{*command.load*, *command.count*, *command.terminate*, *obtain_image*, *display_image*, *count_and_display_holes*}

$\mu X.$ (*command.load* → *obtain_image* → *display_image* → X
   |
   command.count → *count_and_display_holes* → X
   |
   command.terminate → *SKIP*)

The recursive nature of the specification, and the terminating condition, can both be clearly seen.

Review Question 13.1   Express in your own words the meaning of the specification of *SYSTEM*.   ▫

Review Question 13.2   Remove the μ operator from the specification of *SYSTEM* to give an explicitly recursive specification.   ▫

13.3 Refinement

So far, we have developed a top-level specification in accordance with the techniques of Parts I and II. There lies ahead the task of generating an algorithmic description of

SYSTEM. In this section we shall try to give a feel for the stages through which a specification must be transformed before executable code is produced. A top-level specification, as produced by process analysis, must be *refined* through various stages until the required level of detail is achieved. The refinement steps entail an element of design to the extent that the additional detail is not laid down in the statement of requirements. The final design document will be in a form such that it can be transformed in a straightforward manner to executable Occam code. Of course, each refinement step must be checked for correctness, because increasing the level of detail can lead to the introduction of errors.

We refine the specification of a process into subprocesses using concurrency, interleaving and sequencing. The idea is to use process analysis and CSP iteratively, increasing the detail until we reach a CSP description in terms of atomic events. At each stage of the iteration one identifies a particular node (representing a component process) of the process network at the current level. Explosion of this node is achieved by subjecting it to process analysis. The CSP specification of the corresponding process is also refined into the specification of the appropriate concurrent processes. We shall apply this technique to our case study.

Consider the top-level process network (Figure 13.1). Exploding the node *SYSTEM* involves the introduction of component processes, linked by new channels, and refining the accompanying CSP description. This is illustrated in Figure 13.2 as an explosion where one process is replaced by three in parallel:

SYSTEM = CONTROLLER || CELLS || FUNNEL

In an exploded process network, we indicate the composite process by a grey boundary.[1]

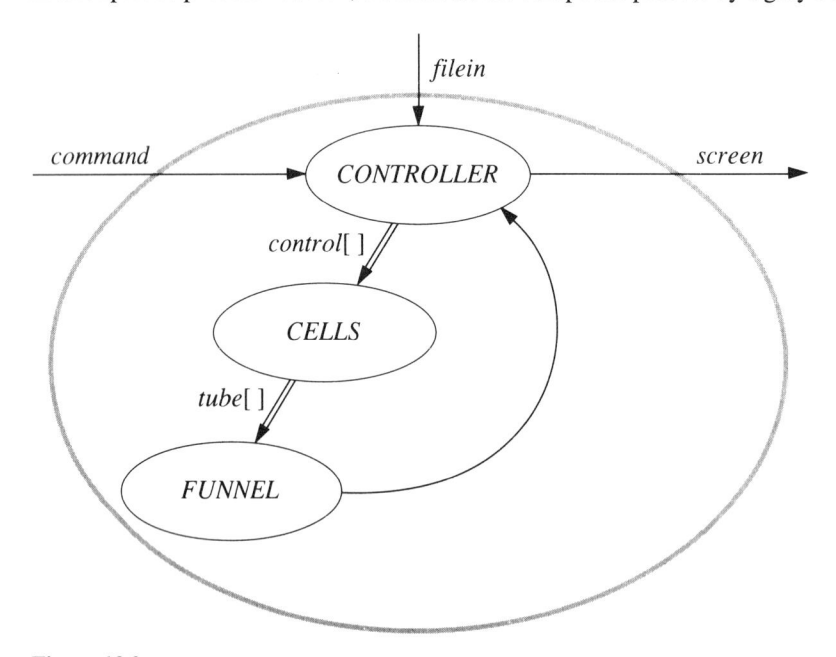

Figure 13.2

---

[1] When drawing exploded diagrams by hand, use a dashed boundary for the composite process.

The *CONTROLLER* process performs the control activities that we have already analysed in our top-level specification. In addition, the alphabet of *CONTROLLER* must include communication events along the new channels that are attached to *CONTROLLER*. We therefore replace the events in the specification of *SYSTEM* by subprocesses *LOAD_IMAGE* and *COUNT_HOLES* in the refinement of *CONTROLLER*. Termination will now require some communication between *CONTROLLER* and the other components, as they also have to be terminated; we introduce a subprocess *TERMINATE* to deal with any new events that may have to be introduced:

CONTROLLER =
 (*command.load* → *LOAD_IMAGE* ; *CONTROLLER*
 |
 command.count → *COUNT_HOLES* ; *CONTROLLER*
 |
 command.terminate → *TERMINATE*)

This completes our consideration of *CONTROLLER* at the current level of refinement. The detailed design of the new subprocesses introduced here will be left until Chapter 15.

The other two components shown in Figure 13.2 are *CELLS* and *FUNNEL*. At this stage we shall not identify the arrangement of the individual pixel processes; *CELLS* is a single process which handles all events that concern the current image. Finally, the additions that will be required for the hole-counting algorithm are performed by the process *FUNNEL*, which adds the numbers on all its entry channels and sends the sum on its exit channel.

13.4 The main channels

The process network for the exploded process (Figure 13.2) indicates the channels between the component processes. The exit channel from the *FUNNEL* process carries a single value—the hole count—for each image analysed. The other channels are indicated by double lines; these represent multiple channels and are named with a special notation, using brackets. We call such a set of multiple channels a **channel array**.

The channel array *tube*[ ] from *CELLS* to *FUNNEL* carries the integers generated by the patterns in the hole-counting algorithm; *FUNNEL* is a multiple adder, and so it requires multiple entry channels.

The channel array *control*[ ] is used to enable communication from *CONTROLLER* to *CELLS*. Without making any detailed assumptions about the nature of the *CELLS* process, we can make the general observation that it will be exploded into a network of concurrent processes, each describing the behaviour of an individual pixel. Since *CONTROLLER* may have to communicate with each of these pixel processes, it is desirable to incorporate a multiplicity of channels into this level of the design.

13.5 Exploding the *CELLS* process

We shall consider next the refinement of *CELLS*.

It was suggested in Section 4.2 that an image can be represented satisfactorily as a rectangular array of pixels. (This is a design decision.) We shall associate a local cell process to each pixel.[2] These local cell processes are essentially identical, differing only in the names of the channels to which they are attached. When we have a set of identical processes we may number them in a logical fashion; we then refer to the whole set of processes as a *process array*. In our case we can explode *CELLS* into a two-dimensional process array. A typical local process node, corresponding to the pixel in cell position (i, j), is identified as $CELL(i, j)$ as shown in Figure 13.3. Suppose that, using the notation of Chapter 4, the number of rows in the array is *rows*, and the number of columns is *cols*. Then:

$0 \leq i \leq rows - 1$

$0 \leq j \leq cols - 1$

The total number of local cell processes is given by:

$cells = rows \times cols$

We may refer to a typical component process in the array as a *CELL* process.

The effect of this explosion is to express *CELLS* as a parallel combination of the *CELL* processes. We could perhaps write this out as:

$CELLS = CELL(0, 0) \parallel CELL(0, 1) \parallel CELL(0, 2) \parallel \ldots \parallel CELL(rows - 1, cols - 1)$

but this is clumsy as well as being imprecise. We therefore prefer to use the **replicated concurrency operator**, which is written before the component processes, as follows:

$CELLS = \parallel_{\substack{0 \leq i < rows \\ 0 \leq j < cols}} CELL(i, j)$

The two inequalities appended to the concurrency operator specify the range of values of i and j for the component processes $CELL(i, j)$. This notation may be used whenever we have an indexed collection of processes combined in parallel.

Now we must establish the channels through which the local cell processes communicate. Before dealing with channels between these cell processes, we shall tidy up the arrangements for communications between a typical local process $CELL(i, j)$ and the processes *CONTROLLER* and *FUNNEL*. The channels from *CONTROLLER* are shown in Figure 13.3 as $control[i, j]$—each channel is indexed in the same way as the process $CELL(i, j)$ to which it leads. As i and j range over all permitted values, we obtain all the channels from *CONTROLLER* to *CELLS*.

The labelling of the channels from *CELLS* to *FUNNEL* is slightly more complicated. When we come to examine the *FUNNEL* process, we shall see that it takes its inputs from a one-dimensional channel array, which we call $tube[\ ]$. Each value input to *FUNNEL* is generated as an output from one of the local *CELL* processes. Thus the exit channels from the array of *CELL* processes must form the channel array $tube[\ ]$.

Exercise

13.1 The number of *CELL* processes is *cells*, so the channels from *CELLS* to *FUNNEL* are $tube[0], \ldots, tube[cells - 1]$. Establish a formula for identifying the channel $tube[r]$ that links the process node $CELL(i, j)$ with the *FUNNEL* process.

---

[2]In practice it is unrealistic to assign a process to each pixel. Each local process would handle a block of pixels and be placed on a transputer, the number of processes matching the number of available transputers. The local processes could then be refined further in order to derive program code.

SPECIFICATION AND DESIGN   155

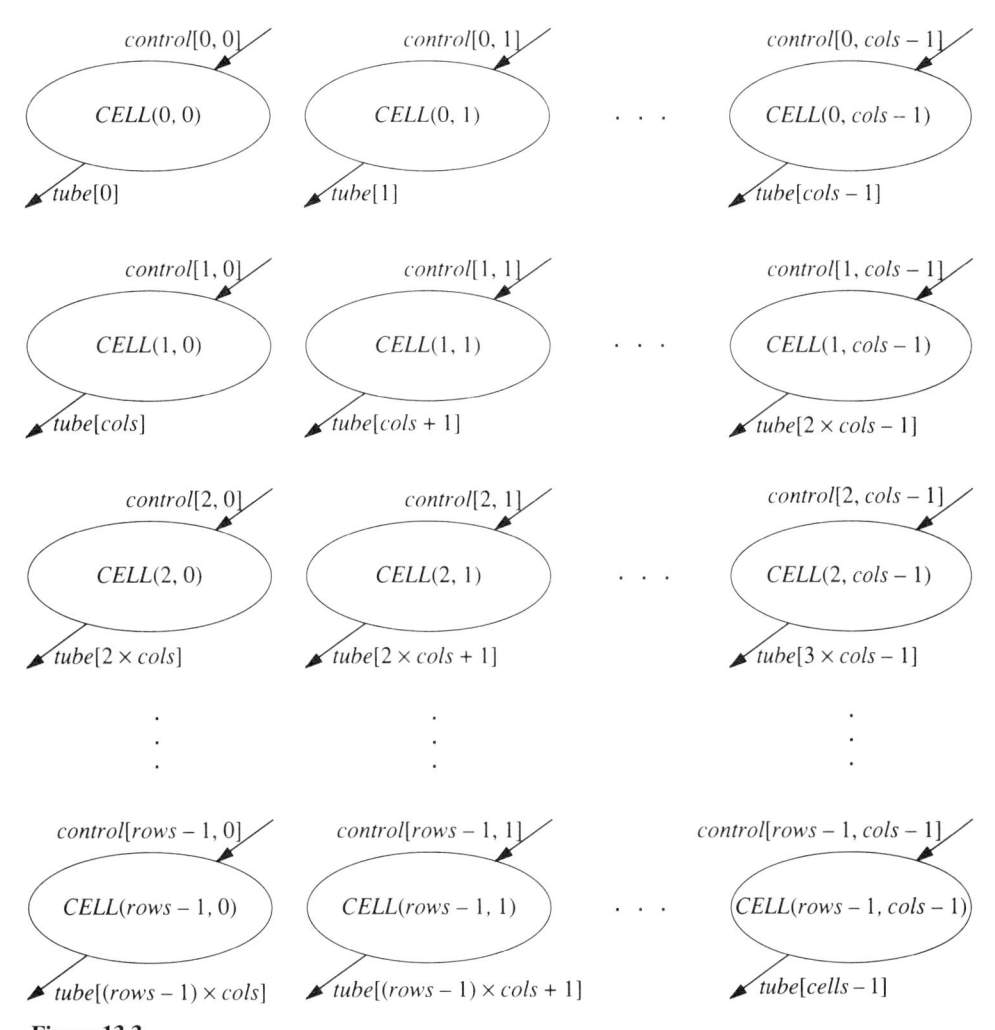

Figure 13.3

Solution 13.1 Essentially we have to find a means of relabelling a two-dimensional array so that it becomes a one-dimensional array. We can achieve this by labelling consecutively along successive rows, as shown in Figure 13.3, starting from the first.

Since the number of processes in each row is *cols*, the process $CELL(i, j)$ becomes associated with the $[(i \times cols) + j]$th channel. Thus one suitable formula for labelling the channel from $CELL(i, j)$ to *FUNNEL* is $tube[(i \times cols) + j]$.

□

13.6 Internal communication within *CELLS*

Our process analysis is not yet complete. We have designed the process *CELLS* as a parallel composition of an array of *CELL* processes, and we have identified the channels between $CELL(i, j)$ and the subprocesses *CONTROLLER* and *FUNNEL*; but we have not yet established the channels between the local *CELL* components.

To complete the process analysis it is necessary to make inter-cell communications explicit. In other words, we need to identify the channels that are used to exchange information between neighbours.

(a)

(b)

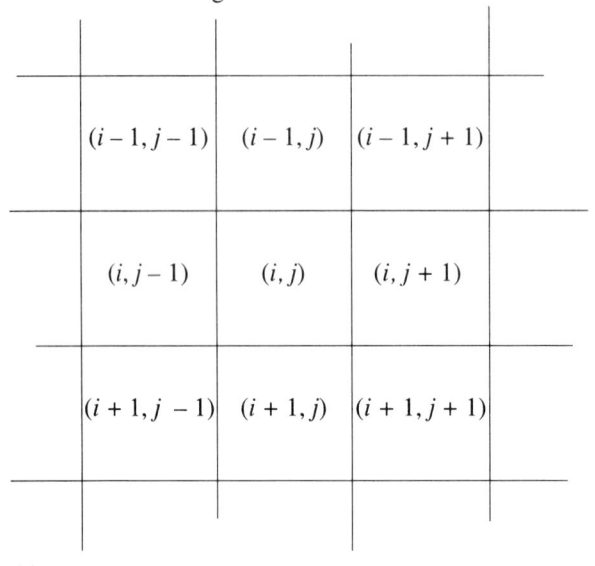

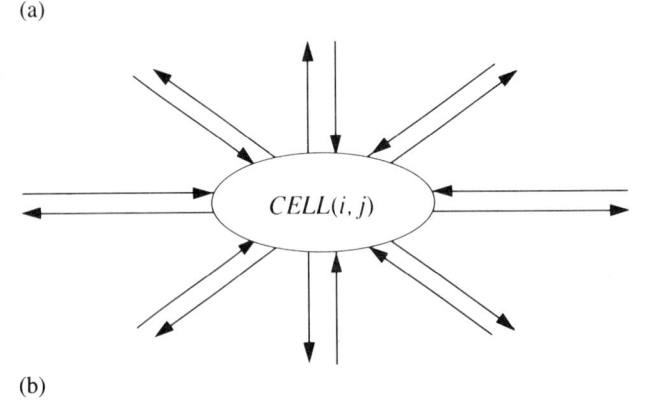

Figure 13.4

Figure 13.4(a) shows a rectangular array in which a typical cell has eight neighbours. Inter-cell communication takes place along eight entry channels and eight exit channels; see Figure 13.4(b). We may use the eight principal compass bearings to label the exit channels from a given process node $CELL(i, j)$. Thus the channel leaving $CELL(i, j)$ in a northerly direction will be called $north[i, j]$, and so on, as shown in Figure 13.5.

Since a similar set of eight exit channels is required for each cell, we set up a two-dimensional channel array for each of the eight geographic directions.

Each process node will also have eight corresponding entry channels—these are the exit channels of the appropriate neighbouring cells. The labelling of these channels is straightforward, except possibly near the edges of the array. For example, the channel entering $CELL(i, j)$ from the north is just $south[i-1, j]$, since it is the channel leaving $CELL(i-1, j)$ in a southerly direction.

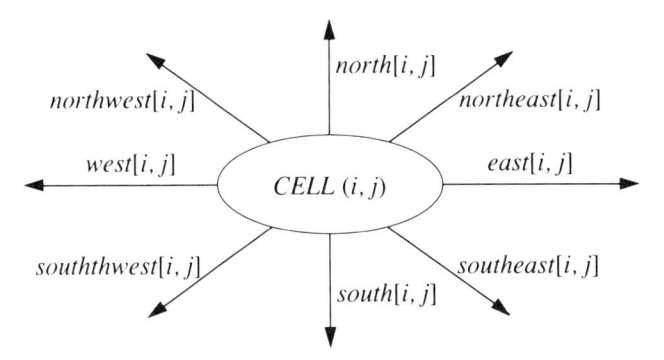

Figure 13.5

Exercise

13.2 Give the complete labelling of the incoming channels for an internal process node $CELL(i,j)$.

Solution 13.2 The solution is shown in Figure 13.6.

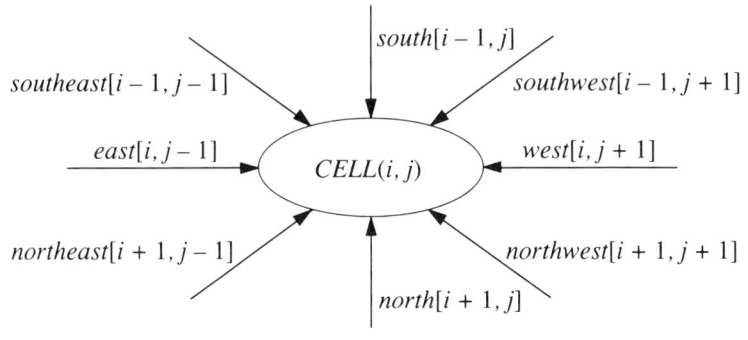

Figure 13.6

Wraparound

In labelling the inter-cell channels, we were careful to refer to *internal* cells. This is because cells on the edge of the array do not have a full complement of neighbours. Without doubt, for an image processing application the correct procedure is to treat the edge (and corner) cells separately.

However, the price of this careful treatment is the complication of handling edge cells as special cases. There is an alternative—we may link the opposite pairs of edges.[3] For example, a north channel leaving a cell on the top edge of the array enters the opposite cell on the bottom edge from the south, as shown in Figure 13.7. While this gives an incorrect treatment of the edge cells, it has the very significant advantage that all the processes $CELL(i, j)$ are identical, irrespective of the values of i and j. In practice, this strictly

---

[3] This is a familiar dodge to mathematicians, and amounts to thinking of the image as wrapped around a *torus* (a ring doughnut).

incorrect treatment of the edges frequently does not have any effect on the results of processing the image, as it is possible to arrange that the image does not occupy any of the cells on the boundary of the grid.

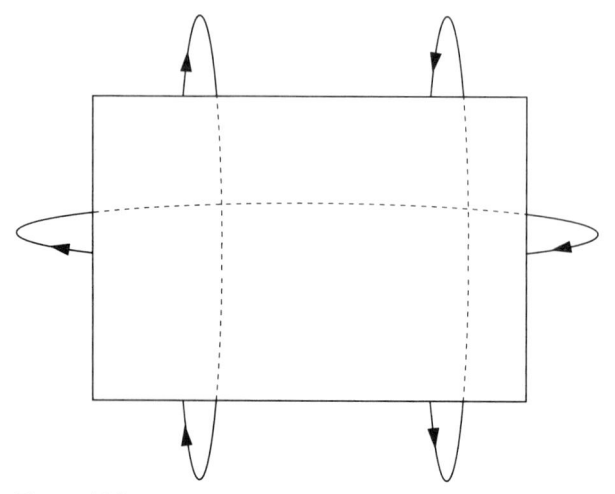

Figure 13.7

This matching of opposite edges is put into effect using modular arithmetic. Formally:

$i \oplus 1$ means $(i+1)$ mod *rows*

$i \ominus 1$ means $(i-1)$ mod *rows*

$j \oplus 1$ means $(j+1)$ mod *cols*

$j \ominus 1$ means $(j-1)$ mod *cols*

Where (i, j) is an internal pixel, the meanings of $\oplus$ and $\ominus$ are identical with $+$ and $-$ respectively. Do not spend too much time worrying about the details here. The important point to grasp is that a suitable labelling system can be constructed.

Review Question 13.3 Given a complete listing of the internal channels of a process, what fundamental condition is required to be satisfied?

13.7 Process replication

A process array consists of a number of indexed replicas of a given process. In Section 13.5 we saw how a process array may be combined using the replicated concurrency operator:

$$CELLS = \|_{\substack{0 \leq i < rows \\ 0 \leq j < cols}} CELL(i, j)$$

When the ranges of values of i and j can be inferred from a suitable context we may omit them and write more briefly:

$$CELLS = \|_{ij} CELL(i, j)$$

We might also wish to compose elements of a process by interleaving. For example, when the *CONTROLLER* process receives the command *load*, it could forward the command along the channel array *control*[ ] to the process array *CELLS*, using the following interleaved composition of processes:

$BCLOAD =$
    $control[0, 0].load \rightarrow SKIP |||$
    $control[0, 1].load \rightarrow SKIP |||$
    $control[0, 2].load \rightarrow SKIP |||$
    .
    .
    .
    $control[1, 0].load \rightarrow SKIP |||$
    .
    .
    .

In this case we can abbreviate the specification using the **replicated interleaving operator**, thus:

$BCLOAD = |||_{ij} \, control[i, j].load \rightarrow SKIP$

On the other hand, we may wish to compose a process array by sequencing. Consider the process:

$LDPIXEL(i, j) = filein.black \rightarrow control[i, j].black \rightarrow SKIP$
                              |
                $filein.white \rightarrow control[i, j].white \rightarrow SKIP$

which receives a pixel value on the channel *filein* and transmits it to the process *CELL(i, j)*. The process specified by the sequential composition:

$LDPIXEL(0, 0) \, ; \, LDPIXEL(0, 1) \, ; \, LDPIXEL(0, 2) \, ; \, \ldots$
$LDPIXEL(1, 0) \, ; \, LDPIXEL(1, 1) \, ; \, LDPIXEL(1, 2) \, ; \, \ldots$
    .
    .
    .

may be abbreviated using the **replicated sequencing operator** Σ as follows:

$\Sigma_{ij} LDPIXEL(i, j)$

We shall have occasion to use these notations in the development of our case studies.

13.8 Summary

Let us review progress so far. Starting from our statement of requirements, we have proceeded to the following level of design, with a process network given by Figure 13.2 and amplified in Figure 13.3:

$SYSTEM = CONTROLLER \parallel CELLS \parallel FUNNEL$

$CONTROLLER =$
$\qquad (command.load \rightarrow LOAD\_IMAGE; CONTROLLER$
$\qquad \mid$
$\qquad command.count \rightarrow COUNT\_HOLES; CONTROLLER$
$\qquad \mid$
$\qquad command.terminate \rightarrow TERMINATE)$

$CELLS = \parallel_{\substack{0 \leq i < rows \\ 0 \leq j < cols}} CELL(i,j)$

This process description includes the expansion of *CELLS* as a two-dimensional array of concurrent processes. The channels that connect *CELLS* to *FUNNEL* and *CONTROLLER* form channel arrays.

We have introduced notations for replicated composition of process arrays using concurrency, interleaving and sequencing.

The next stage of our development method will be to design the subprocesses of *CONTROLLER*, the individual processes of the *CELL* array and the process *FUNNEL*. These points will be addressed in Chapter 15, where we complete the CSP design of our image-processing system.

14 MORE CSP

Before we can continue with the refinement of the process components of *SYSTEM*, we need to introduce some further elements of CSP notation. First we shall show how local variables are used, especially in the context of choice by input value. We then study the two-place buffer as an exercise in deadlock analysis. We also specify a funnel adder of the type needed for the case study. Finally we introduce some more notation for the composition of a process array.

14.1 Input, output and variables

When two processes P and Q are capable of participating in a mutual communication, this event appears in the alphabet of both processes in the form $c.s$ where c identifies the communication channel and s identifies the signal communicated. The use of this notation makes it abundantly clear that two processes participate in the same event. However, the CSP description does not indicate which of P or Q is transmitting and which is receiving. Where the communication is a simple handshake, that is, an event used solely to synchronize the two processes, this does not matter. In general, though, it is desirable to indicate whether a particular communication event serves as an input event or as an output event.

Example

14.1 Consider the following process:

$P = left.a \rightarrow right.a \rightarrow P$

What does this process do? In the absence of a process network we cannot be sure. We know that P has two channels, *left* and *right*, but we have no way of knowing whether they are entry or exit channels.

Thus any of the following descriptions of P might be valid:

- repeatedly inputs the value a on channel *left* and then outputs it on channel *right*—this is a one-place buffer which accepts the value a only;
- repeatedly outputs the value a on channel *left* and then inputs the value a on channel *right*—this first outputs a and then acts as a buffer;

161

- repeatedly inputs the value *a* alternately from channels *left* and *right*—this is a sink which absorbs the value *a* from alternate channels in sequence;
- repeatedly outputs the value *a* alternately on channels *left* and *right*.

This example illustrates the desirability for a notation to distinguish entry and exit channels. It also highlights another point. The interpretation of *P* as a buffer is limited—it is a special-purpose buffer which can handle just the one value *a*. In order to specify a general-purpose buffer it is necessary to use a choice mechanism.

□

Exercise

14.1 Figure 14.1 is a process network for a one-place buffer. Specify *BUFF* in CSP if the only values acceptable by the buffer are *a* and *b*.

$$\xrightarrow{\textit{left}} \boxed{BUFF} \xrightarrow{\textit{right}}$$

Figure 14.1

Solution 14.1

$$BUFF = \textit{left}.a \rightarrow \textit{right}.a \rightarrow BUFF \mid \textit{left}.b \rightarrow \textit{right}.b \rightarrow BUFF$$

The choice by input value ensures that the value output on *right* is identical to that previously input on *left*.

⊡

We shall now introduce a notation which will enable us to take care of the points we have raised. Suppose we are considering a process, with exit channel *c*, which includes the events *c.f*, *c.g* and *c.h* in its alphabet. An output event will be denoted by:

$$c!e$$

where *e* is a variable which can take any of the values *f*, *g* or *h*. More generally, if the messages (values) allowed on channel *c* comprise a certain set, *e* may be any expression which evaluates to a member of that set.

Now let us consider the process whose entry channel is *c*. A *choice* of input event will be denoted by:

$$c?v$$

where *v* is a local variable of the process, which is assigned the value transmitted on the channel *c*. Thus the value of *v* is determined by the corresponding output event of the process that has *c* as its exit channel.

Example

14.2 The buffer process of Exercise 14.1 can now be expressed as:

$$BUFF = \textit{left}?s \rightarrow \textit{right}!s \rightarrow BUFF$$

This may be written as the following boxed specification:

```
┌──────── BUFF ────────────────────────────┐
│ {left.s, right.s | s = a ∨ s = b}        │
├──────────────────────────────────────────┤
│ μX. left ?s → right !s → X               │
└──────────────────────────────────────────┘
```

Note that the events are still written with dots in the alphabet; it is only in the process descriptions that we use ? (choice by input) and ! (output value). The alphabet uses standard set notation to describe a set with certain properties, which are stated following the short vertical bar |. The symbol ∨ is the logic symbol for 'or'. □

It may help you to remember the new notation by thinking of the question mark as asking for a value from the channel. The symbol following the question mark must be a variable; the value received by this variable is used to choose the subsequent behaviour of the process. The expression following the exclamation mark must evaluate to a definite value which is to be output. This expression may contain variables that have already been given values.

Example

14.3 A process *MULT_3* repeatedly accepts numeric input on the channel *in*, and outputs three times the input value on the channel *out*. A specification of *MULT_3* is given by the following:

$$MULT\_3 = in?temp \to out!(3 \times temp) \to MULT\_3$$

Note the use of parentheses to enclose the output expression. □

Review Question 14.1 Specify a process *AVERAGE* which repeatedly accepts two values on the channel *pair* and outputs their average on the channel *out*. ⊡

Review Question 14.2 Specify a process *SQUARE* which repeatedly accepts a number on the channel *in*, squares the number, and outputs the result on channel *out*. ⊡

Example

14.4 Consider the parallel combination illustrated in Figure 14.2, where the subprocesses *U* and *V* communicate along channel *c*. If:

$$U = c!a \to P$$

and

$$V = c?v \to Q$$

then

$$U \parallel V = c.a \to (P \parallel Q)$$

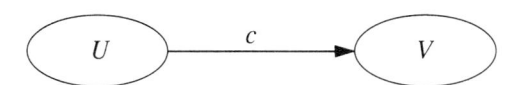

Figure 14.2

This is the communication rule that we mentioned in Section 10.2, but we now have a notation to distinguish input and output. In the expansion of $U \parallel V$ we still write $c.a$ as this is an internal communication of $U \parallel V$. We use ? or ! only when specifying an external communication.

□

Parametrized processes

When the first event of a process is a choice by input value, it is often convenient to think of the input value as determining a *state* of the process. We may then name the subprocess that describes the subsequent behaviour using the state value as a *parameter*. Thus we write:

$$P = c?v \rightarrow Q_v$$

This means that the first event of P is an input communication, and the subsequent behaviour of P is given by the process Q_v, where the values of v act as parameters for a set of processes. For example, let $\{a, b\}$ be the set of communications on the channel *left* in Figure 14.1, and define the set of two processes:

$$Q_v = right!v \rightarrow SKIP$$

for $v \in \{a, b\}$. Then we may write:

$$BUFF = left?v \rightarrow Q_v\,;BUFF$$

14.2 Double buffers

We now expand the discussion so that we can examine some of the more common instances of deadlock and its avoidance. In particular we shall consider a double buffer, which may be represented as a pipeline of two simple buffers.

A **double buffer** or *two-place* buffer can store up to two values. Input of values takes place on the channel *in*; the values may be output on the channel *out*, in the sequence in which they were input. As shown in Figure 14.3 the two-place buffer may be exploded into two concurrent one-place buffers.

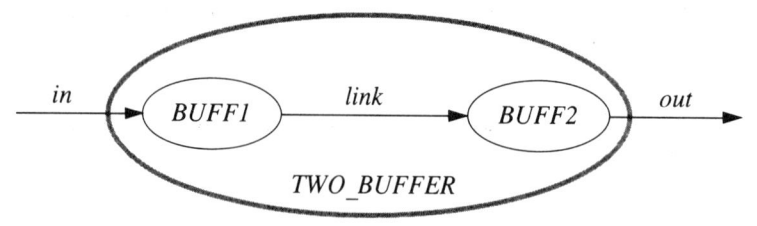

Figure 14.3

Exercises

14.2 Express the process *TWO_BUFFER* of Figure 14.3 in terms of its subprocesses.

Solution 14.2

$$TWO\_BUFFER = BUFF1 \parallel BUFF2$$

$$BUFF1 = in?x \rightarrow link!x \rightarrow BUFF1$$
$$BUFF2 = link?x \rightarrow out!x \rightarrow BUFF2$$

MORE CSP 165

Although we have chosen the same variable name x in both processes *BUFF1* and *BUFF2*, this will not cause any problems.

All variable names are considered to be local to their processes.

⊡

14.3 Use the rules for the concurrency operator to expand *TWO_BUFFER*.

Solution 14.3

$$\begin{aligned}
TWO\_BUFFER &= (in?x \to link!x \to BUFF1) \parallel (link?x \to out!x \to BUFF2) \\
&= in?x \to link.x \to (BUFF1 \parallel out!x \to BUFF2)
\end{aligned}$$
by internal event rule and communication rule

⊡

Review Question 14.3 Suppose the first value available on channel *in* of *TWO_BUFFER* is a. What is the trace with two events?

⊡

We shall now analyse the process *TWO_BUFFER*, using a state-based approach. We shall label the states with names written in small capitals; in each state there is a corresponding subprocess which describes the subsequent evolution of the double buffer.

The process *TWO_BUFFER* does not exist in isolation. It must be a component of a larger process, being linked to another component or components on the channels *in* and *out*. We call the collection of processes which communicate with a given process the *environment* of the process.

Suppose for simplicity that the environment of *TWO_BUFFER* determines that the only possible value of the input on *in* is a. How does the process *TWO_BUFFER* now behave? We shall show a buffer whose next event is an output communication as a black node (it is full) and a buffer whose next event is an input communication as a white node (it is empty). There are four possible states: EE, FE, EF and FF, as illustrated by Figure 14.4.

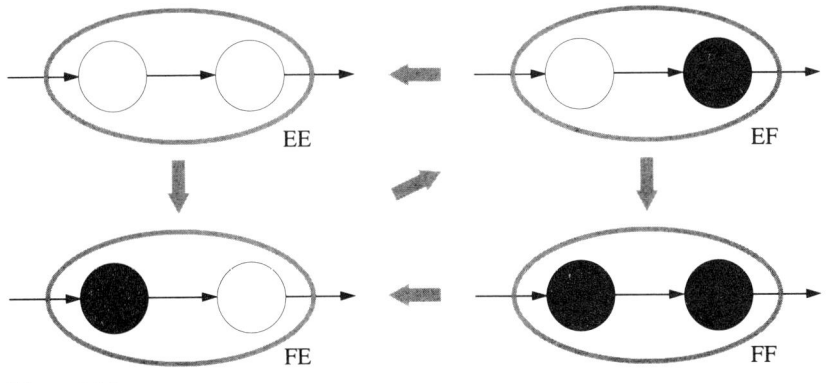

Figure 14.4

The initial state of the process is EE. Let the corresponding process be *EE*. Then:

$$EE = TWO\_BUFFER = in.a \to link.a \to (BUFF1 \parallel out!a \to BUFF2)$$

using the result of Exercise 14.3. Note that *in.a* does not use a ? because a is not a variable (it is a specific value) and that *link.a* is an internal event of *TWO_BUFFER*.

So in the state EE the next event must be *in.a*. The new state is therefore FE. In this state, both *BUFF1* and *BUFF2* must next perform *link.a*. After *link.a* has taken place, the process is in state EF.

At this stage there is a choice. Either the value *a* can be output by *BUFF2* or *BUFF1* starts again, with the input of *a*. Indeed, both might happen simultaneously. The order might be determined by the environment, which could impose a particular sequence (say *out.a* → *in.a* →…); otherwise we have no way of knowing which will happen first, and the choice is non-deterministic. If *out.a* occurs first, the process reverts to its initial state EE with both buffer processes awaiting input. The future evolution of the process is as already stated.

If, on the other hand, *in.a* occurs first we have further input, leading to state FF with both buffer components ready to output. In this latter case the next event that must happen is *out.a*, so that the second buffer outputs, leading to state FE. As already explained, the next event in state FE is that the first buffer passes its data on to the second, leaving *TWO_BUFFER* in state EF.

The transition from one state to another is triggered by a communication event on one of the channels *in*, *link* or *out*; these transitions are summarized in the state transition diagram, Figure 14.5.

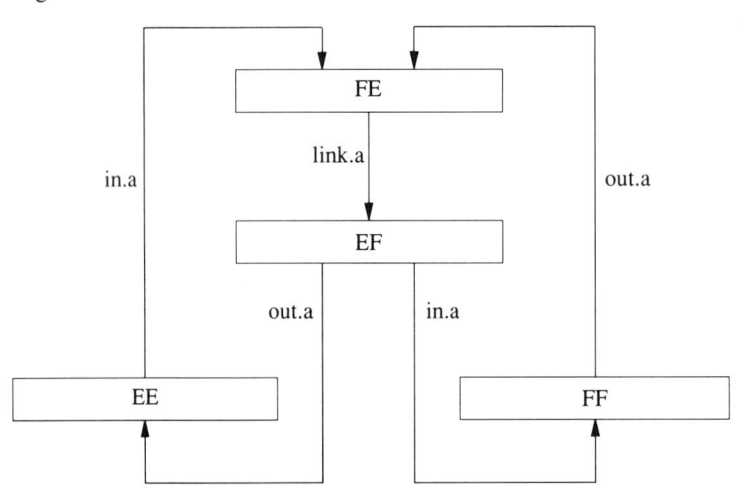

Figure 14.5

Note in particular that the system keeps on returning to the choice point EF. We shall now look at the process *EF* that describes the future behaviour of the double buffer when it is in the state EF.

Exercises

14.4 Expand the specification of the process *TWO_BUFFER* as far as the state EF.

Solution 14.4 Recalling that the initial state of *TWO_BUFFER* is EE, we have:

$$TWO\_BUFFER = EE = in.a \to link.a \to EF$$

where

$$EF = (BUFF1 \parallel out!a \to BUFF2)$$

14.5 Derive a recursive specification of the process *EF*.

Solution 14.5 The first two events must be *in.a* and *out.a*, but *EF* does not care in which order they occur. The subprocess that describes this behaviour is an interleaving of the corresponding single-event processes, that is:

$(in.a \rightarrow SKIP) \;|||\; (out.a \rightarrow SKIP)$

Subsequently the system is in the state FE that is given by:

$FE = link.a \rightarrow EF$

This gives the process definition:

$EF = (in.a \rightarrow SKIP) \;|||\; (out.a \rightarrow SKIP) \;;\; link.a \rightarrow EF$

☐

The results of the Exercises 14.4 and 14.5 have given us a description of the process *TWO_BUFFER* that may be interpreted as follows: *TWO_BUFFER* begins by initializing the buffer to the state EF, and then evolves recursively. The above expansion is typical of how we analyse specifications involving parallelism. We may use this analysis to see if the process definition for *TWO_BUFFER* is deadlock-free. We make the following observations.

The single communication event *in.a*, unconstrained by choice, cannot, on its own, cause deadlock. The process *TWO_BUFFER* can wait patiently until its partner process in the environment is ready to communicate. The internal event *link.a* also cannot be the cause of deadlock. Thus the transition from the initial state EE of *TWO_BUFFER* to EF is free of deadlock. If we can show that the transition from EF back to EE is deadlock-free, this will imply that our process definition is itself deadlock-free.

Now the first event of *EF* is a free choice between *in.a* and *out.a*, which can cause no problems. Either event can take place. However, the next event (the one of *in.a* and *out.a* which has not yet happened) may cause deadlock. For example, if the environment insists on engaging in event *out.a* when the buffer is in state EE and therefore can perform only *in.a*, then deadlock will ensue.

Review Question 14.4 Which other situation is liable to cause deadlock?

☐

Deadlock caused by insisting on reading an empty buffer (or writing to a full buffer) can be avoided in two ways. One method is to link the channels *in* and *out* to a pair of non-communicating processes. These processes evolve asynchronously, so they wait as long as necessary until engaging in their next event. On the other hand, if the environment of *TWO_BUFFER* is a single process (or a set of communicating processes) to which the channels *in* and *out* are linked, then a suitable protocol must be observed. The protocol for a two-place buffer must ensure that the number of events on the channel *in* is never less than the number of events on the channel *out*, but never exceeds that number by more than two. Thus *TWO_BUFFER* allows one or two values to be input (on *in*) and eventually outputs them (on *out*) in the same order. In other words, the concurrent composition of two one-place buffer processes is indeed a two-place buffer process. This approach could be extended to a pipeline consisting of any finite number of one-place buffers.

168 SPECIFICATION AND DESIGN OF CONCURRENT SYSTEMS

Exercise
14.6 Determine whether the following processes are deadlock-prone:
(a) $((a?x \to b?y \to SKIP) \square (b?y \to a?x \to SKIP)) \parallel (a!1 \to SKIP) \parallel (b!1 \to SKIP)$
(b) $((a?x \to b?y \to SKIP) \sqcap (b?x \to a?y \to SKIP)) \parallel (a!1 \to SKIP) \parallel (b!1 \to SKIP)$
(c) $((a?x \to b?y \to SKIP) \sqcap (b?y \to a?x \to SKIP)) \parallel (a!1 \to b!1 \to SKIP)$

Solution 14.6

(a) There are two possible evolutions of this process. Since channels a and b are both ready to output, the choice by channel will be made randomly. If a is chosen then the process will evolve as follows:

$$a.1 \to (b?y \to SKIP) \parallel SKIP \parallel (b!1 \to SKIP)$$
$$= a.1 \to b.1 \to SKIP \parallel SKIP \parallel SKIP$$
$$= a.1 \to b.1 \to SKIP$$

This evolution has the successful trace:

$< a.1, b.1 >\checkmark$

On the other hand if channel b is chosen for input then we have:

$$b.1 \to (a?x \to SKIP) \parallel (a!1 \to SKIP) \parallel SKIP$$
$$= b.1 \to a.1 \to SKIP \parallel SKIP \parallel SKIP$$
$$= b.1 \to a.1 \to SKIP$$

with the successful trace:

$< b.1, a.1 >\checkmark$

Either way there is no possibility of deadlock.

(b) In this case we obtain:

$$(a?x \to b?y \to SKIP \sqcap b?y \to a?x \to SKIP) \parallel (a!1 \to SKIP) \parallel (b!1 \to SKIP)$$
$$= (a.1 \to b.1 \to SKIP) \sqcap (b.1 \to a.1 \to SKIP)$$

and there is no risk of deadlock. In fact, in part (a) we had a choice between two channels which were both ready to transmit, giving an effectively non-deterministic choice.

(c) In this process, the first branch of the non-deterministic choice reduces successfully, but if the second branch is taken there is a classic deadlock:

$$(a?x \to b?y \to SKIP \sqcap b?y \to a?x \to SKIP) \parallel (a!1 \to b!1 \to SKIP)$$
$$= (a.1 \to b.1 \to SKIP) \sqcap STOP$$

Proof obligations

We have approached the specification of *TWO_BUFFER* in a somewhat informal way. A buffer process is specified by the relationship between the input and output streams. Firstly, the output stream must at all times be an *initial segment* of the input stream; that is, it must match the input stream from the beginning up to some point. For a single buffer, it is additionally true that the length of the output stream must be the same as, or one less than, the length of the input stream. In the case of a double buffer, the corresponding condition is that the length of the output stream is equal to, or more than, two less than the length of the input stream. Consequently the explosion of *TWO_BUFFER* into the parallel composite *BUFF1* ∥ *BUFF2* generates a *proof obligation*—to ensure that the composite does indeed satisfy the criteria for a double buffer. The use of traces in CSP allows this proof obligation to be discharged formally. We shall rely on the informal exposition given here.

14.3 Specifying a funnel adder

One of the components in our design of the image-processing system is the multiple addition process *FUNNEL*. We shall take a detailed look here at how to design a process which adds a collection of numbers; in this way we shall avoid being deflected from the task in hand when performing the design of our image-processing system. This will provide further practice in refinement using the ? and ! notation for communication events.

A simple adder

We took a brief look at multiple addition in Chapter 3. Let us start with a *simple adder*, which accepts a stream of integers on each of its two entry channels. The adder takes each pair of integers, one from each stream, and delivers their sum on its exit channel.

Exercise
14.7 Figure 14.6 is a process network for a simple adder. Give the corresponding CSP specification.

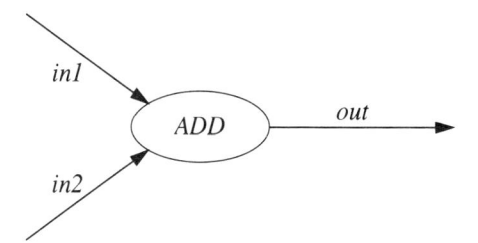

Figure 14.6

Solution 14.7

$$\begin{array}{l} \text{ADD} \\ \{in1.z, in2.z, out.z \mid z \in \mathbb{Z}\} \\ \\ \mu X. ((in1?x \rightarrow SKIP) \,|||\, (in2?y \rightarrow SKIP)); out!(x + y) \rightarrow X \end{array}$$

A multiple adder

Next, we consider a process with four entry channels and one exit channel, as shown in Figure 14.7; the function of the process is to add four streams of integers whose values are supplied on its entry channels, and supply the sums on the exit channel.

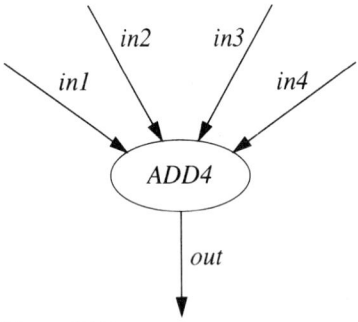

Figure 14.7

Exercise

14.8 Develop the process *ADD4* of Figure 14.7 as a CSP specification.

Solution 14.8

ADD4

$\{in1.t, in2.t, in3.t, in4.t, out.t \mid t \in \mathbb{Z}\}$

$\mu X. ((in1\,?w \rightarrow SKIP) \,|||\, (in2\,?x \rightarrow SKIP) \,|||\, (in3\,?y \rightarrow SKIP) \,|||\, (in4\,?z \rightarrow SKIP));$
$out\,!(w + x + y + z) \rightarrow X$

Suppose now that we wish to build the process *ADD4* from simple adders. The specification of the multiple adder *ADD4* tells us precisely what the output should be, but it does not help us to construct such an adder from other components. The next step is therefore to refine the process *ADD4*—this takes us into the design phase.

To add four numbers requires three additions but, as we saw in Chapter 3, there is more than one way of linking simple adders to generate the required sum. (In fact, the associativity law of arithmetic guarantees that any network of three simple adders which has no loops will correctly add four numbers.) We did suggest though that, on grounds of efficiency, a funnel configuration was desirable, as shown in Figure 14.8. In the exploded process network, a grey boundary is used to indicate the composite process.

The three simple adders are specified identically, differing only in the names of their channels. Thus:

$FUNNEL4 = (ADD(0) \,\|\, ADD(1) \,\|\, ADD(2))$

It will be convenient to index the array of *ADD* processes from 0. Implicit in this

MORE CSP 171

specification of *FUNNEL4* is an appropriate labelling of the channels, as shown in Figure 14.8, to form a *channel array*.

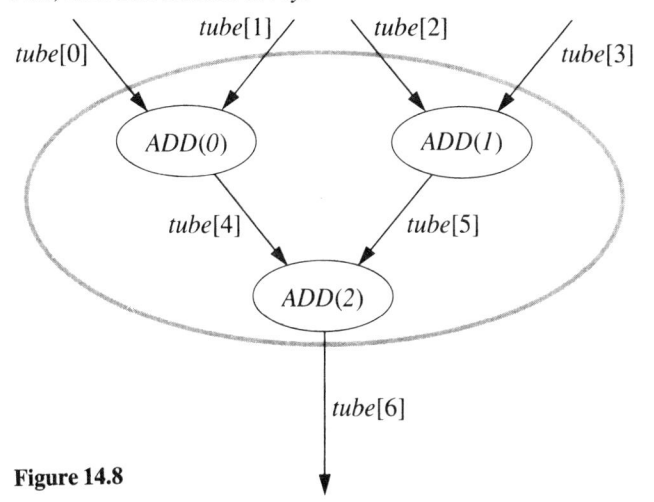

Figure 14.8

Exercise
14.9 Specify the processes *ADD(r)*, where $r = 0, 1, 2$.

Solution 14.9 We note that the channels have been labelled consistently so that, for each value of r, the entry channels to *ADD(r)* are *tube[2r]* and *tube[2r + 1]*, and its exit channel is *tube[r + 4]*. Therefore:

$$ADD(r) = ((tube[2r]?x \to SKIP) \;|||\; (tube[2r + 1]?y \to SKIP)) ;$$
$$tube[r + 4]!(x + y) \to ADD(r)$$

▫

Once again, it is possible to prove formally that *FUNNEL4* meets the specification of *ADD4*.

We can use a similar procedure to construct a funnel adder for any number of inputs. The primary entry channels can be labelled *tube[0]*, ..., *tube[N − 1]*, where *N* is the number of inputs, and *N* − 1 simple adders are needed, *ADD(0)* to *ADD(N − 2)*. The entry channels to *ADD(r)* will be *tube[2r]* and *tube[2r + 1]*, and its exit channel is *tube[r + N]*, just as in Figure 14.8. The total number of channels in the *FUNNEL* process is $2N − 1$, so the final output from *FUNNEL* appears on channel *tube[2N − 2]*. Thus we obtain the following process description for *FUNNEL*:

$$FUNNEL = \|_{0 \le r \le N-2} ADD(r)$$

$$ADD(r) = (tube[2r]?x \to SKIP \;|||\; tube[2r + 1]?y \to SKIP) ;$$
$$tube[r + N]!(x + y) \to ADD(r)$$

To avoid the excessive use of parentheses we have adopted the convention that the prefixing operator binds more closely than the parallel operators.

Review Question 14.5 Let the number of inputs be $N = 8$. Draw a diagram to verify that the processes *ADD(0)*, ..., *ADD(6)*, connected by channels *tube[0]*, ..., *tube[14]* as described above, implement a funnel adder with input on *tube*[0], ..., *tube*[7] and output on *tube*[14].

14.4 Summary

We have introduced the notations ? and ! for input and output events in a CSP process description. Note that ? is used with a local variable to represent choice by input value and ! is used with an evaluatable expression (which may be a constant or a variable). When a definite input event is required or when describing an internal communication we continue to use the dot notation. We also use the dot notation for a communication event in the alphabet of a process and in traces.

The use of ? for choice by input value is frequently followed by a parametrized process:

$c?v \rightarrow P_v$

Here *v* may take any allowable value which can be transmitted on channel *c*. The use of a parameter in the name of a process indicates that the behaviour of the process depends on the value of the parameter.

We illustrated the use of the ? and ! notations in the context of a double buffer, and discussed the conditions for deadlock. We also examined a specification for a funnel adder; this will be used in performing the additions demanded by our hole-counting algorithm.

15 DETAILED DESIGN

We are now going to tackle the detailed design of our image-processing system. Recall that we designed the overall system as the following parallel composite:

SYSTEM = CONTROLLER || CELLS || FUNNEL

In Chapters 13 and 14 we began to analyse these subprocesses. Our aim in the next phase of the development is to produce a CSP description of the system in terms of events each of which is an executable action.

15.1 The strategy

In order to perform the next level of refinement of the design, we need to have an overview of the strategy of communication. The channel array *control*[ ] links *CONTROLLER* to *CELLS* and the channels *tube*[0], ..., *tube*[*cells* – 1] link *CELLS* to *FUNNEL*. Since the number of entry channels to *FUNNEL* is *cells*, the exit channel from *FUNNEL* (that leads to *CONTROLLER*) is *tube*[2 × *cells* – 2].

An informal data flow analysis will help us see our way forward. The CSP system design document must model the behaviour of the system in response to the three system commands LOAD IMAGE, COUNT HOLES and TERMINATE listed in the statement of requirements.

The action to be taken in response to LOAD IMAGE is to initiate the transfer of data representing the next image in the filestore to the *CELLS* process and to the display screen. When the COUNT HOLES command is issued, the hole-counting algorithm must be initiated. This entails the *CELLS* process identifying the relevant patterns and passing on the corresponding numeric values (1, –1 or 0) to the adder process *FUNNEL*. The latter process adds up all its inputs and conveys the sum to *CONTROLLER*, which issues the appropriate message on the *screen* channel.

Finally, the effect of the TERMINATE command is to close down all components of the system. It is therefore necessary for *CONTROLLER* to notify *CELLS* and *FUNNEL* to close down. The termination signal must then be forwarded by *FUNNEL* on to *CONTROLLER*, which itself closes down, thus terminating *SYSTEM* successfully.

Review Question 15.1 Which of the three component processes of *SYSTEM* are involved in describing each of the system commands LOAD IMAGE, COUNT HOLES and TERMINATE required by the statement of requirements?

Review Question 15.2 Identify the channels along which the main data flows take place in response to each of the system commands.

In the light of the description of the behaviour of the system, we now look at each component process in turn.

15.2 The process *CONTROLLER*

The *CONTROLLER* process acts as the command handler and also triggers activity in the *CELLS* process. We shall deal with the latter aspect first. Here is the specification of *CONTROLLER*:

$CONTROLLER =$
$\quad (command.load \rightarrow LOAD\_IMAGE\ ;\ CONTROLLER$
$\quad |$
$\quad command.count \rightarrow COUNT\_HOLES\ ;\ CONTROLLER$
$\quad |$
$\quad command.terminate \rightarrow TERMINATE)$

Each of the system commands is represented in CSP by a signal—*load*, *count* or *terminate*—on the *command* channel to *CONTROLLER*, leading in turn to the appropriate subprocess. For each of these subprocesses—*LOAD_IMAGE*, *COUNT_HOLES* and *TERMINATE*—it is necessary to convey the command signal to each of the individual processes *CELL*(i, j). This behaviour may be described by introducing the new subprocess *BROADCAST*, defined as follows:

$BROADCAST_{cmd} = |||_{ij} control[i,j]!cmd \rightarrow SKIP$

This process sends the signal that is the current value of the variable *cmd* in parallel to each of the process components *CELL*(i, j).

The main subprocesses of *CONTROLLER* can now be expressed in terms of *BROADCAST*. We shall first expand *COUNT_HOLES* and *TERMINATE*, leaving *LOAD_IMAGE* until last.

When *CONTROLLER* receives the *count* signal the next event of *CONTROLLER*, after the command signal has been passed on to *CELLS*, is to receive the hole count from *FUNNEL* along the channel $tube[2 \times cells - 2]$. In fact, if a is the number of Type A blocks and b is the number of Type B blocks, the number of holes is $b - a + 1$. It will turn out to be more convenient to allow *FUNNEL* to transmit the value $b - a$ and let *CONTROLLER* add the final 1 before transmitting the hole count on the *screen* channel. Thus:

$COUNT\_HOLES =$
$\quad BROADCAST_{count}\ ;\ tube[2 \times cells - 2]?x \rightarrow screen!(x+1) \rightarrow SKIP$

The use of x as an input variable here indicates that any integer value received on the channel from *FUNNEL* will be acceptable.

Similarly, in the case of *terminate*, the command must be passed from *CONTROLLER* to *CELLS*, and the next event of *CONTROLLER* is to receive a response from *FUNNEL* to indicate that *CELLS* and *FUNNEL* had closed down:

$TERMINATE = BROADCAST_{terminate}\,;tube[2 \times cells - 2].terminate \rightarrow SKIP$

We still have to consider the process *LOAD_IMAGE* that handles the *load* command signal. In order to load an image, *CONTROLLER* notifies each of the processes *CELL(i, j)*, using the process $BROADCAST_{load}$, so that *CELL(i, j)* is prepared to receive a pixel value. *CONTROLLER* then arranges to transmit the relevant pixel value to each *CELL* process.

$LOAD\_IMAGE = BROADCAST_{load}\,;LOAD\_CELLS$

The process *LOAD_CELLS* takes an image from the filestore, displays it on the screen and distributes it amongst the processes *CELL(i, j)*. The specification of *LOAD_CELLS* depends on the interface with the filestore. We have already made the assumption that an image is stored as a rectangular array of pixels, with a predetermined number of rows and columns. However, we do not know how this data is transmitted from the filestore. Since the filestore is external to the system that we are developing, this is actually an omission from the statement of requirements. We assume that whenever we want a new image one is available and can be input sequentially on the channel *filein*. As each pixel value is received, it is output to corresponding *CELL* process. We can assume further that the image data is transmitted row by row. Thus all the data for row 0 is transmitted, followed by all the data for row 1, and so on until the data for row *rows* − 1(the last row) is sent. The row and column position for the current pixel may be denoted respectively by variables *i*, taking values between 0 and *rows* − 1, and *j*, with values between and 0 and *cols* − 1.

In summary, the process *LOAD_CELLS* receives a sequence of pixel values on the channel *filein* and transmits each one on the *screen* channel and on the appropriate channel *control[i, j]*. We shall consider *LOAD_CELLS* to be composed of a sequence of subprocesses *LOAD_CELL(i, j)*, each of which obtains a single pixel value and transmits it on the channels *screen* and *control[i, j]*. The first event of *LOAD_CELL(i, j)* is to receive a pixel value on the channel *filein*; the only allowable pixel values are *black* and *white*. This value is then transmitted on both the *screen* and the appropriate *control* channels. We might therefore write:

$LOAD\_CELL(i, j) = filein?pixel \rightarrow screen!pixel \rightarrow control[i,j]!pixel \rightarrow SKIP$

Here we have assumed that the pixel value is sent first to the screen and then to the appropriate process *CELL(i, j)*. However, there is no reason why these two events should not happen in parallel; we therefore introduce the subprocess array:

$DISPLAY_{pixel}(i, j) = (screen!pixel \rightarrow SKIP \,|||\, control[i,j]!pixel \rightarrow SKIP)$

This is an array of processes, each of which can be in one of two states—*black* and *white*. In either state, the appropriate colour is transmitted to the screen and to the corresponding cell process, in no particular order.

176 SPECIFICATION AND DESIGN OF CONCURRENT SYSTEMS

Exercise

15.1

(a) Give a CSP specification of the process *LOAD_ROW(i)* that loads a complete row of pixel values.

(b) Use your answer to (a) to give a CSP specification of *LOAD_CELLS*.

Solution 15.1

(a) $LOAD\_ROW(i) = filein?pixel \rightarrow DISPLAY_{pixel}(i, 0)$;
$filein?pixel \rightarrow DISPLAY_{pixel}(i, 1)$;
$filein?pixel \rightarrow DISPLAY_{pixel}(i, 2)$;
...

$filein?pixel \rightarrow DISPLAY_{pixel}(i, cols-1)$

This can be written more compactly using the replicated sequencing operator:

$$LOAD\_ROW(i) = \sum_{j=0}^{cols-1} (filein?pixel \rightarrow DISPLAY_{pixel}(i, j))$$

(b) We may now write:

$$LOAD\_CELLS = \sum_{i=0}^{rows-1} LOAD\_ROW(i)$$

□

Exercise

15.2 One of the requirements is that the system should be configured initially with a blank image (all cells white). Give a specification of the process *INIT* that fulfils this requirement.

Solution 15.2 Initially, a blank image should appear on the screen, and each local *CELL* process should hold the corresponding pixel value, *white*. We note that, before a value can be transmitted on *control[i, j]*, it must be preceded by the warning signal *load*:

$$INIT = BROADCAST_{load} ; \sum_{i=0}^{rows-1} \sum_{j=0}^{cols-1} DISPLAY_{white}(i, j)$$

The process *INIT* first sends the signal *load* to all the *CELL* components, in parallel; it then transmits the pixel value *white*, in sequence, to each *CELL* component and to the screen (in parallel).

□

Exercise

15.3 Give a complete CSP design for *CONTROLLER*.

DETAILED DESIGN

Solution 15.3

CONTROLLER

$\{command.load, command.count, command.terminate\} \cup$
$\{tube[2 \times cells - 2].x \mid x = terminate \lor x \in \mathbb{Z}\} \cup$
$\{filein.v \mid v = black \lor v = white\} \cup \{screen.y \mid y = black \lor y = white \lor y \in \mathbb{Z}\} \cup$
$\{control[i, j].w \mid 0 \leq i < rows, 0 \leq j < cols, w \in \{black, white, load, count, terminate\}\}$

$INIT;$
$\mu X. (command.load \rightarrow BROADCAST_{load} ; LOAD\_CELLS; X$
$\quad |$
$\quad command.count \rightarrow BROADCAST_{count} ; tube[2 \times cells - 2]?x \rightarrow screen!(x + 1) \rightarrow X$
$\quad |$
$\quad command.terminate \rightarrow BROADCAST_{terminate} ; tube[2 \times cells - 2].terminate \rightarrow SKIP)$

where

$INIT = BROADCAST_{load} ; \sum_{i=0}^{rows-1} \sum_{j=0}^{cols-1} DISPLAY_{white}(i, j)$

$BROADCAST_{cmd} = \underset{ij}{|||} control[i, j]!cmd \rightarrow SKIP$

$LOAD\_CELLS = \sum_{i=0}^{rows-1} \sum_{j=0}^{cols-1} filein?pixel \rightarrow DISPLAY_{pixel}(i, j)$

$DISPLAY_{pixel}(i, j) = (screen!pixel \rightarrow SKIP \mid\mid\mid control[i, j]!pixel \rightarrow SKIP)$

☐

Review Question 15.3 The processes defined in the solution to Exercise 15.1 use the sequencing operator. Could a parallel operator have been used?

☐

15.3 The process *CELLS*

We now come to the process *CELLS*; as stated in Chapter 13, this is designed as a concurrent combination of an array of *CELL* processes. Each local process in the array has the same behaviour, with appropriate labelling of its channels.

A sequence of events in which $CELL(i,j)$ engages is triggered by a command on the channel $control[i,j]$. Thus we have:

$$CELL(i,j) = control[i,j] ?cmd \rightarrow C_{cmd}(i, j)$$

where the process component C_{cmd} describes the subsequent behaviour of *CELL* after receiving a command. We shall consider the possible values of *cmd* in turn.

Loading a pixel

On receiving the command *load*, $CELL(i,j)$ must next engage in the event $control[i,j]?pixel$ that inputs the value of the pixel (i,j) for the current image. This value will then have to be stored so that it is available for subsequent processing (by the hole-counting algorithm). Finally, the process $CELL(i,j)$ must return to the state in which it can receive further commands on its *control* channel.

A suitable method of storing a single value is a one-place buffer. We therefore associate such a local *BUFFER* process with each *CELL* process. We therefore revise our refinement of *CELLS* as follows:

$$CELLS = \|_{ij} (CELL(i,j) \| BUFFER(i,j))$$

The new channels between the cell process and the local buffer may be called *inbuffer*[i, j] and *outbuffer*[i, j], as shown in Figure 15.1. (These channels are in addition to the channels introduced in Section 13.4.)

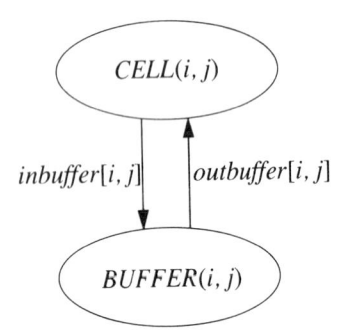

Figure 15.1

Thus we might expect:

$$C_{load}(i,j) = control[i,j]?pixel \rightarrow inbuffer[i,j]!pixel \rightarrow CELL(i,j)$$

Unfortunately this is a recipe for deadlock. In addition to receiving values from C_{load}, the buffer also needs to output these values to C_{count}. There is no requirement that these alternate in orderly fashion; the user may load several images without counting any of them, or may issue the command to count the same image more than once. The buffer can know nothing of this—its only reasonable mode of behaviour is to alternately input and output values. We shall therefore establish the following *buffer protocol*: whenever a *CELL* process wishes to communicate with a *BUFFER* process, it engages in a linked pair of communications—an output from *BUFFER* followed by an input to *BUFFER*. (We shall leave the initialization of *BUFFER* until the end of this section.) In the case of C_{load} the old value that was stored in the buffer is overwritten, so it is just output and discarded. Thus:

$$C_{load}(i,j) = \\ outbuffer[i,j]?x \rightarrow control[i,j]?pixel \rightarrow inbuffer[i,j]!pixel \rightarrow CELL(i,j)$$

Terminating CELL

Consider next the behaviour of $C_{terminate}(i,j)$. Each process *CELL*(i, j) receives the input *terminate* (from *CONTROLLER*). To terminate successfully, it must convey the instruction to the corresponding *ADD* process in *FUNNEL*. We leave the details as an exercise. Bear in mind that the local *BUFFER* process must also be terminated successfully.

Exercise
15.4 Complete the specification of $C_{terminate}(i,j)$.

DETAILED DESIGN 179

Solution 15.4 The exit channel from *CELL(i, j)* to *FUNNEL* is *tube[i × cols + j]*, as we saw in Exercise 13.1.

$C_{terminate}(i,j) =$
  outbuffer[i, j]?*x* →
  (*inbuffer[i, j]*!*terminate* → *SKIP* ||| *tube[i × cols + j]*!*terminate* → *SKIP*)

$C_{terminate}$ begins by receiving the current value from the process *BUFFER(i, j)*, according to the buffer protocol. This value is discarded. It then transmits signals, in parallel, to close down *BUFFER(i, j)* and *FUNNEL*.

Calculating the local count

Now we come to the important function of *CELL*, the execution of the hole-counting algorithm. This will appear in the specification of C_{count}. We need to establish what the individual processes *CELL(i, j)* do to produce the global answer. Each of these processes outputs a number, and these numbers are passed to the *FUNNEL* process to be summed, the final sum being returned to the *CONTROLLER*.

In Section 12.3 we described the algorithm in detail. Rather than determining a number for each cell, the algorithm associates a number with each 2 × 2 block of cells, as illustrated in Figure 15.2.

Type A [A] ➡ –1   Type B [B] ➡ 1

Figure 15.2

We shall somehow have to identify each *CELL* process with a block. This turns out to be very straightforward. All we have to do is to associate each block with one of its cells. We shall make the arbitrary decision of associating each block with its top left-hand corner, as shown in Figure 15.3. Each of the other cells in the block will have to communicate its current value to the process associated with the top left-hand cell, which must then draw the appropriate conclusions.

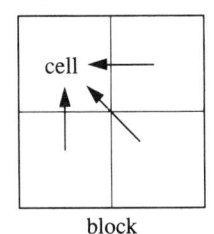

Block-to-cell communication
Figure 15.3

Hence the controlling cell in each block receives communications from three neighbouring cells. Each cell belongs to a number of blocks, and must transmit its value to the controlling cell in each of those blocks.

Exercise
15.5 How many blocks does a given cell belong to? Along which channels does it need to output its own pixel value?

180 SPECIFICATION AND DESIGN OF CONCURRENT SYSTEMS

Solution 15.5 The cell belongs to three blocks other than the one it controls. It must output its own value along channels *west*, *northwest* and *north*, as shown in Figure 15.4.

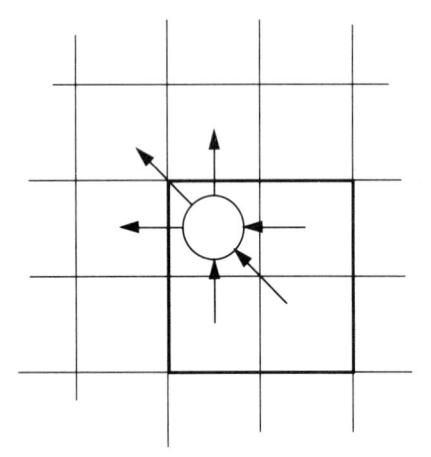

Figure 15.4

To work out the count for the block it controls, *CELL* must receive certain information, and to assist other *CELL* processes it must send information. It would be silly to impose some ordering on these communications; clearly *CELL* should be allowed to send and receive when it is ready. Hence sending and receiving must be specified in parallel. Obviously all three neighbouring values must be received before calculating the local count.

Exercise
15.6 Identify the communication events in which $C_{count}(i,j)$ engages.

Solution 15.6 The current pixel value of the cell is obtained from the local buffer. This value is then held in the local variable *pixel*. To avoid deadlock, each communication with the buffer must be bi-directional, that is, it must consist of reading the buffer followed by writing to the buffer. Thus the communications are:

outbuffer[i,j]?*pixel*
inbuffer[i,j]!*pixel*
north[i,j]!*pixel*
northwest[i,j]!*pixel*
west[i,j]!*pixel*
north[$i \oplus 1, j$]?*southpixel*
northwest[$i \oplus 1, j \oplus 1$]?*southeastpixel*
west[$i, j \oplus 1$]?*eastpixel*
tube[$i \times cols + j$]!*localcount*

The variables *southpixel*, *southeastpixel* and *eastpixel* hold the pixel values of the neighbouring cells in the block; these will be used to compute the block value that is added in to the global sum by *FUNNEL*.

We may make the following observations about the events listed in Solution 15.6. The input on *outbuffer* must precede the outputs on *inbuffer*, *north*, *northwest* and *west*; the

DETAILED DESIGN 181

latter may occur in any order. Also, the calculation and output of the block value must occur after receiving all the inputs, which themselves may occur in any order. We shall define $C_{count}(i,j)$ in terms of the following subprocesses:

$SEND(i,j)$ sends the local pixel value to neighbours and to local buffer

$RECEIVE(i,j)$ receives the pixel values of other cells in block

$CALCULATE(i,j)$ performs the calculation and output of the block value

Hence a specification of this process is:

$C_{count}(i,j) =$
 $outbuffer[i,j]?pixel \rightarrow (SEND_{pixel}(i,j) \,|||\, (RECEIVE(i,j)\,;\, CALCULATE(i,j)))\,;$
 $CELL(i, j)$

$SEND_{pixel}(i,j) =$
 $(inbuffer[i,j]!pixel \rightarrow SKIP) \,|||$
 $(north[i,j]!pixel \rightarrow SKIP) \,|||$
 $(northwest[i,j]!pixel \rightarrow SKIP) \,|||$
 $(west[i,j]!pixel \rightarrow SKIP)$

$RECEIVE(i,j) =$
 $(north[i \oplus 1, j]?southpixel \rightarrow SKIP) \,|||$
 $(northwest[i \oplus 1, j \oplus 1]?southeastpixel \rightarrow SKIP) \,|||$
 $(west[i, j \oplus 1]?eastpixel \rightarrow SKIP)$

In order to specify the subprocess $CALCULATE(i,j)$ we shall temporarily resort to the use of **if-then-else**. We shall meet the formal CSP notation in Chapter 16. (The logic symbol $\wedge$ means **'and'**)

$CALCULATE(i,j) =$
 if $(pixel = white) \wedge (southeastpixel = black) \wedge (eastpixel = southpixel)$
 then if $eastpixel = white$
  then $tube[i \times cols + j]!(-1)$
  else $tube[i \times cols + j]!1$
 else $tube[i \times cols + j]!0$

We remark that it is now evident that only three of the eight potential exit channels from $CELL(i, j)$ are actually needed to specify the hole-counting algorithm: $north[i, j]$, $northwest[i, j]$ and $west[i, j]$. The complete process network for $CELL(i, j) \,\|\, BUFFER(i, j)$ is shown in Figure 15.5.

Completing the design of CELLS

We are almost ready now to gather the threads and present the complete design of *CELLS*. The one thing we have failed to do is to specify the local buffer operation. The local buffer process operates concurrently with $CELL(i,j)$, communicating along channels *inbuffer* and *outbuffer*. In normal operation, the buffer will output a value and then input a value. We must initialize the buffer though, because its first communication will, in accordance with the buffer protocol, be on its exit channel. Thus:

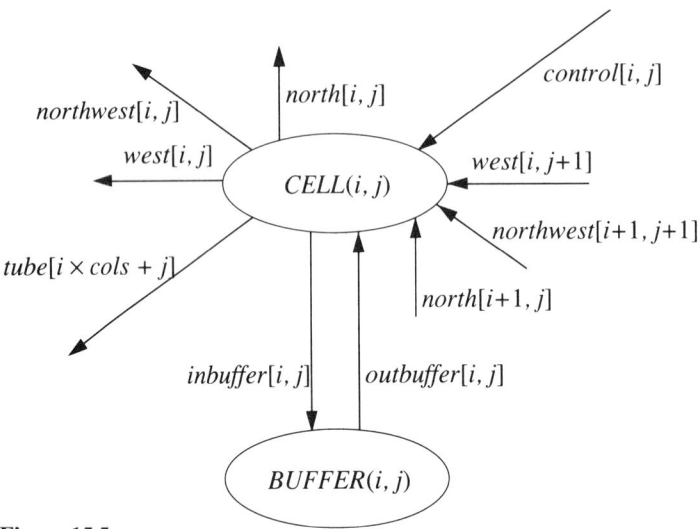

182 SPECIFICATION AND DESIGN OF CONCURRENT SYSTEMS

Figure 15.5

$BUFFER(i,j) = outbuffer[i,j]!init \rightarrow inbuffer[i,j]?pixel \rightarrow B_{pixel}(i,j)$

$B_{white}(i,j) = outbuffer[i,j]!white \rightarrow inbuffer[i,j]?pixel \rightarrow B_{pixel}(i,j)$
$B_{black}(i,j) = outbuffer[i,j]!black \rightarrow inbuffer[i,j]?pixel \rightarrow B_{pixel}(i,j)$
$B_{terminate}(i,j) = SKIP$

Review Question 15.4 What happens to the first signal, *init*, which is output by *BUFFER*? □

Exercise
15.7 Give the complete design of *CELLS*.

Solution 15.7

CELLS

$\{control[i,j].w \mid w \in \{black, white, load, count, terminate\}\} \cup$
$\{outbuffer[i,j].x, inbuffer[i,j].x \mid x \in \{init, black, white, terminate\}\} \cup$
$\{tube[r].c \mid 0 \leq r < cells, c \in \{-1, 0, 1, terminate\}\} \cup$
$\{north[i,j].pixel, northwest[i,j].pixel, west[i,j].pixel \mid pixel \in \{black, white\}\}$
  $(0 \leq i < rows, \; 0 \leq j < cols)$

$\|_{ij}(CELL(i,j) \| BUFFER(i,j))$
where
$CELL(i,j) = control[i,j]?cmd \rightarrow C_{cmd}(i,j)$
$C_{load}(i,j) =$
  $control[i,j]?pixel \rightarrow outbuffer[i,j]?x \rightarrow inbuffer[i,j]!pixel \rightarrow CELL(i,j)$
$C_{count}(i,j) =$
  $outbuffer[i,j]?pixel \rightarrow (SEND_{pixel}(i,j) \|\| (RECEIVE(i,j); CALCULATE(i,j)));$
  $CELL(i,j)$

(continued overleaf)

$C_{terminate}(i, j) =$
  $outbuffer[i, j]\,?x \rightarrow$
    $(inbuffer[i, j]\,!terminate \rightarrow SKIP \;|||\; tube[i \times cols + j]\,!terminate \rightarrow SKIP)$
$SEND_{pixel}(i, j) =$
  $(inbuffer[i, j]\,!pixel \rightarrow SKIP) \;|||\; (north[i, j]\,!pixel \rightarrow SKIP) \;|||$
  $(northwest[i, j]\,!pixel \rightarrow SKIP) \;|||\; (west[i, j]\,!pixel \rightarrow SKIP)$
$RECEIVE(i, j) =$
  $(north[i \oplus 1, j]\,?southpixel \rightarrow SKIP) \;|||\; (west[i, j \oplus 1]\,?eastpixel \rightarrow SKIP) \;|||$
  $(northwest[i \oplus 1, j \oplus 1]\,?southeastpixel \rightarrow SKIP)$
$CALCULATE(i, j) =$
  if $(pixel = white) \wedge (southeastpixel = black) \wedge (eastpixel = southpixel)$
  then if $eastpixel = white$
      then $tube[i \times cols + j]\,!(-1)$
      else $tube[i \times cols + j]\,!1$
  else $tube[i \times cols + j]\,!0$
$BUFFER(i, j) = outbuffer[i, j]\,!init \rightarrow inbuffer[i, j]\,?pixel \rightarrow B_{pixel}(i, j)$
$B_{white}(i, j) = outbuffer[i, j]\,!white \rightarrow inbuffer[i, j]\,?pixel \rightarrow B_{pixel}(i, j)$
$B_{black}(i, j) = outbuffer[i, j]\,!black \rightarrow inbuffer[i, j]\,?pixel \rightarrow B_{pixel}(i, j)$
$B_{terminate}(i, j) = SKIP$

15.4 The process *FUNNEL*

The basic internal operation of *FUNNEL* has already been covered in Section 14.3. We have, for a perpetual funnel adder with *cells* inputs:

$FUNNEL = \|_{0 \leq r \leq cells-2} ADD(r)$

$ADD(r) = (tube[2r]\,?x \rightarrow SKIP \;|||\; tube[2r+1]\,?y \rightarrow SKIP);$
    $tube[r + cells]\,!(x + y) \rightarrow ADD(r)$

The communications between *FUNNEL* and the other components *CONTROLLER* and *CELLS* are carried by the channels $tube[0]$ to $tube[cells - 1]$ and $tube[2 \times cells - 2]$.

Review Question 15.5 How many *ADD* components are there in *FUNNEL*? Why? How many additions are performed?

Further analysis reveals that this version of *ADD(r)* is not completely adequate, because it makes no allowances for receiving an instruction to terminate.

Our specification therefore needs modification to allow successful termination when the input values are *terminate*. These values are transmitted to *FUNNEL* by each of the *CELL* processes, so each *ADD* process which is linked to a *CELL* process will receive the signal *terminate* on both entry channels. If each in turn sends *terminate* on its exit channel, this provides a consistent behaviour for all the *ADD* processes. Thus we obtain

$ADD(r) = (tube[2r]\,?x \rightarrow SKIP \;|||\; tube[2r+1]\,?y \rightarrow SKIP); A_{x,y}(r)$

$A_{terminate, terminate}(r) = tube[r + cells]\,!terminate \rightarrow SKIP$
$A_{x,y}(r) = tube[r + cells]\,!(x + y) \rightarrow ADD(r)$ when $x, y \in \mathbb{Z}$

Note that the final process *ADD(cells −2)* also outputs *terminate*; this signal will be received by *CONTROLLER*, which must not terminate before receiving it.

Exercise

15.8 Complete the CSP design of *FUNNEL*.

Solution 15.8

FUNNEL

$\{tube[r].x \mid 0 \leq r \leq 2 \times cells - 2, x \in \mathbb{Z} \vee x = terminate\}$

$FUNNEL = \|_{0 \leq r \leq cells - 2} ADD(r)$
$ADD(r) = (\ tube[2r]?x \rightarrow SKIP \,\|\|\, tube[2r+1]?y \rightarrow SKIP)\ ; A_{x,y}(r)$
$A_{terminate,\,terminate}(r) = tube[r + cells]!\,terminate \rightarrow SKIP$
$A_{x,y}(r) = tube[r + cells]!(x + y) \rightarrow ADD(r)$ when $x, y \in \mathbb{Z}$

☐

15.5 Summary

We have now completed the design of our image-processing system. The whole system is specified by:

$SYSTEM = CONTROLLER \,\|\, CELLS \,\|\, FUNNEL$

where *CONTROLLER* has channels which link it to the external processes representing the input device, filestore and screen. The complete alphabet of *SYSTEM* consists of the union of the alphabets of its three component processes. The communication events between these three processes belong to the alphabets of both the processes that share in the communication; the events that belong to only one process are internal to that process. The individual detailed designs have been presented in Exercises 15.3, 15.7 and 15.8.

We derived the designs by refining the process networks and considering the flow of data consequent upon each of the command signals, *load*, *count* and *terminate*. We also had to make provision for the initialization of the system. The storage function of each component of *CELLS* was achieved by introducing a local process *BUFFER(i, j)* which is concurrent with each process *CELL(i, j)*. Communication between the cell handler and its buffer is governed by a strict buffer protocol to prevent deadlock.

16 SELECTION AND REPETITION

Our whole thrust so far has been to emphasize those aspects of specification and design that are modelled by processes and the communications between them. Our target programming language, Occam, makes provision for processes and communication channels in the context of an imperative or procedural programming style. The basic programming unit is the process, and the basic data object is the variable. Conventional constructs of imperative programming languages, namely selection by Boolean expression and repetition (iteration), are the control mechanisms provided within processes.

In this chapter we shall introduce notations for incorporating assignment to variables, selection and repetition within a CSP document. We shall use these notations to transform our system design to a form whereby it may be implemented, in a fairly direct fashion, in Occam code.

One particular concern of ours will be the replacement of recursion in a CSP description by iteration. At the time of writing, current versions of Occam do not make provision for implementing recursive processes. We therefore provide a formal method of removing recursion from a system design. By using a set of rules and formal definitions, you will learn how to transform a CSP process into an equivalent design in extended CSP.

16.1 Assignment, variables and arrays

We have already used variables in the context of input and output to and from processes. However, it would be convenient if variables could be manipulated using assignment. In our case study, we had to introduce local buffers to support the hole-counting algorithm. Your experience of conventional programming styles may have suggested an alternative approach using assignment to a variable to hold intermediate results.

In an implementable design we shall use a number of extensions to CSP, of which the assignment notation is the first. We shall introduce subprocesses that assign the value of an expression to an identifier, without a formal process specification. Thus it will be understood that the subprocess:

$x := <\text{expression}>$

computes the value of <expression> and assigns this value to the variable x. The scope of the variable x is the current process.

These assignment processes can be combined with other processes in the usual way. We shall enclose an assignment process in parentheses when necessary to avoid ambiguity.

Example

16.1 Let P denote the process that receives two successive numbers on its entry channel, adds them, and outputs the cube of their sum. Calling the entry channel *in* and the exit channel *out*, we may write:

$$P = in?x \rightarrow in?y \rightarrow z := x + y; out!(z \times z \times z) \rightarrow SKIP$$

The variables x, y and z are in scope throughout P.

□

Example

16.2 The process Q, with entry channel *in* and exit channel *out*, inputs a value to the variable x and outputs, in order, the square, cube and fourth power of x. Using assignments to variables to store intermediate results, we have:

$$Q = in?x \rightarrow (square := x \times x) ;$$
$$(out!square \rightarrow SKIP \;|||\; cube := x \times square \;|||\; fourth := square \times square) ;$$
$$(out!cube \rightarrow out!fourth \rightarrow SKIP)$$

□

A further possible saving can be made, in appropriate circumstances, by the use of arrays of variables. If the powers of x are stored in the array of variables:

$$p[1], p[2], p[3], p[4], \ldots$$

then we can use replicated sequential composition to generalize the above specification to cope with an arbitrary power.

Example

16.3 The specification of the process that inputs a value and outputs, in order, all its powers up to the tenth power is given by:

$$P_{10} = in?x \rightarrow (p[1] := x); \sum_{i=2}^{10} (p[i] := x \times p[i-1] \;|||\; out!p[i-1] \rightarrow SKIP); out!p[10] \rightarrow SKIP$$

□

16.2 Selection

The evolution of a process is frequently determined by the value received on an entry channel. This is handled in CSP by using choice by input value. In extended CSP we introduce a notation for a selection construct which can handle choice by input value as a special case.

If P and Q are processes, and *bool* is a Boolean expression then the notation:

$$P \triangleleft bool \triangleright Q$$

denotes the process that behaves either like P (if *bool* evaluates to *true*) or like Q (if *bool* evaluates to *false*). This process has the following meaning:

if *bool* **then** *P* **else** *Q*

We shall see later that the use of infix notation will prove advantageous when we wish to make a selection based on several Boolean expressions.

Example
16.4 The process

$$SKIP \triangleleft (message = quit) \triangleright output!message \rightarrow CONTINUE$$

in which *message* is a variable, will terminate successfully if *message* has the value *quit*, otherwise it will transmit *message* on the *output* channel.

Exercise
16.1 Specify a process *SQPOS* which accepts a stream of numbers on the channel *in*. Each input is followed by transmitting on the channel *out* the square of the input if it is positive, or the unchanged input if it is negative.

Solution 16.1

$$SQPOS = in?x \rightarrow (out!(x \times x) \rightarrow SQPOS \triangleleft x > 0 \triangleright out!x \rightarrow SQPOS)$$

16.2 Specify a simple buffer which terminates successfully on receipt of the specific value *terminate*.

Solution 16.2

$$BUFF = in?x \rightarrow out!x \rightarrow (SKIP \triangleleft (x = terminate) \triangleright BUFF)$$

Note that the buffer passes the message on even when the input value of *x* is *terminate*. This behaviour is essential if we are to be able to close down a multiple buffer formed from simple buffers acting in parallel.

The precedence of $\triangleleft \triangleright$ will be governed by the following conventions:

$$a \rightarrow P \triangleleft bool \triangleright b \rightarrow Q = (a \rightarrow P) \triangleleft bool \triangleright (b \rightarrow Q)$$
$$P; Q \triangleleft bool \triangleright R; S = P; (Q \triangleleft bool \triangleright R); S$$

The following results concerning Boolean choice are straightforward, and are given here without formal proof.

Rule 16.1

For any processes *S* and *T*:

$$S \triangleleft true \triangleright T = S$$

Rule 16.2

For any *P*, *Q*:

$$(P \triangleleft x = a \triangleright Q) = (Q \triangleleft x <> a \triangleright P)$$

Rule 16.3

For any *P, Q, S*, and any Boolean expression *bool*:

$(P \triangleleft bool \triangleright Q) ; S = (P ; S) \triangleleft bool \triangleright (Q ; S)$

Rule 16.4

For any non-terminating *P*, we have $P ; Q = P$. Consequently:

$(P \triangleleft bool \triangleright Q) = (P \triangleleft bool \triangleright SKIP) ; Q$

Multiple selection

A finer degree of control may be achieved as follows. The process:

$P \triangleleft bool1 \triangleright (Q \triangleleft bool2 \triangleright R)$

behaves like *P* if *bool1* is *true*, otherwise it behaves like:

$(Q \triangleleft bool2 \triangleright R)$

Note that in general this will not be identical with:

$(P \triangleleft bool1 \triangleright Q) \triangleleft bool2 \triangleright R$

We shall write:

$P \triangleleft bool1 \triangleright Q \triangleleft bool2 \triangleright R$

without any brackets to denote:[1]

$P \triangleleft bool1 \triangleright (Q \triangleleft bool2 \triangleright R)$

> **Review Question 16.1** Construct a table to illustrate the values of *bool1* and *bool2* for which the process:
>
> $P \triangleleft bool1 \triangleright Q \triangleleft bool2 \triangleright R$
>
> behaves like each of *P*, *Q* and *R*. □

It is clear how this notation can be generalized to even more nested choices. Where there are many conditions, we simplify the notation as follows:

P	$\triangleleft bool1 \triangleright$
Q	$\triangleleft bool2 \triangleright$
R	$\triangleleft bool3 \triangleright$
S	

The behaviour of such a process is found by working your way down to the first Boolean expression that is *true*. The process directly preceding this expression is activated. If none of the Boolean expressions are *true* then the last process will be activated. In particular, if the Boolean expressions are mutually exclusive, the construct behaves much like a case statement in Pascal.

It is worth noting that the Boolean choice operator has to have a catch-all process—*S* in

---

[1] This is described formally by saying that the infix operator $\triangleleft bool \triangleright$ associates to the right.

the list above—which describes the behaviour when all the Boolean expressions evaluate to *false*. This is quite different from the choice mechanisms introduced previously—choice by input value and choice by channel—which only describe the behaviour following one of a prescribed list of events.

Exercise

16.3 Specify a process *TSQPOS* which passes on numbers unchanged if they are negative, outputs the square of the input if it is positive, and terminates on receiving a suitable input.

Solution 16.3

$$TSQPOS = \mu P.\ in?x \rightarrow$$
$$(out!terminate \rightarrow SKIP \quad \triangleleft x = terminate \triangleright$$
$$out!(x \times x) \rightarrow P \quad \triangleleft x > 0 \triangleright$$
$$out!x \rightarrow P)$$

16.3 The while construct

Recursion is a very powerful and useful construction in CSP, which often arises naturally in the description of a process; indeed, many of the specifications that we have met are defined recursively. Unfortunately recursion is not fully supported in Occam, the language of the transputer. However, as we shall see in the next chapter, Occam does include a while construct. That is, a terminating process *P* can be repeated indefinitely while some Boolean expression has the value *true*. Before each activation of the process *P*, the Boolean expression is tested; if the value of the Boolean expression has become *false*, *P* is no longer repeated.

In this section we introduce the CSP while construct, which allows a process to be defined iteratively by a **loop**. We shall then see, in Section 16.4, how a recursive process specification may be replaced by an equivalent loop. The CSP while construct has the syntax:

$$b*P$$

where *b* is a Boolean expression and *P* is a terminating process; it denotes the process whose behaviour is described by:

while *b* **do** *P*

Formally, we define:

$$b*P = \mu X.\ ((P\ ;\ X) \triangleleft b \triangleright SKIP)$$

In words, $b*P$ is the process that repeatedly tests the value of *b*, behaving like *P* if *b* is *true*, but terminating when *b* is *false*. It is to be understood that the value of *b* may change as a result of the activation of *P*.

The definition of $b*P$ is equivalent to saying that if:

$$X = (P\ ;\ X) \triangleleft b \triangleright SKIP$$

then

$$X = b*P$$

We shall have occasion to make use of this form of the definition. Note that:

$$false*P = SKIP$$

Non-terminating loops

As a special case of the while construct, consider the process:

$Q = true * P$

where P is a terminating process. Applying the formal definition:

$Q = \mu X. ((P; X) \triangleleft true \triangleright SKIP)$

Therefore, by Rule 16.1:

$Q = \mu X. (P; X)$

Since P is a terminating process, the behaviour of Q is the continual repetition of P. We may alternatively write:

$Q = P; Q$

Exercise

16.4 Express the non-terminating process defined by:

$R = a \rightarrow R$

in extended CSP notation using a while construct.

Solution 16.4 We have:

$R = a \rightarrow R$
$ = a \rightarrow SKIP; R$

so let:

$P = a \rightarrow SKIP$

Thus:

$R = P; R$

which is equivalent to:

$R = true * P$
$ = true * (a \rightarrow SKIP)$

☐

Review Question 16.2 In the solution to Exercise 16.4, why can we not simply write the following?

$R = true * a$

☐

Review Question 16.3 The following process definition was given in the solution to Exercise 16.1:

$SQPOS = in?x \rightarrow (out!(x \times x) \rightarrow SQPOS \triangleleft x > 0 \triangleright out!x \rightarrow SQPOS)$

Give a definition of the process $SQPOS$ using the while construct.

☐

Terminating loops

The main use of the while construct is to express the behaviour of a loop which repeats until a Boolean expression becomes *false*; that is, it is used to express the behaviour of a *terminating loop*.

Let us consider again a buffer which remains active until it receives the signal *terminate*. A process description for such a buffer was given in the solution to Exercise 16.2 by:

$BUFF = in?x \to out!x \to (SKIP \triangleleft (x = terminate) \triangleright BUFF)$

Since termination occurs when the input has the value *terminate*, a suitable Boolean expression to control the iteration of the loop is:

$x <> terminate$

It would appear that a possible definition of *BUFF* using a while construct might be:

$BUFF = (x <> terminate)*(in?x \to out!x \to SKIP)$

Exercise
16.5 How does this definition fail to agree with the recursive specification of *BUFF*?

Solution 16.5 The problem here is that before the first iteration of the loop, the expression $(x <> terminate)$ must be evaluated, but at this stage it cannot be evaluated because the variable x has not been initialized. □

It turns out that a correct specification, including initialization, is:

$BUFF = in?x \to out!x \to (x <> terminate)*(in?x \to out!x \to SKIP)$

We shall give a formal proof of this in the next section. Note that our buffer process has been specified so that it will certainly transmit the first value that it receives, even if that value is *terminate*. The semantics of a while loop allow the possibility that the body of the loop is never activated.

16.4 Removing recursion

In order to derive a correct iterative process definition which is equivalent to a given recursive specification, it is necessary to have a formal method of derivation. In this section we shall prove some results which will allow us to systematically replace recursion by iteration in our process designs.

Recursion rule 1

If:

$P = (Q;P) \triangleleft b \triangleright S$

then:

$P = b*Q;S$

Proof
Since $X = b*Q$ is equivalent to:

$$X = (Q \,;\, X) \triangleleft b \triangleright SKIP$$

we may write:

$$b*Q \,;\, S = ((Q \,;\, b*Q) \triangleleft b \triangleright SKIP) \,;\, S$$
$$= (Q \,;\, b*Q \,;\, S) \triangleleft b \triangleright S \qquad \text{by Rule 16.3}$$

Consequently, $b*Q \,;\, S$ satisfies the equation:

$$X = (Q \,;\, X) \triangleleft b \triangleright S$$

in other words, $b*Q \,;\, S = P$.

Recursion rule 2

If Q is a terminating process and:

$$P = Q \,;\, (R \,;\, P) \triangleleft b \triangleright S$$

then:

$$P = Q \,;\, b*(R \,;\, Q) \,;\, S$$

Proof

Let:

$$T = (R \,;\, P) \triangleleft b \triangleright S$$

then:

$$P = Q \,;\, (R \,;\, P) \triangleleft b \triangleright S$$
$$= Q \,;\, T$$

This expression for P can be substituted inside the parentheses, giving:

$$P = Q \,;\, (R \,;\, Q \,;\, T) \triangleleft b \triangleright S$$

and so:

$$Q \,;\, T = Q \,;\, (R \,;\, Q \,;\, T) \triangleleft b \triangleright S$$

Since Q is a terminating process, it follows that:

$$T = (R \,;\, Q \,;\, T) \triangleleft b \triangleright S$$

and so, by *Recursion rule 1*:

$$T = b*(R \,;\, Q) \,;\, S$$

Finally:

$$P = Q \,;\, T$$
$$= Q \,;\, b*(R \,;\, Q) \,;\, S$$

Exercise

16.6 Apply *Recursion rule 2* to give a formal derivation of the terminating buffer process:

$$BUFF = in?x \rightarrow out!x \rightarrow (SKIP \triangleleft (x = terminate) \triangleright BUFF)$$

in terms of the while construct.

Solution 16.6 We may use Rule 16.2 to write:

$BUFF = in?x \to out!x \to (BUFF \triangleleft x<> terminate \triangleright SKIP)$

Take:

$Q = in?x \to out!x \to SKIP$
$b = (x <> terminate)$

Thus:

$BUFF = Q\,; (BUFF \triangleleft b \triangleright SKIP)$

and so, by *Recursion rule 2* (with $R = SKIP$):

$BUFF = Q\,; b*Q$
$\qquad = in?x \to out!x \to SKIP;\, (x<> terminate)*(in?x \to out!x \to SKIP)$

as required. □

Exercise

16.7 Remove recursion from the following process description:

$X = in?x \to (SKIP \triangleleft x<0 \triangleright out!x \to X\,)$

Explain briefly how this process evolves.

Solution 16.7 By Rule 16.2:

$X = in?x \to (out!x \to X \triangleleft x \geq 0 \triangleright SKIP)$

Let:

$Q = in?x \to SKIP$
$R = out!x \to SKIP$
$b = (x \geq 0)$

so that:

$X = Q\,; (R\,; X \triangleleft b \triangleright SKIP)$

Applying *Recursion rule 2*:

$X = Q\,; b*(R\,; Q)\,; SKIP$
$\quad = in?x \to (x \geq 0)*(out!x \to in?x \to SKIP)$

This process acts as a buffer which receives integers on its entry channel and repeatedly outputs any non-negative values it has received. When a negative number is received it is not transmitted, and the process terminates. □

Review Question 16.4 To which simple processes are the following specifications equivalent?

(a) $Q1 = false*(in?x \to out!x \to SKIP)$
(b) $Q2 = (x := 0)\,; (x > 0)*(in?x \to out!x \to SKIP)$

□

194 SPECIFICATION AND DESIGN OF CONCURRENT SYSTEMS

The essence of a recursive process which can terminate is the presence of a terminating condition. If the process can be expressed in the form:

$$P = Q; (R; P) \triangleleft b \triangleright S$$

it can be reduced directly to a while loop using the rules above. We cannot assume though that it will be possible to write every recursive process in this form. In practice, we can still adopt a systematic approach to a large class of recursively defined processes. Provided the recursive activation of P is the last subprocess in a particular choice, it is possible to give a general method for deriving an equivalent while construct. This method is best illustrated by an example.

Example
16.5 In Exercise 16.3 we considered the process specified by:

$TSQPOS = \mu P.\ in?x \rightarrow$
$\qquad (out!terminate \rightarrow SKIP \qquad \triangleleft x = terminate \triangleright$
$\qquad out!(x \times x) \rightarrow P \qquad\qquad\quad \triangleleft x > 0 \triangleright$
$\qquad out!x \rightarrow P)$

We could transform this using *Recursion rule 2* to obtain:

$TSQPOS = in?x \rightarrow$
$\qquad (x <> terminate)*$
$\qquad (out!(x \times x) \rightarrow in?x \qquad \triangleleft x > 0 \triangleright$
$\qquad out!x \rightarrow in?x);$
$\qquad out!terminate \rightarrow SKIP$

An alternative method of transforming this specification is by introducing a control variable, which we shall call *running*. There are three steps:

1. initialize *running* to *true* and replace the expression $\mu P.$ by *running**;
2. replace each *SKIP* by the terminating condition (*running* := *false*);
3. replace each recursive call of the process—that is, each recurrence of P in the body of the specification—by *SKIP*.

We are then left with the following equivalent form of the specification:

$TSQPOS = (running := true) ;$
$\qquad running*$
$\qquad (in?x \rightarrow$
$\qquad (out!terminate \rightarrow (running := false) \qquad \triangleleft x = terminate \triangleright$
$\qquad out!(x \times x) \rightarrow SKIP \qquad\qquad\qquad\qquad \triangleleft x > 0 \triangleright$
$\qquad out!x \rightarrow SKIP))$

☐

Review Question 16.5 Write down the successful trace of *TSQPOS* when the sequence of values 1, 2, −5, *terminate* is available on the channel *in*.

Exercise
16.8 Derive an iterative version of the process X by introducing a control variable:

$X = in1?x \rightarrow Y\ [\!]\ in2?y \rightarrow SKIP$
$Y = in3?x \rightarrow SKIP\ [\!]\ in4?y \rightarrow X$

Solution 16.8 Since:

$$X = in1?x \rightarrow (in3?x \rightarrow SKIP$$
$$\square$$
$$in4?y \rightarrow X)$$
$$\square$$
$$in2?y \rightarrow SKIP$$

we can write:

$$X = running := true;$$
$$running*$$
$$(in1?x \rightarrow (in3?x \rightarrow running := false$$
$$\square$$
$$in4?y \rightarrow SKIP)$$
$$\square$$
$$in2?y \rightarrow running := false)$$

16.5 Summary

This chapter completes our discussion of the CSP formalism. We have looked at several extensions to CSP that enable processes to be transformed so that they may more closely resemble the structures of Occam, which will be introduced in Chapter 18.

We have looked in particular at a simplified, conventional notation for an assignment process, and we have also introduced notations for selection and repetition of processes. We saw how together these notations can be used to replace choice by input value with Boolean choice, and to replace recursion in a specification with iteration in simple cases.

Here are the new notations that we use in the description of processes.

Assignment

The notation:

$$v := e$$

specifies a subprocess which evaluates an expression e and assigns its value to the variable v, which is local to the current process.

Selection (Boolean choice)

The notation:

$$P \triangleleft b \triangleright Q$$

defines the process that behaves like P if the Boolean expression b has the value *true*, and like Q otherwise. Several selections may be nested to give a case-by-case selection. We gave four rules for reasoning about processes that involve Boolean choice.

Repetition (while construct)

If b is a Boolean expression and P is a process, the process:

$b * P$

is defined as:

$\mu X . (P ; X \triangleleft b \triangleright SKIP)$

It follows that:

$b * P = (P ; b * P) \triangleleft b \triangleright SKIP$

Recursion rule 2 states that the recursive process P given by:

$P = Q ; (R ; P \triangleleft b \triangleright S)$

can be expressed iteratively as:

$P = Q ; b * (R ; Q) ; S$

An alternative method of removing recursion from a CSP specification requires the introduction of a control variable.

17 TRANSFORMING THE DESIGN

We shall now make use of the new notations introduced in Chapter 16 to transform our CSP design into a more suitable format, making use of assignment, selection and repetition; in particular we shall remove all the formal recursion from the design. As in Chapter 15, we shall treat each of the component processes separately. The remaining phase, writing program code, will then be a direct translation from the transformed CSP design into Occam code.

17.1 The process *CONTROLLER*

We start with the process *CONTROLLER* defined as follows:

$CONTROLLER =$
  $INIT;$
  $\mu X. (command.load \rightarrow BROADCAST_{load}; LOAD\_CELLS; X$
    $|$
    $command.count \rightarrow BROADCAST_{count};$
      $tube[2 \times cells - 2]?x \rightarrow screen!(x+1) \rightarrow X$
    $|$
    $command.terminate \rightarrow BROADCAST_{terminate};$
      $tube[2 \times cells - 2].terminate \rightarrow SKIP)$

The specifications of *INIT*, *BROADCAST*, *LOAD_CELLS* and *DISPLAY* were given in the solution to Exercise 15.3 and are fairly straightforward, but the recursive definition at the top level of *CONTROLLER* will have to be transformed into a while construct, and the choice by input value has to be transformed into Boolean choice.

We shall first transform the choice by input value in the process *CONTROLLER* to Boolean choice. In the form given above, the choice by input value does not have a catch-all value, so it will need to be tailored in order to be converted to Boolean choice. However, our assumption that only three messages can be carried on the *command* channel effectively means that if the message is neither *load* nor *count*, it must be *terminate*. We thus obtain the following version:

198 SPECIFICATION AND DESIGN OF CONCURRENT SYSTEMS

$CONTROLLER =$
$\quad INIT;$
$\quad \mu X. \; command?cmd \rightarrow$
$\quad\quad ((BROADCAST_{load}; LOAD\_CELLS; X) \qquad \triangleleft cmd = load \triangleright$
$\quad\quad (BROADCAST_{count}; tube[2 \times cells - 2]?x \rightarrow screen!(x+1) \rightarrow X)$
$\quad\quad\qquad\qquad\qquad\qquad\qquad\qquad\qquad\qquad \triangleleft cmd = count \triangleright$
$\quad\quad (BROADCAST_{terminate}; tube[2 \times cells - 2]?x \rightarrow SKIP))$

We now make the following useful observation. Whichever value of *cmd* is received, the first thing to take place will always be $BROADCAST_{cmd}$ with the appropriate value of *cmd*. We may therefore simplify the specification, without changing its meaning, as follows:

$CONTROLLER =$
$\quad INIT;$
$\quad \mu X. \; (command?cmd \rightarrow BROADCAST_{cmd};$
$\quad\quad ((LOAD\_CELLS; X) \qquad\qquad\qquad \triangleleft cmd = load \triangleright$
$\quad\quad (tube[2 \times cells - 2]?x \rightarrow screen!(x+1) \rightarrow X) \quad \triangleleft cmd = count \triangleright$
$\quad\quad (tube[2 \times cells - 2]?x \rightarrow SKIP)))$

Exercise

17.1 Use the method of Example 16.5 to eliminate recursion from the CSP design for *CONTROLLER*.

Solution 17.1

$CONTROLLER =$
$\quad INIT;$
$\quad (running := true);$
$\quad running * (command?cmd \rightarrow BROADCAST_{cmd};$
$\quad\quad (LOAD\_CELLS; SKIP \qquad\qquad\qquad \triangleleft cmd = load \triangleright$
$\quad\quad tube[2 \times cells - 2]?x \rightarrow screen!(x+1) \rightarrow SKIP \quad \triangleleft cmd = count \triangleright$
$\quad\quad tube[2 \times cells - 2]?x \rightarrow (running := false)))$

17.2 The process *CELLS*

We now examine the next component, *CELLS*. Here is an extract from the design developed in Chapter 15:

$CELLS = \parallel_{ij} (CELL(i,j) \parallel BUFFER(i,j))$

$CELL(i,j) = control[i,j]?cmd \rightarrow C_{cmd}(i,j)$

$C_{load}(i,j) =$
$\quad outbuffer[i,j]?x \rightarrow control[i,j]?pixel \rightarrow inbuffer[i,j]!pixel \rightarrow CELL(i,j)$

$C_{count}(i,j) =$
$\quad outbuffer[i,j]?pixel \rightarrow$
$\quad\quad (SEND_{pixel}(i,j) \;\vert\!\vert\!\vert\; (RECEIVE(i,j); CALCULATE(i,j))); CELL(i,j)$

$C_{terminate}(i,j) =$
  $outbuffer[i,j]?x \to$
    $(inbuffer[i,j]!terminate \to SKIP ||| tube[i \times cols + j]!terminate \to SKIP)$

$CALCULATE(i,j) =$
  if $(pixel = white) \wedge (southeastpixel = black) \wedge (eastpixel = southpixel)$
  then if $eastpixel = white$
    then $tube[i \times cols + j]!(-1) \to SKIP$
    else $tube[i \times cols + j]!1 \to SKIP$
  else $tube[i \times cols + j]!0 \to SKIP$

$BUFFER(i,j) = outbuffer[i,j]!init \to inbuffer[i,j]?pixel \to B_{pixel}(i,j)$
$B_{white}(i,j) = outbuffer[i,j]!white \to inbuffer[i,j]?pixel \to B_{pixel}(i,j)$
$B_{black}(i,j) = outbuffer[i,j]!black \to inbuffer[i,j]?pixel \to B_{pixel}(i,j)$
$B_{terminate}(i,j) = SKIP$

We have omitted details of *SEND* and *RECEIVE* here as they involve neither choice nor recursion. Let us consider first the process $CELL(i,j)$.

Exercise

17.2 Replace the choice by input value in $CELL(i,j)$ by Boolean choice.

Solution 17.2

$CELL(i,j) = control[i,j]?cmd \to$
  $(C_{load}(i,j)$ $\triangleleft cmd = load \triangleright$
  $C_{count}(i,j)$ $\triangleleft cmd = count \triangleright$
  $C_{terminate}(i,j))$

In order to perform the next stage of the transformation, we introduce the subprocess *NONTER* that handles the non-terminating commands. Here $NONTER_{cmd}$ deals with the values *load* and *count* of *cmd* until the recursive call to $CELL(i,j)$:

$NONTER_{cmd} =$
  $outbuffer[i,j]?x \to control[i,j]?pixel \to inbuffer[i,j]!pixel \to SKIP$
                                                                    $\triangleleft cmd = load \triangleright$
  $outbuffer[i,j]?pixel \to (SEND_{pixel}(i,j) ||| (RECEIVE(i,j); CALCULATE(i,j)))$

We can then write:

$CELL(i,j) = control[i,j]?cmd \to$
  $((NONTER_{cmd}; CELL(i,j))$ $\triangleleft cmd <> terminate \triangleright$ $C_{terminate}(i,j))$

Exercise

17.3 Use *Recursion rule 2* of Chapter 16 to remove recursion from $CELL(i,j)$.

Solution 17.3 The result states that if:

$P = Q;(R;P) \triangleleft b \triangleright S$

then:

$$P = Q ; b*(R ; Q) ; S$$

Here we have:

$Q = control[i,j] ?cmd \rightarrow SKIP$
$b = (cmd <> terminate)$
$R = NONTER_{cmd}$
$S = C_{terminate}(i, j)$

Therefore:

$CELL(i,j)$
  $= control[i,j]?cmd \rightarrow SKIP;$
    $(cmd <> terminate)*(NONTER_{cmd} ; control[i,j] ?cmd \rightarrow SKIP) ;$
    $C_{terminate}(i,j)$

□

Exercise
17.4 Reformulate $CALCULATE(i, j)$ using the Boolean choice operator.

Solution 17.4

$CALCULATE(i,j) =$
  $(tube[i \times cols + j]!(-1) \rightarrow SKIP$ ◁ $eastpixel = white$ ▷
  $tube[i \times cols + j]!1 \rightarrow SKIP)$
    ◁ $(pixel = white) \wedge (southeastpixel = black) \wedge (eastpixel = southpixel)$ ▷
  $tube[i \times cols + j]!0 \rightarrow SKIP$

□

Finally let us consider $BUFFER(i,j)$. The channel $inbuffer[i,j]$ is capable of carrying just three values: *white*, *black* and *terminate*. Consequently we can write the process as follows, using the Boolean choice operator.

$BUFFER(i,j) = outbuffer[i,j]!init \rightarrow inbuffer[i,j]?pixel \rightarrow B_{pixel}(i,j)$

$B_{pixel}(i,j) =$
  $(outbuffer[i,j]!pixel \rightarrow inbuffer[i,j]?pixel \rightarrow B_{pixel}(i,j)$
                                                      ◁ $pixel <> terminate$ ▷
  $SKIP)$

Exercise
17.5 Rewrite $B_{pixel}(i,j)$ replacing recursion by a while construct.

Solution 17.5

By the definition of the while construct:

$B_{pixel}(i,j) =$
  $(pixel <> terminate)*(outbuffer[i,j]!pixel \rightarrow inbuffer[i,j]?pixel \rightarrow SKIP)$

□

As a result of Exercise 17.5, we can now write $BUFFER(i,j)$ as follows:

$BUFFER(i,j) =$
  $outbuffer[i,j]!init \rightarrow inbuffer[i,j]?pixel \rightarrow$
  $(pixel <> terminate)*(outbuffer[i,j]!pixel \rightarrow inbuffer[i,j]?pixel \rightarrow SKIP)$

This completes the treatment of *CELLS*.

17.3 The process *FUNNEL*

Finally we must examine *FUNNEL* to replace choice by input and recursion. Here is the CSP specification of *FUNNEL* as developed in Chapter 15:

$FUNNEL = \|_{0 \le r \le cells-2} ADD(r)$

$ADD(r) = (tube[2r]?x \rightarrow SKIP \,\|\|\, tube[2r+1]?y \rightarrow SKIP) ; A_{x,y}(r)$
$A_{terminate,\,terminate}(r) = tube[r+cells]!terminate \rightarrow SKIP$
$A_{x,y}(r) = tube[r+cells]!(x+y) \rightarrow ADD(r)$ if $x, y \in \mathbb{Z}$

During normal running, *ADD* receives an integer on each of its two entry channels and sends the sum on its exit channel. Termination of *ADD* is triggered by a dual input of *terminate* and the output of *terminate*. We may therefore express the termination condition as follows:

$(x = terminate) \land (y = terminate)$

Exercise

17.6 Give a design for $ADD(r)$ using Boolean choice.

Solution 17.6

$ADD(r) = (tube[2r]?x \rightarrow SKIP \,\|\|\, tube[2r+1]?y \rightarrow SKIP) ;$
    $(tube[r+cells]!(x+y) \rightarrow ADD(r)$
               $\triangleleft \mathbf{not}((x = terminate) \land (y = terminate)) \triangleright$
    $tube[r+cells]!terminate \rightarrow SKIP)$

Exercise

17.7 Rewrite the design of $ADD(r)$ without recursion.

Solution 17.7

$ADD(r) =$
    $(tube[2r]?x \rightarrow SKIP \,\|\|\, tube[2r+1]?y \rightarrow SKIP) ;$
    $\mathbf{not}((x = terminate) \land (y = terminate))*$
    $(tube[r+cells]!(x+y) \rightarrow$
        $(tube[2r]?x \rightarrow SKIP \,\|\|\, tube[2r+1]?y \rightarrow SKIP));$
    $tube[r+cells]!terminate \rightarrow SKIP$

17.4 Summary

In this chapter we have taken our CSP design one stage further. Choice by input value and recursion have been removed in favour of Boolean choice and iteration using while loops.

Bringing together the designs of the individual processes would now provide a detailed design document which can be used to write an Occam program for the image-processing system. This final task forms the subject matter of Chapter 18.

18 AN OCCAM VERSION OF *SYSTEM*

We are now almost in a position to write an Occam program for the image-processing system. What is missing is a familiarity with the syntax of Occam. We shall present the Occam code corresponding to each of our CSP designs, with the intention that you should acquire a reading knowledge of Occam. A summary of the syntax of Occam is presented in the Appendix.

18.1 Atomic processes

An Occam program is a *process*, with a **declarations part** and an **actions part**. The declarations part names the constants and variables that appear in the process, as well as the internal channels of the process. The actions part expresses the process in terms of subprocesses, using various control structures, which we shall meet in Section 18.2. Ultimately each process must be expressed in terms of communication events and **atomic processes**, which can be executed by the Occam environment. The following processes are atomic:

```
SKIP
STOP
v := e
```

Here, v stands for a variable name and e stands for any expression which evaluates to a legitimate value. The communication events in Occam are:

```
c ? v
c ! e
```

where c stands for a channel name. Note that in Occam the use of ? and ! to distinguish input and output is obligatory. Consequently, an input event must use a variable, even if there is only one legitimate value for the input signal.

Every process name will have been declared as such in a declarations part. However, it is desirable for processes to be clearly identifiable within programs. We achieve this by using lower-case letters throughout for events and beginning all process names with an upper-case letter.

18.2 The main control structures

Occam provides a number of control structures to support the process operations available in CSP. Each control structure in Occam is introduced by a suitable reserved word, called a *constructor*. The following is a list of the constructors used in Occam:

PAR	concurrency or interleaving
SEQ	sequential combination
IF	Boolean choice
ALT	choice by channel
WHILE	while loop

We shall now illustrate the use of these constructors. For PAR we consider the specification of *SYSTEM*:

SYSTEM = CONTROLLER ‖ CELLS ‖ FUNNEL

The corresponding code in Occam is:

```
PAR
  Controller
  Cells
  Funnel
```

Note carefully that each process is written on a separate line, and is indented two spaces from the constructor PAR. This layout is a syntactical requirement of the Occam programming language.

We now give examples of how the other constructors are used. The sequential CSP process:

P ; Q ; R

is written in Occam as:

```
SEQ
  P
  Q
  R
```

The SEQ constructor is also used for prefixing processes with events. For example:

command?load → filein?image → X

becomes, in Occam:

```
SEQ
  command ? load
  filein ? image
  X
```

The IF constructor is used to code Boolean choice. Its syntax is similar to the use of **case** in Pascal. For example, the CSP process:

$$P \quad \triangleleft b1 \triangleright$$
$$Q \quad \triangleleft b2 \triangleright$$
$$R$$

is coded in Occam as follows:

```
IF
  b1
    P
  b2
    Q
  TRUE
    R
```

Note that each Boolean expression is indented two spaces from `IF`, and each choice of process is indented two spaces from the Boolean expression that selects it. The semantics of this structure are that each of the Boolean expressions is evaluated in turn; as soon as one evaluates to `TRUE` the corresponding process is activated, and all subsequent Boolean expressions are ignored. It is necessary for the programmer to ensure that at least one Boolean expression in an `IF` structure evaluates to `TRUE`. This is frequently achieved by using the value `TRUE` for the final branch of the structure.

Since our CSP design document for the image-processing system does not include a choice by channel, we shall leave an example of the use of `ALT` until Part IV.

The `WHILE` constructor is used to code a while loop; thus:

$$b*P$$

becomes:

```
WHILE b
  P
```

Control structures can be nested; for example:

$$b*(P\,;Q\,;(R\,\|\,S))$$

will become:

```
WHILE b
  SEQ
    P
    Q
    PAR
      R
      S
```

`WHILE b` is always followed by a single process, which may however be a structured process introduced by a constructor. The indentation rules must be observed strictly, as they delineate the scope of the constructors.

18.3 Defining a named process

We saw in Section 18.2 how the process description of *SYSTEM* may be written in Occam as a parallel composition of named processes. We cannot tell yet from the code whether the component processes are truly concurrent or whether they are interleaved. This is determined by *declaring* the channels that appear in the process network (or in the alphabets of the component processes).

Figure 13.1 indicated the channels *command*, *filein* and *screen*. These channels are declared using CHAN:

    CHAN command, filein, screen :

A ***declaration*** begins with a declaration symbol and ends with a colon. When we need to use a channel array, we have the following forms of declaration:

    CHAN tube[N] :

Here the index N indicates an array of *N* channels labelled 0, ..., N – 1. For a two-dimensional array we write the declaration in the form:

    CHAN control[rows][cols] :

The declaration symbols are:

    CHAN   for declaring names of channels

    DEF   for declaring names of constants

    VAR   for declaring names of variables

A process description may be preceded by one or more declarations. The scope of the names in the declarations is the process description that follows them.

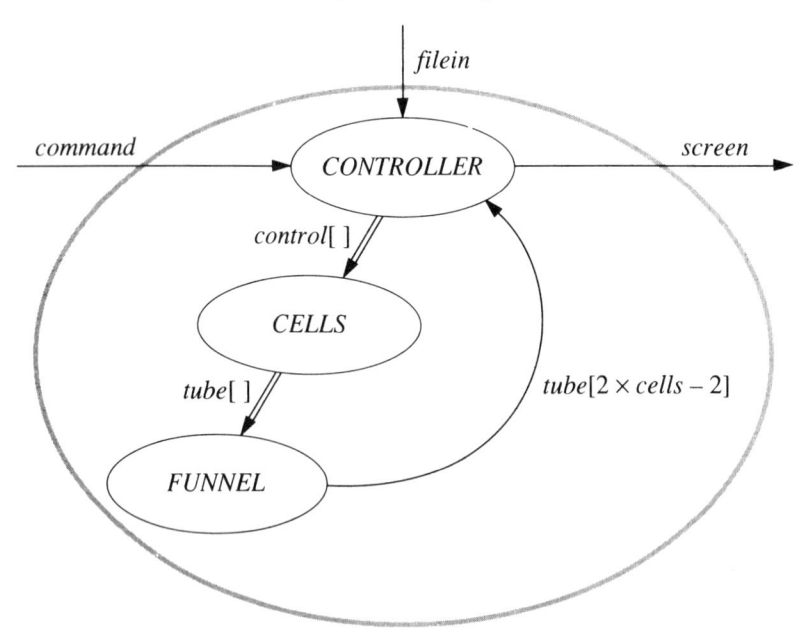

Figure 18.1

Figure 18.1 is a process network for the exploded *SYSTEM*. In order to provide declarations for the channel arrays, we must first establish values for the constants *rows*, *cols* and *cells*. Such constants are defined in Occam with DEF. Suppose we are dealing with an image represented as an array with 20 rows and 40 columns. We write:

```
DEF rows = 20, cols = 40, cells = rows * cols :
```

We also need to provide declarations to name the constants that are transmitted between the components of System. For these declarations, we need to make some assumption about the format in which the inputs arrive. In Occam, a quoted character stands for its ASCII value. We could therefore write:

```
DEF load = 'l', count = 'c', terminate = 't',
    black = 'b', white = 'w' :
```

Here we assume that the characters 'l', 'c', and 't' are input on the command channel and the characters 'b' and 'w' are input on the filein channel.

An Occam process communicates with its environment via external channels which are declared as formal parameters in the process header.

The CSP process *SYSTEM* may now be coded as follows:

```
PROC System(CHAN command, screen, filein) =
  DEF rows = 20, cols = 40, cells = rows * cols :
  CHAN control[rows][cols], tube[2 * cells - 1] :
  DEF load = 'l', count = 'c', terminate = 't',
    black = 'b', white = 'w' :
  PAR
    Controller
    Cells
    Funnel :
```

The process is given the name System by using the PROC symbol, followed by the name and any formal parameters, and an equals sign. The declarations and process body are indented two spaces relative to the symbol PROC. The final line of the process body ends with a colon. Note also that, as for example in the declaration of tube[ ], the size of an array can be declared as an expression rather than a simple constant.

The constants and channel names declared here at the topmost level are available for use at lower levels.

18.4 The process Controller

We shall now see how the first component, *CONTROLLER*, is coded. Here is the final version of *CONTROLLER* as developed in Exercise 17.1 (we have removed a redundant *SKIP*):

CONTROLLER =
  INIT ; (*running* := *true*) ;
  running*(*command*?*cmd* → *BROADCAST*$_{cmd}$;
  (*LOAD_CELLS*   ◁ *cmd* = *load* ▷
  tube[2 × *cells* − 2]?*x* → *screen*!(*x* + 1) → *SKIP*   ◁ *cmd* = *count* ▷
  tube[2 × *cells* − 2]?*x* → (*running* := *false*)))

Let us first establish the declarations required for the Controller process.

Exercise

18.1 Which names need to be declared in the `Controller` process?

Solution 18.1 We shall need the variable names `running`, `cmd`, `x`.
The channel names `command`, `tube`, `screen` and the constant names `cells`, `load`, `count`, `terminate` are available from the enclosing process, `System`.

□

The *CONTROLLER* process is defined in terms of Boolean choice. It can be coded using the `IF` construct as follows, using the Boolean constants `TRUE` and `FALSE`. Note that in Occam a parametrized process is activated with the actual parameter in parentheses:

```
PROC Controller =
  VAR running, cmd, x :
  SEQ
    Init
    running := TRUE
    WHILE running
      SEQ
        command ? cmd
        Broadcast(cmd)
        IF
          (cmd = load)
            Load_cells
          (cmd = count)
            SEQ
              tube[2 * cells - 2] ? x
              screen ! (x + 1)
          (cmd = terminate)
            SEQ
              tube[2 * cells - 2] ? x
              running := FALSE :
```

The final option is controlled by the Boolean expression (`cmd = terminate`), that must be written explicitly in the Occam code. This condition will be reached only if (`cmd = load`) and (`cmd = count`) have failed. In these circumstances `cmd` must take the value `terminate`, so the final option will indeed be selected. If none of the Boolean expressions in an `IF` construct has the value `TRUE`, a run-time error will occur.

The code for `Controller` includes activations of three subprocesses: `Init`, `Broadcast` and `Load_cells`. We shall first consider `Broadcast` and see how parameters are specified in Occam.

The subprocess `Broadcast`

The process definition of `Controller` uses the parametrized subprocess `Broadcast`. The allowable values of the parameter are `load`, `count` and `terminate`. An Occam process definition may specify one or more *formal* parameters, enclosed in parentheses. Each formal parameter is given a local name in the process definition, and must be preceded by one of the specifiers VALUE (for a constant parameter), VAR or CHAN. This is similar to the way in which formal parameters of procedures are specified in Pascal. The process definition for Broadcast therefore begins with the header:

```
PROC Broadcast(VALUE cmd) =
```

The name cmd here is a local constant; x or y could have been chosen but cmd seems more expressive. It should not be confused with the variable cmd that appears as the *actual* parameter when Broadcast is activated from Controller.

The CSP specification of *BROADCAST* includes a parallel composition over a number of identical processes:

$$BROADCAST_{cmd} = |||_{ij} control[i,j]!cmd \rightarrow SKIP$$

Occam allows for this situation by using a **replicator**. A replicator has the general form:

```
r = [a FOR b]
```

in which r is a variable called the *replicator index*, a is an expression which provides the initial value of r, and b is an expression whose value is the number of replicated processes. Thus the set of values taken by r is:

```
a, a + 1, a + 2, ..., a + b - 1
```

We are now in a position to code the process Broadcast. It should be borne in mind though that the parallel combination over *i* and *j* is actually a double replication. Since $0 \leq i < rows$, $0 \leq j < cols$, we have:

```
PROC Broadcast(VALUE cmd) =
  PAR i = [0 FOR rows]
    PAR j = [0 FOR cols]
      control[i][j] ! cmd :
```

Note that a replicator does not need to be declared and the trailing SKIP can be omitted in Occam. Also, each index of an element in a two-dimensional array is enclosed in a separate pair of brackets.

Review Question 18.1 Write this parallel combination in an alternative way.

The subprocess Init

Here is the CSP definition of *INIT* that we obtained in Section 15.2:

$$INIT = BROADCAST_{load}; \sum_{i=0}^{rows-1} \sum_{j=0}^{cols-1} DISPLAY_{white}(i,j)$$

This is a sequential combination of processes, which is introduced in Occam by the control symbol SEQ. Once again the process array is combined in Occam using a replicator.

The Occam process definition of Init is:

```
PROC Init =
  SEQ
    Broadcast(load)
    SEQ i = [0 FOR rows]
      SEQ j = [0 FOR cols]
        Display(white, i, j) :
```

The process definition of *DISPLAY* is:

$$DISPLAY_{pixel}(i, j) = (screen!pixel \rightarrow SKIP \;|||\; control[i,j]!pixel \rightarrow SKIP)$$

We shall code both the CSP parameter *pixel* and the indexes *i* and *j* of the process array *DISPLAY* as VALUE parameters in Occam. The channel `screen` has already been specified as a parameter of the process `System`, and the channel array `control[ ]` was declared in `System`:

```
PROC Display(VALUE pixel, i, j) =
  PAR
    screen ! pixel
    control[i][j] ! pixel :
```

The process header indicates that `pixel`, `i` and `j` are all VALUE parameters of `Display`.

The subprocess Load_cells

The final subprocess to consider is *LOAD_CELLS*, whose CSP specification is:

$$LOAD\_CELLS = \sum_{i=0}^{rows-1} \sum_{j=0}^{cols-1} filein?pixel \rightarrow DISPLAY_{pixel}(i, j)$$

This may be implemented in the same way as `Init`.

Exercise
18.2 Give a process definition for `Load_cells`.

Solution 18 We obtain:

```
PROC Load_cells =
  VAR pixel :
  SEQ i = [0 FOR rows]
    SEQ j = [0 FOR cols]
      SEQ
        filein ? pixel
        Display(pixel, i, j) :
```

Review question 18.2 When is it appropriate to enumerate the processes in a PAR or SEQ combination, and when is it appropriate to use a replicator?

AN OCCAM VERSION OF SYSTEM 211

18.5 The process `Cells`

We now come to the second component of *SYSTEM*, the *CELLS* process. We obtained the following in Chapter 17:

$$CELLS = \|_{ij}(CELL(i,j) \| BUFFER(i,j))$$

The internal channels in *CELLS* were given in the solution to Exercise 15.7; they are *inbuffer*[ ], *outbuffer*[ ], *north*[ ], *northwest*[ ] and *west*[ ].

Exercise

18.3 Give an Occam process definition for *CELLS*.

Solution 18.3

```
PROC Cells =
  CHAN north[rows][cols], west[rows][cols],
    northwest[rows][cols],
      inbuffer[rows][cols], outbuffer[rows][cols] :
  PAR i = [0 FOR rows]
    PAR j = [0 FOR cols]
      PAR
        Cell(i, j)
        Buffer(i, j) :
```

Here the channel declarations occupy more than one line; when this happens the subsidiary line must be indented two (or more) spaces.

□

We must now look at the process definition for *CELL*.

$CELL(i,j) =$
  $control[i,j] \, ?cmd \to$
    $(cmd <> terminate)*(NONTER_{cmd} ; control[i,j] \, ?cmd \to SKIP) ;$
  $C_{terminate}(i,j)$

$NONTER_{cmd} =$
  $outbuffer[i,j] \, ?x \to control[i,j] \, ?pixel \to inbuffer[i,j] \, !pixel \to SKIP$
    $\triangleleft cmd = load \triangleright$
  $outbuffer[i,j]?pixel \to (SEND_{pixel}(i,j) \, \| \, (RECEIVE(i,j) ; CALCULATE(i,j)))$

$C_{terminate}(i,j) =$
  $outbuffer[i,j]?x \to$
    $(inbuffer[i,j]!terminate \to SKIP \, \| \, tube[i \times cols + j]!terminate \to SKIP)$

Note that we were somewhat cavalier in our definitions of *RECEIVE* and *CALCULATE*. Strictly speaking, they require some mechanism to convey the values of the variables *pixel*, *southpixel*, *southeastpixel* and *eastpixel*. We shall introduce appropriate parameters into the Occam implementation of these processes.

We may now derive the code for `Cell(i, j)`. We shall incorporate the subprocesses $NONTER_{cmd}$ and $C_{terminate}$ into the process definition:

```
PROC Cell(VALUE i, j) =
  VAR cmd, pixel,x, s, se, e :
  SEQ
    control[i][j] ? cmd
    WHILE cmd < > terminate
      SEQ
        -- NONTER
        IF
          cmd = load
            SEQ
              control[i][j] ? pixel
              outbuffer[i][j] ? x
              inbuffer[i][j] ! pixel
          cmd = count
            SEQ
              outbuffer[i][j] ? pixel
              PAR
                Send(pixel, i, j)
                SEQ
                  Receive(s, se, e, i, j)
                  Calculate(pixel, s, se, e, i, j)
        Control[i][j] ? cmd
    -- C_terminate
    SEQ
      outbuffer[i][j] ? x
      PAR
        inbuffer[i][j] ! terminate
        tube[i*cols + j] ! terminate :
```

We have inserted two comment lines in the code; these begin with a double hyphen - -. We have also omitted some redundant instances of SKIP. Note that each of the parallel processes Cell(i, j) uses local variables cmd and pixel. Since each variable is declared locally there is no name clash.

The subprocesses Send, Receive and Calculate

There now remains the problem of coding the subprocesses Send, Receive and Calculate. First we repeat the specifications of these subprocesses:

$SEND_{pixel}(i,j) =$
   $(inbuffer[i, j]!pixel \rightarrow SKIP) \; ||| $
   $(north[i, j]!pixel \rightarrow SKIP) \; ||| $
   $(northwest[i, j]!pixel \rightarrow SKIP) \; ||| $
   $(west[i, j]!pixel \rightarrow SKIP)$

$RECEIVE(i, j) =$
  $(north[i \oplus 1, j]?southpixel \rightarrow SKIP) \;|\|\|$
  $(northwest[i \oplus 1, j \oplus 1]?southeastpixel \rightarrow SKIP) \;|\|\|$
  $(west[i, j \oplus 1]?eastpixel \rightarrow SKIP)$

$CALCULATE(i, j) =$
  $(tube[i \times cols + j]!(-1) \rightarrow SKIP$ $\triangleleft eastpixel = white \triangleright$
  $tube[i \times cols + j]!1 \rightarrow SKIP)$
  $\triangleleft (pixel = white) \wedge (southeastpixel = black) \wedge (eastpixel = southpixel) \triangleright$
  $tube[i \times cols + j]!0 \rightarrow SKIP$

Remember that a communication from the south comes via a channel *north*, and so on. The subprocess Send should cause no difficulties:

```
PROC Send(VALUE pixel, i, j) =
  PAR
    inbuffer[i][j] ! pixel
    north[i][j] ! pixel
    northwest[i][j] ! pixel
    west[i][j] ! pixel :
```

Receive is a more problematical, as it involves modular arithmetic. For this purpose Occam provides the remainder operator \ . For example:

  7 \ 3 evaluates to 1
  11 \ 4 evaluates to 3

In our context, we write:

  (i + 1) \ rows for $i \oplus 1$
  (j + 1) \ cols for $j \oplus 1$

Exercise

18.4 Derive the Occam code for Receive and Calculate.

Solution 18.4 Receive has three parameters—southpixel, southeastpixel, eastpixel—whose values are the colours of the pixels in the block labelled by (i, j). These must be VAR parameters so that they can be passed on to Calculate:

```
PROC Receive(VAR southpixel, southeastpixel,
    eastpixel, VALUE i, j) =
  VAR iplusone, jplusone :
  SEQ
    iplusone := (i + 1) \ rows
    jplusone := (j + 1) \ cols
    PAR
      north[iplusone][j] ? southpixel
      northwest[iplusone][jplusone] ? southeastpixel
      west[i][jplusone] ? eastpixel :
```

The only output from `Calculate` is the value of the block type, which is transmitted along a channel. All its parameters are VALUE parameters. We may simplify the coding by introducing a local variable `localcount`:

```
PROC Calculate(VALUE pixel, southpixel,
   southeastpixel, eastpixel, i, j) =
VAR localcount :
DEF otherwise = TRUE :
SEQ
   IF
      (pixel = white)
            AND (southeastpixel = black)
            AND(eastpixel = southpixel)
         IF
            eastpixel = white
               localcount := -1
            eastpixel = black
               localcount := 1
      otherwise
         localcount := 0
      tube[i * cols + j] ! localcount :
```

□

The subprocess `Buffer`

Finally we shall deal with the implementation of the *BUFFER* process. We have:

BUFFER(*i, j*) =
   outbuffer[*i, j*]!*init* → *inbuffer*[*i, j*]?*pixel*→
   (*pixel* < > *terminate*)*(*outbuffer*[*i, j*]!*pixel* → *inbuffer*[*i, j*]?*pixel* → *SKIP*)

This may be coded as follows:

```
PROC Buffer(VALUE i, j) =
   DEF init = 0 :
   VAR pixel :
   SEQ
      outbuffer[i][j] ! init
      inbuffer[i][j] ? pixel
      WHILE pixel < > terminate
         SEQ
            outbuffer[i][j] ! pixel
            inbuffer[i][j] ? pixel :
```

The actual value of the constant `init` is immaterial as it is discarded.

18.6 The process `Funnel`

The *FUNNEL* process consists of the parallel composition of a number of *ADD* processes:

$FUNNEL = \|_{0 \leq r \leq cells-2} ADD(r)$

$ADD(r) =$
$\quad (tube[2r]?x \rightarrow SKIP \;|||\; tube[2r+1]?y \rightarrow SKIP) \,;$
$\quad \textbf{not}((x = terminate) \wedge (y = terminate))*$
$\quad (tube[r + cells]!(x + y) \rightarrow (tube[2r]?x \rightarrow SKIP \;|||\; tube[2r+1]?y \rightarrow SKIP)) \,;$
$\quad tube[r + cells]!terminate \rightarrow SKIP)$

Note that the number of *ADD* processes in this definition is $cells - 1$.

Exercise

18.5 Implement the processes *FUNNEL* and *ADD* in Occam.

Solution 18.5

```
PROC Funnel =
  PAR r = [0 FOR cells - 1]
    Add(r) :

PROC Add(VALUE r) =
  VAR x, y :
  SEQ
    PAR
      tube[2 * r] ? x
      tube[2 * r + 1] ? y
    WHILE NOT((x = terminate)AND(y = terminate))
      SEQ
        tube[r + cells] ! (x + y)
        PAR
          tube[2 * r] ? x
          tube[2 * r + 1] ? y
    tube[r + cells] ! terminate :
```

18.7 Summary

In this chapter we have taken you on a lightning tour of the Occam programming language. We have taken our detailed CSP design document and implemented it as a set of Occam processes. The complete Occam program could now be obtained by collecting all the process definitions of this chapter.

An Occam process consists of a number of communication events and atomic processes combined using constructors. Where the processes form an array, the constructor must be followed by a replicator of the form:

```
r = [a FOR b]
```

The names of constants, variables and channels used in the process must be declared before the process definition or they must be known from the environment of the process (a higher-level process).

A process may be named so that it can be activated one or more times. Named processes can convey parameters much like procedures in sequential programming languages.

SUMMARY OF PART III

We have followed the image-processing case study through its long journey. Starting from an embryonic statement of requirements, we developed a CSP specification. We employed the explosion technique to refine this specification into a system design. This required a systematic analysis of the component processes and the communications between them. We introduced variables, and the ? and ! notation for input and output, to aid the development. The complete design was given in Chapter 15. Amongst the topics covered we included a discussion of how to use a special message, *terminate*, which is propagated to all component processes in order that they may close down in an orderly fashion.

We then developed extensions to CSP by introducing notations for Boolean choice and while loops, as well as assignment to variables. These notations were used, in a systematic manner, to remove choice by input value and recursion from our design.

Finally, we gave a rapid introduction to Occam, and showed how to code the component processes and subprocesses.

SOLUTIONS TO PART III REVIEW QUESTIONS

12.1 It will work perfectly unless we are unlucky enough to come across an image of a nut resting on its edge, as, for example, in the figure below:

12.2

(a) In Fig. 12.6(a), we can identify one Type A block and two Type B blocks, yielding $-1 + 2 + 1 = 2$ holes.

(b) In Fig. 12.6(b), we can identify one Type A block and two Type B blocks, yielding $-1 + 2 + 1 = 2$ holes.

13.1 A message is received on the *command* channel. If the message is *load* the events *obtain_image* and *display_image* take place, in sequence, after which the whole process starts up again. If the message is *count* the event *count_and_display_holes* takes place, after which the whole process starts up again. If the message is *terminate* the process comes to a successful conclusion.

13.2 $SYSTEM =$
$(command.load \rightarrow obtain\_image \rightarrow display\_image \rightarrow SYSTEM$
$|$
$command.count \rightarrow count\_and\_display\_holes \rightarrow SYSTEM$
$|$
$command.terminate \rightarrow SKIP)$

SOLUTIONS TO PART III REVIEW QUESTIONS   219

13.3 It is vital that each channel appears exactly twice in the complete listing of the channels, once as an output and once as an input. You should be able to see that our labelling scheme for the internal channels of *CELLS* achieves this.

14.1 $AVERAGE = pair?x \rightarrow pair?y \rightarrow out!((x + y)/2) \rightarrow AVERAGE$

14.2 $SQUARE = in?x \rightarrow out!(x \times x) \rightarrow SQUARE$

14.3 <*in.a*, *link.a*>

14.4 If the environment insists on engaging in the event *in.a* when the buffer is in state FF.

14.5

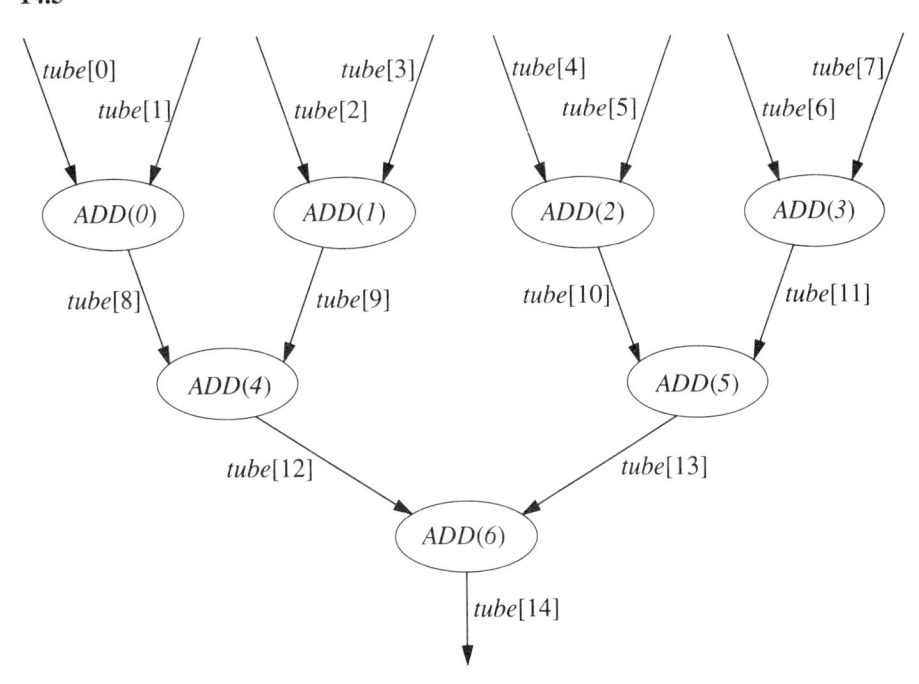

```
\tube[0]    /tube[3]/     \tube[4]    /tube[7]/
  tube[1]/    tube[2]/      tube[5]/    tube[6]/
     ↓  ↓        ↓  ↓          ↓  ↓        ↓  ↓
    ADD(0)      ADD(1)        ADD(2)     ADD(3)
    tube[8]\    /tube[9]      tube[10]\   /tube[11]
         ↓    ↓                    ↓    ↓
         ADD(4)                    ADD(5)
              tube[12]\       /tube[13]
                      ↓    ↓
                      ADD(6)
                       |tube[14]
                       ↓
```

15.1 The command LOAD IMAGE is achieved using *CONTROLLER* and *CELLS* only; it does not trigger any event in *FUNNEL*.

The commands COUNT HOLES and TERMINATE require the participation of all three components: *CONTROLLER*, *CELLS* and *FUNNEL*.

15.2 The command LOAD IMAGE will use the channel array *control*[ ] since the processes *CELL*(*i*, *j*) store the image data and must be told what the new image is. It will also use *filein* and *screen*.

The command COUNT HOLES uses the channel array *control*[ ] since the current image, which must be consulted, is stored by the array of *CELL* processes. The calculation will be performed by the *FUNNEL* process and so data must be passed to it along the array *tube*[ ]. The final result will be passed back to *CONTROLLER* along the channel $tube[2 \times cells - 2]$.

TERMINATE will bring all processes to a successful conclusion. An instruction must be passed down the channel array *control*[ ] to tell the processes *CELL(i, j)* to terminate. They in turn must use the array *tube*[ ] to tell the *FUNNEL* process to terminate. Finally the termination signal must travel along *tube*[2 × *cells* − 2].

15.3 The input on *filein* arrives in sequence and so must be read in sequence. Also, the output from *CONTROLLER*—the pixel values that make up the image—on the single channel *screen,* cannot be shared between parallel processes. (It would be possible to introduce a refinement in which the *screen* channel were replaced by a channel array; the resulting process array could perform all the outputs in parallel.)

15.4 The event that begins the initialization of *CELL* is *control*[*i, j*].*load* which is sent by *INIT*. This is followed by C_{load} whose first event on *outbuffer*[*i, j*] is *outbuffer*[*i, j*]?*x*, where the value of *x* is discarded. Thus the signal *init* is discarded.

15.5 The *ADD* components form a process array indexed from 0 to *cells* − 2; thus there are *cells* − 1 components. Since the number of inputs to *FUNNEL* is *rows* × *cols* = *cells*, the number of additions required is *cells* − 1.

16.1 The process behaves like:
    P   if *bool1* is *true*
    Q   if *bool1* is *false* and *bool2* is *true*
    R   if *bool1* is *false* and *bool2* is *false*

16.2 The syntax of ∗ requires that the first operand is a Boolean expression and the second operand a process. Since *a* is an event and not a process, the proposed expression is inadmissible in CSP.

16.3 By Rule 16.3, the process may be rewritten as:

SQPOS = *in*?*x* → (*out*!(*x* × *x*) → *SKIP* ◁ *x* > 0 ▷ *out*!*x* → *SKIP*) ; *SQPOS*

This is of the form:

SQPOS = *P* ; *SQPOS*

The process definition is therefore equivalent to:

SQPOS = *true*∗(*in*?*x* → (*out*!(*x* × *x*) → *SKIP* ◁ *x* > 0 ▷ *out*!*x* → *SKIP*))

16.4

(a) Since the condition is always *false* it fails immediately and the process terminates successfully. Hence:

Q1 = *SKIP*

(b) After initialization the condition (*x* > 0) fails immediately and the process terminates. So:

Q2 = (*x* := 0) ; *SKIP*

This is effectively just another *SKIP*, since the local variable *x* is no longer accessible after *Q2* terminates, so the assignment is not observable.

16.5

<1, 5, −5, *terminate*>

18.1 We can interchange the enumeration of rows and columns to give:

```
PAR j = [0 FOR cols]
  PAR i = [0 FOR rows]
    control[i][j] ! cmd :
```

Since the processes are all activated in parallel, this is completely equivalent to the version in the text.

18.2 A CSP infix operator becomes an enumerated PAR or SEQ in Occam. The prefix form in CSP, Σ or $\|$ or $\|\|$, is implemented using a replicator.

PART IV

CONCURRENCY CASE STUDIES

19 A MODEL OF A SIMPLE TELEPHONE NETWORK

We now wish to illustrate as many features as possible of the development method ODM. Our chosen vehicle is a pair of case studies. The first of these, which occupies the bulk of Part IV, is a telephone network, somewhat more elaborate than the two-telephone system discussed in Part I. You may find it helpful to glance back to that discussion before commencing work. In this chapter we carry the case study through from a statement of requirements, via process analysis and a CSP system specification, to a CSP design document. In particular, we make use of the communications protocol introduced in Part I to ensure the two-phone system did not deadlock.

In the course of evaluating the initial version of the design we shall discover a defect, which may be remedied by the introduction of *soft switching*, a topic which is covered in Chapter 20. We also introduce a further CSP design construct, *guarded* choice by channel. Using these new concepts, we complete the CSP design for a small telephone network in Chapter 21.

This design is now almost in the form where it can be implemented as an Occam program. However, the design includes recursive specifications that have to be transformed before it is suitable for the generation of code.

The transformation of our design into Occam code occupies Chapter 22, which begins with two aspects of writing Occam programs that were not dealt with in Part III: the folding editor and the role of channel parameters in replicating Occam processes.

Chapter 23 is associated with the second of our case studies. This takes the form of obtaining a concurrent solution to a familiar problem—the Towers of Hanoi—which is developed using ODM.

19.1 The scope of the model

In Chapter 5 we illustrated our model of communication with a simple telephone system for two users. We are now going to expand and enlarge this model, which is a good example of a system which has inherent temporal parallelism. During the course of the analysis we shall encounter a significant basic problem which may arise in concurrent systems, and a new technique for coping with it. This case study will also widen our experience of networks of parallel processes.

We start by outlining the scope of the enlarged model in the form of an informal statement of customer requirements. Next we introduce the first attempt at specifying a telephone network to service four users. By using the development method we show that although our initial specification does not result in deadlock, the system is prone to a problem which leaves users in a state of suspense.

The customer requires a model of a four-telephone network. The communication protocols for the network must be designed and checked to ensure that the network functions correctly. Other requirements are enumerated as follows:

```
Each user must be able to connect to each other user
on a one-to-one basis. There is to be no conferencing
facility, and no crossed lines. There is no need for
a central exchange.

Each user has a handset to communicate across the
network, and a push-button facility to select a
destination. A user whose handset is being called
must be alerted to the incoming call by a buzzer.

The network must not subject users to undue delay.
For example when a user calls a phone which is
already in use, an engaged signal must be received
promptly.

The network should be permanently running; it does
not have to be switched off periodically, nor should
it be subject to breakdown or deadlock.
```

It turns out that the customer is primarily concerned with the logical flow of control through the network, and so, for simplicity, the transmission of actual data (conversation) can be ignored in this model.

Ambiguities and omissions in the customer's requirements will emerge during the course of developing our formal specification of the model.

Discussion

We must stress here that our model will be very simplistic, and will have little to do with a real-world telephone system. Real-world systems are very much more complicated, with millions of users. Nevertheless, it is surprising how complicated our four-telephone model turns out to be.

In a real system it would be highly impractical to connect each user to every other user. Instead, users in a given area are all connected to a local exchange, through which they may contact each other. For long-distance calls there is a network of trunk exchanges to which local exchanges are connected. This hierarchy of exchanges continues, with yet more exchanges to handle, for example, international calls. The routeing of such a call can be quite a complex procedure.

Despite the simplifications of our model we shall nevertheless at times draw upon our intuition of how a telephone system might be expected to behave. For example, we shall not elaborate on the meaning of an engaged signal, as mentioned above. This reliance on intuition would not be possible in the development of a large piece of commercial software, and the developer would need to discuss such matters at length with the customer, in order to clarify points of detail. For our purposes, though, by using a little of our everyday experience of telephones, we can save time and space so that we can concentrate on the formal development issues.

19.2 Initial process analysis

Bearing in mind the customer requirements, we can commence with the first stage in ODM, process analysis. The network must service four users; a top-level process network is shown in Figure 19.1.

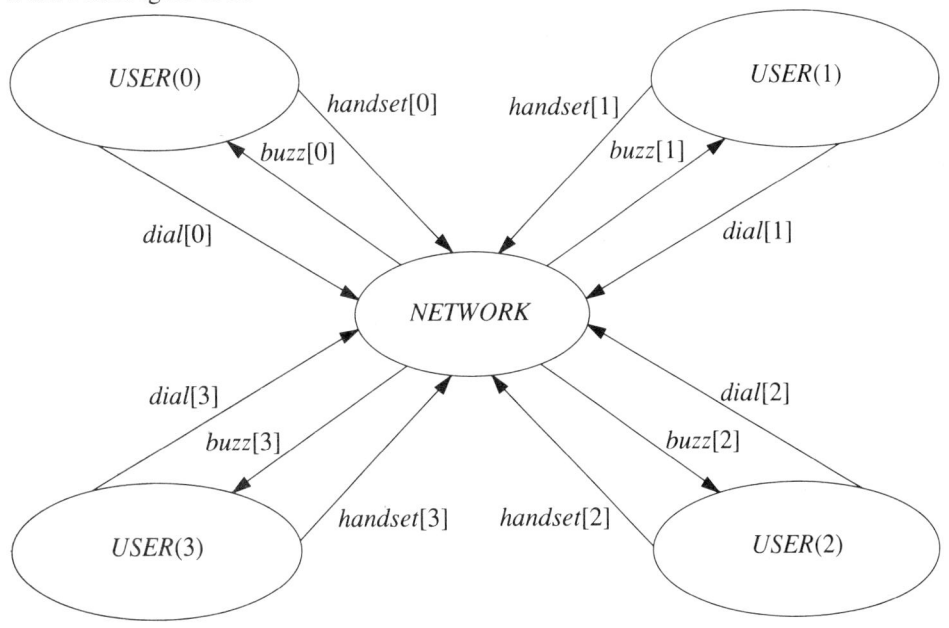

Figure 19.1

In this diagram we have labelled the channels with the names of the devices that enable the network to communicate with its environment. For each of the four users this involves a handset, a dial (this anachronistic name still persists) and a buzzer (to alert the user to an incoming call). Since each user has an identical set of channels, we have set up the channels as arrays indexed according to the number of the corresponding *USER* process.

Our next task is to clarify and specify in sufficient detail the behaviour of these external channels. We can enumerate the messages that will be transmitted along each of the channels depicted.

A handset is effectively a toggle switch by which the user can begin and end a session of telephone use. Thus we allow each *handset* channel to carry the two messages *up* and *down*. We call the set of messages that may be transmitted on a channel the ***alphabet*** of the channel. Thus the channel *handset* has the alphabet {*up*, *down*}. There is a further requirement that these two values must alternate on the channel *handset*—the handset cannot be picked up twice without first being put down.

As far as the dials are concerned, there is an immediate lack of clarity about the customer's intent. Discussion with the customer may reveal that there need be no provision for dialling non-existent numbers, and so the only values passed on each *dial* channel will be integers in the range 0–3.

Finally, we need to know what signals are required on the *buzz* channels. Suppose the customer is happy for a single pulse to alert the user of an incoming call; we shall call this value *noise*.

Review Question 19.1 Write down the part of the alphabet of *NETWORK* that consists of the external events.

▫

Review Question 19.2 Suppose the customer required the buzzer to continue sounding, on receipt of an incoming call alert, until the handset is lifted or the alert is cancelled. How would this affect the set of messages on the *buzz* channels?

▫

19.3 Refinement of the process *NETWORK*

We begin our first attempt at refinement by exploding the node *NETWORK*. The simplest way to service four users is to provide each user with a separate telephone process, and connect the processes together to enable communication. The telephone processes are essentially identical in behaviour; we name them $T(i)$ where $i = 0, 1, 2, 3$.

In the process network diagram shown in Figure 19.2 each node represents a telephone

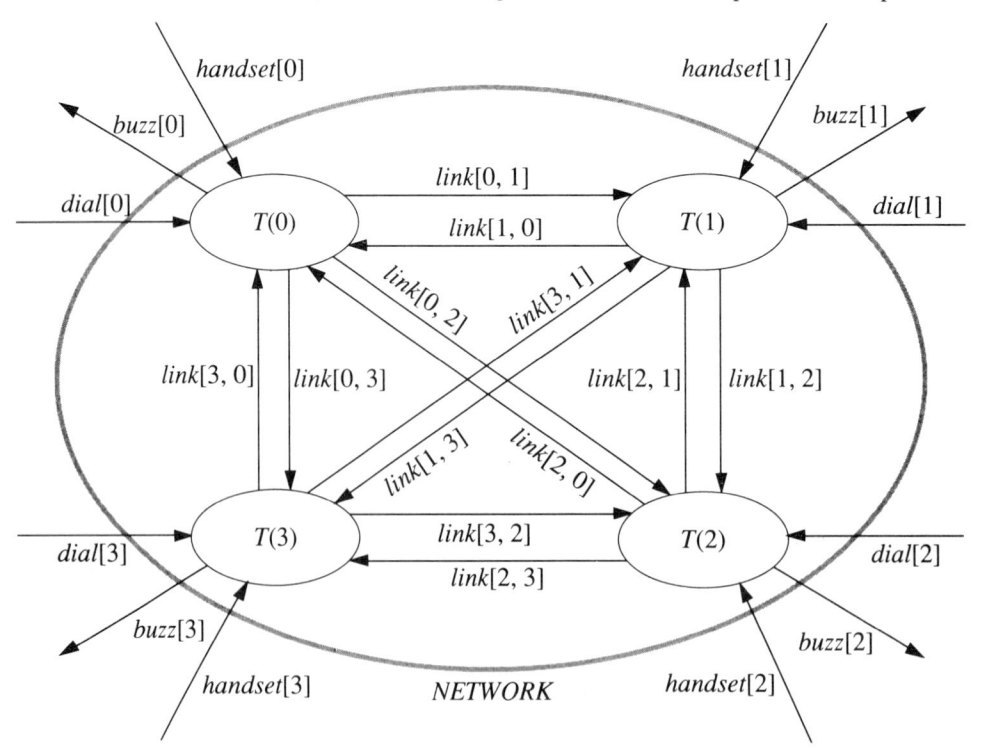

Figure 19.2

process; the diagram shows pairs of channels linking each phone to each other (as well as the previous links to the environment). Each telephone process has its own local environment, which consists of the remainder of the network together with the phone's own USER.

To interconnect the processes $T(i)$ we have introduced a doubly indexed array of channels denoted $\{link[i,j] \mid 0 \le i, j \le 3, i \ne j\}$, where the channel $link[i,j]$ carries communications from $T(i)$ to $T(j)$. The nature of the values that are to be communicated on these channels will be investigated presently.

Review Question 19.3 Identify the channels along which $T(0)$ can receive messages.

Review Question 19.4 Use the CSP formalism to express the process NETWORK in terms of the processes $T(0)$, $T(1)$, $T(2)$, $T(3)$.

19.4 A state-based description

Our next task is to give informal descriptions of the behaviour of each individual telephone, and to do this we shall use the same state-based approach that we employed in Chapter 5. When we are discussing a single process $T(i)$, we shall (as far as possible) refer to it merely as T, without its index. Initially the network is in a dormant state, in which all handsets are down. Let the process DOWN describe the behaviour of a telephone from its dormant state until it returns to that state. In particular, DOWN may engage in some sequence of events, eventually returning to the initial state; when this happens, the process DOWN terminates successfully. Bearing in mind that the system is to run for ever, we may expect to define T as a recursive process.

Exercise
19.1 Express T in terms of DOWN in CSP notation.

Solution 19.1

$T = \mu X. (DOWN; X)$

In words, T is the process that first behaves likes DOWN and then repeats itself.

We shall use names in small capitals for the states of a telephone. A dormant phone is in state DOWN, and has two possible patterns of behaviour. Either its USER can require it to make an outgoing call, or another USER can try to ring in. In order to make an outgoing call, USER communicates with the phone via the channel *handset*, and in this case the telephone process enters a new state which we call DIAL. This state DIAL might lead to other states but eventually, perhaps when the user has completed the call, the telephone will revert to the initial state DOWN.

On the other hand if, when $T(i)$ is in the state DOWN, another USER (with index j) tries to connect to $T(i)$, the latter moves to a different state which we call BUZZING$_j$. Notice that the origin of the incoming call must now be distinguished in the state name. Before making this latter state transition, $T(i)$ must acknowledge receipt of the request from $T(j)$ and issue a signal on the channel *buzz*[i]. Like the state DIAL, the state BUZZING$_j$ leads to a sequence of events, but eventually the process T will revert to the state DOWN.

Enumerating the states

It is becoming clear that this development is leading to a complex description of the evolution of each telephone process. As in Part I, it is helpful to enumerate the various states of a telephone:

DOWN   The dormant state, in which the handset is down and the telephone is not linked with any other telephone.

DIAL   The dialling state of the telephone, in which a number can be dialled.

$CALLING_j$ The state of a telephone when it has just been used to dial telephone j.

$TALK_j$ The state of a telephone when contact has been established with telephone j so that both users can talk to each other.

$BUZZING_j$ The state of a telephone when it has just been dialled from telephone j.

Each telephone in our network has eleven possible states. For example, telephone 0 can be in any of the states DOWN, DIAL, $CALLING_1$, $CALLING_2$, $CALLING_3$, $TALK_1$, $TALK_2$, $TALK_3$, $BUZZING_1$, $BUZZING_2$, $BUZZING_3$. Possible transitions between states are shown in Figure 19.3. (In order to avoid excessive complexity the states $CALLING_3$, $TALK_3$ and $BUZZING_3$ are not shown.)

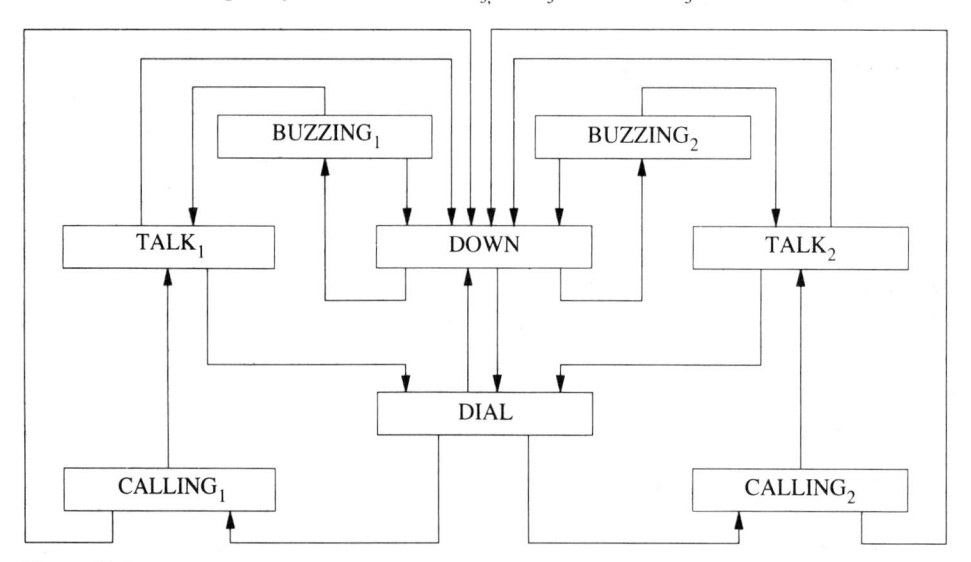

Figure 19.3

Review Question 19.5 Write down a possible sequence of states for a telephone from DOWN to DOWN, based on Figure 19.3.

You should note that most paths through the state diagram lead back to the home state DOWN. We shall find it convenient to define a subprocess of T corresponding to each state. We shall adopt the convention that each such subprocess describes the behaviour of a telephone until it returns to its home state. So, for example, the process *DOWN* describes the complete behaviour of the system through any one cycle of the state diagram from the home state back to the home state. Since T commences in the home state we may express this using CSP as follows:

$T = DOWN\,;\,T$

In a similar way, $CALLING_j$ describes the behaviour of a telephone from the state CALLING$_j$ to the state DOWN. Since the state CALLING$_j$ may be reached from the state DOWN, it follows that $CALLING_j$ is a subprocess of $DOWN$.

The state DOWN

Figure 19.3 shows that any state may lead to two or more other possible states. The choice between the available transitions is influenced by the environment of T. In each state the first event will be the receipt of a communication along an entry channel. This entry channel determines the evolution of T to its next state. In general, at any given time a communication is likely to be available on only one entry channel. If, however, more than one input communication is available, the choice between them is exercised non-deterministically by T in accordance with the rules for choice by channel.

When a telephone i is in state DOWN, the possible courses of events may lead to either BUZZING$_j$ or DIAL. The transition to DIAL is initiated by a signal on the channel *handset*; the transition to BUZZING$_j$ is initiated by a signal on the channel $link[j, i]$ where, of course, $i \neq j$. Thus the initial event of $DOWN$ will be determined by a choice by channel.

> **Review Question 19.6** Which channel carries the signal which causes telephone 0 to change state from DOWN to BUZZING$_2$?
>
> ▫

> **Review Question 19.7** Which transitions between states are triggered by each of the following events:
>
> (a) *handset.up*
>
> (b) *handset.down*
>
> ▫

As we have already said, the channel *handset* can carry two messages: *up* and *down*. There are two basic forms for a communication on a channel $link[j, i]$; we assign named values to each, as follows:

alert   an attempt to establish a connection, or confirmation that a connection already exists;

break   an attempt to disconnect, or confirmation that no connection exists.

When $USER(j)$ rings $USER(i)$, the process $T(i)$ receives the request $link[j, i].alert$, indicating that $USER(j)$ has picked up the handset and dialled through to $USER(i)$. This request is acknowledged by the event $link[i, j].break$, showing that the handset of telephone i is, as yet, still firmly down.

Specifying the process DOWN

We shall now begin to write down CSP specifications of the state subprocesses, making use of the process annotations that we obtained in Chapter 5. Although we must now introduce subscripts to keep track of which other telephone is being contacted, the basic descriptions still stand.

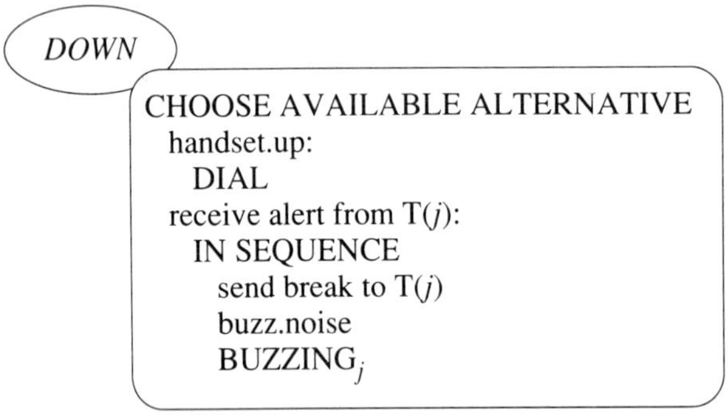

232 SPECIFICATION AND DESIGN OF CONCURRENT SYSTEMS

DOWN
> CHOOSE AVAILABLE ALTERNATIVE
> handset.up:
>   DIAL
> receive alert from T(j):
>   IN SEQUENCE
>   send break to T(j)
>   buzz.noise
>   BUZZING$_j$

Figure 19.4

Figure 19.4 gives a process annotation for *DOWN*.
In order to write down the CSP specification of *DOWN*, we shall need a notation to exercise a choice amongst an arbitrary number of channels. Suppose that *ch* is an entry channel for a process and *d*[ ] is an entry channel array. In a manner with which you should by now be familiar we introduce the ***replicated fetbar operator*** and write, for example:

$$\square_i d[i].b \to Q_i$$

for the process that exercises choice between the channels in the array *d*[ ] and then proceeds according to the channel selected. We also use the notation:

$$(ch.a \to P) \square (\square_i d[i].b \to Q_i)$$

for the process that selects any available input communication, on either *ch* or one of the *d*[*i*], and proceeds accordingly. Note that the syntax requires that the first event of each process that is an operand of $\square$ is an input communication.

We shall also adopt a further convention regarding the use of fetbar $\square$. If the alphabet of a channel has a choice of acceptable messages, the dot notation *ch.a* or *d*[*i*].*b* is replaced by *ch*?*v* or *d*[*i*]?*w*. We then write, for example:

$$ch?v \square d[1]?w$$

or, if appropriate:

$$ch?v \square d[1].b$$

We may also write:

$$\square_i d[i]?w \to Q_{w,i}$$

for the process that exercises choice between the channels in the array *d*[ ] and then proceeds according to the channel selected and the message received.

Exercise
19.2 Give a CSP specification of *DOWN*(*i*) in terms of processes *DIAL*(*i*) and *BUZZING$_j$*(*i*).

Solution 19.2

$$DOWN(i) = handset[i].up \to DIAL(i)$$
$$\square$$
$$\square_{j \neq i} link[j, i].alert \to link[i, j]!break \to buzz[i].noise \to BUZZING_j(i)$$
□

19.5 The state DIAL

The next task is to consider in more detail each of the remaining states; we shall start with DIAL, the state of a telephone once the handset is raised.

In the state DIAL a user has two courses of action—either to abandon the attempt to make a call by replacing the handset, or to dial a number. In the former case the telephone returns to its dormant state, but in the latter it is necessary to alert the destination and then proceed in an appropriate manner. The process annotation in Figure 19.5 is based on the one that we wrote down in Chapter 5.

```
DIAL
    CHOOSE AVAILABLE ALTERNATIVE
        handset.down:
            DOWN
        dial.number:
            IN SEQUENCE
                IN PARALLEL
                    send alert to T(number)
                    receive response from T(number)
                IF
                    response = break
                        CALLING_number
                    response = alert
                        TALK_number
```

Figure 19.5

Review Question 19.8 How does the process *DIAL* know which choice of action its user has made?

If the destination that has been alerted responds with *break* (because its handset is down), telephone i now is in state $CALLING_{number}$ where *number* is the number just dialled.

Exercise
19.3 Write a CSP specification of *DIAL(i)*.

Solution 19.3 Here is a possible solution:[1]

$DIAL(i) =$
　　$handset[i].down \rightarrow SKIP$
　　$[]$
　　$dial[i]?number \rightarrow$
　　　　$(link[i, number]!alert \rightarrow SKIP \;|||\; link[number, i]?reply \rightarrow SKIP)$;
　　　　$CALLING_{number}(i)$ 　　$\triangleleft\; reply = break \;\triangleright\; TALK_{number}(i)$

The process *SKIP* that appears in the specification of *DIAL* in Solution 19.3 indicates that, after the occurrence of the event $handset[i].down$, the process *DIAL* has successfully terminated. In the context of the overall process *T* this results in a return to state DOWN.

Generally speaking, the process *SKIP* in some part of the description indicates that the telephone reverts to some other previously defined state.

Review Question 19.9 What happens when a user dials her own number?

Review Question 19.10 In what way should the alphabet for channel $dial[i]$ be constrained?

Self dialling

Should provision be made for the users dialling their own numbers? There is no reference to this in the initial statement of requirements, so any implementation of this facility becomes a design issue. Our representation makes no provision for this facility. The underlying assumption is presumably that the hardware of each telephone receiver disables the button that dials itself.

Alternatively, the matter could be treated as an omission from the statement of requirements which has to be taken up with the customer.

Exercise
19.4 Suppose that the customer advises that the hardware cannot be modified to disable self dialling. Suggest two plausible courses of behaviour for *DIAL(i)* on receipt of the communication $dial[i].i$.

Solution 19.4 Either the signal is ignored, and the process remains in the state DIAL, or this case may be treated as being identical to dialling the number of a different phone which is already busy.

Drawing on our own experience of real telephone systems we shall consider what adaptation is needed for our description to conform with the second course of behaviour in Solution 19.4. In this case, the only option open to the user is to replace the handset. This situation is described by the process:

　　$handset[i].down \rightarrow SKIP$

---
[1] Remember that the prefix operator binds more closely than the interleaving operator.

Exercise

19.5 Rewrite $DIAL(i)$ to accommodate the situation where the user dials his own number.

Solution 19.5

$DIAL(i) =$
  $handset[i].down \rightarrow SKIP$
  $\square$
  $dial[i]?j \rightarrow$
    $(handset[i].down \rightarrow SKIP \quad \triangleleft j = i \triangleright$
    $(link[i,j]!alert \rightarrow SKIP \;|||\; link[j,i]?reply \rightarrow SKIP)\,;$
    $CALLING_j(i) \quad \triangleleft reply = break \triangleright \quad TALK_j(i))$ □

19.6 The states CALLING, TALK and BUZZING

After dialling a remote user, the preferred outcome is a transition to the state CALLING. We consider this state next.

There are two possibilities: either the remote phone answers the call, or the user who originated the call tires of waiting and hangs up. If the call is answered our convention demands that an acknowledgement must be passed to the remote phone. In this case the two users are connected, leading to the state TALK. If the originator hangs up the remote phone must be informed accordingly. This is summarized in Figure 19.6.

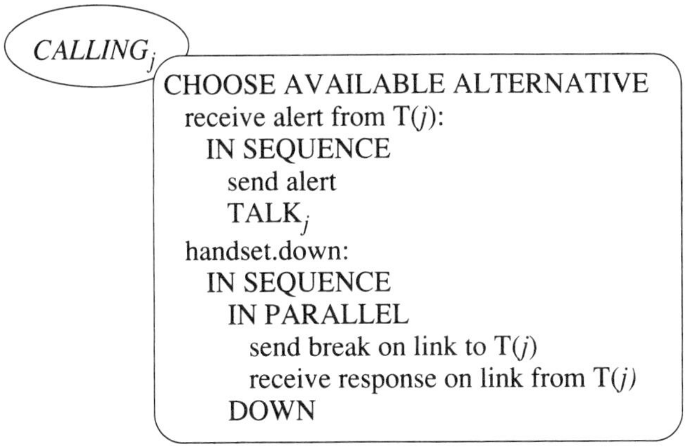

CALLING$_j$

CHOOSE AVAILABLE ALTERNATIVE
  receive alert from T(j):
    IN SEQUENCE
      send alert
      TALK$_j$
  handset.down:
    IN SEQUENCE
      IN PARALLEL
        send break on link to T(j)
        receive response on link from T(j)
      DOWN

Figure 19.6

Notice that in parallel with telling the remote telephone that the local telephone (*i*) has hung up, telephone *i* must receive a reply; whatever reply is received, telephone *i* returns to the state DOWN.

The initial choice is by channel, and we have:

$CALLING_j(i) =$
  $link[j,i].alert \rightarrow link[i,j]!alert \rightarrow TALK_j(i)$
  $\square$
  $handset[i].down \rightarrow$
    $(link[i,j]!break \rightarrow SKIP \;|||\; link[j,i]?any \rightarrow SKIP)$

Review Question 19.11 Why in the first alternative of $CALLING_j$ are the two communications sequential while in the second they are in parallel?

To complete our analysis of an outgoing call we must specify the process $TALK_j(i)$. Either party may terminate the call by hanging up; the telephone that is hung up then goes into state DOWN. We assume that if the remote phone terminates the connection before we hang up then our phone enters the state DIAL. (This is not what usually happens when you use a British Telecom telephone line. However, it is a reasonable simplification.) We then have the following:

$TALK_j(i) =$
  $handset[i].down \rightarrow (link[i,j]!break \rightarrow SKIP \,|||\, link[j,i]?any \rightarrow SKIP)$
  $\Box$
  $link[j,i].break \rightarrow link[i,j]!alert \rightarrow DIAL(i)$

Notice that the actual acknowledgement sent to the phone that terminates the call is unimportant—we have chosen *alert*.

The final subprocess to be developed is *BUZZING*. The process *BUZZING* corresponds to an incoming call. As usual, there are two possible patterns of progress, with a choice by channel between the possible initial events.

Review Question 19.12 Which events can take place when a phone is in the state $BUZZING_j$?

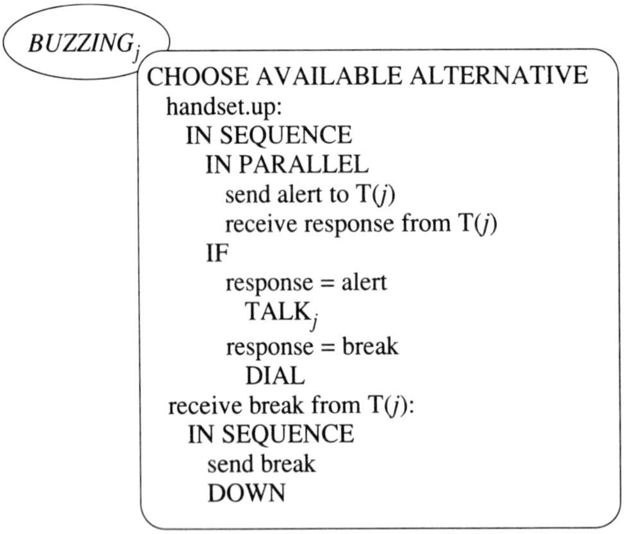

$BUZZING_j$
CHOOSE AVAILABLE ALTERNATIVE
  handset.up:
    IN SEQUENCE
      IN PARALLEL
        send alert to T(j)
        receive response from T(j)
      IF
        response = alert
          $TALK_j$
        response = break
          DIAL
  receive break from T(j):
    IN SEQUENCE
      send break
      DOWN

Figure 19.7

A suitable process annotation for $BUZZING_j$ is shown in Figure 19.7. This may be formalized into the following CSP design:

$BUZZING_j(i) =$
  $handset[i].up \rightarrow (link[i,j]!alert \rightarrow SKIP \,|||\, link[j,i]?reply \rightarrow SKIP)$;
    $TALK_j(i) \triangleleft reply = alert \triangleright DIAL(i)$
  $\Box$
  $ink[j,i].break \rightarrow link[i,j]!break \rightarrow SKIP$

Review Question 19.13 To what do the two choices of channel in $BUZZING_j$ correspond?

19.7 The process *NETWORK*

Let us summarize our progress to date, and then validate the resulting specification against the original requirements. A CSP system design for the four-telephone network is shown below.

We shall examine what happens when a user calls a phone which is already in use, and see whether a prompt response is received.

NETWORK
{ *handset*[*i*].*up*, *handset*[*i*].*down*, *link*[*i*, *j*].*alert*, *link*[*i*, *j*].*break*,
  buzz[*i*].*noise*} ∪ { *dial*[*i*].*n* | 0 ≤ *n* ≤ 3 }   (0 ≤ *i*, *j* ≤ 3 *j* ≠ *i*)

$T(0) \parallel T(1) \parallel T(2) \parallel T(3)$
where
$T(i) = \mu X. (DOWN(i) ; X)$

$DOWN(i) =$
  (*handset*[*i*].*up* → *DIAL*(*i*))
  □
  $\Box_{j \neq i}$ *link*[*j*, *i*].*alert* → *link*[*i*, *j*]!*break* → *buzz*[*i*].*noise* → *BUZZING*(*i*)

$DIAL(i) =$
  handset[*i*].*down* → SKIP
  □
  dial[*i*]?*j* →
    (*handset*[*i*].*down* → SKIP   ◁ *j* = *i* ▷
    (*link*[*i*, *j*]!*alert* → SKIP ⦀ *link*[*j*, *i*]?*reply* → SKIP);
    CALLING(*i*)   ◁ *reply* = *break* ▷ *TALK*(*i*))

CALLING(*i*) =
  link[*j*, *i*].*alert* → *link*[*i*, *j*]!*alert* → *TALK*(*i*)
  □
  handset[*i*].*down* →
    (*link*[*i*, *j*]!*break* → SKIP ⦀ *link*[*j*, *i*]?*reply* → SKIP);

TALK(*i*)=
  handset[*i*].*down* →
    (*link*[*i*, *j*]!*break* → SKIP ⦀ *link*[*j*, *i*]?*reply* → SKIP);
  □
  link[*j*, *i*].*break* → *link*[*i*, *j*]!*alert* → *DIAL*(*i*)

BUZZING(*i*) =
  handset[*i*].*up* →
    (*link*[*i*, *j*]!*alert* → SKIP ⦀ *link*[*j*, *i*]?*reply* → SKIP);
    TALK(*i*) ◁ *reply* = *alert* ▷ *DIAL*(*i*)
  □
  link[*j*, *i*].*break* → *link*[*i*, *j*]!*break* → SKIP

Review Question 19.14 Suppose $USER(0)$ has dialled $USER(1)$. Give the corresponding trace of $NETWORK$.

Exercise

19.6 If $USER(0)$ has just called $USER(1)$, and $USER(1)$ has not yet responded, the state of the network is now described by the following process:

$$(CALLING_1(0)\,;\,T(0)) \parallel (BUZZING_0(1)\,;\,T(1)) \parallel T(2) \parallel T(3)$$

(a) What are the next two events that $CALLING_1(0)$ can engage in?

(b) What are the next two events that $BUZZING_0(1)$ can engage in?

(c) What happens if $USER(2)$ now tries to call $USER(0)$?

Solution 19.6

(a) The next two events are either:

<$\ldots$ $link[1,0].alert,\ link[0,1].alert$>
or <$\ldots$ $handset[0].down,\ link[0,1].break$>
or <$\ldots$ $handset[1].down,\ link[1,0].alert$>

(b) The next two events are either:

<$\ldots$ $handset[1].up,\ link[1,0].alert$>
or <$\ldots$ $handset[1].up,\ link[0,1].break$>
or <$\ldots$ $link[0,1].break,\ link[1,0].break$>

(c) In a word, nothing! Or at least, nothing yet. Expanding the process:

$$(CALLING_1(0)\,;\,T(0)) \parallel (BUZZING_0(1)\,;\,T(1)) \parallel T(2) \parallel T(3)$$
we obtain:

$(CALLING_1(0)\,;\,T(0)) \parallel (BUZZING_0(1)\,;\,T(1)) \parallel$
$(handset[2].up \to dial[2].0 \to link[2,0]!alert \to CALLING2(0)\,;\,T(2)) \parallel T(3)$

The first two events of $T(2)$ pose no problems, but the output event $link[2,0]!alert$ cannot take place until $CALLING_1(0)$ is prepared to participate; the answer to part (*a*) shows that this will not occur until the connection between telephone 0 and telephone 1 is successfully concluded.

Let us consider now the situation in part (c) of Exercise 19.6, when $USER(0)$ has called $USER(1)$, and now $USER(2)$ attempts to call $USER(0)$. As we have seen, process $T(2)$ is unable to proceed. This is not deadlock, because there is a possibility that a future development will resolve the situation, namely that the call between $T(0)$ and $T(1)$ will end. Nevertheless it is a violation of one of the system requirements—that the users must not experience undue delays. In a real telephone system it would certainly not be reasonable to dial the number of a busy phone and receive no response whatsoever—remaining in limbo without even being able to hang up effectively—until the call at the other end was ended.

What we need is some means of allowing $T(0)$ to signal $T(2)$ that it is busy. In order to achieve this, we shall introduce a neutral process which acts in parallel with each T process and informs all callers that the associated phone is engaged. Of course, we shall need some mechanism to switch this process on and off as required.

Since the new neutral process has to communicate with the other telephone processes, it seems most sensible to make use of the existing array of channels *link*[ ] between the processes *T*(*i*). However, this will mean that, in some sense, each *T* process and its paired neutral process are sharing the channels to the other telephones. We shall need to take a break from the development of the telephone network system to develop this concept.

19.8 Summary

We have introduced our telephone network case study as a set of four intercommunicating telephones. After establishing a minimal set of user requirements, we drew a top-level process network which we exploded into a set of four identical communicating telephone processes. With the process annotations for the two-telephone system of Part I in mind, we wrote down a CSP design for a working system. Our formal description incorporated the communications protocol of Part I, whereby each transmission along a *link* channel is accompanied by a parallel input on the reverse *link* channel.

Although our description could be used to build a working telephone network, it suffers from an undesirable feature: when a user dials a telephone which is already in use, the network stores the call. The calling telephone is effectively disabled until the stored call can be dealt with, leaving the caller in an unsatisfactory state of suspense. In fact, the statement of requirements for our telephone system expressly ruled out this situation, and demanded a telephone system where all actions lead to a swift response so that no one is left with the problem of being forced to hang on.

We therefore seek a modification of our telephone system which can handle this situation. The method of circumventing our problem is discussed in the next chapter.

20 BLOCKERS AND SOFT SWITCHING

In a real-time system, such as the telephone system we are modelling, it is often the case that one process needs to interrogate another (perhaps in order to discover its state). More often than not the target process will have work of its own to do. Unless we make specific provision to monitor regularly requests for information as part of the detailed design of the process, these requests will go unanswered for varying periods of time. In order to rectify this defect, we introduce a useful concept called *soft switching*. This chapter is a short interlude to describe the idea in some detail. In particular we shall make use of a new CSP concept, *guarded choice by channel*.

20.1 The blocker

In order to enable a process to monitor requests, we introduce another, subordinate, process whose sole job is to monitor and respond to such requests, and let it run concurrently with the original process. A process network, as shown in Figure 20.1 will make this clearer.

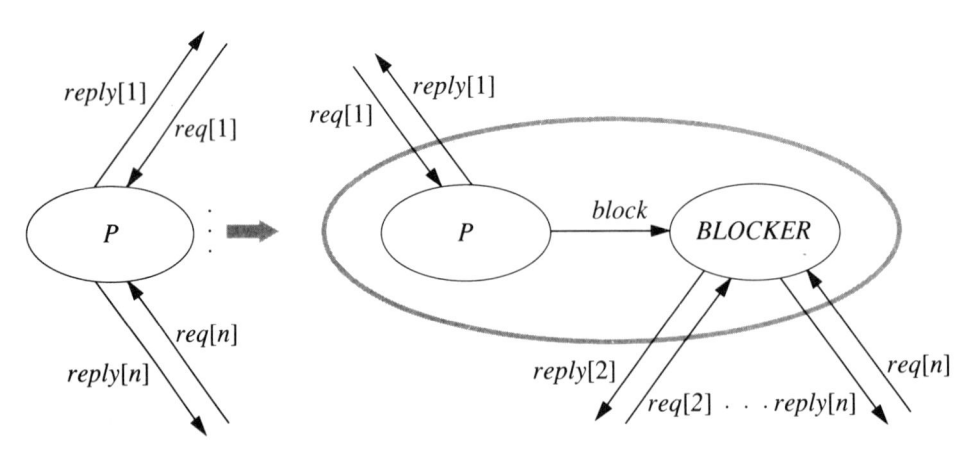

Figure 20.1

The process P shown on the left has two-way communication with n other processes. At any time a status request may be ready on one of the channels req[i]; this should be accepted without undue delay, and a response provided on the channel reply[i]. If P has a variety of other tasks to perform, it is very difficult to organize all these tasks in such a way as to comply with this requirement. On the right we have replaced P by a parallel composition P ∥ BLOCKER, with a single channel block connecting the two processes. In the diagram P is depicted as being connected to the channels req[1] and reply[1], whilst BLOCKER is dealing with the remaining channels {req[i]} and {reply[i]}. In fact the possibilities are much more general than this. P can elect to deal with any subset of the entry/exit channel pairs, and can instruct BLOCKER to look after the remainder. The subset dealt with by P changes from time to time; at any time BLOCKER deals with the currently remaining channels. The duty of the BLOCKER process is as follows:

(a) it accepts a new command from P, thus determining its subsequent behaviour; or

(b) if a request is received on one of the entry channels for which it currently has responsibility it makes an appropriate response on the corresponding exit channel.

The specification of BLOCKER might seem straightforward, but in fact it will bring to light a fundamental problem of concurrent systems which can be just as undesirable as deadlock. Since the division of channels between P and BLOCKER is not static but varies throughout the evolution of the process, a process network which ties individual channels to either P or BLOCKER is not appropriate. The situation is best illustrated as in Figure 20.2, which reflects the use of the channels {req[i]} and {reply[i]}.

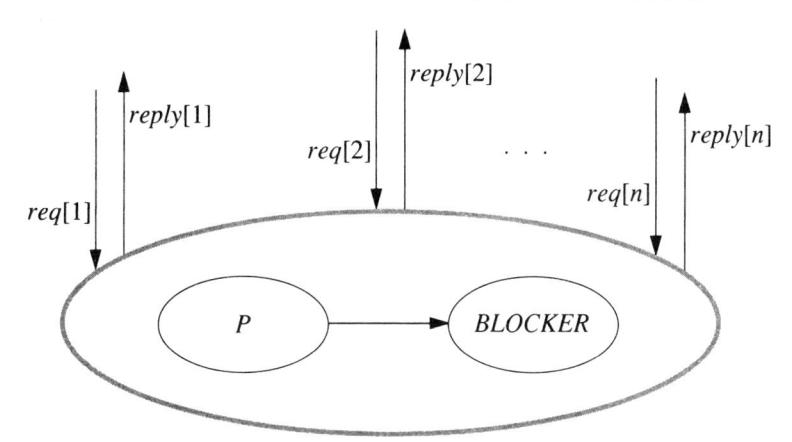

Figure 20.2

At any stage there is a subset J of the full set of indexes {1, 2, ..., n} which label the channels req[j] that have to be intercepted by BLOCKER. In order to achieve this P sends a suitable message on block. If, at a later time, P decides that the set J should be changed it informs BLOCKER accordingly. Of course if at any time J is the empty set then BLOCKER has nothing to do but await a further communication from P.

We may identify the following states of BLOCKER:

NONE   No channels to be intercepted

J   Channels $\{req_j\}_{j \in J}$ to be intercepted, where J is any non-empty subset of {1, 2, ..., n}

Exercise
20.1 Why is the channel *block* essential for controlling the behaviour of *BLOCKER*?

Solution 20.1 Because *P* and *BLOCKER* are parallel processes, if they are to communicate at all (in our model of concurrency) then it must be by channel. Since the allocation of channels between the processes *P* and *BLOCKER* changes with time, these processes share channels. So it is essential that they communicate in order to avoid the fatal error of both trying to use a channel simultaneously. The easiest way to do this is to let one process, *P*, control the other. In general, if any process is to exert control over the behaviour of another process, then there must be a channel to convey the instructions. □

Exercise
20.2 Write a CSP specification for *BLOCKER*.

Solution 20.2

$$BLOCKER = block?set \rightarrow BLOCKER_{set}$$

$$BLOCKER_{none} = block?set \rightarrow BLOCKER_{set}$$

$$BLOCKER_J = (block?set \rightarrow BLOCKER_{set})$$
$$\square$$
$$\square_{j \in J} req[j]?query \rightarrow reply[j]!busy \rightarrow BLOCKER_J)$$

The variable *set* takes as its value the subset of $\{1, 2, ..., n\}$ identified by the input message on *block*. When *set* ≠ *none*, *BLOCKER* accepts requests on the appropriate *req* channels and it responds with the *busy* signal on the corresponding *reply* channel. □

In the case of our telephone network each phone process will have its own *BLOCKER*, which will take care of unwanted incoming alerts while the phone is connected to another phone. In addition there are times when the *BLOCKER* should intercept *all* incoming lines; for example, whilst a user is preparing to dial.

Review Question 20.1 Write down the values that might be sent by $T(0)$ to its blocker. □

Soft switching

The idea of a controlled switching of processes that intercept a set of entry channels in this way is called ***soft switching***. The controlling process *P* sends a message, on the channel *block*, which acts as a soft switch which re-allocates the channels. At first sight, the idea of soft switching may appear to contradict a basic relationship between processes and channels, since until now a channel has always connected two fixed processes point-to-point—channels have not been shared. However, there is no real contradiction as the channel arrays *req*[ ] and *reply*[ ] still link the uniquely defined process *P* ∥ *BLOCKER* to its environment. *P* and *BLOCKER* are in fact subprocesses of *P* ∥ *BLOCKER*. In this sense it is possible to have soft switching between such subprocesses. Nevertheless we must still be very cautious. A strict protocol must be observed so that a process and its blocker never try to communicate with the environment on the same channel at the same time. The observance of this protocol is under the control of process *P*. But this is entirely in keeping with the nature of the blocker, which only wishes to respond to those channels that the main process does not care to receive. In the case of such an incoming message the blocker returns a *busy* reply and the requirement of rapid response is met. At any time the channels that are to be blocked are under the control of the process *P,* and the blocker is informed about what to block by messages along the channel *block*.

20.2 Guarded communications

The purpose of soft switching is to allow a process to control the circumstances in which certain channels will be handled by a subordinate process. As we have seen, the essential behaviour of the process *BLOCKER* is to issue a standard response to any message received on a given set of channels; the set of channels is varied from time to time under the control of the master process.

In Part III we used variables to hold values in the CSP description of the evolution of a process. In particular, we used a variable to stand for a communication received on an entry channel; the value of the variable is then used in a choice by input value construction. We shall now see how variables may also be used in the description of soft switching.

With each channel in the set of switchable entry channels we associate a ***guard***. This guard may be *open* or *closed*. When a guard is open, its channel may be selected for input in the usual way. However, a channel whose guard is closed may not be selected for input, *even if a communication is waiting on the channel.* An entry channel guard is denoted in CSP by a Boolean expression followed by an ampersand (&). Let *P* be a process with entry channels *c* and *d*. If *bool1* and *bool2* stand for two Boolean expressions, the following notation defines *P* as a ***guarded choice by channel*** (in terms of the subprocesses *P1* and *P2*):

$$P = (bool1 \& c.v1 \rightarrow P1 \; [] \; bool2 \& d.v2 \rightarrow P2)$$

The behaviour of the process *P* depends on the values of the guard expressions *bool1* and *bool2* as follows:

bool1	*bool2*	*P*
true	*true*	$c.v1 \rightarrow P1 \; [] \; d.v2 \rightarrow P2$
true	*false*	$c.v1 \rightarrow P1$
false	*true*	$d.v2 \rightarrow P2$
false	*false*	*STOP*

An open guard is one where *bool* evaluates to *true*; if it evaluates to *false* the guard is closed. The guard expressions must be evaluated before the process *P* commences. Once evaluated they cannot be changed before the choice has been determined. As usual the notation can be extended to include a choice between several channels. A multiple guarded choice by channel is indicated by the notation:

$$[] \, (\, bool \, \& \, chan.var \,) \rightarrow \ldots$$

This indicates a choice by channel which can only be made if the Boolean expression *bool* evaluates to *true*. Let us see now how we can apply guarded choice to the description of a blocker.

Corresponding to the array *req*[ ] of entry channels we use an array *b*[ ] of Boolean variables. Let *J* be the set of channels to be intercepted by *BLOCKER*. Then, for each *j* in *J*, set the corresponding *b*[*j*] to be *true* and, for each *i* not in *J*, set *b*[*i*] to be false. The Boolean variables can now act as guards to determine precisely which channels are handled by *BLOCKER*. This gives us the following design:

$$BLOCKER = (|||_{1 \leq i \leq n} b[i] := false) ; B$$

$$B = block?set \rightarrow RESET_{set} ; B$$
$$\square$$
$$|||_{1 \leq i \leq n} b[i] \& req[i]?query \rightarrow reply[i]!busy \rightarrow B$$

$$RESET_{set} = |||_{1 \leq i \leq n} (b[i] := true \triangleleft i \in set \triangleright b[i] := false)$$

In this specification, the variables *b*[*i*] are initialized to *false*. In this state all the guards are closed and *B* cannot respond to any channel, except *block*. As soon as a value *set* is communicated by the master process, the subprocess *RESET* assigns new values to the guards so that the guards for the values of *i* in *set* are now open, but the other guards are closed. The process *B* is now able to respond to inputs on the corresponding *req*[*i*] channels. *B* remains in this state until a new instruction is received on *block*.

We shall use a variant of this specification in our development of the *NETWORK* process.

Example
20.1 This example illustrates how the same channel may have more than one guard.

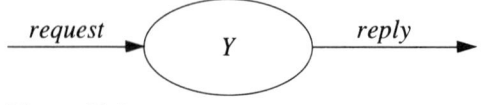

request → Y → *reply*

Figure 20.3

Figure 20.3 shows a process which has only one entry channel *request*, with alphabet {*alert*}, and one exit channel *reply*, with alphabet {*engaged, ok*}. Its behaviour is described as follows:

$$Y =$$
$$\quad (busy \ \& \ request.alert \rightarrow reply!engaged \rightarrow P$$
$$\quad \square$$
$$\quad \textbf{not } busy \ \& \ request.alert \rightarrow reply!ok \rightarrow Q \ )$$

Only one of the guards *busy* or **not** *busy* will be *true*, and depending on which it is the reply to an *alert* will be *engaged* or *ok*.

$$\square$$

Review Question 20.2 Give an alternative (but equivalent) design for the process *Y* of Example 20.1 in terms of an unguarded input event followed by a Boolean choice.

$$\boxdot$$

20.3 Infinite starvation

The *BLOCKER* is a very neat and effective way of avoiding delays in certain types of process network, but nevertheless is prone to a particular problem. Consider a situation where process *P* wants to use the channels *req*[1] and *reply*[1]. Whilst it is doing so, *BLOCKER* has been instructed to intercept and reply to incoming requests on the remaining channels {*req*[*j*]}. Eventually *P* may successfully conclude the sequence of events which engage the channels *req*[1] and *reply*[1]. The process *BLOCKER* must now be instructed to go dormant until further notice. There is however a possible snag—*P* may find itself unable to communicate with *BLOCKER*! For if there is a constant deluge of requests on the remaining channels {*req*[*j*]}, there is nothing in the specification of *BLOCKER* to prevent these requests from being serviced in preference to the communication on channel *block*. The upshot is that *P* may now be willing to accept communications on some or all of the channels, but may nevertheless not succeed in engaging in any such communication as a result of external factors beyond its control. This unsatisfactory state of affairs is referred to as **infinite starvation**, which is a form of *livelock*. In general the symptom is that one or more processes are capable of progressing but are prevented from doing so by other processes that deny them access to a necessary resource.

Infinite starvation refers to a situation where a process is waiting for a communication which *will* become available, but will be one of a choice of several input communications. These communications are subject to choice by channel under the control of the receiving process. If a communication is ready on more than one channel, the receiving process may legitimately choose to be unfair and always avoid one particular process, which becomes the victim of starvation.

The problem of infinite starvation may be overcome by the use of *prioritized choice by channel*, which we introduced in Part II (Section 8.2). The notation:

$$(a \rightarrow P \boxplus b \rightarrow Q)$$

denotes a process which behaves exactly like:

$$(a \rightarrow P \,\square\, b \rightarrow Q)$$

except that if the event *a* is ready it will be selected in preference to the event *b*.

Prioritized choice provides a way out of the starvation problem that afflicts the process *BLOCKER*. The specification may be amended so that commands on the channel *block* are given priority over all other requests. You could perhaps think of prioritized choice in the following way: as soon as a communication is available on the priority channel, an implicit guard on each of the other channels is closed.

The telephone blocker

Let us apply what we have learned to the blocker for the telephone process $T(0)$, with entry channels $link[k, 0]$ for $k = 1, 2, 3$. We may call the blocker $BL(0)$. This blocker may have to handle various sets of values of *k*, according to the input message on the channel *block*:

Message	*Set of phones*	*State of T*
none	{ }	in the DOWN state
all_but_1	{2, 3}	when connected to telephone 1
all_but_2	{1, 3}	when connected to telephone 2
all_but_3	{1, 2}	when connected to telephone 3
all	{1, 2, 3}	when dialling

Exercise

20.3 Write down a CSP specification of *BL*(0) for the telephone system using the operator ⇸ and the variable *cmd* (which takes values *none*, *all*, *all_but_1*, ... describing the set of blocked channels). The value of *cmd* is updated by a message from *T*(0) on the channel *block*; the initial value transmitted is *cmd* = *none*.

Solution 20.3 An incoming request must be *alert*, to which the response from the blocker will always be *busy*—the telephone is not available.

As before, we introduce a Boolean array *b*[ ]; *b*[*k*] takes the value *true* when *k* is in the blocking set and *false* otherwise. For example, when *b*[1] has the value *true* the channels *link*[0,1] and *link*[1,0] are blocked. We may set out the CSP specification as follows:

$BL(0) =$

$\quad block?cmd \rightarrow RESET_{cmd} ;\ BL(0)$

$\quad ⇸$

$\quad \Box_{1 \le k \le 3}\ b[k] \& link[k, 0].alert \rightarrow link[0, k]!busy \rightarrow BL(0))$

$RESET_{cmd} =$

$\quad (|||_{1 \le k \le 3} b[k] := false) \quad \lhd cmd = none \rhd \quad |||_{1 \le k \le 3} b[k] := true) ;$

$\quad (b[1] := false \quad \lhd cmd = all_but_1 \rhd$

$\quad\ b[2] := false \quad \lhd cmd = all_but_2 \rhd$

$\quad\ b[3] := false \quad \lhd cmd = all_but_3 \rhd$

$\quad\ SKIP)$

The state information is contained in the current array of values *b*[*k*] that is passed in the recursive call to *BL*(0).

□

Review Question 20.3 Describe in your own words the behaviour of the following process.

$\Box_{1 \le k \le 3}\ b[k] \& link[k, 0].alert \rightarrow link[0, k]!busy \rightarrow BL(0)$

□

20.4 Summary

We have introduced the concept of a blocking subprocess which runs concurrently with a real-time process; the sole function of the blocker is to respond rapidly to all incoming requests with a *busy* signal. The main process controls the blocker through a command channel which from time to time carries signals notifying the blocker which channels to handle. Such dynamic re-allocation of channels to a subprocess is called soft switching. The command channel must be given priority over all external channels lest the command signals be choked off by infinite starvation.

We introduced guarded communications using Boolean expressions and saw how an array of Boolean variables may be used to describe soft switching in CSP by means of a guarded choice by channel.

21 REVISED SPECIFICATION OF THE TELEPHONE NETWORK

Bearing in mind that our original specification failed we must re-design the telephone process T, by incorporating the idea of a blocker process discussed in the previous chapter. We find ourselves in a situation which is by no means uncommon in the development of software. In the course of validating our process design for *NETWORK* against the statement of requirements we have discovered the need for a modification to the system specification. As a result it becomes necessary to examine each component of the design so far to ensure that it satisfies the modified specification.

The process network of Figure 21.1 reflects the fact that each phone process $T(i)$ has control of a blocker process $BL(i)$, with which it communicates along a channel *block*. The function of $BL(i)$ is to respond promptly to unwanted incoming calls. Strictly speaking you would expect the channel *block* to be identified by a subscript i; however, we shall not bother to do this, as each *block* channel occurs locally within the exploded version of a particular telephone process.

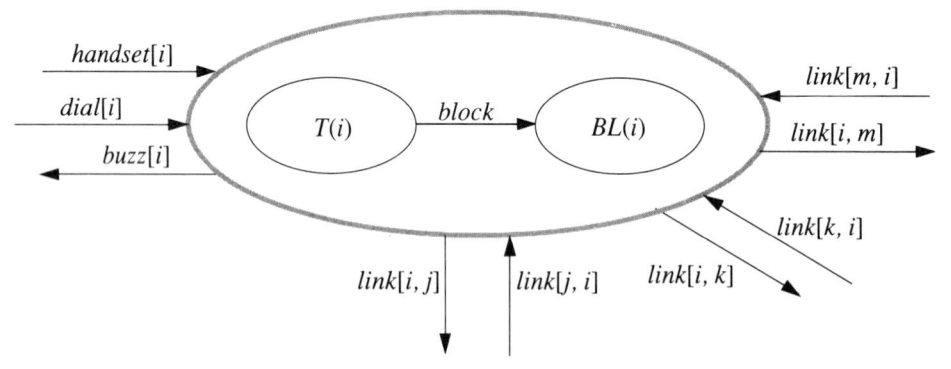

Figure 21.1

We begin this chapter by establishing a CSP design for *BL*. This is followed by a discussion to establish that the resulting design for *NETWORK* will be free of deadlock. The remainder of this chapter is devoted to obtaining a modified design for each of the sub-processes of the *T* process.

21.1 The process *BL*

We shall begin our revised specification of *NETWORK* by considering the behaviour of *BL*.

Review Question 21.1 In our network of four telephones, how many incoming *link* channels might each *BL* process have to handle? ▫

We shall assume that the possible messages on each channel *block* are *all, all_but_0, all_but_1, all_but_2, all_but_3, none*. As soon as a telephone enters a new state, the corresponding *T* process sends the appropriate message on its *block* channel.

In Section 20.3 we obtained the following specification for *BL*(0):

$BL(0) =$
 $(block\,?\,cmd \rightarrow RESET_{cmd}; BL(0)$
 ▷
 $\square_{1 \leq k \leq 3} b[k]\,\&\,link[k, 0].alert \rightarrow link[0, k]!busy \rightarrow BL(0))$

$RESET_{cmd} =$

$(|||_{1 \leq k \leq 3} b[k] := false) \quad \triangleleft cmd = none \triangleright \quad |||_{1 \leq k \leq 3} b[k] := true);$
$(b[1] := false \quad\quad\quad\quad \triangleleft cmd = all\_but\_1 \triangleright$
$b[2] := false \quad\quad\quad\quad \triangleleft cmd = all\_but\_2 \triangleright$
$b[3] := false \quad\quad\quad\quad \triangleleft cmd = all\_but\_3 \triangleright$
$SKIP)$

Note that the alphabet of each *link* channel has been extended to include the message *busy*. We must now generalize this for each of the *BL*(*i*). Channels *link*[*i, k*] exist provided $i \neq k$, so we can write the following:

$BL(i) =$
 $(block\,?\,cmd \rightarrow RESET_{cmd}; BL(i)$
 ▷
 $\square_{k \neq i} b[k]\,\&\,link[k, i].alert \rightarrow link[i, k]!busy \rightarrow BL(i))$

This specification is valid for each value of *i* ($0 \leq i \leq 3$) and the choice by channel is over values of $k \neq i$ in the range $0 \leq k \leq 3$. We shall also rewrite the subprocess *RESET* as follows:

$RESET_{cmd} =$

$(|||_{0 \leq k \leq 3} b[k] := false) \quad \triangleleft cmd = none \triangleright \quad |||_{0 \leq k \leq 3} b[k] := true;$
$(b[0] := false \quad\quad\quad\quad \triangleleft cmd = all\_but\_0 \triangleright$
$b[1] := false \quad\quad\quad\quad \triangleleft cmd = all\_but\_1 \triangleright$
$b[2] := false \quad\quad\quad\quad \triangleleft cmd = all\_but\_2 \triangleright$
$b[3] := false \quad\quad\quad\quad \triangleleft cmd = all\_but\_3 \triangleright$
$SKIP)$

This version of *RESET* can be used by each of the processes *BL*(*i*)—in each case one of the values of *b*[*k*] is redundant, but this is a small price to pay for the simplicity of sharing a single version of *RESET* between the four *BL* processes.

21.2 Deadlock analysis

One of the reasons for developing a formal specification is to be able to reason about the system being developed. The state and transition based style of specification that we are using does much of the work for us. It enables us to specify each telephone process in terms of its expected behaviour; that is, if a telephone is in a particular state and an allowable event happens, then the specification tells us exactly how the process responds and the state in which it finishes.

Each telephone process can be specified in an internally self-consistent manner. So what is there left to prove—what can go wrong? Parallel processes operate asynchronously and so there is no problem—until they try to communicate. The problem is that communication is two-way and though the internal specification of each process is correct, the order in which the communications take place may not match up between the two communicating processes. The most obvious way for this to happen is when a process wishes to communicate but the target process is unable to do so—deadlock. Unfortunately deadlock is not the only problem that can arise—there is also the problem of livelock and its variants. The classic case of livelock is when processes are still functioning but they are only performing tedious internal communications and nothing of interest is happening. Equally disastrous is the problem of infinite starvation, where all the processes are still functioning and interesting things are going on, but one process which has something equally interesting to perform is being starved of action.

Finally and even more subjective is the problem of delay, whereby everything is proceeding but some things are not proceeding quickly enough. However, as long as all the processes are still functioning, there should be no undue delay, since this is the one thing we took into account when we introduced the blocker processes.

When the system is commissioned it is described by the following process:

NETWORK = *PHONE*(0) || *PHONE*(1) || *PHONE*(2) || *PHONE*(3)
PHONE(*i*) = *T*(*i*) || *BL*(*i*)

Our aim is to design the process *NETWORK* with structures that are guaranteed not to lead to deadlock. We now proceed to justify the absence of deadlock in our approach. The introduction of blocker subprocesses renders it impossible for a process to be deadlocked through waiting to output. For, suppose process $T(i)$ is trying to send a message to process $T(j)$ while $T(j)$ is itself attempting to send a message. There are two possibilities. Either $T(j)$ is engaged in communicating with some other telephone process, or is itself attempting to communicate with $T(i)$.

In the former case, $T(i)$ need not worry about getting a response—the subprocess $BL(j)$ will provide one! This cannot lead to deadlock since the possibility of the communication taking place has been catered for, and it will even be acknowledged.

The next review question asks you to consider the alternative case.

Review Question 21.2 Suppose $T(j)$ is trying to communicate with $T(i)$; explain why there is no likelihood of deadlock.

□

A further source of deadlock on output arises when a process attempts to communicate with another process which has already terminated. All the telephone processes in the network recur forever, so there is no chance of a process trying to communicate with another that has terminated.

What about input—can a telephone process become deadlocked when attempting to accept input that cannot arrive? There are three situations to consider.

Firstly, the possible events in each state allow a choice by channel. Since a message on the channel *handset* is acceptable in any state, the process cannot become deadlocked. Each of the subprocesses *DOWN*, *DIAL*, *CALLING*, *TALK* and *BUZZING* is willing to accept input on its *handset* channel.

Secondly, a process may await a response to a communication it has just sent. Once again, our communications protocol ensures that such a response will eventually be forthcoming, so its recipient is not deadlocked.

Review Question 21.3 How can $T(i)$ be sure that a response will always be forthcoming when it needs one?

□

Thirdly, the blocker process always has a choice between taking input on the *link* channels and on *block*. Any communication to *PHONE(i)* will either be available to $T(i)$, which will then send a signal on *block*, or will be directed to the *BL(i)* in parallel with a request for a response.

In summary, provided that:

(a) all output is done in parallel with obtaining a response;

(b) any input is acknowledged; and

(c) all entry channels are eventually serviced;

a process cannot arrive at a situation where it is unable to communicate. Of course this ignores the possibility of hardware failure.

21.3 The processes *DOWN* and *BUZZING*

We must now describe each of the states of a typical phone process T, taking into account the role of the blocker process. In re-formulating the design we must ensure that the *BL* process is informed of its duties as quickly as possible. The intention is to provide a prompt response to incoming calls. Thus the first event of each subprocess describing a state of a telephone should be a communication to its blocker, putting the blocker in the appropriate state. We shall relate this discussion to the original version of *NETWORK* derived in Section 19.7.

The initial behaviour of *PHONE(i)* is given by:

$DOWN(i) \parallel BL(i)$

The first event of $DOWN(i)$ should be to switch its blocker off, because at this stage we are willing to accept any incoming calls. However, as soon as the process $T(i)$ receives an input—either from the local user or from a remote phone—it will enter a new state in which the blocker will be informed to be prepared for appropriate action. Thus we commence with:

252 SPECIFICATION AND DESIGN OF CONCURRENT SYSTEMS

$DOWN(i) =$
  $block!none \to$
    $(handset[i].up \to DIAL(i)$
    $[]$
    $[]_{j \neq i} link[j, i].alert \to link[i, j]!break \to buzz[i].noise \to BUZZING_j(i))$

The only change to the previous version of *DOWN* is the event *block!none*. Note that *DOWN* is prepared to accept *alert* on any input *link* channel.

The next step will be to re-design the processes $DIAL(i)$ and $BUZZING_j(i)$. (Since our previous specification was erroneous, we must re-examine each component which arose earlier.) The most drastic changes to our original design are required for the process $DIAL(i)$. We shall therefore defer the re-design of this process until Section 21.4.

The process $BUZZING_j(i)$ corresponds to an incoming call. Remember that the message *all_but_j* on the *block* channel instructs the blocker to handle the *link* channels from telephones other than *j*. The process $BUZZING_j(i)$ therefore begins with the transmission of the message *all_but_j* on *block*; this is the only change from the previous version. The fact that the blocker is notified on entering each new state will, as we have seen, ensure that it handles the correct subset of *link* channels.

Here is a revised CSP specification for $BUZZING_j(i)$:

$BUZZING_j(i) =$
  $block!all\_but\_j \to$
    $(handset[i].up \to$
      $(link[i, j]!alert \to SKIP ||| link[j, i]?reply \to SKIP) ;$
      $TALK_j(i) \triangleleft reply = alert \triangleright DIAL(i)$
    $[]$
    $link[j, i].break \to link[i, j]!break \to SKIP)$

21.4 The processes *DIAL* and *TALK*

We now consider the specification of the remaining processes.

The process *DIAL* commences with the event *block!all*. As soon as the number *j* has been dialled *DIAL* must be prepared to receive a response from telephone *j*, so the blocker must be sent the message *all_but_j*. However, the evolution of the process is no longer as simple as it was in Chapter 19. There are several possible outcomes of dialling another number. As before, the response *alert* is handled by proceeding directly to the state TALK, and the response *break* causes the telephone of the called party to buzz. There is also a third and new possibility: the response could be *busy*.

> **Review Question 21.4** How could the response *busy* arise?
>
> ☐

To handle this new situation we introduce the state ENGAGED. A telephone enters this state when the number it has just dialled is busy. While in this state, the telephone cannot communicate with any other phone until its handset is replaced. Its blocker must consequently be sent the message *all*.

In order to accommodate the modifications to the version of *DIAL* given in Section 19.7

REVISED SPECIFICATION OF THE TELEPHONE NETWORK 253

to include the communications on the channel *block* and the response *busy*, we shall introduce the subprocess $DIALLING_j$.

$DIAL(i) =$
  $block!all \to$
   $handset[i].down \to SKIP$
  $\square$
  $dial[i]?j \to$
   $(handset[i].down \to SKIP \quad \triangleleft j = i \triangleright \quad DIALLING_j(i))$

$DIALLING_j(i) =$
  $block!all\_but\_j \to$
   $(link[i, j]!alert \to SKIP \;|||\; link[j, i]?reply \to SKIP)\;;$
  $CALLING_j(i) \qquad \triangleleft reply = break \triangleright$
  $ENGAGED(i) \qquad \triangleleft reply = busy \triangleright$
  $TALK_j(i)$

Notice that as soon as a number has been dialled it is necessary to take control of the *link* channels to the dialled phone away from the blocker, so that the subprocess *DIALLING* can handle the communication with the distant phone. The parallel nature of the inter-phone communication, coupled with the certainty of obtaining some response, will prevent deadlock as long as we make adequate provision for all possible responses.

Our next task is to consider the processes that result from making a call. We start with the process $CALLING_j(i)$. This process arises solely from the process $DIALLING_j(i)$. Thus the blocker is already handling all the *link* channels to *i* except the one from *j*, and so no new message on *block* is required. Consequently the process $CALLING_j(i)$ requires no modification.

The process *ENGAGED* also arises solely from the process $DIALLING_j$, after a *busy* message is received. It must now instruct the blocker to handle all calls—even one from telephone *j*. The telephone can then do only one thing—wait for the handset to be replaced so that it can revert to state DOWN.

Exercise
21.1 Specify the process *ENGAGED*.

Solution 21.1

  $ENGAGED(i) = block!all \to handset[i].down \to SKIP$

                                ⊡

Exercise
21.2 What changes are needed to the CSP design for *TALK*?

Solution 21.2 The process $TALK_j$ is invoked by the processes $BUZZING_j$, $DIALLING_j$ and $CALLING_j$. The two former processes send the message *all_but_j* and the latter only arises from $DIALLING_j$. Consequently when $TALK_j$ begins the most recent message received by the blocker is *all_but_j*, and the blocker is already handling the correct set of channels. Thus no change is needed to the original design.

                                     ⊡

Review Question 21.5 Since the *SKIP* in *ENGAGED* leads back to the next recursion of *DOWN*, why is the event *block!all* necessary?

21.5 Summary

We have now developed a complete specification of a telephone network for four users. You may perhaps notice that the number four is not intrinsic to our development, which could have been performed equally for a larger number of telephones with minimal amendment to our specification.

An important result which we incorporated into our modified design was the blocker that acts as a slave process to handle signals that cannot be dealt with immediately by the main process. The processes *DOWN, BUZZING, DIAL, DIALLING* and *ENGAGED* begin by resetting the state of the blocker. The processes *CALLING* and *TALK* are unamended from the version designed in Chapter 19.

In order to build the software for our network, we must implement our design in Occam. Most of the design is already sufficiently detailed for this purpose; but our specification is recursive. We have seen in Part III that recursive specifications must be recast into iterative designs in order to be coded in Occam. This will form part of our work in Chapter 22, where we obtain an Occam version of the network with four telephones.

22 CODING THE TELEPHONE NETWORK

We have now seen a complete specification of the telephone network. In this chapter we shall develop Occam code for the network. As we saw in Part III, we shall have to refine some of the general CSP constructions in order to be able to convert them to Occam code. In the course of our development, we shall introduce one or two useful tools that aid the writing of Occam programs.

22.1 The Occam folding editor

Our development method has very much a top-down flavour to it. We define a process in a fairly general way, and then explode it into several parallel processes that are individually specified. Occam programming systems provide a *folding editor* which allows code to be written at the higher levels of the design process in a manner which allows its automatic incorporation into the final program. A folding editor allows a text file to be viewed like a sheet of paper which can be folded so that parts of the sheet are hidden from view. The position of the hidden text appears as a *fold line*, and is identified by a *fold header*; the editor displays the fold line as three full stops followed by the fold header. The editor thus allows gaps in programs—that is, sections of code that have not yet been written—to be allocated a named position in the code. The portion of text represented by a fold line is called a *fold*. As the coding proceeds in a top-down fashion, each fold is opened out and coded individually.

We defined the process NETWORK in the previous chapter as a parallel combination of telephone and blocker processes. By considering this process definition, we are able to write a top-level Occam code fragment for it. We have:

$NETWORK = \|_{0 \leq i \leq 3} PHONE(i)$
$PHONE(i) = T(i) \| BL(i)$

We see from the process network in Figure 19.2 that the channels of PHONE(i) are *handset*[i], *dial*[i], *buzz*[i], and *link*[j, k] where either j or k is equal to i.

The corresponding Occam code may be developed as follows:

```
PROC Network =
  CHAN handset[4], dial[4], buzz[4], link[4][4] :
  ...     PROC Phone
  PAR i = [0 FOR 4]
    Phone( i, handset[i], dial[i], buzz[i], link ) :
```

This piece of code contains several new elements, which we shall now proceed to explain.

It begins with the declaration of the channels that are needed. We have had to define a complete channel array `link`, including some channels (such as `link[1][1]`) that do not exist.

The process `Phone` is left completely undefined at this stage. It is represented by a fold line which reserves a place in the final listing and has the associated descriptive comment `PROC Phone`. We shall return to the contents of this fold later.

The `Network` process is defined as the replication of a process `Phone`, which is assumed to have five parameters. This is not the only possibility, but one that will serve our purposes here. The number of the telephone is passed to the process `Phone` in terms of the index `i`, and we have given the individual channels `handset[i]`, `dial[i]` and `buzz[i]` explicitly. However, for simplicity, the entire channel array `link[ ][ ]` is passed to each `Phone`, though it will use only those channels specifically connected to it according to the process network.[1]

22.2 The process `Phone`

The generation of Occam code is achieved by repeatedly making explicit code that has been relegated to folds. We have just seen a code fragment with a fold for the definition of `PROC Phone`, which we must fill in now. At the top level we know that *PHONE* is a parallel composition of a telephone process *T* and a blocker process *BL*.

Here is the top-level code for `PROC Phone`:

```
{ { {    PROC Phone
PROC Phone ( VALUE i, CHAN hhandset, ddial, bbuzz,
link[][] ) =
  DEF alert = ***, break = ***, busy = *** :
  CHAN block :
  DEF none = ***, all = ***, all_but_0 = 0, all_but_1
= 1, all_but_2 =2, all_but_3 = 3 :
  ...     PROC Tel
  ...     PROC Block
  PAR
    Tel( hhandset, ddial, bbuzz, link, block)
    Block( block, link) :
} } }
```

In expanding a fold, two *crease lines* are introduced. The top crease begins with { { {

---

[1] This is a major simplification and one which may cause problems if we were to implement this program by distributing it across a transputer network; but for the purposes of our case-study it will suffice.

CODING THE TELEPHONE NETWORK   257

followed by the name attached to the fold line that identifies the fold. The bottom crease } } } marks the end of the fold. These crease lines are ignored by the compiler; they serve only to identify the fold to the editor to simplify the writing and amendment of program code.

The formal channel parameters of Phone are given names that correspond to the actual channels that replace them in the activation of the Phone process. The formal channel array parameter is written as link[ ][ ]; in an activation of the process Phone it is replaced by the name of the channel array — link. It is appropriate at this stage to include the alphabet of the channel array link[ ][ ] through which messages are transmitted between the processes Phone(i). The indication *** is used within constant definitions to indicate (distinct) values that can be arbitrarily chosen and do not affect the validity of the code.

The formal parameter i will be used in the refinement of Phone to identify the relevant channels in the array link[ ]; for convenience it is not passed explicitly to Tel and Block but is accessed globally. Since the channel is local to Phone it does not matter that the same name is used whenever a Phone process is activated. The alphabet of the channel block must also be defined at this stage to ensure consistency in the values transmitted.

The four processes that behave like Phone are activated in the body of the top-level process Network. However, the definition of the process Phone stands on its own, and could be used in other situations if required.

Now we need to code the processes Tel and Block, whose parameters label the channels to which they are attached; we shall begin with the code for Block, which is the simpler of the two.

22.3 The process Block

Our next task is to obtain an Occam version of *BL(i)*, which is defined in terms of choice by channel. Choice by channel is implemented in Occam using the constructor ALT. For example, the process:

handset?sig → P ▯ dial?number → R

becomes:

```
ALT
   handset ? sig
      P
   dial ? number
      R
```

The modified fetbar ⇾ is implemented in Occam using the constructor PRI ALT. For example:

block?cmd → P ⇾ link?message → Q

is coded as:

```
PRI ALT
   block ? cmd
      P
   link ? message
      Q
```

The ALT constructor can also be used with a replicator; for example, the process:

$$\square_{1 \leq k \leq 3} link[k, 0]?message \rightarrow link[0, k]!busy \rightarrow SKIP$$

is coded as follows:

```
ALT k= [1 FOR 3]
   link[k][0] ? message
      SEQ
         link[0][k] ! busy
         SKIP
```

Here is the CSP design for the blocker process that we saw in Section 21.1:

$BL(i) =$
$\quad (block?cmd \rightarrow RESET_{cmd}$
$\quad \boxplus$
$\quad \square_{k \neq i} b[k] \& link[k, i].alert \rightarrow link[i, k]!busy \rightarrow SKIP)$;
$\quad BL(i)$

$RESET_{cmd} =$
$\quad |||_{0 \leq k \leq 3} (b[k] := false) \quad \triangleleft cmd = none \triangleright \quad |||_{0 \leq k \leq 3} (b[k] := true)$;
$\quad b[0] := false \quad\quad\quad\quad \triangleleft cmd = all\_but\_0 \triangleright$
$\quad b[1] := false \quad\quad\quad\quad \triangleleft cmd = all\_but\_1 \triangleright$
$\quad b[2] := false \quad\quad\quad\quad \triangleleft cmd = all\_but\_2 \triangleright$
$\quad b[3] := false \quad\quad\quad\quad \triangleleft cmd = all\_but\_3 \triangleright$
$\quad SKIP$

The specification of *BL* consists of a fourfold choice by channel followed by a recursive call to the process. The last three alternatives are guarded by Boolean variables. The first alternative assigns a value to the variable *cmd*, followed by variable assignments that establish the state of the process.

We use a WHILE constructor to remove recursion in the specification for the process $BL(i)$. Block has a channel parameter and a channel array parameter, as indicated in the top-level code for PROC Phone:

```
{ { {    PROC Block
PROC Block( CHAN block, link[ ][ ] ) =
   VAR cmd, any, b[3] :
   WHILE TRUE
      PRI ALT
         block ? cmd
            SEQ
               IF
                  cmd = none
                     SEQ k = [0 FOR 4]
                        b[k] := FALSE
                  TRUE
                     SEQ k = [0 FOR 4]
                        b[k] := TRUE
```

```
                    IF
                        cmd = all_but_0
                            b[0] := FALSE
                        cmd = all_but_1
                            b[1] := FALSE
                        cmd = all_but_2
                            b[2] := FALSE
                        cmd = all_but_3
                            b[3] := FALSE
                        TRUE
                            SKIP
                ALT k = [0 FOR 4]
                    b[k] & link[k][i] ? any
                        link[i][k] ! busy :
}}}
```

There are a number of further points to note in the definition of PROC Block. Guarded choice by channel is implemented just as in CSP, with a Boolean expression followed by &. The interleaved assignments are coded using SEQ, as PAR is very inefficient for assignments. The identity of the process is determined by the value of the global parameter i.

Notice also the use of the variable any when we are expecting a specific input on a channel and we do not need to check its value. Although the specification tells us that the input value on channel *link*[*k*, *i*] will be *alert*, an Occam input process has the syntax:

```
channel ? v
```

where v is a variable.

We have coded a general-purpose blocker which applies to the four cases we need, according to the value of the global parameter i. On each activation, one of the possible values of cmd = all_but_j is redundant, but nothing is lost by including it.

22.4 The process Tel

In Chapter 21 we saw how the telephone process could be specified in terms of a set of subprocesses describing the individual states. The subprocess designs are collected here for convenience:

$T(i) = \mu X . (DOWN(i) ; X)$

$DOWN(i) =$
    $block!none \rightarrow$
        $(handset[i].up \rightarrow DIAL(i)$
        $\square$
        $\square_{j \neq i} link[j, i].alert \rightarrow$
            $link[i, j]!break \rightarrow buzz[i].noise \rightarrow BUZZING_j(i))$

$DIAL(i) =$
    $block!all \rightarrow$
        $handset[i].down \rightarrow SKIP$
        $\square$
        $dial[i]?j \rightarrow$
            $(handset[i].down \rightarrow SKIP \quad \triangleleft j = i \triangleright \quad DIALLING_j(i))$

$DIALLING_j(i) =$
$\quad block!all\_but\_j \rightarrow (link[i,j]!alert \rightarrow SKIP ||| link[j,i]?reply \rightarrow SKIP) ;$
$\quad CALLING_j(i) \quad \triangleleft reply = break \triangleright$
$\quad ENGAGED(i) \quad \triangleleft reply = busy \triangleright$
$\quad TALK_j(i)$

$CALLING_j(i) =$
$\quad link[j,i].alert \rightarrow link[i,j]!alert \rightarrow TALK_j(i)$
$\quad \Box$
$\quad handset[i].down \rightarrow (link[i,j]!break \rightarrow SKIP ||| link[j,i]?any \rightarrow SKIP)$

$ENGAGED(i) = block!all \rightarrow handset[i].down \rightarrow SKIP$

$TALK_j(i)=$
$\quad handset[i].down \rightarrow (link[i,j]!break \rightarrow SKIP ||| link[j,i]?any \rightarrow SKIP)$
$\quad \Box$
$\quad link[j,i].break \rightarrow link[i,j]!alert \rightarrow DIAL(i)$

$BUZZING_j(i) =$
$\quad block!all\_but\_j \rightarrow$
$\quad\quad (handset[i].up \rightarrow (link[i,j]!alert \rightarrow SKIP ||| link[j,i]?reply \rightarrow SKIP) ;$
$\quad\quad\quad TALK_j(i) \quad \triangleleft reply = alert \triangleright \quad DIAL(i)$
$\quad\quad \Box$
$\quad\quad link[j,i].break \rightarrow link[i,j]!break \rightarrow SKIP)$

We shall approach the coding of a telephone process as follows. Each subprocess corresponding to a state will be coded within a fold. The main process code for the process *T* will therefore consist of the constant definitions (for the alphabets of the external channels `hhandset` and `ddial`), variable declarations, folds for the state process definitions, and a fold for the process *DOWN*.

Exercise

22.1 Write the top-level code for PROC Tel.

Solution 22.1

```
{ { {    PROC Tel
PROC Tel( CHAN hhandset, ddial, bbuzz, link[ ][ ],
block) =
  DEF up = ***, down = ***, noise = *** :
  VAR any, reply :
   ...      PROC Buzzing
   ...      PROC Dial
   ...      PROC Dialling
   ...      PROC Calling
   ...      PROC Talk
  SEQ
    WHILE TRUE
        ...      Down
} } }
```

CODING THE TELEPHONE NETWORK 261

The simple recursion in *T* has been removed by using the WHILE constructor.

We now look at the fold Down. This will be coded directly from the specification given above. Since the process *DOWN* is only activated from Tel we shall not code it as a named process; we just write the process definition in the fold, where the compiler will treat it as in-line code:

```
{ { {    Down
SEQ
   block ! none
   ALT
      hhandset ? any
         Dial
      ALT j = [0 FOR 4]
         link[j][i] ? any
            SEQ
               link[i][j] ! break
               bbuzz ! noise
               Buzzing(j)  :
} } }
```

Notice again the use of the variable any when the input can take only one value, and the redundant entry channel link[i][i] that never carries any message. Since the fold Down completes the process definition for Tel it must end with a colon. The activation of the processes Dial and Buzzing(j) omit the channel names, which are available globally throughout Tel.

We shall now ask you to determine the contents of the folds that contain the definitions of the processes Buzzing, Dial and Dialling.

Exercises

22.2 By looking at the specification of $BUZZING_i(i)$, derive the code for PROC Buzzing(j). (Remember that the value of i is available globally.)

Solution 22.2

```
{ { {    PROC Buzzing
PROC Buzzing(VALUE j) =
   DEF all_but_j = j :
   SEQ
      block ! all_but_j

      ALT
         hhandset ? any
            SEQ
               PAR
                  link[i][j] ! alert
                  link[j][i] ? reply
               IF
                  reply = break
                     Dial
                  TRUE
```

```
            Talk(j)
     link[j][i] ? any
        link[i][j] ! break :
} } }
```

Exercise
22.3 Derive the code for PROC Dial from the specification of *DIAL(i)*.

Solution 22.3

```
{ { {      PROC Dial
PROC Dial =
  VAR j :
  SEQ
    block ! all
    ALT
      hhandset ? any
        SKIP
      ddial ? j
        IF
          j = i
            hhandset ? any
          TRUE
            Dialling(j) :
```

Exercise
22.4 Obtain the code for PROC Dialling(j).

Solution 22.4

```
   { { {     PROC Dialling
PROC Dialling(VALUE j) =
  DEF all_but_j = j :
  SEQ
    block ! all_but_j
    PAR
      link[i][j] ! alert
      link[j][i] ? reply
    IF
      reply = break
        Calling(j)
      reply = busy
        . . .    Engaged
      TRUE
        Talk(j) :
} } }
```

The code for the fold Engaged is quite straightforward:

```
{{{    Engaged
block ! all
hhandset ? any
}}}
```

We may implement the subprocess *CALLING$_j$(i)* as follows:

```
{{{    PROC Calling
PROC Calling(VALUE j) =
  ALT
    link[j][i] ? any
      SEQ
        link[i][j] ! alert
        Talk(j)
    hhandset ? any
      PAR
        link[i][j] ! break
        link[j][i] ? any :
}}}
```

22.5 Implementing the process *TALK*

We have been able to put off much of the hard work of implementing the network to the last moment. We now come to the subprocess *TALK*, whose specification entails a recursive call to the subprocess *DIAL*.

Review Question 22.1 Why do we call the activation of *DIAL* within *TALK* a recursive call?

Since Occam does not support recursive processes, we transform our recursive specifications into iterative form using the star operator *.

Recall that our state-based specification involves various states in which a telephone may find itself. The transitions between the states occur due to communications between the phone and its environment (the user and the other phones). A convenient version of the state transition diagram is shown in Figure 22.1.

Our main task at this stage is to identify recursion in the processes that describe these states. Recursion may be identified by closed loops in the state transition diagram, since these correspond to processes that ultimately reactivate themselves. Clearly there are a number of closed paths through the state DOWN. These correspond to the recursive definition of *T(i)*, which we have already dealt with simply using WHILE TRUE.

Since we have taken the state DOWN as the dormant state the processes *ENGAGED* and *BUZZING$_j$* do not involve any further recursion. These processes effectively terminate when their activation brings the telephone to the state DOWN. It is now sufficient to search for closed cycles that do not include our basic state DOWN. These are shown in Figure 22.2.

Thus we shall have to be careful how we handle the three states CALLING, DIAL and TALK.

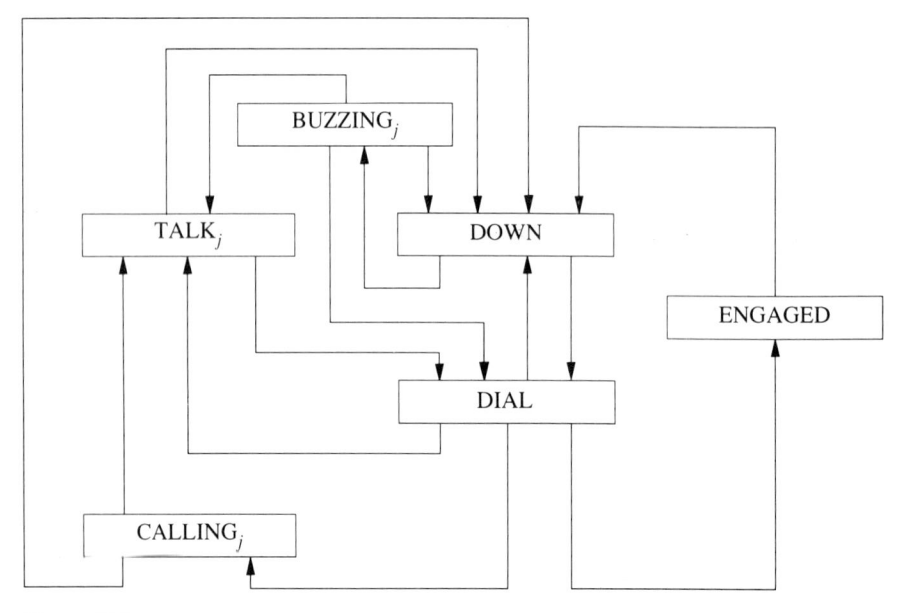

Figure 22.1

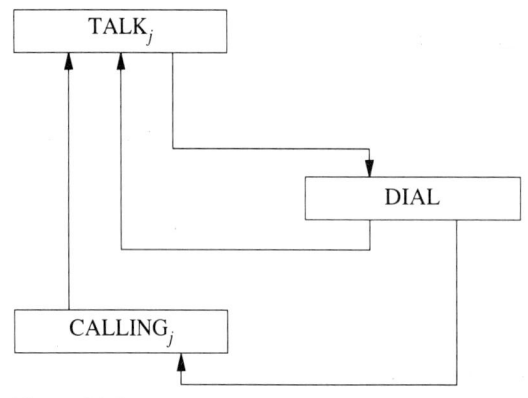

Figure 22.2

In order to decouple a mutually recursive set of specifications, we choose one state as a master, writing out its design as an explicitly recursive process without reference to the others. The recursion in this process will have to be transformed to iteration. The other processes are then coded in terms of the master process.

In our case, we could choose either *TALK* or *DIAL* as the master process. We shall choose *TALK* as the master process; this means that we must remove the reference to *DIAL* within *TALK* accordingly.

Review Question 22.2 Why could we not use *CALLING* as the master process?

To expand the specification of *TALK* given in Section 22.4, we first replace the reference to *DIAL* by its full specification. This gives us the following:

CODING THE TELEPHONE NETWORK   265

$TALK_j(i)=$
    $handset[i].down \to (link[i,j]!break \to SKIP \;|||\; link[j,i]?any \to SKIP)$
    □
    $link[j,i].break \to link[i,j]!alert \to block!all \to$
        $(handset[i].down \to SKIP$
        □
        $dial[i]?j \to$
            $(handset[i].down \to SKIP$ ◁ $j = i$ ▷
            $(block!all\_but\_j \to (link[i,j]!alert \to SKIP \;|||\; link[j,i]?reply \to$
$SKIP)$;
            $CALLING_j(i)$ ◁ $reply = break$ ▷
            $ENGAGED(i)$ ◁ $reply = busy$ ▷
            $TALK_j(i))))$

The call to *ENGAGED* cannot lead to a recursive activation of *TALK* as it is a terminating process. The reference to *CALLING*, however, contains implicit recursion, so it too must be expanded.

When the full definition of *CALLING* is substituted, we shall have a description of *TALK* in terms of terminating processes and explicit recursion. In order to control the explicit recursion we carry out the following procedure. We introduce a Boolean variable *talking* which is initially set to *true*. The recursive specification is now replaced by introducing a while loop, controlled by the variable *talking*. The final references to *TALK* are now replaced by *SKIP*; the recursion is absorbed into the while loop. However, whenever a path through the process description terminates, we must insert the process (*talking := false*), which has the effect of ending the while loop.

The final specification of *TALK* in closed form turns out to be quite lengthy:

$TALK_j(i) =$
    $(talking := true);$
    $talking *$
    $(handset[i].down \to (link[i,j]!break \to SKIP\;|||\; link[j,i]?any \to SKIP)$;
        $(talking := false)$
    □
    $link[j,i].break \to link[i,j]!alert \to block!all \to$
        $(handset[i].down \to (talking := false)$
        □
        $dial[i]?j \to$
            $(handset[i].down \to (talking := false)$ ◁ $j = i$ ▷
            $(block!all\_but\_j \to (link[i,j]!alert \to SKIP\;|||\; link[j,i]?reply \to SKIP);$
            $(link[j,i].alert \to link[i,j]!alert \to SKIP$ †
            □
            $handset[i].down \to$
                $(link[i,j]!break \to SKIP\;|||\; link[j,i]?any \to SKIP) ;$
                $(talking := false))$
                                      ◁ $reply = break$ ▷
            $ENGAGED(i)$; $(talking := false)$
                                      ◁ $reply = busy$ ▷
        $SKIP))))$ †

The two lines marked with a dagger contain the new *SKIP* that replaces the recursive use of *TALK*.

Exercise

22.5 Describe in your own words the basic sequence of state transitions given above.

Solution 22.4 Once the *talking* loop has been entered there is a basic choice between replacing the local telephone handset or having the remote user do so. In the former case the local phone goes immediately into the terminal state DOWN, whereas in the latter one is in state DIAL with various further choices ahead. Either the local phone can be hung up, leading to state DOWN, or the local user can try dialling out. If you erroneously dial your own number you eventually return to DOWN.

If you have dialled a reasonable number which is not busy, the local phone enters state CALLING. In this case either you hang up and enter state DOWN, or you wait until the called telephone is picked up, when the local phone will enter the desired state TALK and begin the loop again. If the called number is busy, the local phone enters the state ENGAGED that must lead to state DOWN.

The only other possibility is that the other telephone is trying to contact you at exactly the same time as you are trying to contact it, in which case the state TALK is entered directly.

You may check that this tallies with the available transitions as shown in Figure 22.1.

□

Having transformed the recursive specification of the process *TALK* to a form involving a loop, we are in a position translate this into code. We shall make use of a local fold to avoid the need for excessive indentation.

As before we shall assume that the channels hhandset, block, ddial, the channel array link[][] and the value i of the local phone are accessible to PROC Talk. The identity of the remote phone is passed as a parameter j. (We include one or two comments; these appear at the end of a line preceded by two dashes.)

```
{{{   PROC Talk
PROC Talk( VAR j ) =
  VAR talking :
  SEQ
    talking := TRUE
    WHILE talking
      ALT
        hhandset ? any
          SEQ
            PAR
              link[i][j] ! break
              link[j][i] ? any
            talking := FALSE
        link[j][i] ? any
          SEQ
            link[i][j] ! alert
            block ! all
```

```
                    ALT
                      hhandset ? down
                        talking := FALSE
                      ddial ? j        -- this is a new number
                        IF
                          j = i
                            SEQ
                              hhandset ? any
                              talking := FALSE
                          TRUE
                            . . .       DIALLING

{ { {   DIALLING
SEQ
  block ! j                           -- since j = all_but_j
  PAR
    link[i][j] ! alert
    link[j][i] ? reply
  IF
    reply = break
      -- CALLING
      ALT
        link[j][i] ? any
          link[i][j] ! alert
        hhandset ? any
          SEQ
            PAR
              link[i][j] ! break
              link[j][i] ? any
            talking := FALSE
    reply = busy
      -- ENGAGED
      SEQ
        block ! all
        hhandset ? any
        talking := FALSE
    TRUE                    - - reply = alert
      SKIP :
} } }
```

22.6 Summary

In this chapter we have completed our real-time case-study. We have gained further experience in translating a suitable CSP design from which recursion has been removed into Occam. In so doing, we mentioned a new technique for isolating recursion in a mutually recursive set of process specifications. We also discussed briefly the folding editor that is a feature of Occam development environments. This editor is a useful tool in allowing programs to be coded in top-down fashion.

In producing the code for the telephone network you have participated in a very substantial piece of work. You should feel that you can cope with small specifications, their refinement and design, and the production of code.

23 THE TOWERS OF HANOI

We have now covered a complete method of developing software for concurrent processes. In this chapter we are going to consider another problem to which these techniques can be applied; this should provide you with an overview which summarizes the techniques taught in this book. The problem is that of the Towers of Hanoi, and you may well be familiar with a sequential treatment. In the following discussion you will learn how a seemingly innocent problem can give rise to very subtle deadlock issues. After we have shown how to resolve these issues you will be able to complete the task of producing an Occam implementation of a valid concurrent algorithm for solving the Towers of Hanoi problem.

23.1 Specification

We are going to set up the Towers of Hanoi problem as a concurrent processing system and develop a CSP specification.

There is a natural description of a recursive solution to the Towers of Hanoi problem. This solution, however, gives little feel about what is the next step at any given stage. It has been shown that the recursive solution is equivalent to a procedure whereby alternate steps consist of moving the smallest disc cyclically—we shall call this 'clockwise'—and moving the smaller of the discs on the other two pegs.

We shall set up the problem in this fashion and perform process analysis, leading up to a CSP description of the solution. We shall also take preliminary steps towards developing code for the problem. Our approach follows the ODM strategy that has been a feature of this book. In order to concentrate on the concurrent processing aspect of the problem we shall ignore the details of outputting the steps in the solution; these may be inserted in a fairly straightforward manner.

The scene is set in Figure 23.1, which shows three vertical pegs; on one of them there are three discs of differing sizes arranged upwards in order of decreasing size. The problem is to determine a sequence of moves, starting with all the discs in order on peg A, and resulting with them all in order on peg B. An allowable move consists of moving the top disc from any peg to another peg, without ever placing a larger disc on a smaller disc. A solution to this problem is illustrated in Figure 23.2.

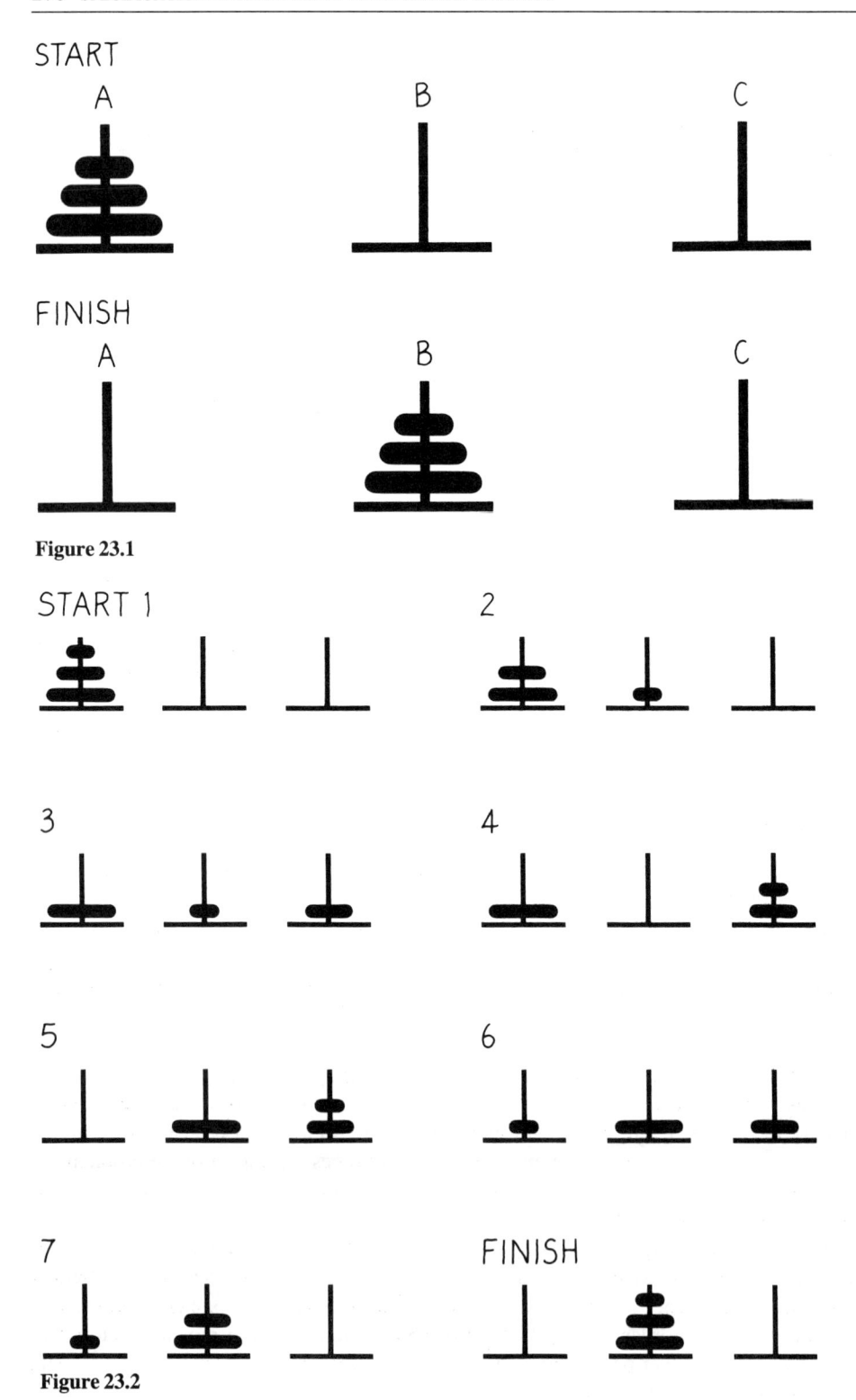

270 SPECIFICATION AND DESIGN OF CONCURRENT SYSTEMS

Figure 23.1

Figure 23.2

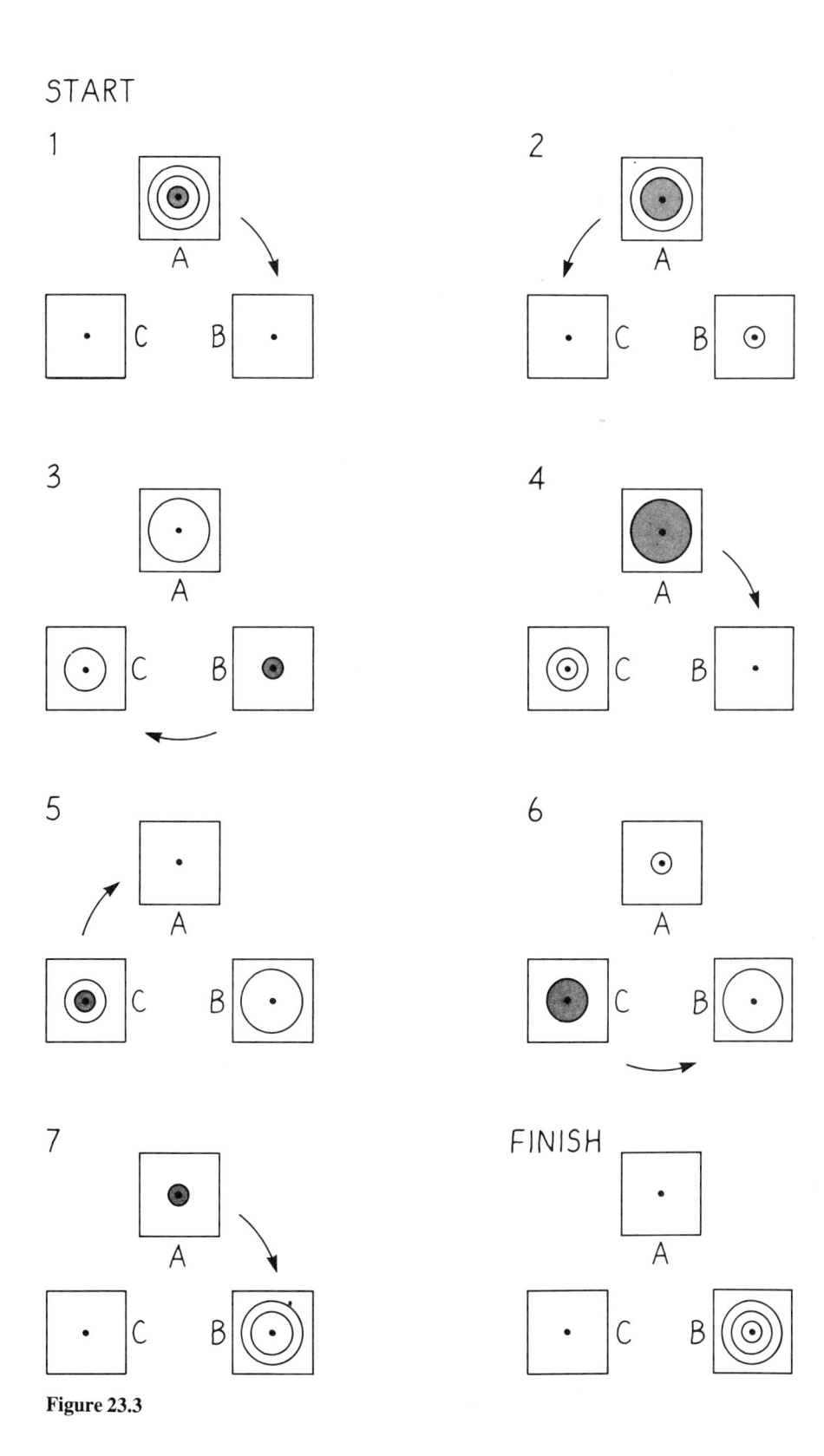

Figure 23.3

272 SPECIFICATION AND DESIGN OF CONCURRENT SYSTEMS

We would like to be able to generalize this solution so that it applies to the Towers of Hanoi problem for any number of discs. It will help if we view the solution for the three-disc problem from above, as shown in Figure 23.3, with the pegs arranged in a circle rather than in a straight line. The disc about to move is highlighted in each case, and an arrow shows the direction of the move.

Note carefully that in each odd-numbered move (in the left-hand column) the smallest disc moves clockwise. In each even-numbered move a disc moves between the two pegs not containing the smallest disc—there is only one allowable move in each case. This gives a simple algorithm: alternately move the smallest disc clockwise and perform another legal move. In the final position two pegs are empty and the problem is solved. This algorithm extends, indeed, to deal with any number of discs.

How can we exploit concurrency in developing a program for this algorithm? At any time each peg holds a pile of discs. We may treat the three pegs as concurrent identical processes, as indicated in the process network of Figure 23.4. Each process *TOWER(i)* has two exit channels *clock*[i] and *anti*[i] and a pair of entry channels, labelled by their source processes.

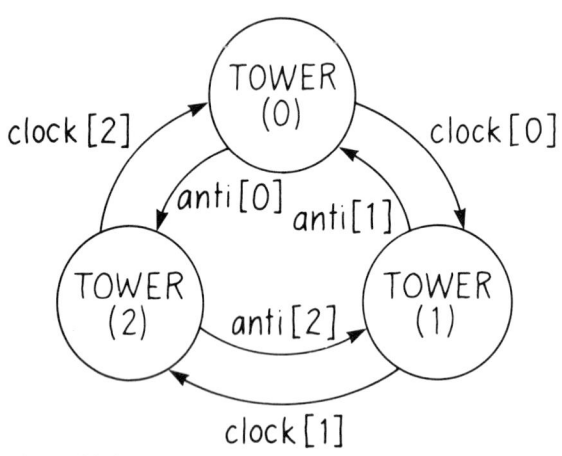

Figure 23.4

Exercise

23.1 Give an initial CSP design for the Towers of Hanoi problem.

Solution 23.1

$HANOI = TOWER(0) \| TOWER(1) \| TOWER(2)$

where the process *TOWER* has yet to be defined.

The corresponding Occam code is:

```
PROC Hanoi =
  CHAN clock[3], anti[3] :
  ...    PROC Tower
  PAR
    Tower(0, clock[0], anti[1], anti[0], clock[2] )
    Tower(1, clock[1], anti[2], anti[1], clock[0] )
    Tower(2, clock[2], anti[0], anti[2], clock[1] ):
```

THE TOWERS OF HANOI 273

The Occam process Tower has an index parameter and four channel parameters arranged systematically in the order exit clockwise, entry anticlockwise, exit anticlockwise, entry clockwise.

The *TOWER* process requires some initialization, followed by a sequences of moves. We shall need to design an appropriate data structure to describe the state of a peg at any time. What data do we need? In the simple case of three discs we may use the representation shown in Figure 23.5.

Data Representation

Disc Values: small, medium, large

Position Variables: top, next, third

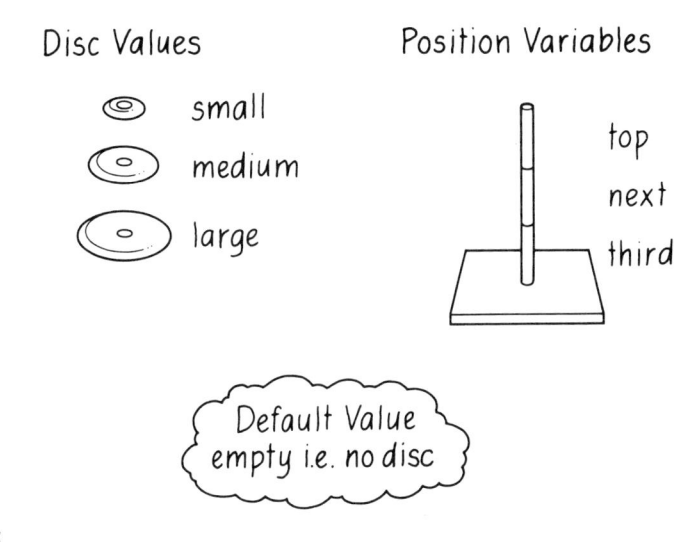

Default Value empty i.e. no disc

Figure 23.5

Initially, the variables associated with peg 0 have the values:

top = small
next = medium
third = large

When a peg holds fewer than three discs some of the position variables hold no values; for example, for a peg holding two discs *third* has the value *empty*.

Exercise
23.2 Code the initialization of Tower (i, ...) in Occam.

Solution 23.2

```
{{{    Init
SEQ
  IF
    i = 0
      SEQ
        top := small
```

```
            next := medium
            third := large
    i < > 0
        SEQ
            top := empty
            next := empty
            third := empty
    running := TRUE
} } }
```

We have included the line `running := TRUE` in anticipation of a repetitive solution to the main body of the problem.

Moving a disc

The significant work in developing our solution lies in a correct design for moving a disc. Let us perform process analysis for a single *TOWER*, based on our analysis of Figure 23.3. The moves occur in pairs.

Exercise

23.3 Give a sequence of messages which describe a pair of moves of discs between the pegs, from the viewpoint of the peg containing the disc *small* .

Solution 23.3 First the disc *small* is passed clockwise—this corresponds to an output message from *TOWER*. The current peg no longer holds the disc *small*; it must now be determined whether the current peg or its anticlockwise neighbour has the smaller top disc—this will require an exchange of information. So *TOWER* sends the value of its new *top* anticlockwise, and awaits a response. This response, on its clockwise entry channel, will be either an acceptance message (in which case the top disc is removed from the current peg), or the value of its neighbour's *top* (in which case this value is added as the new top disc).

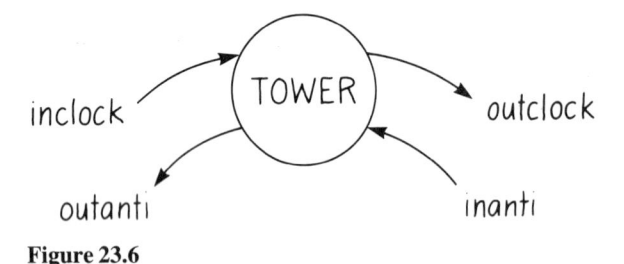

Figure 23.6

The result of this exercise can be expressed as the following (partial) process annotation, using the channel names given in Figure 23.6.

```
IF
  the top disc is small
    IN SEQUENCE
      pass top on outclock
      pass next on outanti
      await a reply on inclock
      IF
        reply = accepted
          THEN record that next has been removed
        otherwise
          use reply as new top
  otherwise
    ?
```

What about the pegs which do not currently have the disc *small*? Clearly for such a peg, *TOWER* can receive the disc *small* (on its clockwise entry channel) or the value of its neighbour's top disc (on its anticlockwise entry channel).

Exercise

23.4 Complete the process annotation, when the top disc is not *small*.

Solution 23.4

```
    .
    .
    .
    otherwise
      CHOOSE AVAILABLE ALTERNATIVE
        inclock.small
          update position variables
        inanti.disc
          IF
            disc is smaller than top
              IN SEQUENCE
                send accepted on outclock
                update position variables
            otherwise
              IN SEQUENCE
                send top on outclock
                update position variables
```

We now need to formalize our process annotation into a CSP design. We may write

$TOWER = INIT; running*MOVE;$
$MOVE = IFSMALL \triangleleft top = small \triangleright IFOTHER$

Exercise

23.5 Give CSP designs for the processes *IFSMALL* and *IFOTHER*.

Solution 23.5

$$IFSMALL = outclock!small \to outanti!next \to inclock?reply \to$$
$$((top := third; next := empty; third := empty)$$
$$\triangleleft reply = accepted \triangleright$$
$$top := reply)$$

$IFOTHER =$
  $inclock?disc \to third := next; next := top; top := small$
  $\Box$
  $inanti?disc \to$
    $((outclock!accepted \to third := next; next := top; top := disc)$
    $\triangleleft disc < top \triangleright$
    $(outclock!top \to top := next; next := third; third := empty))$

Deadlock analysis

We now appear to have all the components of a CSP design, which can be assembled and implemented as Occam code. But first we ought to ensure that when three *TOWER* processes are combined concurrently they will proceed without reaching deadlock. This is an important reason for using the formal notation of CSP. Even our simple process contains sufficient complexity to require detailed analysis. Since initialization includes no communications, let T represent the process *TOWER* immediately after initialization. We therefore consider the following process, which captures the behaviour of *HANOI* after initialization:

$H = T(0) \| T(1) \| T(2)$
$T(0) = c[0]!small \to P$
$T(1) = c[0]?disc \to Q \ \Box \ a[2]?disc \to QQ$
$T(2) = c[1]?disc \to S \ \Box \ a[0]?disc \to SS$
$P = a[0]!medium \to U$

We have labelled the clockwise channels a and the anticlockwise channels c. $T(0)$ contains the small disc, which it wants to pass clockwise before proceeding to its next state, in which it passes its next disc. The other two T processes, not having the small disc, begin by awaiting an input communication.

Exercise

23.6 Expand H to obtain its initial evolution.

Solution 23.6

Since $T(0)$ and $T(1)$ can agree on a communication, we have:

$H = c[0].small \to (P \| Q \| (c[1]?disc \to S \ \Box \ a[0]?disc \to T))$

After updating variables, $T(1)$—which is now in state Q—has *top* = *small* and so must pass it clockwise as its first event. We therefore have:

$Q = c[1]!small \to a[1]!empty \to V$

The evolution of H is now dependent on a choice by channel—and both choices may now be available! Both $T(0)$ and $T(1)$ wish to communicate with $T(2)$, which is willing to accept either. Which choice should be taken? Our preliminary discussion assumed that after the small disc is passed clockwise, the next move is to pass a different disc. However, this has not been captured into our design; we cannot guarantee that the small disc will not be passed again before the other disc is moved. Because of the asynchronous behaviour of the process components, $T(1)$ might send its communication before $T(0)$ makes the second move of its pairs. This is only a possibility, but we do need to guarantee correct behaviour.

Exercise

23.7 Explain how the process evolves if $T(1)$ sends on the small disc before $T(0)$ makes its comparison with $T(2)$.

Solution 23.7

After sending on the small disc to $T(2)$, $T(1)$ is ready to compare with $T(0)$, that is to proceed with $a[1]!empty$. Meanwhile $T(0)$ is still in state P, waiting to proceed with $a[0]!medium$. To cap it all $T(2)$, having received *small*, is only interested in sending it on, that is, $c[2]!small$. All process components wish to transmit, and none wishes to receive—a classic deadlock situation.

□

The result of Exercise 23.7 indicates that is possible for a choice to be made in our design which would result in deadlock. By converting a correct sequential algorithm into a concurrent formulation we have arrived at the possibility of deadlock. We must therefore address this issue.

Let us review the source of the difficulty. The process $T(0)$, whose *top* disc is *small*, must engage in three communications: pass *top* to its clockwise neighbour $T(1)$, pass *next* to its anticlockwise neighbour $T(2)$, and receive a response from $T(2)$. We seek to avoid the situation whereby the *small* disc would get another move in before $T(0)$ and $T(2)$ have a chance to exchange discs. The reason this could happen is that $T(2)$ is willing to receive a message from either neighbour.

The solution is to interchange the two output communications from $T(0)$. Why does this work? Only one of the three communications is with $T(1)$: pass *top*. So the $T(1)$ cannot care whether it receives *top* before or after the $T(2)$ receives *next*. However, the transmission of *next* is part of a two-way exchange which guarantees that $T(2)$ will not communicate with $T(1)$ before the response has been transmitted. This successfully closes off the option which would lead to deadlock.

We must still ensure that we do not land ourselves with the opposite problem of performing the exchange with $T(2)$ before $T(1)$ receives *small*. There is no danger, though, of the exchange taking place before the *small* disc is passed because the exchange requires a second event: *inclock?reply*. Consequently we amend the CSP design of *MOVE* so that:

$IFSMALL = outanti!next \to outclock!small \to inclock?reply \to$
$\qquad ((top := third; next := empty; third := empty)$
$\qquad\qquad \triangleleft reply = accepted \triangleright$
$\qquad top := reply)$

Review Question 23.1 Would prioritizing the choice by channel in *IFOTHER* so that *small* is never accepted when another communication is waiting be an alternative way out of the situation leading to deadlock?

23.2 Coding the Towers of Hanoi

We saw in the previous section that the overall structure for our program is as follows.

```
PROC Hanoi =
  CHAN clock[3], anti[3] :
  ...     PROC Tower
  PAR
    Tower(0, clock[0], anti[1], anti[0], clock[2] )
    Tower(1, clock[1], anti[2], anti[1], clock[0] )
    Tower(2, clock[2], anti[0], anti[2], clock[1] ):
```

The definition of the process Tower has to be inserted into the fold on the second line. Firstly we need a declaration for PROC Tower with the parameters that must be passed to it. In turn we shall need to insert in the definition of PROC Tower declarations of all the identifiers that are local to each instance of the process.

Exercise
23.8 Give the declaration line for PROC Tower and its local constants and variables.

Solution 23.8 The declaration line is

```
PROC Tower( VALUE i, CHAN outclock, inanti, outanti,
  inclock) =
```

This shows that the index i is a value passed to the process and used as a constant in the body of the definition, while outclock, inanti, outanti, inclock are the local names of channels that again can be used throughout the body of the definition. The local constants and variables may be identified from the CSP design. It is an easy task to decide if any particular name refers to a constant or a variable and the resulting declarations are as follows:

```
VAR top, next, third :
DEF small = 1, medium = 2, large = 3, empty = 100 :
VAR running :
VAR disc, reply :
DEF accepted = *** :
```

The first three lines are needed by the Init fold; the other two are needed to implement *MOVE*.

Exercise
23.9 Implement the corrected version of *MOVE* into Occam code.

Solution 23.9

Here is the required code:

```
{ { {     Move
IF
  top = small
                              - - small disc on top
     SEQ
        outanti ! next
        outclock ! small
        inclock ? reply
        IF
          reply = accepted
             SEQ
                              - - remove two discs
                top := third
                next := empty
                third := empty
          reply <> accepted
                              - - replace top disc
                top := reply
  top <> small
                              - - no small disc on top
     ALT
        inclock ? disc
          SEQ
                              - - add small disc to top
             third := next
             next := top
             top := small
        inanti ? disc
          IF
             disc < top
                SEQ
                              - - add disc to top
                   outclock ! accepted
                   third := next
                   next := top
                   top := disc
             TRUE
                SEQ
                              - - lose top disc
                   outclock ! top
                   top := next
                   next := third
                   third := empty :
} } }
```

□

Finally we get the following listing for the process Tower, with the fold Init opened out:

```
PROC Tower( VALUE i, CHAN outclock, inanti, outanti,
  inclock) =
VAR top, next, third :
DEF small = 1, medium = 2, large = 3, empty = 100 :
VAR running :
VAR disc, reply :
DEF accepted = *** :
{ { {    Init
SEQ
    IF
       i = 0
         SEQ
            top := small
            next := medium
            third := large
       i < > 0
         SEQ
            top := empty
            next := empty
            third := empty
    running := TRUE
} } }
    WHILE running
      . . .    Move
```

We remark that our program describes correctly the recursive element of the solution to the problem. It does not, however, address the terminating condition. This would need to be established in order to obtain a complete solution.

SUMMARY OF PART IV

We have discussed concurrent processes in a number of contexts. Concurrent processes may arise naturally as the most apt description of a real-time system, or they may arise from the consideration of a suitable parallel algorithm which arises from separating out the description of components that correspond to spatially distinct objects. Concurrency may also be applied to problems whose solution may be speeded up by the use of several processors.

We call our approach to the formal analysis of concurrent systems ODM. The first step in describing a concurrent system is process analysis. This involves identifying suitable processes and the channels along which they communicate. The customer's requirements for the system are then incorporated into a CSP specification. Further design decisions can also be built in using the CSP notation. The complete CSP design is a formal description which could be implemented in principle. We then develop our design into an algorithmic model using such programming tools as variables and assignment. This enables us to develop a detailed design document.

Our target programming language has been Occam, but a CSP design could be coded in any language that supports parallel processes with a suitable communication model. In order to develop Occam code we found it necessary to make some modifications to our designs. In particular, it is necessary to replace recursion by a provably equivalent iterative construct, in the form of a while loop.

We have worked through two case studies in programming concurrent systems—a telephone network and the solution of the Towers of Hanoi—applying the techniques of ODM to derive an Occam implementation.

In the course of the first case study we met a number of new features—guarded choice by channel in CSP, soft switching and the use of a blocker for real-time systems, and the Occam folding editor. At the same time you should have gained more experience in applying the CSP formalism and transforming it to executable code. We also saw how an error in an initial solution may show up when validating a formal design against the user requirements, and how any modification must be carried through all subsystems.

The second case study allowed us to apply a process formalism to a theoretical problem by identifying concurrent subsystems within the problem description. Once again, the availability of a formal notation allowed us to discover and resolve a defect in the initial design.

SOLUTIONS TO PART IV REVIEW QUESTIONS

19.1 The external events are precisely the communications between *NETWORK* and other nodes of the process network. The other nodes comprise the environment of four users, and the alphabet consists of the following set:

$\{handset[i].up, handset[i].down \mid 0 \leq i \leq 3\} \cup$
$\{dial[i].j \mid 0 \leq i, j \leq 3\} \cup \{buzz[i].noise \mid 0 \leq i \leq 3\}$

19.2 The appropriate messages on the *buzz* channel are *on*, which switches on the buzzer and *off*, which switches it off.

19.3 *handset*[0], *dial*[0], *link*[1, 0], *link*[2, 0], *link*[3, 0]

19.4 Since the processes $T(i)$ are to communicate they must be combined concurrently to give:

$NETWORK = T(0) \parallel T(1) \parallel T(2) \parallel T(3)$

This can be written more compactly as:

$NETWORK = \parallel_{0 \leq i \leq 3} T(i)$

19.5 One possibility is DOWN, DIAL, CALLING$_1$, TALK$_1$, DOWN. There are innumerable others.

19.6 *link*[2, 0]

19.7

(a) DOWN to DIAL, BUZZING$_j$ to TALK$_j$
(b) DIAL to DOWN, CALLING$_j$ to DOWN, TALK$_j$ to DOWN

19.8 The user's choice is communicated to *DIAL* along different channels—*handset* and *dial*.

19.9 Our version of the process *DIAL* ignores this possibility. If *number* = *i* the description would include a communication on the non-existent channel *link*[*i*,*i*].

19.10 The alphabet of *dial*[*i*] should be constrained to allow the event *dial*[*i*].*number* only when *i* ≠ *number*.

19.11 The first alternative describes a situation in which telephone *j* has been called and we are waiting for it to respond to the call; we then acknowledge its response with *alert* and proceed to the TALK state. However, in the second alternative, when we replace the handset after trying to call someone it may be that they are dialling us and so communication needs to be in parallel.

19.12 Either the handset is lifted (to answer the call) or the call is cancelled by the calling party.

19.13 In the first we respond by lifting the handset and sending an *alert* message while awaiting a reply. This reply should be an *alert* to to show that we have got through. On the other hand, though, it could be a *break* message to show that just as we lifted the telephone the other person gave up and hung up. This would leave us only with a dialling tone.

Alternatively, if the other party hangs up before we respond, our phone reverts to the dormant state, DOWN.

19.14 < *handset*[0].*up*, *dial*[0].1 >

20.1 Any of the following sets :{ }, {2, 3}, {1, 3}, {1, 2}, {1, 2, 3}

20.2 $Y = \textit{request.alert} \rightarrow (\textit{reply!engaged} \rightarrow P \triangleleft \textit{busy} \triangleright \textit{reply!ok} \rightarrow Q)$

20.3 This process describes the behaviour of the blocker *BL*(0) when one (or more) of the other telephones is trying to alert telephone 0. If, say, the condition *b*[1] has the value *true*, indicating that the channel *link*[1, 0] is blocked, then the blocker can choose to accept an *alert* signal on this channel and respond with a *busy* signal. If, however, the condition *b*[1] is *false*, the channel *link*[1, 0] is not blocked, then this is not a possible choice of channel for the blocker and an *alert* signal received from telephone 1 must be dealt with elsewhere—by the telephone process *T*(0). Similar remarks apply regarding the values of *b*[2] and *b*[3].

21.1 Each *BL* has a maximum of three incoming *link* channels. When a telephone is in the state DIAL, its blocker must handle all three links; when it is connected to another telephone—in a CALLING, TALK or BUZZING state—the blocker must handle the two remaining links; and when it is in the state DOWN the blocker has no links to handle.

21.2 Owing to the convention that all outputs occur in parallel with obtaining a response, the two processes cannot become deadlocked with both trying to talk and neither listening. Our communications protocol requires that *T*(*j*) receive a reply in parallel with its output, so the output from *T*(*i*) to *T*(*j*) will be successfully received.

21.3 Deadlock occurs only if the partner process wishes to input when $T(i)$ requires it to output. By virtue of the communications protocol, if the original output is accepted, it must either be acknowledged subsequently, or the acceptance must take place in parallel with an output to $T(i)$.

21.4 The response *busy* would be sent to phone i by the blocker of phone j if it were in one of the states DIAL, BUZZING$_k$, CALLING$_k$ or TALK$_k$ ($k \neq i$).

21.5 If the phone that was busy when called decides to phone back, the corresponding *link* channel will not be attached to the blocker. It will not be dealt with by *ENGAGED* either, which is only willing to accept the handset event. To avoid the new caller being held in limbo until the handset is replaced, we make sure the blocker sends a *busy* signal to all calling phones.

22.1 The process *DIAL* itself activates *TALK*, so a subsequent activation of *DIAL* from within *TALK* is recursive.

22.2 The use of *CALL* as the master process would not eliminate the recursion generated by the loop TALK to DIAL to TALK.

23.1 It would still not guarantee that the anticlockwise communication could not be delayed until after $T(1)$ was ready to transmit *small*, as the processes are asynchronous.

APPENDIX—OCCAM

An Occam program describes a process and its communications in terms of inputs, outputs and assignments. The format of a program is specified by the Occam syntax, and consists of statements which normally occupy a single line. The structure of an Occam program is specified by the indentation of the statements in units of two spaces. An Occam program may include comments. A **comment** is introduced by a pair of hyphens, thus - -

We present the syntax of a simplified Occam here in a form of EBNF[1] notation. (Current implementations run Occam 2 which contains numerous features which would have detracted from the introductory exposition of this book. The essential process features of Occam are covered by our simplified syntax.) The **terminal** symbols are shown in the `Courier` typewriter face that has a serif, and the **non-terminal** symbols are shown in *Times italic*. Each **production rule** may use the following symbols:

=	is defined to be
|	or
{ }$_n$	encloses a group which is repeated *n* or more times
▫▫	introduces a line indented two spaces from the previous line
↵	start a new line

For example:

process = *action* | SKIP | STOP | *construction* | *instance*

means that the non-terminal *process* can be replaced by one of the non-terminals *action*, *construction* or *instance*, each of which is defined by its own production rule, or by one of the terminal symbols SKIP or STOP.

It will be seen that some Occam constructions are required to occupy more than one line, as in the sequence construction:

---

[1] The form of Extended Backus Naur Form used here is an extension of the widely used Backus Naur Form. The main differences are that non-terminals are not enclosed by angle brackets, and that symbols are included for showing new lines and indentation.

sequence = SEQ ↵
    {*process* ↵}₂

This means that the non-terminal *sequence* can be replaced by the terminal symbol SEQ followed on a new line indented by two spaces and a *process*, followed on a new line indented by the same two spaces and a *process*, followed possibly by similar new lines.

Specific examples will be given of the particular constructions being defined.

A.1 Data types

You have seen in this and previous courses that computer languages are concerned with the representation of data types. Typically in initial specifications we feel free to use any data type with which we are familiar and which best suits our purposes. However, as we refine the design and approach implementable code we convert everything to those data types which are available in the target implementation language. A range of complex data types is allowed in Occam 2.

Primitive data types

Here are the primitive data types, with some typical examples:

integer	0, 10, −2394
character	'a', '9', '?'
bool	TRUE, FALSE
string	"hello world"

For the purpose of writing code these data types are represented as in the above examples. These representations are referred to as **literals**.

The characters are simply those in the ASCII character set and are represented internally by the numbers 0–255. Since any number in the range 0–255 can be represented by an 8-bit byte we sometimes refer to characters as bytes:

    character = *byte*

The objects in the above data types are used to describe Occam processes. These processes communicate using channels, which may be thought of as the data type *channel*, in the same way that we think of the other classes of objects as forming data types. An external channel to the real-world environment (such as the keyboard or VDU display) is represented as an integer which is defined by the local implementation.

Arrays

For each base type it is possible to construct arrays of values, such as the composite data type *array of integer*. All data types, including *channel*, may be used as a base type to construct arrays. An individual element of an array is selected by means of a subscript. Occam adheres to the convention that all arrays have a subscript range beginning at 0.

Though *string* is treated as a primitive data type, you should be aware that it can also be considered as an array of characters:

    string = *array_of_characters*

Names

It is possible to refer to data objects by *abbreviations*, that is by suitably chosen **names**. These names are used to make a program readable, and in order to enable constant values in processes to be modified with ease and security. In the case of channels names are essential since the underlying channel is often virtual. A name must begin with an alphabetic character, and may then contain any number of alphabetic, dot, or digit characters up to an implementation-dependent limit, e.g. `alpha`, `digit10`, `another.name`. (In the course units we avoid the use of dots in Occam names to prevent confusion with the very different convention for the use of dots in CSP.)

A.2 Declarations

Names are something introduced by the user, and so they must be made explicit in the code in the form of a *declaration*. There are four types of declaration:

declaration =
  definition_declaration | *channel_declaration* |
  variable_declaration | *process_declaration*

Definition declarations

To begin we have:

definition_declaration =
  DEF *integer_name* = *integer* : | DEF *character_name* = *character* : |
  DEF *string_name* = *string* :

Here are some examples:

```
DEF space = 32 :
DEF char1 = 'a' :
DEF greeting = "hello" :
```

Channel declarations

channel_declaration =
  CHAN *channel_name* : |
  CHAN *channel_array_name* { [*arraysize*] }$_1$:

The array subscripts range from 0 to (*arraysize* – 1).
  For example:

```
CHAN control.to.worker :
CHAN link[10] :
```

In the latter example the channel array has 10 elements, `link[0],...,link[9]`.

Variable declarations

An Occam program is executed using *variables*; these are names which stand for an object of a particular data type whose value can change during the execution of a program. Occam is only weakly typed. Though variables must be declared, the declaration does not include the type of the variable though in some cases clues are given. The types of variable declarations that may appear in code are integers and integer arrays, characters, Booleans and strings.

The corresponding declarations are given below.

> *variable_declaration* =
>   VAR *integer_variable* : | VAR *character_variable* : | VAR *bool_variable* : |
>   VAR *string_variable* [BYTE *arraysize*] : |
>   VAR *integer_array_variable* { [*arraysize*] }$_1$:

In the case of a string variable, the 0th element is always the length of the string. For example, if `message` is a string variable whose current value is "`Bye`", then the elements of message have the following values:

```
message[0] = 3
message[1] = 'B'
message[2] = 'y'
message[3] = 'e'
```

Process declarations will be covered in Section A.7.

A.3 Expressions

Literals, abbreviations and variables can be formed into expressions which may be evaluated in a way that needs very little explanation. Here we only consider a small selection of the constructions available in Occam and only describe their evaluation where it is not obvious. The range of expressions is given by the following rule:

> *expression* = *integer_expression* | *character_expression* | *bool_expression*

Integer expressions

> *integer_expression* =
>   *integer* | *integer_name* | *integer_variable* | *integer_array_variable*[*index*] |
>   *string_variable* [0] |
>   (*integer_expression* + *integer_expression*) |
>   (*integer_expression* − *integer_expression*) |
>   (*integer_expression* * *integer_expression*) |
>   (*integer_expression* / *integer_expression*) |
>   (*integer_expression* \ *integer_expression*)

Here

> *index* = *integer_expression*

and the value of the expression is a suitable positive integer.

Character expressions

character_expression =
    character | character_name | character_variable | string_variable [index]

where the value of *index* is a suitable positive integer.

Boolean expressions

bool_expression =
    bool | bool_name | bool_variable |
    (*bool_expression* AND *bool_expression*) |
    (*bool_expression* OR *bool_expression*) |
    NOT *bool_expression*

Channel expressions

Channels can also be obtained from expressions which for simplicity we distinguish from the above evaluatable expressions:

channel = TIME | *channel_name* | *channel_array_name* [*index*]

Here the value of *index* is a suitable non-negative integer, and TIME is a special clock channel which is not discussed further here.

A.4 Actions

Actions are concerned with input, output and assignment:

action = input | output | assignment

These terms are defined as follows:

Operator	General form	Example

?	*input = channel ? variable*	`chan1 ? x`
		`link[3][1] ? cmd`
		`chan[2] ? row[4]`

!	*output = channel ! expression*	`out ! (x + y) + z`
:=	*assignment = variable := expression*	`x := x + diff`

A.5 Processes

Having described an *action*, the simplest type of process, we are in a position to describe more complex constructions. We have:

process = action | SKIP | STOP | *construction* | *instance*

The rule for *construction* is given in Section A.6. An *instance* is a call to a previously defined process:

instance = process_name (*actual* {, *actual* }₀) | *process_name*

actual = channel_name | *channel_array_name* [ ] | *expression*

{, *actual* }₀ represents a sequence of 0 or more *actuals* separated by commas.
An example of an *instance* is:

```
buffer(link[0], link[1])
```

A.6 Constructions

Constructions are processes formed using the constructors SEQ, IF, WHILE, PAR and ALT:

construction = sequence | *conditional* | *loop* | *parallel* | *alternation*

Any construction may be replicated:

replicator =
    integer_variable = [*integer_expression1* FOR *integer_expression2*]

The process is replicated for each possible value of the integer variable from the value of *integer_expression1* to the value of:

integer_expression1 + *integer_expression2* − 1

and *integer_expression2* is positive.
For example, the replicated process:

```
i = [ base FOR 5 ]
P(i)
```

is equivalent to the array of five processes:

```
P(base)
P(base + 1)
P(base + 2)
P(base + 3)
P(base + 4)
```

Sequence construction

sequence = SEQ ↵
    ₀₀{*process* ↵}₂|
    SEQ *replicator* ↵
    ₀₀*process* ↵

Here ₀₀{*process* ↵}₂ represents a sequence of two or more processes each indented by two spaces from the keyword SEQ and followed by a new line, where *process* has been defined previously.

Examples:

```
SEQ
  out ! 3
  in ? x
```

Note that the construction:

```
SEQ i = [ 2 FOR 3 ]
    out ! row[i]
```

is equivalent to:

```
SEQ
    out ! row[2]
    out ! row[3]
    out ! row[4]
```

Conditional construction

$$conditional =$$
$$\quad IF \lrcorner$$
$$\quad\quad _{\square\square}\{choice \lrcorner\}_2 |$$
$$\quad IF\ replicator \lrcorner$$
$$\quad\quad _{\square\square}choice$$

Here:

$$choice = guarded\_choice \mid conditional$$

$$guarded\_choice = bool\_expression \lrcorner$$
$$\quad\quad\quad _{\square\square}process$$

Examples:

(a)
```
IF
   x = 1
     out ! x
   TRUE
     SKIP
```

(b)
```
IF
   x = 1
     IF
       y = 2
         out ! 2
       TRUE
         out ! 1
   TRUE
     SKIP
```

(c)
```
IF i = [ 1 FOR 2 ]
   x = i
     out ! row[i]
```

Loop construction

$$loop = \text{WHILE } \lrcorner \\ _{\square\square} process$$

For example:

```
WHILE running
   SEQ
      in ? x
      out ! x
```

Parallel construction

$$parallel = \\ \quad \text{PAR } \lrcorner \\ \quad _{\square\square} \{process \lrcorner\}_2 \mid \\ \quad \text{PAR } replicator \lrcorner \\ \quad _{\square\square} process$$

Examples:

(a)
```
PAR
   buffer(in, mid)
   buffer(mid, out)
```

(b)
```
PAR i = [ 0 FOR 3 ]
   buffer(link[i], link[i + 1])
```

Alternation

$$alternation = \\ \quad \text{ALT}\lrcorner \\ \quad _{\square\square} \{alternative \lrcorner\}_2 \mid \\ \quad \text{ALT } replicator\lrcorner \\ \quad _{\square\square} alternative$$

Here

alternative = guarded_alternative | alternation

$$guarded\_alternative = \\ \quad guard \lrcorner \\ \quad _{\square\square} process$$

$$guard = \\ \quad input \mid \\ \quad bool\_expression \text{ \& } input \mid \\ \quad bool\_expression \text{ \& SKIP}$$

Examples:

(a)
```
ALT
    in1 ? x
        out ! x
    in2 ? y
        out ! y
```

(b)
```
ALT i = [ 1 FOR 2 ]
    in[i] ? row[i]
        out ! row[i]
```

(c)
```
ALT
    (n < 4) & in1 ? x
        SEQ
            out ! x
            n := n + 1
    in2 ? y
        out ! y
```

(d)
```
ALT
    in ? x
        out ! x
    TRUE & SKIP
        out ! 0
```

A.7 Process definitions

We mentioned in Section A.5 that a process can be an *instance*, that is, an actual call to a formal definition of a process; as such, it can be considered as similar to a procedure call in other high-level languages. In order to define named processes we need the following formal declaration:

process_declaration =
  PROC *process_name*(formal {,formal}$_0$) = ↵
   $_{\square\square}${declaration ↵}$_0$
   $_{\square\square}$body :

body = *process*

formal =
  CHAN *channel_name* | CHAN *channel_array_name* { [ ] }$_1$ |
  VALUE *expression* | VAR *primitive_variable* | VAR *array_variable* { [ ] }$_1$

In a process call, the values of expressions are passed to corresponding formal parameters, and actual variables are to be identified with corresponding formal variables, while channels are also given possibly similar local names.

Example:

```
PROC buffer(CHAN in, out) =
   VAR running :
   SEQ
      running := TRUE
      WHILE running
         SEQ
            in ? x
            out ! x :
```

A.8 Occam programs

We have now described all the ingredients of the Occam language, in terms of which an Occam program takes the following simple form:

program =
    PROGRAM *program_name*
    {*declaration*}$_0$
    body

GLOSSARY OF TERMS

alphabet	The set of events associated with a process, or a channel.
buffer	A process which takes input values and outputs those values unchanged.
channel	A directed communications link between two processes.
compose	To construct a process from two or more processes.
concurrent system	A system which is composed of several identifiable processes which are active at the same time.
deadlock	The situation where one or more processes are for ever prevented from further progress because they cannot agree on a communications link.
environment	The unspecified processes attached to the external channels of a given process.
event	The occurrence of an activity of interest.
formal methods	The use of a formal language for specification and design, and of mathematical proof for verification.
funnel	An arrangement of processors which cascade a result down to a final process.
guard	A Boolean expression whose value determines whether a communication is available for selection.
guarded communication	A communication to which a guard is attached.
implementation	The process of turning a detailed design into program code. It is often referred to as programming, or, less frequently, as coding.
link interface controller	The part of a transputer which is used for communication with other transputers.
livelock	A situation in concurrent processing where the second party to a communication may never participate in the communication, but is not prevented from doing so.

mailbox model	A model of processing where processes communicate with each other by passing messages to a mailbox.
non-deterministic choice	Describes the position where choice is made according to factors which are beyond the current level of process refinement.
parallel composition	Where a single process is equivalent to a number of processes combined and executed concurrently.
pipe	A process which has a single input channel and single output channel.
pipeline	A sequence of pipes placed end to end.
post-fragmentation	The process of defining and designing a system of processes based on the inherent concurrency in a problem and subsequently allocating those processes to processors.
pre-fragmentation	A description of the process of breaking up a problem bearing in mind the arrangement of processors on which the resulting code will be executed.
process	System which is capable of engaging in some activity or observable behaviour.
process network	A diagram of a system as a collection of processes with synchronized communication.
recursive process	Is a process whose action is defined in terms of itself.
refinement	Decomposition of a process by explosion.
requirements analysis	The process of examining and checking a statement of requirements to produce the system specification.
response	The way in which a system reacts to an event.
selection	A programming construct that allows choice among several courses of action.
sequential composition	A process equivalent to two processes which evolve one after another.
set	An unordered collection of distinct elements.
sink	A process which consumes data from a channel.
SKIP	A subprocess of a process which does nothing but terminates successfully.
softswitching	The controlled reallocation of a channel between parallel subprocesses.
source	The process which provides data to a channel.
state	A mode of system behaviour which is externally observable.
statement of requirements	The document which expresses, in customer terms, what is required from a system.
state transition	The act of changing from one state to another. During a transition between states the system may perform some.
state transition diagram	A state transition diagram specifies the allowable transitions between states and the events which trigger those transitions.

STOP	A process which starts but does nothing else. In particular, it never terminates.
synchronous message passing	A processing model in which the sender and recipient must synchronize for communication to take place.
system	A system is a collection of components which are related in some manner in order to achieve some desirable effect.
systolic array	An array of processors in which the flow of signals is entirely one way.
time slicing	The allocation of short time slices to each of a number of processes.
trace	A record of the sequence of events of a process as seen by a hypothetical observer.
Turing machine	An abstract machine capable of being in any one of a number of states, a read-write head, a tape on which symbols can be stored and a state transition function.

INDEX

actions part, 203
adder, 169
alphabet, 79, 295
alphabet of channel, 227
associative rule, 107
asynchronous, 20
atomic processes, 203

blocked (process), 20, 68, 93
box notation, 83
buffer, 27, 164

central processing unit, 6
channel, 14
channel array, 123, 153
choice:
    by channel, 134, 203, 240, 243
    of input event, 162
    by input value, 134
choice-by-channel rule, 119
closed (guard), 243
comment lines, 212
comms protocol, 22, 63, 65
communication event, 78
concurrency operator, 114, 119, 135
concurrent, 3
constructor, 204
crease lines, 256
CSP, ix, 79, 82, 185

deadlock, 21–23, 121, 250
deadlock rule, 121
declarations part, 203

electronic funds transfer, 4

entry channel, 16
environment, 15, 17, 165, 229
event, 19, 78
evolution (of a process), 19, 79
exit channel, 16
explode, 150, 152
external channel, 16

fetbar, 98, 102
fold, 256
fold line, 256
folding editor, 255
fragmentation, 11, 146
funnel, 30

geometric parallelism, 42
guard, 96, 243
guarded choice by channel, 243
guarded expression, 97

inter-process communication, 19
interleaving operator, 110, 135
internal event, 78
internal event rule, 119

livelock, 21–23, 250
local variable, 162
loop, 189

message passing, 11
multiprogramming, 7

non-deterministic choice, 135

Occam, 11, 203, 255, 285

Occam environment, 207
Open Development Method (ODM), 9, 11, 143
open (guard), 243

parallelism, 42, 57
parametrized process, 164
pipe, 27
pipeline, 27, 29
pixels, 4
precedence, 95, 187
prefix rule, 107
prefixing, 81
prioritized choice by channel, 102, 245
process, 3, 13
process analysis, 10
process annotation, 24
process array, 154
process header, 207
process network, 15
proof obligation, 169

recursive definition, 127, 135
refinement, 151
replicated concurrency operator, 154
replicated fetbar operator, 232
replicated interleaving operator, 159
replicated sequencing operator, 159
replicator, 209

replicator index, 209

selection, 45
sequential composition, 105
SKIP, 86
SKIP rule, 107
slave process, 254
soft switching, 242
starvation, 245, 250
state, 13, 79, 81, 164
state transition diagram, 93, 230
STOP rule, 107
subprocess, 80
successful termination, 86
synchronization, 11, 20

temporal parallelism, 57
terminating loop, 191
thinbar, 95
thresholding, 46
trace, 90
transputer, 5, 8
Turing machine, 5

von Neumann, 6–7

while construct, 189
wraparound, 44